CANADA AND THE
THIRD WORLD

CANADA AND THE
THIRD WORLD

Overlapping Histories

EDITED BY

KAREN DUBINSKY, SEAN MILLS,

AND SCOTT RUTHERFORD

UNIVERSITY OF TORONTO PRESS

LIBRARY AND ARCHIVES CANADA CATALOGUING IN PUBLICATION

Canada and the Third World : overlapping histories / edited by Karen Dubinsky, Sean Mills, and
Scott Rutherford.

Includes bibliographical references and index.

Issued in print and electronic formats.

ISBN 978-1-4426-0806-1 (bound).—ISBN 978-1-4426-0687-6 (paperback).—
ISBN 978-1-4426-0688-3 (pdf).—ISBN 978-1-4426-0689-0 (html).

1. Canada—Relations—Developing countries. 2. Developing countries—Relations—Canada.
I. Dubinsky, Karen, author, editor II. Mills, Sean, 1978–, author, editor III. Rutherford, Scott,
1979–, author, editor

FC244.T55C35 2016   327.710172'4   C2015-905287-4
                                                  C2015-905288-2

We welcome comments and suggestions regarding any aspect of our publications—please feel free
to contact us at news@utphighereducation.com or visit our Internet site at www.utppublishing.com.

North America
5201 Dufferin Street
North York, Ontario, Canada, M3H 5T8

2250 Military Road
Tonawanda, New York, USA, 14150

ORDERS PHONE: 1-800-565-9523
ORDERS FAX: 1-800-221-9985
ORDERS E-MAIL: utpbooks@utpress.utoronto.ca

UK, Ireland, and continental Europe
NBN International
Estover Road, Plymouth, PL6 7PY, UK
ORDERS PHONE: 44 (0) 1752 202301

ORDERS FAX: 44 (0) 1752 202333
ORDERS E-MAIL: enquiries@nbninternational.com

Every effort has been made to contact copyright holders; in the event of an error or omission,
please notify the publisher.

This book is printed on paper containing 100% post-consumer fibre.

The University of Toronto Press acknowledges the financial support for its publishing activities of
the Government of Canada through the Canada Book Fund.

Printed in the United States of America.

Contents

List of Illustrations   vii

Acknowledgements   ix

Contributors   xi

Introduction   1
KAREN DUBINSKY, SEAN MILLS, AND SCOTT RUTHERFORD

1 Indigenous Peoples, Colonialism, and Canada   15
SCOTT RUTHERFORD

2 Immigration Policy, Colonization, and the Development of a White Canada   37
BARRINGTON WALKER

3 Canadian Businesses and the Business of Development in the "Third World"   60
KAREN DUBINSKY AND MARC EPPRECHT

4 Canada and the Third World: Development Aid   88
MOLLY KANE

5 From Missionaries to NGOs   120
RUTH COMPTON BROUWER

6 Foreign Policy, Diplomacy, and Decolonization   155
DAVID WEBSTER

7 Military Intervention and Securing the Third World, 1945–2014   193
IAN MCKAY AND JAMIE SWIFT

8 A Decade of Change: Refugee Movements from the Global South and the Transformation of Canada's Immigration Framework   217
LAURA MADOKORO

9 Popular Internationalism: Grassroots Exchange and Social Movements   246
SEAN MILLS

Glossary   267

Index   273

Illustrations

Figures

1.1 Crown–Aboriginal treaties in Canada, 1763–2005   21
2.1 J.S. Woodsworth's *Strangers Within Our Gates* (1908)   45
3.1 Community members from La Union, El Estor, Guatemala   78
6.1 Image from the cover of Carl Berger's book *The Sense of Power*   159
8.1 Tsering Dorjee Wangkhang and Jampa Dorjee Drongotsang reporting for training   218
8.2 Cliff Shaw, the 14th Dalai Lama, and James George   233

Table

4.1 Timeline of selected global events and Canada's aid program   112

Boxes

1.1 Culture and colonialism: Orientalism   20
3.1 A native perspective of gold mining in Guatemala and its devastating impacts on our brothers and sisters, the Mayans   80
5.1 From *To Plow with Hope*   148
6.1 Racialized perceptions in Canadian foreign policy making   182
8.1 Timeline of humanitarian assistance in 1970s' Canada   240
9.1 Kari Levitt and the idea of Canadian dependency   254

Acknowledgements

IT HAS BEEN OUR GREAT GOOD FORTUNE to have worked together, on various projects and in various capacities, for some years. Most recently we've shared countless discussions about the undergraduate courses we teach and about our frustrations that there isn't a single, concise book we can use to introduce students in Development Studies or History courses to issues pertaining to relations between Canada and the countries of the Global South. So we decided to write one. We quickly realized, however, that this was a task that far exceeded our collective knowledge and capabilities. So our first thank you is to the other contributors to this book, who brought their areas of expertise to this project in the form of well-written, introductory-level chapters, delivered within the page limit and on time. You can't ask more from contributors than that. Our second thank you is to several years of undergraduate students to whom we have taught many of the issues that this book addresses. Eduardo Galeano once wrote, with characteristic irony, "The division of labour in our world is that some nations specialize in winning and others in losing." We offer this book to our students in the hopes that they will take up the challenge of finding their way, ethically and intelligently, in the project of making a better world.

The Department of Global Development Studies and the History Department at Queen's University and the History Department at the University of Toronto gave us the security of institutional homes. Thanks to the University of Toronto History Department and the Queen's Fund for Scholarly Research and Creative Work and Professional Development for financial support. All the people at the University of Toronto Press Higher Education Division have been enthusiastic and helpful about this book. Thanks especially to Megan Pickard, Natalie Fingerhut, Ashley Rayner, Anna Del Col, and copy editor Eileen Eckert. Photographer James Rodríguez (MiMundo.org) generously gave us permission to use some of his evocative images. Helen Picard helped with some of the initial formatting. Thanks to the friends and family who debated these issues with us: Susan Belyea, Mary Caesar, Sayyida Jaffer, Paul Kelley, Susan Lord, Freddy Monasterio, Désirée Rochat, Rodney Saint-Eloi, Anna Shea, and Zaira Zarza.

Contributors

Ruth Compton Brouwer, Professor Emerita of History, King's University College, Western University, Canada, has written extensively on women and missions and, more recently, on secular NGO work. Her most recent book is *Canada's Global Villagers: CUSO in Development, 1961–86* (2013).

Karen Dubinsky teaches in the departments of Global Development Studies and History at Queen's University. She is the author and editor of several books, including *Within and Without the Nation: Transnational Canadian History* (2015, co-editors Adele Perry and Henry Yu), *My Havana: The Musical City of Carlos Varela* (2014, co-editors Caridad Cumana and Xenia Reloba), and *Babies Without Borders: Adoption and Migration across the Americas* (2010).

Marc Epprecht has a PhD in history from Dalhousie University, and has published books and articles on the history of gender, sexuality, and development, mostly in southern Africa. Marc developed the original Canada and the "Third World" course at Queen's University in 2000.

Molly Kane has over 30 years' experience in the field of social justice, human rights, and international cooperation. Since 2011 she has been Researcher in Residence at the Centre International de recherche en développement international et société, Université du Québec à Montréal (CIRDIS-UQAM).

Laura Madokoro is Assistant Professor in the Department of History and Classical Studies at McGill University. Her research explores the intersection of race, humanitarianism, and migration in the twentieth century. Her work has appeared in the *Canadian Historical Review, Modern Asian Studies, Journal of the Overseas Chinese, Refuge, Journal of Refugee Studies*, and *Histoire Sociale*.

Ian McKay has taught history at Queen's University since 1988. His recent publications include *Reasoning Otherwise: Leftists and the People's Enlightenment in Canada, 1890–1920* (2008), *In the Province of History: The Making of the Public Past in Twentieth-Century Nova Scotia* (2010, with Robin Bates); and *Warrior Nation: Rebranding Canada in an Age of Anxiety* (2012, with Jamie Swift).

Sean Mills teaches in the History department at the University of Toronto. His book, *The Empire Within: Postcolonial Thought and Political Activism in Sixties Montreal* (2010), received the Quebec Writers' Federation First Book Award in 2010 as well as an Honourable Mention for the Canadian Historical Association's Sir John A. Macdonald Award in 2011. His book *A Place in the Sun: Haiti, Haitians, and the Remaking of Quebec* is scheduled for publication in 2016.

Scott Rutherford teaches in the Global Development Studies department and in the Cultural Studies program at Queen's University. His research explores the history of Aboriginal protest in Canada. He was the co-editor of *New World Coming: The Sixties and the Shaping of Global Consciousness* (2008) and a special issue of the journal *Race and Class* (2010).

Jamie Swift is the author of a dozen books, including, most recently, *Warrior Nation: Rebranding Canada in an Age of Anxiety* (2012, with Ian McKay). He teaches at the Queen's School of Business and works as a social justice and peace advocate.

Barrington Walker is Associate Professor of History at Queen's University. A historian of modern Canada, his research focuses upon blacks, immigration, the law, and the formation of the racial state. He is the author of *Race on Trial: Black Defendants in Ontario's Criminal Courts, 1858–1958* (2010) and the editor of *The African Canadian Legal Odyssey: Historical Essays* (2012).

David Webster is Associate Professor of History at Bishop's University. He is the author of *Fire and the Full Moon: Canada and Indonesia in a Decolonizing World* (2009) and collection editor of *East Timor: Testimony* (2004).

Introduction

KAREN DUBINSKY, SEAN MILLS, AND SCOTT RUTHERFORD

EVERY TIME CANADIANS USE THEIR CELL PHONES, put on their jeans or sneakers, savour tropical fruits, plan their winter vacations, send remittances to relatives in other countries, or consider donating money to an international charity, they are participating in foreign relations, most likely with that part of the planet sometimes known as the Third World (a controversial term we'll address in this introduction). Canadian relations with the Third World are varied and complicated, and clearly there is no single view about their meaning. Some of us might see these relationships, past and present, as shining examples of Canada's distinctive, peace-oriented global leadership. For others they represent just another example of Western domination and Canada's active participation in exploitative, colonial relations. Either way, we are past the time when one could argue that Canada's only important ties are with other Western countries such as the United States or the United Kingdom.

This book starts from the perspective that the ties between Canada and the Third World are all around us. They are obvious in the $23 billion sent home annually in remittances from Canada to India, China, Pakistan, and other far-away countries.[1] So too are they tragically apparent in the flag-draped coffins of Canadian soldiers killed in Afghanistan. The ties exist in foreign aid, business, mining, and the many incarnations of the Canadian International Development Agency (CIDA; now part of Foreign Affairs, Trade and Development Canada). They form the basis of ongoing discussions about race, gender, religion, and "Canadian" or "Quebec" values. They exist in Haitian restaurants in Montreal and in the vibrant diversity of Toronto's suburbs, Vancouver's Chinatown, and countless other places in both rural and urban Canada. These relations are not new; their histories are deep, long, and multifaceted. Yet even if we are generally aware of the Third World in our daily lives, most Canadians know relatively little about the historical foundations of the complex nature of the country's entanglements with non-Western societies.

There are a handful of well-known Canadians whose ties to countries of the Third World are recognized. Doctors Norman Bethune and Samantha Nutt, rapper K'naan, politician Stephen Lewis, writers Rohinton Mistry and Austin Clarke, and filmmaker Deepa Mehta are all public figures in Canada whose biographies overlap with the Third World. But there are others about whom our knowledge seems to stop at our national borders. Plenty of Canadians know about Sir William Van Horne, former president of the Canadian Pacific Railway, and thus present at the famous driving of the "last spike" in 1885—an iconic moment that has graced Canadian history textbooks for generations. Fewer Canadians know there was another dimension to Van Horne: he also went on to build railroads in Cuba and Guatemala. These ties come back to us daily in the form of Chiquita bananas that are still transported from Guatemala through the railroad systems Van Horne oversaw.[2] Many Canadians are also aware of the legendary circus performer William Hunt, the "Great Farini." Farini thrilled audiences by crossing Niagara Falls on a tightrope in the 1860s, even once performing in front of the visiting Prince of Wales. His subsequent career is less well known and certainly less celebrated. In the 1880s he became one of the many entrepreneurs who harnessed European racial hierarchies to his advantage, bringing Asians, Africans, and Aboriginal people from North America to the stages of London to display them as curiosities.[3] Even that most horribly famous Canadian mass murderer Marc Lépine, perpetrator of the Montreal Massacre of December 6, 1989, has a more complex, less national origin than we remember, which reflects Canadian–Third World histories. Lépine was born Gamil Gharbi, son of Monique Lépine and Rachid Liass Gharbi, an Algerian Muslim immigrant. Lépine changed his name to separate himself from his abusive father and because he was, according to his mother, fed up with the anti-Arab racism he encountered in 1970s Montreal. The story is further complicated by the bitter history of Lépine's father. Rachid Gharbi came to Canada after surviving electric shock torture at the hands of the French military during the Algerian War, a conflict in which Canada tacitly supported the French over the Algerians (support that included military equipment).[4] This war provided theorist Frantz Fanon with the inspiration for his classic manifesto of decolonization and national liberation, *The Wretched of the Earth.*

All three cases provide examples of the same point: even the most iconic people or events or moments exist in a big, interconnected world. By looking outside our customary framework of the nation, such stories or events often become larger, more complex, and more global than we first realized. These are all examples of "Canadian" stories that, as a recent anthology about transnational Canadian history put it, link this country "to a host of nations, events, ideologies, political systems, cultures of meaning, and relationships well beyond Canada's borders."[5]

We know less than we should know about the complex lives of figures such as Van Horne, Farini, or Lépine because Canadian history—as it is presented in government narratives and school textbooks, and even in much writing by university professors—is often thought of as being separate from the world, and most especially the Third World. The story of Canada's development is understood predominantly in terms of relations with Britain, France, and, later, the United States. This is both a product and a reiteration of some narrowly racialized assumptions about what Canada is (a country composed of white people) and what matters in its past (relations with the "mother countries"). This perspective imagines Canadian development as distinct from the many processes that went into the making of the societies of the South. Historically, the Third World is portrayed as being a land far removed from the dominant paths of Canadian history. This leaves the impression that Canada's relationship to the Third World has a present but not a past. The authors of this collection hope to offer a different, more historically grounded view of Canadian–Third World relations. Although coming from many different perspectives, all of the authors of this collection believe that Canada's history has long been bound up with the broader world, and this world is one that stretches far beyond the North Atlantic triangle within which its foreign relations have generally been understood. Long before *Canada* and the *Third World* existed as categories, those living in North America had multiple contacts with non-European and non-white peoples, not the least of which were the many Aboriginal societies colonized by settlers and by the Canadian state. We can see how relations on reserves, in movements such as Idle No More, and in the ongoing tragedies of missing Aboriginal women and girls are among the many legacies of colonialism that shape all parts of the country.

Canada's relationships with the societies of the Third World are therefore fundamentally shaped by its own colonial history. After conquering New France in 1759, the British empire gained control of the colonies that would become Canada, and settlers occupied and took control over the land. The new dominion created in 1867 expanded westward across the continent, bringing the West and the Aboriginal peoples who lived there under its political control. Throughout the twentieth century Canada slowly gained independence from Britain while simultaneously coming into the orbit of the growing power of the United States. In the opening chapter of this book, Scott Rutherford explores the imperial context of the origins of Canada and the geographies of empire in which the architects of the Canadian state understood themselves. Canada historically played a subordinate role to Britain and the United States: "Miss Canada" to the matronly Mother England or all-knowing Uncle Sam, as the cartoonists used to depict it. Historically, therefore, Canada's relationship to the Third World was always filtered through the imperial ambitions of those two countries. In a forerunner to modern-day international development, in 1929 the British Imperial

Office wrote the British Colonial Development Act, a directive that was used to discuss resource development across the empire.[6] Canada and Kenya may now seem like completely different places, but in the minds of British colonial officials, the distance between the two young dominions was not so great as we might now presume. Canada itself is the product of empire, and this history played a fundamental role in how it would approach other colonized and formerly colonized societies. While Canada was an active part of the British and American empires and their various imperial projects, it has always also had its own internal forms of colonialism, and individual Canadians and the Canadian government forged their own relationships with the Third World that were tied to but never completely controlled by the larger imperial players.

A variety of Canadian governments and individuals from many different backgrounds have maintained just about every sort of relationship with the people and societies of the Third World—from the intimate to the military, and from business encounters to joint participation in campaigns for human rights and international solidarity. When we think about "Canadian–Third World relations," most Canadians probably have in mind the history of Canadian foreign policy or government-to-government relations. On this score, the Canadian government has, as this book will show, a rather mixed record. As Barrington Walker discusses in this book, for much of its history the Canadian state tried to keep people from what we would now call the developing world at arm's length. Canada—the famous "nation of immigrants"—was built on escalating degrees of racial exclusion, as racially restrictive immigration laws sought to keep Canada white, helping to draw a global colour line between the world's white societies and all of its "others." In the aftermath of World War II, Canada became involved in many of the efforts of colonial powers to maintain Western hegemony in the Third World. As David Webster shows in his chapter, Canada often walked a conflicted, at times duplicitous, path between its self-perception as a voice for justice and independence and its firm commitment to Cold War–era alliances. Canadian arms were sold to France, even though Canadian officials knew that these arms would be used against Algerians during the Algerian war of independence.[7] When it came to South Africa's apartheid system of white minority government, Webster argues that Canada combined strong words with carefully constrained actions. Canada manufactured weapons—including Agent Orange—to be used by the American forces in Vietnam. And, as Ian McKay and Jamie Swift argue in their contribution, in the twenty-first century the Canadian government has sought to develop a new warrior image that has fuelled its participation in the invasion and occupation of Afghanistan.

This book has much to say about Canadian government policy with respect to Third World peoples and places. However, our second major aim is to expand our focus. Who makes foreign relations? We think that plenty of people do. To more fully understand Canadian–Third World relations, we need to consider the ties created and the forms of power exerted not only by the state but also by individuals and nonstate actors such as nongovernmental organizations (NGOs), churches, tourists, and others. In this book we will see that many different individuals and organizations—from missionaries to NGOs to CEOs—have created ties to the Third World. Their actions have varied, but often their self-image has not. They believed in their own altruism. They believed that they had come to the Third World to help alleviate poverty and promote social justice. However, their actions often contradicted their altruistic proclamations. Even the best-intentioned individuals had trouble imagining that the people that they hoped to help had minds, not to mention cultures and histories, of their own. Like parents presiding over their impulsive or immature children, Canadians' relations with Third World people have often been paternalistic. Altruistic intentions or gestures have often given way to actions that demonstrate how Western cultural superiority continues to motivate. People and organizations change, of course, and, as Ruth Compton Brouwer discusses here, missionaries of earlier periods became actively involved in international solidarity movements in the 1960s and 1970s. But just as there was change, there was also continuity. Many would argue, as do Molly Kane and others in this book, that NGOs working in the Third World today are not completely divorced from the missionary sensibilities of earlier periods.[8]

Two stories, both drawn from the history of Canadian/Guatemalan relations, help to highlight what we mean when we speak of the complexity and variety of Canadian interventions in the Third World. Both took place during the 1980s, when the long civil war in Guatemala was at its most brutal. Battles between the Guatemalan military and guerrillas seeking a more equitable society had turned into a military rampage, which targeted students, church members, journalists, and rural Mayan populations in what Guatemalan courts now recognize as acts of genocide. The brutality of successive Guatemalan governments in the 1970s and 1980s was legendary, so much so that even the United States—which had long funded and trained the Guatemalan armed forces—suspended military aid under President Jimmy Carter in 1977. Ronald Reagan reversed this and resumed military relations with Guatemala in the 1980s, despite the war. However, the United States was not the only game in town. Guatemala's president during the most brutal moments of the war was General Efrain Rios Montt, an active evangelical Protestant. His regime was described by Canada's United

Church *Observer* as "barbarism with a Christian face," but other Canadians were more supportive.[9] Rios Montt used his religious connections to purchase what he needed, including helicopter parts he got—at a discount, he claimed—through unspecified evangelical churches in Canada.[10]

At the same time as some churches inside Canada were aiding the Guatemalan military, other Canadians were actively working to help Guatemalans on the other side of the conflict. French-Canadian missionaries had a long history of working in Latin America and the Caribbean, and by the 1970s many had been radicalized by the ideas of liberation theology and had taken the side of the Latin American poor against right-wing dictatorships. In 1981, 30-year-old Raoul Léger, a lay missionary from Bouctouche, New Brunswick, was killed by the Guatemalan military during a gun battle. Léger, a trained social worker, was in Guatemala with the Quebec Foreign Missionary Society to provide aid to the poor. The Guatemalan military government attempted to portray him as a dangerous, armed revolutionary. His fellow missionaries, as well as many Guatemalan friends, describe him as a committed social worker, carrying out his social mission in a poor neighbourhood in Guatemala City.[11] A decade later, more than a hundred other Canadians, motivated by the same situation in Guatemala, participated in "Project Accompaniment." Their job was to act as witnesses alongside the estimated one million Guatemalans who had been displaced by the war as they returned to their still dangerous country.[12]

These two stories provide convenient and illustrative bookends, and not only about relations between Canadians and Guatemalans. The United Nations Human Development Index tells us that over 85 per cent of the world's population lives in "the developing world."[13] Obviously it is impossible to slot Canadian–Third World relations into a single category, as no one story can capture such complexities. Canada's participation in the broader project of Western imperialism is only part of the story. Stories like those of Raoul Léger or Project Accompaniment are reminiscent of what scholar Leela Gandhi calls "minor forms" of anti-imperialism, based on friendship and mutual recognition of shared humanity. Gandhi, writing about the British empire of the nineteenth and twentieth centuries, asks a question that is equally pertinent to Canadians: "[W]hat ethical imperatives rendered some Europeans immune to the temptations of an empire which was a factory for making imperialist-minded citizens?"[14] Not all First World–Third World encounters are invasions. As David Webster shows here, Canadians sometimes acted in unexpected ways even at the state level. Prime Minister Louis St. Laurent was the only leader of a Western nation to address, via telegram, an important gathering in Bandung, Indonesia, in 1955. The Bandung Conference could be said to signal the "birth" of the Third World as a politically autonomous grouping, distinct from colonial powers. It brought participants from 25 newly decolonized countries to try to form common perspectives on global equality and find an independent path in a bipolar Cold War world. That Canadian Asia experts in Ottawa called the Bandung declaration "a thoughtful and construct[ive] document" says something very important: Canadians—inside and outside government—did not speak with one voice when it came to the Third World. This is as true for the past as it is for the present.

Sean Mills shows in his chapter that Canadians have often refused to accept the actions of their governments when they engage in harmful or destructive activities in the Global South. In the 1960s and 1970s, for example, a variety of social movements emerged that sought to work with people in the Third World against various forms of domination. They opposed the Vietnam War and Canada's implicit involvement in it, and fought to defend the rights of immigrants and refugees who sought to make Canada their home. Quebeckers supported Algerians as they defeated French colonialism and gained independence, and generations of Canadians pressured their government to take action against the white-minority apartheid regime of South Africa. Various groups of Canadians worked in multiple ways to humanize governmental immigration and foreign policies, with varying degrees of success. And indigenous peoples, through varied means, have long refused to accept the colonial imposition of the British Empire and then later the Canadian state. These ideas and actions have ranged from individual acts of resistance to more organized attempts by community organizations and federal bodies to push the Canadian state into relinquishing some of the power it attained during the period of displacement and assimilation in the early twentieth century.

So this book explores Canadian–Third World relations on several levels or dimensions at once: governmental, organizational, and person-to-person. In this book, missionaries, diplomats, politicians, NGO workers, and soldiers—for example—are grouped together as people who "make" Canadian–Third world relations. It is an unusual mix. We also use some unusual terminology. The term **Third World** has been the subject of a great deal of criticism in recent years. There are many who argue that the Third World exists only in the present as a shorthand to stereotype people from outside the West as inherently poor, corrupt, culturally deprived, and trapped in sad, meaningless lives. As a result it confines people into categories first deployed by European colonizers to justify the domination of non-Western people and places. We are constantly inundated with such images across popular media that naturalize poverty and marginalization in non-Western societies.[15] On Twitter, for example, such popular hashtags as #firstworldproblems and #thirdworldproblems are used as shorthand that widens the imagined distance between the lives lived in each place. To pluck another example from the headlines: when Toronto City Council responded to some of the scandals surrounding Mayor Rob Ford in 2013, his brother, Councillor Doug Ford, responded with characteristic bombast: "What's happening today," he declared, "is the overthrow of a democratically elected mayor, illegally. This is what you see in Third World nations. You don't see this in Canada."[16] This statement could be nothing more than a desperate grasp for power by a dying, corrupt political dynasty. But it is a term that is continually used at moments of political crisis, for example when politicians or others refer to problems in Northern Aboriginal communities as "our Third World." Why use the Third World in these ways? What does this phrasing reveal about the common understandings Canadians have about the place they imagine as the "Third World?" Where does the "Third World" fit in the imagination of Canadians?

These examples all make a reluctance to use the term Third World understandable. Yet is it the terminology that is the problem here? Or rather, is it the long and complex history of assumptions of superiority that emanate from Canadians (not only their political leaders) concerning places about which they actually know very little? Using "Third World" to outsource social problems—to assume that issues like poverty or disasters or political conflicts have been imported into places like Canada where they don't belong—is obviously wrong, whatever the terminology. Indeed, this book is premised on the need to close, or at least make more complex, this imagined distance between "us" and "them." Furthermore, the suggested alternatives to "Third World" are problematic in their own ways. Is "developing" (as contrasted to "developed") world any less offensive? It still suggests that some people do not measure up to predetermined universalized standards of the West, and is clearly derived from nineteenth-century evolutionary theory that placed white Europeans atop a hierarchy of racial superiority. More recently people have suggested Global South/Global North as a more appropriate division, and its popularity has grown since the end of the Cold War. In some ways it is a division that is most appropriate if one believes that today's global inequalities are best traced to the rise of neoliberal policies in the late 1980s and 1990s. For this there is ample evidence. Yet it too comes with many problems, not the least of which is the fact that there are countries and peoples in the Northern hemisphere that are poorer than those in the South. Moreover, the richest countries of the Global South have economies that dwarf that of Canada. Where does that leave each in the North-South nexus? Most importantly, the term Global South implies that global inequalities are best explained geographically rather than within and between societies that rarely fit neatly into geographic divides.

Because of all of these difficulties, and despite continued reservations, we have decided to continue to use the term Third World interchangeably with other terms in common usage. Contributors to this book use terms such as "Third World," "Global South," and "developing world" interchangeably. From the 1950s until the early 1990s, the central period of focus in our book, the term "Third World" proved popular among activists, scholars, mainstream media, politicians, development workers, and a range of other commentators. The term was coined by French demographer Alfred Sauvy, who used it to name the tripartite geopolitical tensions that had gripped the planet during the Cold War. The Western pro-capitalist "First World" and the Soviet-led "Second World" fought for power in the colonies and former colonies of Europe, located in Asia, Africa, the Middle East, Latin America, and the Caribbean. Yet the people who lived in such places—people freeing themselves from hundreds of years of often brutal rule by foreign European powers—looked to forge a different future, one that was not conscripted by the narrow range of choices offered by First or Second World powers. Thus the Third World—like the Third Estate of the French Revolution—became a term synonymous with peoples who demanded a rightful place in a world that had long excluded them from exercising power. The term, originally formulated in French, referred not to the "third world" in terms of third place—*tiers monde* rather than *troisième monde*—and our current confusion over the term is partly a result of this inadequate translation.[17]

The term Third World emerges from this history. As Vijay Prashad suggests, the "Third World" was not a place, but a project. "During the seemingly interminable battles against colonialism, the peoples of Africa, Asia and Latin America dreamed of a new world," Prashad writes. "The 'Third World' comprised these hopes and institutions produced to carry them forward." "Unity for the people of the Third World," he continues, "came from a political position against colonialism and imperialism, not from any intrinsic cultural or racial commonalities. If you fought against colonialism and stood against imperialism, then you were part of the Third World."[18] The "Third World" is therefore inextricable from the history of empire and the social and political movements that sought to challenge its power and legacies in the postwar period, and it therefore carries an analytical and political meaning that terms such as "developing world" or "Global South" do not. Because different terminology is required for different contexts, we have used all three terms at different points in the book.

Any exercise in grouping diverse countries together is bound to run into difficulties; what is the common bond that makes sense across vast geographies, histories, and linguistic groups? In attempting to define what constitutes the

Third World, should we be following the lead of international organizations such as the World Bank, which partitions countries into income groups (low, middle, and high)? Or should we be more persuaded by some in the international NGO community, who speak of the "two-thirds world" or "majority world," in order to highlight the lopsided nature of global political and economic relations? How should we categorize what some term the BRICS countries (India, Russia, China, Brazil, and South Africa), which, if one's place on the economic hierarchy were the measure for membership in the "developing world," have perhaps moved to a different neighbourhood? In the end, we remain influenced by Prashad's idea of the Third World as a project, not a place, and we also make no claims for comprehensiveness in this small book. This book is not representative of the totality of ties Canada has established over time with all countries that might fit into the category labelled "Third World." Rather, it is an attempt to continue a general conversation about Canada's place in what Uruguayan writer Eduardo Galeano has termed our "upside down world."[19]

Canada and the Third World is an overdue critical and historical introduction of the topic. We think this is a conversation we need to continue because the last such volumes were published decades ago: Peyton Lyon and Tareq Ismael (eds.), *Canada and the Third World* (1976), Robert Clarke and Richard Swift, *Ties That Bind* (1982), and Jamie Swift and Brian Tomlinson (eds.), *Conflicts of Interest: Canada and the Third World* (1991). There are numerous anthologies and single-authored texts on the history of Canadian foreign policy, but these texts often limit their focus to Canada's relations with our traditional political allies, Britain and the United States, while in Quebec most explorations of the province's international engagements have focused on its relationship with France. Books that explore Canada's relationship to empire have, as a general rule, focused on the country's changing relationship to Britain, rather than to the societies of the Third World. There are also many books and articles discussing some aspect of Canada's relations with particular regions or Third World countries.[20] Most recently, scholars of Indigenous history have been keen to link the experience of Indigenous colonization with global projects of colonial domination across European empires.[21] Yet no single text has offered a general history that explores Canada's relationships with the entity that became known as "the Third World." This absence is felt all the more acutely because of the omnipresence of the Third World in our everyday lives.

In contrast to earlier studies of Canada and the Third World, we insist on the need to see the two realms in the same analytical frame, their histories entangled with each other rather than merely connected through economic relations or foreign policy. Analytically speaking, the globe is an interconnected place. While many of the themes of the book will be familiar to students and readers with a background in Canadian social and cultural history, the book will expand upon these fields by maintaining that Canadian history must be understood within a larger international and transnational context. Scholars writing under the "transnational" umbrella explore, as Sven Beckert explained recently, "a whole range of connections that transcend politically bounded territories and connect various parts of the world to one another."[22] Thinking in transnational terms not only makes Canadian–Third World relations more visible, it also widens the lens. Some issues discussed here have been the traditional terrain of scholars of foreign relations. But this book innovates through its focus on the centrality of culture and nonstate actors to forging relationships between Canada and the Third World. By looking at the entangled nature of Canadian history and the Third World, we hope to contribute to the internationalization of Canadian history, and to the ongoing debates about the boundaries and frameworks within which Canadian history should be understood.

Rather than speaking with one voice to discuss all of the different forms of interaction between Canada and the Third World, as editors we have deliberately sought out a multiplicity of voices. Each chapter is authored by a specialist in the given field of study that she or he is writing about. We have written this book as a general introduction to what are clearly very complicated topics. Each contributor offers an introduction from the author's own perspective. We don't all agree with each other, and readers probably won't all agree with us. We are careful researchers, but we aren't neutral. This is an opinionated book about controversial topics. By presenting, sometimes forcefully, sustained arguments rather than a more encyclopedic recitation of fact, we offer a sampling of some of the different perspectives that currently explore how relations to the Third World should be approached. The questions for discussion that accompany each chapter encourage readers to think critically about the perspective each author offers. The various perspectives in this book will occasionally sound different, no doubt, from what we read about Canada in the daily newspapers, or hear in the speeches of Canadian politicians. This anthology might contradict or complement readers' favourite bloggers or Twitter debates. While this book attempts to offer new ways of thinking about Canada's many interactions with the Third World, and while it will offer an introduction to many of the key concepts, events, and individuals who have shaped this relationship, it is not meant to be a complete and comprehensive study of all aspects of these relations. No single book could possibly claim to offer such a complicated and multifaceted history.

One of the presumed difficulties when thinking about Canada and the Third World is that the terms themselves presume a unidirectional flow of knowledge, with ideas and culture flowing outward from the "West" toward countries that are presumed to be without culture and history. This book demonstrates the multidirectional flow of knowledge and influence between different parts of the world. Just as Canada itself was a product of empire, created through the interactions between the ideals of British imperialism and the complex realities of the territory that would later be claimed by the Canadian state, so too has its history always been shaped by cultural forces produced from both within and outside of its borders. In a similar way, Canadian missionaries, soldiers, development workers, and others went out into the world, bringing with them the ideas that they had, but they were forced to confront new realities. At times, they would bring the knowledge that they developed in the broader world back to Canada, or the narratives that they would produce circulated back throughout the country, shaping views and understandings of the world beyond Canada's borders and its traditional relationships.

Our hope in writing this book is that by better understanding the history of the complex relations we recount in these pages, readers and students will be in a stronger position to make sense of the historical foundations of our present moment, and better positioned to build a more equitable future. This book will help, we believe, to make the conversation about Canada and the Third World more complex than it sometimes has been, helping us to move past ridiculous stereotypes of either Third World savagery or Canadian goodness or superiority. This generation of Canadian students— the people we teach—is already beginning to understand, often through their own experience, the complexities of these relations. *Generation NGO*, as authors Alisha Apale and Valerie Stam dubbed them, refers to the huge growth in international experiential learning opportunities for Canadian students throughout the developing world. International educational programs, volunteer opportunities, and development tourism have all generated an enormous debate among students and educators alike, many of whom are critical of the often superficial and touristic nature of such activities.[23] It is our hope that books like this will help Canadians think with more complexity and reflection about the experiences that many are having.

Further Readings

Austin, David. *Fear of a Black Nation: Race, Sex, and Security in Sixties Montreal.* Toronto: Between the Lines, 2013.

Beaudet, Pierre. *Qui aide qui? Une brève histoire de la solidarité internationale au Québec.* Montreal: Les Éditions du Boréal, 2009.

Burman, Jenny. *Transnational Yearnings: Tourism, Migration, and the Diasporic City.* Vancouver: University of British Columbia Press, 2010.

Demers, Maurice. "Introduction—D'un anti-impérialisme à l'autre: Représentations des nations dominées et colonisées au Canada français." *Mens: revue d'histoire intellectuelle et culturelle* 13, no. 1 (automne 2012): 7–18. http://dx.doi.org/10.7202/1019696ar.

Dubinsky, Karen. *Babies Without Borders: Adoption and Migration across the Americas.* Toronto: University of Toronto Press, 2010.

Granger, Serge. *Le lys et le lotus. Les relations du Québec avec la Chine de 1650–1950.* Montreal: VLB Éditeur, 2005.

Hastings, Paula. "Fellow British Subjects or Colonial 'Others'? Race, Empire, and Ambivalence in Canadian Representations of India in the Early Twentieth Century." *American Review of Canadian Studies* 38, no. 1 (Spring 2008): 3–26. http://dx.doi.org/10.1080/02722010809481818.

LeGrand, Catherine, "L'axe missionnaire catholique entre le Québec et l'Amérique latine. Une exploration préliminaire." Trans. Stéphanie Roesler. *GLOBE: Revue Internationale d'Etudes Quebecoises* 12, no. 1 (2009): 43–66. http://dx.doi.org/10.7202/1000769ar.

Price, John. *Orienting Canada: Race, Empire, and the Transpacific.* Vancouver: University of British Columbia Press, 2011.

Spooner, Kevin A. *Canada, the Congo Crisis, and UN Peacekeeping, 1960–64.* Vancouver: University of British Columbia Press, 2009.

Webster, David. *Fire and the Full Moon: Canada and Indonesia in a Decolonizing World* Vancouver. University of British Columbia Press, 2009.

Notes

1 Aniket Bhusan, "Beyond Aid: Trade, Investment and Remittances between Canada and Developing Countries," *North South Institute Research Report* (June 2013), http://www.nsi-ins.ca/publications/page/4/.

2 Peter McFarlane, *Northern Shadows: Canadians and Central America* (Toronto: Between the Lines, 1989), 25–38.

3 Shane Peacock, *The Great Farini: The High Wire Life of William Hunt* (Toronto: Penguin, 1996), 315–19.

4 Karen Dubinsky, Adele Perry, and Henry Yu, "Canadian History, Transnational History," in *Within and Without the Nation: Canadian History as Transnational History*, ed. Karen Dubinsky, Adele Perry, and Henry Yu (Toronto: University of Toronto Press, 2015). On Canada's role in the Algerian war, see Robin S. Gendron, "Tempered Sympathy: Canada's Reaction to the Independence Movement in Algeria, 1954–1962," *Journal of the Canadian Historical Association / Revue de la Société historique du Canada* 9, no. 1 (1998): 222–41.

5 Dubinsky, Perry, and Yu, "Canadian History, Transnational History," 4.

6 Arturo Escobar, *Encountering Development: The Making and Unmaking of the Third World* (Princeton, NJ: Princeton University Press, 2012 [1995]), 73.

7 Gendron, "Tempered Sympathy," 238.

8 Molly Kane, "International NGOs and the Aid Industry: Constraints on International Solidarity," *Third World Quarterly* 34, no. 8 (2013): 1505–15; Firoze Manji and Carl O'Coill, "The Missionary Position: NGOs and Development in Africa," *International Affairs* 78, no. 3 (2002): 567–83; Nikolas Barry-Shaw and Dru Oja Jay, *Paved with Good Intentions* (Halifax: Fernwood Books, 2012).

9 Katheryn Anderson, *Weaving Relationships: Canada-Guatemala Solidarity* (Waterloo, ON: Wilfrid Laurier University Press, 2003), 17.

10 Kirsten Weld, *Paper Cadavers: The Archives of Dictatorship in Guatemala* (Durham, NC: Duke University Press, 2014), 284.

11 For a look at French-Canadian missionaries in Latin America, see Catherine LeGrand, "Les réseaux missionnaires et l'action sociale des Québécois en Amérique latine, 1945–1980," *Études d'histoire religieuse* 79, no. 1 (2013): 93–115. On Leger see *Raoul Leger, The Elusive Truth*, dir. Renée Blanchar (National Film Board, 2002).

12 Anderson, *Weaving Relationships*.

13 http://hdr.undp.org/en/content/human-development-index-hdi.

14 Leela Gandhi, *Affective Communities: Anticolonial Thought, Fin-de-Siècle Radicalism, and the Politics of Friendship* (Durham, NC: Duke University Press, 2006), 2.

15 See, for example, Nandita Dogra, *Representations of Global Poverty: Aid, Development and International NGOs* (London: I.B. Tauris, 2014).

16 Betsey Powell, "Rob Ford: Dispute Erupts at Council Meeting," *Toronto Star*, November 18, 2013, http://www.thestar.com/news/gta/2013/11/18/rob_ford_council_proposal_to_curb_mayors_power_moves_ahead.html.

17 Vijay Prashad, *The Darker Nations: A People's History of the Third World* (New York: New Press, 2007), 6–11.

18 Ibid., xv, 34.

19 Eduardo Galeano, *Upside Down: A Primer for Our Looking Glass World* (New York: St. Martin's Press, 2001).

20 For the latest examples, see John Price, *Orienting Canada: Race, Empire, and the Transpacific* (Vancouver: University of British Columbia Press, 2011); Jenny Burman, *Transnational Yearnings: Tourism, Migration, and the Diasporic City* (Vancouver: University of British Columbia Press, 2010); Lisa Rose Mar, *Brokering Belonging: Chinese in Canada's Exclusion Era, 1885–1945* (Toronto: University of Toronto Press, 2010); David Webster, *Fire and the Full Moon: Canada and Indonesia in a Decolonizing World* (Vancouver: University of British Columbia Press, 2009).

21 Ken Coates, *A Global History of Indigenous Peoples: Struggle and Survival* (New York: Palgrave Macmillan, 2004).

22 C.A. Bayly, Sven Beckert, Matthew Connely, Isabel Hofmeyr, Wendy Kozol, and Patricia Seed, "AHR Conversation: On Transnational History," *American Historical Review* 111, no. 5 (2006): 1442.

23 Alisha Nicole Apale and Valerie Stam, eds., *Generation NGO* (Toronto: Between the Lines, 2011); Rebecca Tiessen and Robert Huish, eds., *Globetrotting or Global Citizenship: Perils and Potential of International Experiential Learning* (Toronto: University of Toronto Press, 2014).

1

Indigenous Peoples, Colonialism, and Canada

SCOTT RUTHERFORD

Introduction

Approximately six million people in North America identify as having Indigenous ancestry. This chapter offers a brief introduction to some of the histories of global imperialism and colonialism that are formative in our understanding of Canada and to the historical experiences of Indigenous peoples.[1] Examining some of the ideas that drove colonialism will help readers better understand the way the past continues to shape daily experience for Indigenous peoples in Canada. The final section of this chapter introduces some of the ways Indigenous peoples, individually and collectively, have challenged and looked to change the historical inequalities born out of the colonial project. The suggested readings and discussion questions at the end of this chapter ask us to consider the attitudes and practices that shape the contemporary relations that Canada continues to have with the colonial project.

The Global Imperial System

For at least 10,000 years prior to their first sustained contact with European merchants and traders, Indigenous peoples occupied the various regions of what is now North America. Some estimates suggest that upwards of 90 million people may have lived on the land that became known as North America. Other scholars offer a lower number, suggesting that the population was likely between 2 and 10 million.[2] Regardless of the exact figures, North America was a widely diverse place, with competing social customs and worldviews, hundreds of different languages being spoken, and periods of cooperation and conflict between and within communities. For Indigenous peoples, life before European colonization was not without complications. In the thirteenth century CE, for example, communities across the eastern half of the continent began suffering from what historians have termed "a long period of climatic deterioration."[3] In turn, these environmental changes set off periods of disease and corresponding social dislocation, ravaging many communities before European arrival. Christopher Columbus did not "discover" a peaceful paradise when he arrived in the

Americas in the late fifteenth century, but instead found societies immersed in complex domestic, cultural, and social relations.

For all of its symbolic power, 1492, the year of Columbus's landing, made little immediate difference for most Indigenous peoples in the Americas (though for the Taino peoples kidnapped and brought back to Spain, the effect was, indeed, immediate).[4] In other words, it took time—centuries for some—for the relationship between Indigenous peoples and European societies in what is now Canada to become such a lopsided affair. Europeans and Indigenous peoples in what became Canada actually came into contact centuries before Columbus. Norse Vikings landed in what is now Newfoundland in the tenth century. Though intent on settling this territory, Vikings were pushed back by Indigenous communities hostile to such incursions (though not before Vikings took captive several Beothuk—or possibly Mi'kmaq). The descendants of the Norse returned and took several Inuit captive in 1420, this time marking their feat by hanging Inuit kayaks in a cathedral in Tromsø, a Norwegian city.[5]

"Canada" exists because Europeans explored, exploited, and colonized territory outside of their own borders. Portuguese and Spanish merchants came to North America at the end of the fifteenth century hoping to establish new trade routes and to expand Christian influence. The middle of the sixteenth century saw the French, British, and Dutch arrive. Robert J.C. Young argues that colonialism "involved an extraordinary range of different forms and practices carried out with respect to radically different cultures, over many different centuries."[6] While this is true, European colonial empires shared some common goals. They believed that colonizing North America would allow for new forms of commerce and trade to emerge, at the time hoping to jumpstart their own stalled economies. They were also motivated by international competition. In other words, the global colonial project was also a game of imperial one-upmanship. If one European power obtained a new technology or resource, such as gunpowder, others had to find a comparable resource to maintain the balance of power between European empires. Other scholars remind us that the colonial project was also greatly influenced by people on the ground, whose own activities were often unsanctioned and often at odds with the wishes of imperial officials. At first these were mainly men involved in commerce and the military who were looking for personal financial gain. Increasingly, however, they were immigrants from Europe who came with promises of private property and new opportunities that often led to the subjugation and displacement of Indigenous peoples.[7] With all of these diverging motivations, it is understandable that we see little unity in the colonial project from the perspective of settler histories. Yet from the perspective of Indigenous peoples, the differing European motivations mattered little as the colonial project led to the dispossession of land and the wide-ranging subjugation of diverse cultural practices and worldviews on a large scale. To help us understand this history we will examine a two-part process: exploitative colonialism and settler colonialism.[8]

Exploitative Colonialism

Exploitative colonialism and imperialism are closely related, somewhat interchangeable concepts. However, for our purposes, colonialism and its modifiers (exploitative and settler) best help us understand the development of Canada as a colonial space. Most European powers first viewed territories in North America, Latin America, and the Caribbean not as places they wanted to live in, but instead as places over which they could rule to generate wealth to be brought back home. They wanted to extract large amounts of resources as cheaply as possible, thus maximizing their profit, a process called exploitative colonialism. Sugar, for example, had become popular in Europe, yet its extraction from the Caribbean required a massive influx of people to do the work. After Indigenous peoples were literally worked to death, enslaved people taken from West Africa became the main source of colonial labour. Indeed, slavery was a key ingredient that helped feed European financial growth from the sixteenth century onward. As Louis XIV of France remarked, "There is nothing which contributes more to the development of the colonies and the cultivation of their soil than the laborious toil of the Negroes."[9] By the early seventeenth century, 900,000 men and women had been brought to the Americas as slaves. Over the next 300 years, close to 14 million more enslaved people would toil in the Americas. The transatlantic slave trade is thus crucial to understanding the origins of colonialism in the Americas, Canada included. Most of us are familiar with the use of slaves in the United States and the Caribbean, yet few recognize the place of slavery in the development of Canada. In the aftermath of King Philip's war in 1676, for instance, Indigenous peoples were captured and moved to ports in Spain, Morocco, and the Caribbean where they were sold into slavery.[10] In the seventeenth and eighteenth centuries both Indigenous and black men and women were enslaved and played an important role in Montreal's commercial district. "[F]ully half of all colonists who owned a home in 1725," Brett Rushforth writes, "also owned an Indian slave."[11] Slavery, as David Austin reminds us, continues to influence our opinions on race in Canada, even if we do not always recognize the connection.[12]

Slavery's abolition by all European powers and the United States did not end the practice of exploitative colonialism. Until the mid-eighteenth century European exploitative colonialism in North America tended to take place around the eastern and southern parts of the continent as the west was still considered "Indian territory."[13] The onset of the fur trade signalled the beginning of sustained commercial relations between Indigenous peoples and outsiders in what is now Canada. This also initiated profound social, political, cultural, and spiritual change for future generations of Indigenous peoples across the burgeoning colonial landscapes of North America. For example, Indigenous peoples participated in the fur trade and adopted tools and technologies imported from Europe.[14] Conversely, fur traders relied upon Indigenous knowledge and kin networks for survival in harsh new lands. As Ken S. Coates reminds us, "[e]arly European settlements on the east coast of the Americas, throughout Africa, and in Asia often experienced strikingly high death rates. Indigenous peoples often came to their assistance by introducing local medical treatments, giving them food, and otherwise assisting the newcomers with their adaption to strange lands."[15]

Indigenous peoples also proved key allies during the periods of both French-British warfare and British-American warfare. During wars with the United States, for instance, British forces sought out Indigenous allies from the eastern woodlands because the latter were known as fierce warriors. If such alliances implied a balance of power, the "century of diplomacy and warfare," as J.R. Miller calls it, ended with significant dispossession and destabilization for Indigenous communities.[16] The nearly century-long competition between France and Britain for economic and political control along the St. Lawrence River and Eastern Canada contributed significantly to the destabilization of long-term intertribal Indigenous alliances, often resulting in violent conflict between former allies.[17]

European imperial expansion was at its most violent in the period between 1870 and 1945. The scramble to exploit and occupy foreign lands, to revel in the resources and grandeur they provided, created many colonial wars and battles, two of which took place in what is now western Canada. In 1870 and 1885, British and Canadian forces sent some of their most experienced "imperial soldiers" to the west to quell Aboriginal and Métis uprisings. This was part of a "global pattern of conflict over land and resources."[18] With significantly better weapons and much deeper pockets, Europeans emerged victorious in the vast majority of these battles over a variety of Indigenous peoples. After successful stamping out the 1870 rebellion in western Canada, Lord Garnet Wolseley and many of his soldiers travelled the world participating in similar military expeditions, also extinguishing an Ashantee rebellion against British rule in West Africa in 1873.[19]

By 1930 "almost 85 percent of the world's territory either was part of an imperial system or, as in the case of much of Latin America, had formerly been European colonial holdings."[20] Britain took the lead in developing a settler-colonial empire, including British North America (Canada), Australia, and New Zealand, while France treated Algeria as a new form of settlement colony as did Portugal with Brazil.[21]

Settler Colonialism

During the seventeenth century, immigrants from Europe began to arrive with the intention of permanent settlement. Though European powers still valued colonies for their richness of natural resources, they also began to see them as valuable places for the relocation and settlement of their own people. Populating the colonies with Europeans was believed to have several benefits. In theory it would open up new markets for domestic European goods, which were being manufactured rapidly thanks to the advent of factories and new technologies. It also came at a moment when government policy makers and scholars were increasingly worried about "overpopulation" of their home territory. Settlement, or the facilitation of permanent migration from the United Kingdom to British North America (and then Canada), would help solve such problems. In conjunction with the drive for settlement, colonial governments were also concerned with transforming Indigenous peoples into "modern" subjects. By the nineteenth century, European thinkers believed that this transformation could only emerge with the knowledge, disposition, and institutions that they possessed.

By the late 1800s the United States and the newly confederated dominion of Canada were well into the west, into "Indian territory." The dispossession of land from Indigenous peoples was not a quick process. During the era of the fur trade, but especially as it ended, this took place through several strategies: violent attacks, negotiation, forced relocation, and policies that sought total assimilation of European values.[22] This was part of the sustained pressure that "Indigenous peoples have faced . . . to limit cultural and biological pluralism" and to force integration into "a single global system whose primary medium is universalized capitalism."[23] Attempts to secure land, limit pluralism, and assimilate Indigenous people into capitalism often took shape through treaties and formal agreements. These agreements were foundational to the creation of Canada as a modern settler state.

Land and Settler Colonialism

Empire- and nation-building were predicated on gaining land, which in most cases meant actively taking it away from the original inhabitants. "Territoriality," according to Patrick Wolfe, "is settler colonialism's specific, irreducible element."[24] This is how Canada came into existence. Specific notions about the relationship of land development to private ownership deeply shaped settler colonial mentality. This view held that Indigenous peoples were not using the land "properly" and were not capable of doing so without the enlightened guidance of European knowledge.[25] European conceptions about land and improvement were shaped by widely circulating imagery and ideas about Indigenous peoples as "savage" and "untamable" objects, attributes that made them appear as animals more than as human beings. This helped foster the sense that when a person left overcrowded European cities they were arriving on "virgin" soil—*terra nullis*, in other words. This ignored ways that Indigenous peoples had conceptualized and used land for centuries before European arrival (and afterwards during the fur-trade era). Europeans not only came with ideas about the sanctity of private property and land use but also with the means to implement their vision. New rules of law emerged as a key tactic of land control, helping shape the racial organization of Canada as a "white settler" colony.[26] "At each stage," writes Sherene Razack, "the story installs Europeans as entitled to the land, a claim that is codified in law."[27] When Europeans took control of peoples that they had been portraying as uncivilized, it seemed to confirm that myth and reality were the same.

Box 1.1 Culture and Colonialism: Orientalism

In his famous book *Orientalism* (1978), noted postcolonial scholar Edward Said showed how the European colonial project generated a body of knowledge—a perceived set of truths and convictions— about the identity of Westerners based on the portrayal of peoples and societies from the East, or "the Orient." Said demonstrated how through commonly reproduced *discourse* and *imagery* Westerners created an entrenched structure of binary attitudes that reduced whole groups of people to a number of essential characteristics that were used to explain group behaviour, values, attitudes, and cultural practices (Indigenous peoples were most often described with negative characteristics, while Europeans were described with positives). This helped Westerners imagine that the colonial project was necessary in order to help uplift the colonized out of an inferior state of being. Another important postcolonial theorist, Frantz Fanon, argued that colonial domination took shape because the colonized also internalized a sense of inferiority. These insights are particularly important when we consider how Canadian policies toward Indigenous peoples developed and the lasting legacies of such policies and attitudes.

Figure 1.1 Crown–Aboriginal treaties in Canada, 1763–2005

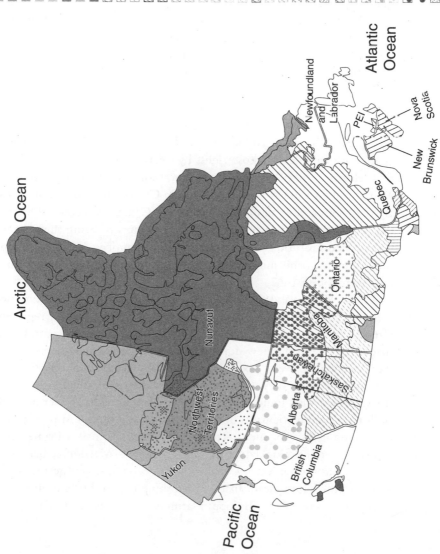

Yukon First Nations traditional territories (1993)
Inuvialuit settlement region (1984)
Sahtu (1994)
Tlicho (2003)
Gwich'in settlement region (1992)
Tsawwassen First Nation (2007)
Maa-nulth First Nation (2007)
Nisga'a First Nation (2000)
Nunavut settlement area (1993)
Nunavik Marine Region (1975,1978)
Nunatsiavut settlement area (2005)
Eeyou Marine Region (2002)
James Bay and northern Quebec (1975,1978)
Treaty No. 7 (1877)
Treaty No. 6 (1876)
Treaty No. 5 (1875)
Treaty No. 4 (1874)
Treaty No. 2 (1871)
Treaty No. 1 (1871)
Treaty No. 3 (1873)
Treaty No. 9 (1905)
Robinson-Superior (1850)
Robinson-Huron (1850)
Willams Treaties (1923)
Southern Ontario (1764–1862)
Peace and Friendship Treaties (1725–1779)
Treaty No. 8 (1899)
Treaty No. 9 (1929–1930)
Treaty No. 10 (1906)
Treaty No. 6 (1889)
Treaty No. 11 (1921)
Douglas Treaties (1850–1854)
Treaty No. 5 (1908)

Treaties are formalized records of negotiated agreements between parties. They can exist between states or between people.[28] Treaty making with Indigenous peoples was central to the foundation of Canada. These negotiated settlements, along with assimilation policies enacted through the *Indian Act*, became the instruments that helped strengthen Canada's colonization of Indigenous peoples as the dispossession of land took place not only through seizure, but also through "engaged legal processes," according to historian John C. Weaver, "ones manipulated by colonizers."[29] Three types of land acquisitions helped shape Canada's development. Early agreements, such as those between First Nations of the western plains and the Hudson's Bay Company, were commercial compacts that, in exchange for material goods and protections, allowed Europeans to trade. A second type were the formalized military alliances between Indigenous peoples and the British imperial government. The final, and arguably most consequential today, were the territorial treaties that began to emerge in the 1760s and continued to be negotiated through the 1920s, and which were again resumed in the 1970s.

One of the most important early treaties was the Royal Proclamation of 1763. Issued by England's King George III, the Royal Proclamation recognized "the rights and lands of Indigenous groups and established the system of surrendering those rights by treaty."[30] It is a treaty with continued relevance. In 2013, for example, the Indigenous rights group Idle No More invoked 1763 as a formative year in Crown and Indigenous relations. By the 1850s almost all of southern Upper Canada was covered by treaties that transferred land to the Crown. The attempts to bring the west under Canada's control took place through a similar process. This led to what is now known as the numbered treaties, agreements made after Canadian confederation in 1867.

From 1871 until 1877, First Nations from across what is now northwestern Ontario, Manitoba, Saskatchewan, and parts of Alberta, representing Cree, Ojibwa, Assiniboines, Sarcees, Blackfoot, Bloods, Stoneys, and Piegans, made treaty with the new dominion of Canada. These agreements, which were negotiated over a six-year period, were not monolithic (local context mattered), but they did generally reorganize the political geography of the Canadian west. Indigenous peoples and the Canadian government were both motivated participants in this process. While European powers looked to Africa and Asia for their territorial expansion, Canada's Prime Minister John A. Macdonald looked to the western prairies. Macdonald believed that the west was the source of Canada's future economic prosperity. However, securing this future meant first extinguishing the land title from the hands of Indigenous peoples so European farmers would have a place to settle and economically develop the land. As part of his National Policy, he also argued for a railway, a way to get these new settlers out to the west and to join Canada from coast to coast.

Like the Crown, Indigenous peoples were also motivated to enter into treaty. With rapidly depleting food sources, such as bison, prairie First Nations saw treaty as a way to ensure a future existence. In exchange for land they would receive some form of social assistance.[31] Those who negotiated Treaty No. 3 in the Kenora-Rainy River area in 1873, for example, feared not only further European settlement but also impending starvation. They also understood that their land had both material wealth, in the form of minerals, and strategic value to Canada. Because of the Indian wars in the United States, the path from Lake Superior to the Red River was of great strategic importance to the Canadian state.[32] This was obvious in the late 1800s when Métis communities rebelled against the appearance of railway and telegraph surveyors in what is now Manitoba. The numbered treaty process, along with attempts to suppress the rebellions led by Louis Riel in 1870 and 1885, was part of a pattern of intensified conflict over land and resources that was global in scope, as noted earlier.

If both parties came to the negotiating table as motivated participants, they did not do so with equal power. Moreover, significant disagreement remains regarding the terms agreed to in the numbered treaties, especially the word "cede." Oral histories suggest that the written version of treaties often narrowed the agreement's intended spirit. Instead of interpreting "cede" to mean the sharing of nonreserve land for mutual hunting and gathering activities, the Canadian state interpreted it as the total surrender of land in return for small parcels of land called reserves. Rather than being accidental misinterpretations, such changes always favoured the Canadian government. The written version of Treaty No. 1 signed by Saulteaux and Cree leaders in 1871 reportedly leaves out several clauses regarding the size of reserve lands, promises of hunting rights, and promises of assistance that would have benefited local Indigenous communities.[33]

When Indigenous peoples agreed to cede lands, they did so with promises that they would have land reserved specifically for them to live on while they would retain hunting and fishing rights elsewhere. Reserves in which Indigenous populations were separated from white Europeans were commonplace across the British Empire. There were numerous motivations behind this tactic. One was the belief that the state was protecting "inferior" peoples from being annihilated by mass settlement. This form of paternalism suggested that over time the "Indian" could be eliminated in favour of gradual assimilation in "citizenship." Reserves also cleared the way for industrial and agricultural development. This was especially true in western Canada (from the western shores of Lake Superior to Vancouver Island). Unlike in parts of Africa and Latin America where settler societies were interested in the surplus value of native labour, Canada was a settler society "far more interested in native land."[34]

Contrary to common belief, reserves are not only rural settlements but are also located in urban settings. The Kitsilano and Musqueam reserves, for example, were created in the middle of Vancouver, and neither group ceded the territories upon which city development took place.[35] Whether they are urban or rural, the press and the general public often speak of reserves in demeaning terms. According to scholars such as Jordan Stanger-Ross, calling reserves "waste lands," for example, "evoked a longstanding conviction that Aboriginal people failed to possess property in a fashion that settlers were bound to respect."[36] Reserves are some of the poorest places in Canada and are often likened to Third World slums. Life on reserves is difficult and made more so by the structural conditions that continue to not only hamper day-to-day survival, but also shape social relations within communities. Yet reserves are also centres of political organizing, the rebirth of Indigenous languages, and sites of burgeoning resistance and concern for environmental degradation—from tar sands in Alberta to clear-cutting in northwestern Ontario.

Missionaries

[H]istory shows the missionary system to be colonialism in the name of Christ. The foundation of colonial Christianity rests on its power to monopolize definitions: who is godless, godly, and most godly[.][37]
—*William Baldridge*

At its core, settler colonialism is about the ability of one group of people to impose their worldview and themselves upon another group of people. If the reserve is one of the physical manifestations of this "civilizing" process, another key element is missionaries, the foot soldiers of empire's civilizing mission.

In the effort to bring "civilization" to their new territories, Europeans employed religion. In 1512, 20 years after Columbus's landing, Pope Julius II, after some consternation, finally got around to deciding that, yes, "Indians" were indeed human beings, and as human beings it was possible for them to be converted to Christianity.[38] Following the lead of Spanish and Portuguese colonizers, the British and French also brought Christianity to the New World to help the civilizing goals of the colonial project. Indeed, the period of rapid European imperial expansion coincides with the "greatest age of Christian expansion since apostolic times." Because Christianity had a "virtually limitless interest in all sides of human behavior," missionaries worked both to convert and to convey the assumptions of a new civilization.[39] Before there were embassies and diplomatic corps there were missionaries, helping to transmit knowledge and information back and forth between different nations. Missionaries, who came to Canada as part of the fur trade, were "among the chief sponsors of imperial contact and one-to-one encounter in this period."[40] J.R. Miller writes that in the seventeenth century "France in particular would be stimulated to maintain contacts with aboriginal people because of a desire to convert them to Christianity." The English, Spanish, and Portuguese all participated in similar endeavours.[41] The Roman Catholic Oblate order provides a good example of how missionary activity in Canada was part of a global movement, partly spurred on by divisions between the Protestant and Catholic churches. Oblates were active not only in Eastern Canada, but also in Texas, parts of Africa, and Sri Lanka. They also were responsible for the majority of residential schools in Canada, a topic returned to below.[42]

The attempt to convert Indigenous peoples to Christianity reshaped social and familial practices. It also ignored the spiritual lives and traditions that already existed in all First Nations communities. From their stations, missionaries combined conversion with other interventions. In doing so, "[t]hey disrupted traditional forms of self-government, realigned local and regional work patterns, and, not least, sought to refashion a wide variety of indigenous domestic, child-rearing, healing, and bodily practices."[43] Much like other soldiers of the empire, missionaries plied their trade across the globe—from Kenya to British Columbia, imagining themselves as the "buffers" between Indigenous populations and settlers. Jesuits, for example, were active across Latin America, India, China, Japan, and, by the early seventeenth century, Eastern Canada. As in South America, Jesuits in Eastern Canada were, at times, critical of "colonialist exploitation." However, they took advantage of the trade routes and contacts established by fur traders to evangelize, particularly to Algonquian and Iroquoian communities. While Jesuits saw themselves as a more humane force than many of their colonial colleagues, Indigenous peoples saw them as part of the larger French presence. Accordingly, writes historian Allan Greer, the relationships established by missionaries with Indigenous peoples "must always be seen as one aspect of a wider process of colonization."[44] In part, this is because, as Ruth Compton Brouwer elaborates later in this book, missionaries looked to fundamentally reshape Indigenous societies. They brought "presumptions about the right gender order" and ideals about "work, domesticity, conjugality, and virtue" to new colonial spaces.[45]

Assimilation through Genocide: The *Indian Act* and Residential Schools

In 1876 the Canadian government created legislation called the *Indian Act*. Although amended several times since, it continues to have significant control over the lives of Aboriginal peoples. The *Indian Act* consolidated previous policies, grounded the state's assimilationist approach toward Indigenous peoples, and strengthened control over them. It operated upon almost every facet of Aboriginal life, from property rights, to political governance, to defining who could and could not be an Indian. One important example of this latter point: Aboriginal women were stripped of their Indian status if they married non-Aboriginal men, a regulation that remained on the books until 1985. For legal scholar Karen Engle, the *Indian Act*'s approach to property, territory, and identity mirrored the "general devaluation of indigenous culture and a desire to assimilate as many Indians as possible."[46] The pervasive racist ideologies that influenced the creation of this legislation have led some scholars to note the similarities between the *Indian Act* in Canada and the development of the apartheid state in South Africa during the twentieth century.[47]

The Canadian government imagined the *Indian Act* as a tool that would help transition Aboriginals from being "Indians" to being "Canadian citizens." Residential schools stand out as one of the *Indian Act*'s most destructive attempts at assimilating Indigenous peoples into dominant Canadian culture. They were operated as a partnership between the Department of Indian Affairs and Christian missionary bodies, and were an important tool in the government's attempts at assimilating Indigenous peoples into mainstream culture. These schools were the result of the official amalgamation of industrial schools and boarding schools in 1923, though in many ways this was merely a formality. By the early 1950s, one-third of all Aboriginal children were at residential schools, which were run by the Anglican, Catholic, Presbyterian, and United churches.[48] When the last of the schools closed in the 1990s, 150,000 children had passed through the nearly 140 Indian residential schools that had been in operation. According to Ronald Niezen, "[t]here are some 86,000 people alive today who once spent time as a child in an Indian residential school."[49] Many more people across generations, however, live with the consequences of this era.

The entire school system was premised on the belief that aboriginality could and should be replaced with Euro-Canadian identity. The aim was, as they put it at the time, to "kill the Indian in the child." For example, teachers often physically reprimanded those students who continued to speak their native language. The missionary zeal for using schooling to assimilate

Indigenous peoples had a long history in Canada, stretching back to the early-nineteenth-century missionary schools in Upper Canada. Residential schools were particularly terrible, though, as nuns and missionaries not only failed to provide basic academic instruction but also often treated children in their care poorly. The food was awful, and both physical and sexual abuse was common. Some children resisted by running away, stealing food, or drinking sacramental wine. Others resorted to arson. According to interviews with former students, in general the experience was one of "solitary shame in which they saw themselves as personally flawed and therefore responsible for the acts of which they were victims."[50] They had internalized the narrative of the colonizer. In May 2015, Supreme Court Chief Justice Beverley McLachlin called residential schooling an attempt by the government to commit "cultural genocide."[51]

Residential schools reflected widely held norms in Canada until the last of them was closed in the 1990s.[52] However, this was not the only effort to assimilate Indigenous peoples through the regulation of culture and societal practice. Alterations to the *Indian Act* in 1885, for instance, led to the prohibition of many cultural and spiritual practices for Indigenous peoples. The West Coast potlatch ceremonies were one of the first spiritual practices prohibited. Central to the social, economic, and political lives of Nuu-chah-nulth and Kwakwaka'wakw peoples, missionaries and government officials feared such ceremonies were anti-private property, detrimental to material progress and spiritual enlightenment, and a danger to recent Aboriginal converts to Christianity.[53] The government adopted a similar approach for many political and legal practices. In 1876, it used the *Indian Act* to legislate its right to depose hereditary chiefs; in 1880 it imposed elected band councils; and in 1884 it began deposing chiefs it did not like. The intent was clear: to "reinforce the notion that Euro-Canadian society considered native ways inferior."[54]

Only in 1951 did the government lift its ban on ceremonies and the ability to raise money to pursue land claims and other political goals. Wars, dispossession, and assimilative policies have taken a toll on Indigenous peoples. Anthropologist Douglas Ubelaker, for example, suggests that Indigenous populations declined 78 per cent in North America over the period between 1650 and 1985 and more than 200 unique languages were made extinct.[55] Because assimilation was used so blatantly to destroy the integrity of Indigenous cultures, scholars and Aboriginal leaders today are increasingly calling the provisions of the *Indian Act* acts of cultural genocide. The dual processes of exploitative colonialism (imperialism) and settler colonialism also profoundly reshaped almost every aspect of Indigenous life, including diet and subsistence practices, housing and settlement, social interaction, and kinship relations.

Indigenous Movements: Canada and the Americas

Famed Canadian media pundit Rex Murphy recently scolded those who use categories such as "colonialism and racism and genocide" to describe Canada's treatment of Indigenous peoples. He felt that this not only misrepresented reality but that it also proved disrespectful "of many—most—Canadians" who only wanted to help Indigenous peoples. According to Murphy, this was the type of "razor rhetoric" that equates attitudes of the nineteenth century with today.[56] Murphy's arguments came on the heels of a new upsurge in Indigenous activism, including those organizing under the banner of Idle No More. These groups insist on using pointed words such as "colonialism" to describe how Indigenous people are treated by the Canadian government as well as by many Canadian citizens and corporations.[57] From the late 1950s onward, these processes were inspired by and intersected with global movements for change worldwide, as Indigenous peoples located their struggles in a broader international framework of colonialism, industrialization, and capitalism.

Indigenous people and their supporters are unconvinced by arguments by Murphy and many others, which neatly separate the past and present. In the early 1960s, Métis and Aboriginal intellectuals began making explicit links between past and present, writing about how their world was profoundly shaped by structures and attitudes of the nineteenth century. They did so partly out of frustration with the poor standards of living many endured daily. Conditions on reserves were deplorable—many still did not have running water, electricity, or proper toilet facilities. Welfare dependency rates, for example, were 10 times the national average, reflecting the difficulty Indigenous peoples had finding well-paid, permanent employment, and the mortality rate was double what it was for non-Aboriginals.

When Lester B. Pearson's Liberals took power in Ottawa in 1963, they invested time and money in the idea that community development projects and less restrictive enfranchisement could help fix the problems faced by Indigenous communities. In this they were continuing a process already initiated by John Diefenbaker's Progressive Conservative government.[58] In 1960, the same year as it enacted its Bill of Rights, the Canadian government extended the federal franchise to registered Indians.[59] For Ellen Fairclough, the Minister of Citizenship, the vote would "remove in the eyes of the world any suggestion that in Canada race or colour places any citizen in an inferior category to other citizens of the country."[60] Indigenous peoples in Canada, however, did not unanimously support this gesture. "The issue of the franchise," argues historian Anthony Hall, "was, and still is, at the symbolic core of some of the central strategic questions facing virtually all Indigenous peoples in nation-states not of their own making."[61] It quickly became a point of contention for several provincial Indigenous organizations, especially in Saskatchewan and Alberta, and a point of protest by Mi'kmaq and Mohawks in Eastern Canada.[62] In 1969 the federal government issued a "White Paper" (the *Statement of the Government of Canada on Indian Policy*), a document many perceived to be a move to privatize and municipalize reserves, terminate treaties, and dismantle the infrastructure of Indian Affairs, all in the name of equality. Aboriginal leaders called it "cultural genocide." In essence, the White Paper was proposed as a civil rights initiative but fulfilled longstanding assimilationist aims.

During the post–World War II period, a number of federal, provincial, and treaty organizations began taking a prominent role as representatives of Indigenous peoples, including status and non-status Indians. By the late 1960s, calls for Indigenous nationhood and sovereignty in North America gave rise to a movement sometimes called "Red Power." As with the other "power" movements of the late 1960s, Red Power activists, in groups such as the American Indian Movement, Native Alliance for Red Power, and the Ojibway Warriors Society, included a number of young Indigenous men and women who were fed up with the state of Aboriginal life in Canada and inspired by global movements for social change.

Of course not all people with Indigenous ancestry have become political activists. As is the case with all marginalized groups, many have attempted simply to adapt, survive, and make do. However, since the 1960s there has been a noticeable upsurge in the numbers of Indigenous organizations that have adopted a range of tactics and strategies to publicize their discontent. Sociologist Howard Ramos estimates that during the 1960s and 1970s there were at least 300 such demonstrations in Canada. This ranged from small petitions to more sensational actions such as road blockades.[63]

There is no one category in which we can locate such protests. Indeed, local issues are simultaneously also wrapped up in provincial and federal policies, Crown relations, and more abstract legacies of the global colonial project. For instance, beginning in the early 1970s, the James Bay Cree in northern Quebec adopted a series of strategies to fend off both Quebec's and Canada's attempts at hydroelectric development on their territory. Over the course of decades of conflict with various levels of government, the Cree of James Bay came to see themselves as a nation of people who, according to Jenson and Papillon, demanded "recognition of collective rights, particularly Aboriginal title." The demand of the Cree "to be treated as a people with its own identity, history, and culture" not only represented Canada as a "multinational country" but also "rejected" the popularly shared notion that "Canadians are all equal citizens, distinguished only by categories such as language, gender, ethnicity, or socioeconomic status."[64]

The loss of land (treaty and unceded), economic development, education rights, and cultural rights have been the focus of many Indigenous organizations and individuals. While situated locally, intellectuals and activists have stressed their identity as Indigenous peoples within a more global framework. Increasingly, they recognize their issues are part of a larger pattern of the effects of industrialization and capitalism worldwide. Around the world, Indigenous peoples have begun to recognize their shared common cultural characteristics as well as their similar experiences with colonization. This has led to a wide range of Indigenous organizing and self-expression, which included protests. "Aboriginal protest," writes Coates, "helped weave thousands of local struggles into a series of national, regional, and ultimately international organizations."[65] North American Indigenous groups are frequently considered on the global scale to be most closely related to the Indigenous groups of Australia and New Zealand, due primarily to the similarities of their colonial histories.[66] Yet, in the pursuit of redress, acknowledgement, and cultural survival, Indigenous peoples in Canada have been joined by others across the Americas, Africa, Australia, and New Zealand. While there were many important Indigenous actors and thinkers during the 1960s and 1970s, Howard Adams and Lee Maracle stand out as two social justice advocates who highlighted the similarities between Third World decolonization and the attempts of Indigenous peoples in North America to challenge and undo the legacies of the colonial project here.[67]

Since the 1960s and 1970s, Indigenous peoples have adopted a variety of tactics and strategies by which to voice both frustration with the current state of affairs and hope that the future will be better. Global recognition has increased through organizations such as the World Council for Indigenous Peoples along with various initiatives within the United Nations. Highly symbolic declarations such as the United Nations Declaration on the Rights of Indigenous Peoples have put Canada in the awkward position of being one of four countries that, over time, have consistently opposed such initiatives. From symbolic confrontation to very dramatic and real conflict, such as in Oka in 1990, Indigenous communities have continued to face incursions both from the state and from private business on the very little land that First Nations hold. From James Bay in 1973, to Grassy Narrows in the mid-1970s and again since the 1990s, to the Six Nations of Grand River near Caledonia since the mid-2000s, Indigenous communities have needed to engage in high-profile, often times confrontational, tactics in an effort to gain (or simply not lose) control over economic development and resource extraction on traditional lands.

Living Legacies: From Idle No More to #AmINext

> During the Winter we danced, the vast amount of critical and
> creative expressions that took place is like the footprints
> we left in the snow, sand, and earth: incalculable.[68]

The 2010s have witnessed new forms of Indigenous protest and new
demands for recognition and change. Women from many different Indigenous communities have been the focal points of numerous recent high-
profile events. In November 2012, four Indigenous women in Saskatchewan
called a meeting to discuss Bill C-45, a federal "omnibus" bill that included
significant changes to the *Indian Act* and drastic rollbacks on environmental
protection. They organized under the banner "Idle No More," and word of
the meeting and the slogan quickly spread through social media. The group
helped galvanize opposition to Bill C-45 but also helped draw attention to
other pressing issues including the housing crisis in Attawapiskat (which
included a hunger strike by Chief Theresa Spence) and demands for recognition of the inherent and shared rights of Indigenous peoples.[69] The early
months of 2013 were characterized by an array of Idle No More protests:
flashmobs, healing dances, marches, drum circles, blockades, and petitions, to
name a few. Its appeal carried far beyond Canadian borders. An international
day of solidarity in early January 2013 saw 265 simultaneous rallies, in places
such as New Zealand, Bulgaria, the United States, Mexico, and India.[70] This
helps reveal how Indigenous movements could effectively harness the power
of social media to create widespread awareness about the array of problems
facing Indigenous communities in Canada.

Recent campaigns have shown us that the legacies of settler-colonial
policies and attitudes are still alive in Canada. Though it first made news
in the mid-1990s, the vast number of missing and murdered Indigenous
women in Canada has become a topic of public concern. There were 1,186
cases in the 30 years up to May 2014, with 1,026 women presumed dead
and another 160 remaining missing. This number was first believed to be
closer to 500 until an RCMP investigation in 2013 nearly doubled the
figure. Organizations such as the Native Women's Association of Canada
have been vocal about the need for a national inquiry, a demand that Stephen Harper's government steadfastly refused to meet. Prime Minister
Harper's rationale was to characterize these as criminal justice cases, not
sociological ones. However, the cases of missing and murdered Aboriginal
women are inextricably tied to material and cultural histories of settler-
colonialism. Many have argued that the cultural codes of African American
slavery have outlived the actual practice. Similarly, centuries of disrespectful

representations of Indigenous bodies, especially those of women, are related to these criminal disappearances and the subsequent failure to value their lives. As the victims are represented in the press as being on the margins of society (some of the murdered were also sex workers) and as pervasive negative stereotypes associated with Aboriginal women continue to be held, Canadians have generally failed to show the necessary concern that would make these cases a more important political issue for current and past governments.[71]

Conclusion

On August 16, 2014, the body of Tina Fontaine, a 15-year-old girl from Sagkeeng First Nation in Manitoba, was found in a bag and dragged out of the Red River near the Alexander Docks in Winnipeg. She had been missing; now she had been murdered. News of Fontaine's death, her youth, and the recent attention toward such incidents sparked spontaneous acts of remembrance and grief across Canada, but especially in Winnipeg. The day after Fontaine's body was pulled from the river, for example, over 2,000 people gathered for a vigil at the Forks in downtown Winnipeg. Renewed calls for a national inquiry splashed across the editorial pages of newspapers across Canada. The premiers of each province jointly called for, at the very least, a national roundtable with them, Aboriginal leaders and community groups, and the Prime Minister and Minister of Justice. Yet little has happened, except that Indigenous women continue to lose their lives as our political leaders ignore them. We do not hold state parades for those who die under bridges or are beaten and left for dead in the cold November waters of a river in Winnipeg.[72]

The majority of this textbook focuses on the external relations forged between Canada, Canadians, and the "Third World." Yet many of the attitudes and practices of Canadians outside of our borders have long been features that have also shaped our own local, regional, and national histories, including that of missionaries, mercantile and then industrial capitalists, and the displacement and subjugation of a land's first peoples. We would do well to remember that the attitudes that helped shape the colonial encounter—particularly a sense of a naturalized racial hierarchy—have not been consigned to the past, but continue to live today. Such attitudes have helped mute Canada's response to mounting evidence that colonial institutions, particularly residential schooling, were unmitigated travesties. As Canadian historian Adele Perry reminds us, recent reports like that of the Truth and Reconciliation Commission on Residential Schools, "demand we place indigenous peoples' version of the history of residential schooling, *and indeed Canada*, at the centre rather than the margin of the history we tell."

"This is our history," she writes, "all of ours."[73]

Discussion Questions

1) What are the similarities and differences between exploitative colonialism and settler colonialism?

2) How do settler-colonial attitudes influence Canada–Indigenous relations today?

3) What strategies have Indigenous peoples and communities used to help mitigate the effects of Canadian policies, such as those that created residential schooling?

4) As you read other chapters, note the similarities and differences in the ways that Indigenous communities were treated in Canada and how Canadians have historically acted in relation to different peoples in the Third World. What do you think accounts for those similarities? What do you think accounts for the differences?

Further Readings

Daschuk, James. *Clearing the Plains: Disease, Politics of Starvation, and the Loss of Aboriginal Life*. Regina: University of Regina Press, 2013.

The Kino-nda-niimi Collective, ed. *The Winter We Danced: Voice from the Past, the Future, and the Idle No More Movement*. Winnipeg: Arp Books, 2014.

Miller, J.R. *Compact, Contract, Covenant: Aboriginal Treaty-Making in Canada*. Toronto: University of Toronto Press, 2009.

Regan, Paulette. *Unsettling the Settler Within: Indian Residential Schools, Truth Telling, and Reconciliation in Canada*. Vancouver: University of British Columbia Press, 2010.

Simpson, Audra. *Mohawk Interruptus: Political Life Across the Borders of Settler States*. Durham: Duke University Press, 2014.

Willow, Anna T. *Strong Hearts, Native Lands: Anti-Clearcutting Activism at Grassy Narrows First Nation*. Winnipeg: University of Manitoba Press, 2012.

Notes

1   For a thorough discussion on terminology, see http://indigenousfoundations. arts.ubc.ca/home/identity/aboriginal-identity-terminology.html.

2   James Daschuk, *Clearing the Plains: Disease, Politics of Starvation, and the Loss of Aboriginal Life* (Regina: University of Regina Press, 2013), 1; Robert J. Muckle, *Indigenous Peoples of North America: A Concise Anthropological Overview* (Toronto: University of Toronto Press, 2013), 67.

3   Daschuk, *Clearing the Plains*, xvi.

4   Sarah Carter, *Aboriginal People and the Colonizers of Western Canada to 1900* (Toronto: University of Toronto Press, 1999), 23.

5   Jace Weaver, "The Red Atlantic: Transoceanic Cultural Exchanges," *American Indian Quarterly* 35, no. 3 (2011): 424.

6   Robert J.C. Young, *Postcolonialism: An Historical Introduction* (Oxford: Blackwell, 2001), 17.

7   Éric Allina-Pisano, "Imperialism and the Colonial Experience," in *Introduction to International Development: Approaches, Actors, and Issues*, ed. Paul Haslam, Jessica Schafer, and Pierre Beaudet (Toronto: Oxford University Press, 2012), 29–32.

8   I am borrowing this framework that was developed by Young in *Postcolonialism*, especially "Part 1: Concepts in History," 13–70.

9   Louis XIV as quoted by Eric Williams, "Capitalism and Slavery," in *Race and Racialization: Essential Readings*, ed. Tania Das Gupta et al. (Toronto: Canadian Scholars' Press, 2007), 149.

10 Weaver, "The Red Atlantic," 431.

11 Brett Rushforth, "'A Little Flesh We Offer You': The Origins of Indian Slavery in New France," *William and Mary Quarterly* 3rd Series, 60, no. 4 (October 2003): 777.

12 David Austin, *Fear of a Black Nation: Race, Sex and Security in Sixties Montreal* (Toronto: Between the Lines Press, 2013), 7–12.

13 Muckle, *Indigenous Peoples*, 110.

14 Ibid., 116.

15 Ken S. Coates, *A Global History of Indigenous Peoples: Struggle and Survival* (New York: Palgrave Macmillan, 2004), 173.

16 J.R. Miller, "Introduction," in *Aboriginal Peoples of Canada: A Short Introduction*, ed. Paul Robert Magocsi (Toronto: University of Toronto Press, 2002), 23.

17 Bonita Lawrence, "Rewriting Histories of the Land: Colonization and Indigenous Resistance in Easter Canada," in *Race, Space, and the Law: Unmapping a White Settler Society*, ed. Sherene H. Razack (Toronto: Between the Lines Press, 2002), 26–27.

18 Carter, *Aboriginal People*, 101.

19 Edgar Holt, "Garnet Wolseley: Soldier of Empire," *History Today* 8, no. 10 (October 1958): 706–09.

20 Tony Ballantyne and Antoinette Burton, "Empires and the Reach of the Global," in *A World Connecting: 1870–1945*, ed. Emily S. Rosenberg (Cambridge, MA: Harvard University Press, 2012), 285.

21 Young, *Postcolonialism*, 16–17.

22 Muckle, *Indigenous Peoples*, 110.

23 Anthony Hall, *The American Empire and the Fourth World: The Bowl with One Spoon* (Montreal: McGill-Queen's University Press, 2004), 70.

24 Patrick Wolfe, "Settler Colonialism and the Elimination of the Native," *Journal of Genocide Research* 8, no. 4 (2006): 388.

25 John C. Weaver, *The Great Land Rush and the Making of the Modern World, 1650–1900* (Montreal: McGill-Queen's University Press, 2003), 11–12.

26 Ballantyne and Burton, "Empires and the Reach," 309.

27 Sherene Razack, "Introduction," in *Race, Space, and the Law: Unmapping a White Settler Society*, ed. Sherene H. Razack (Toronto: Between the Lines, 2002), 3.

28 Miller, *Introduction*, 3.

29 Weaver, *The Great Land Rush*, 13.

30 Muckle, *Indigenous Peoples*, 113.

31 Daschuk, *Clearing the Plains*, 183.

32 Frank Tough, *As Their Natural Resources Fail: Native Peoples and the Economic History of Northern Manitoba, 1870–1930* (Vancouver: University of British Columbia Press, 2011), 88.

33 J.R. Miller, *Compact, Contract, Covenant: Aboriginal Treaty-Making in Canada* (Toronto: University of Toronto Press, 2009), 164.

34 Cole Harris, "How Did Colonialism Dispossess? Comments from an Edge of Empire," *Annals of the Association of American Geographers* 94, no. 1 (2004): 167.

35 Jordan Stanger-Ross, "Municipal Colonialism in Vancouver City Planning and the Conflict over Indian Reserves, 1928–1950s," *Canadian Historical Review* 89, no. 4 (2008): 547.

36 Stanger-Ross, "Municipal Colonialism," 542.

37 William Baldridge, "Reclaiming Our Histories," in *The Post-Colonial Studies Reader*, 2nd ed., ed. Bill Ashcroft, Gareth Griffiths, and Helen Tiffin (New York: Routledge, 2006), 528.

38 Weaver, "The Red Atlantic," 425.

39 J.M. Roberts and Odd Arne Westad, *The Penguin History of the World*, 6th ed. (Toronto: Penguin Books, 2012), 794

40 Ballantyne and Burton, "Empires and the Reach," 322.

41 Miller, "Introduction," 20.

42 *Honouring the Truth, Reconciling for the Future: Summary of the Final Report of the Truth and Reconciliation Commission of Canada* (Ottawa: Truth and Reconciliation Commission of Canada, 2015), 52.

43 Ballantyne and Burton, "Empires and the Reach," 325.

44 Allan Greer, ed., *The Jesuit Relations: Natives and Missionaries in Seventeenth-Century North America* (Boston: Bedford/St. Martin's, 2000), 6.

45 Brouwer, this volume.

46 Karen Engle, *The Elusive Promise of Indigenous Development: Rights, Culture, Strategy* (Durham, NC: Duke University Press, 2010), 29.

47 Hall, *American Empire*, 503–09.

48 J.R. Miller, *Reflection on Native-Newcomer Relations: Selected Essays* (Toronto: University of Toronto Press, 2004), 184; Paulette Regan, *Unsettling the Settler Within: Indian Residential Schools, Truth Telling, and Reconciliation in Canada* (Vancouver: University of British Columbia Press, 2010), 4.

49 Ronald Niezen, *Truth and Indignation: Canada's Truth and Reconciliation Commission on Residential Schools* (Toronto: University of Toronto Press, 2013), 1–2.

50 Ibid., 26.

51 Gloria Galloway and Bill Curry, "'Cultural Genocide' Cited as Goal of Residential Schools," *Globe and Mail*, June 2, 2015, 1, 10.

52 Niezen, *Truth and Indignation*, 27.

53 Katherine Pettipas, *Severing the Ties That Bind: Government Repression of Indigenous Religious Ceremonies on the Prairies* (Winnipeg: University of Manitoba Press, 1994), 88–92.

54 Miller, "Introduction," 32.

55 Muckle, *Indigenous Peoples*, 119.

56 Rex Murphy, "A Rude Dismissal of Canada's Generosity," *National Post*, October 19, 2013, http://fullcomment.nationalpost.com/2013/10/19/rex-murphy-a-rude-dismissal-of-canadas-generosity/.

57 See, for example, the vast collections of essays and reflections in The Kino-nda-niimi Collective, ed., *The Winter We Danced: Voice from the Past, the Future, and the Idle No More Movement* (Winnipeg: Arp Books, 2014).

58 Hugh Shewell, "'Bitterness Behind Every Smiling Face': Community Development and Canada's First Nations, 1954–1968," *The Canadian Historical Review* 83, no. 1 (2002).

59 Until 1960, only Aboriginal peoples who accepted taxation, lived off-reserve, or were war veterans had been allowed the federal franchise. At the provincial level, they were denied the franchise in New Brunswick and Prince Edward Island until 1963 and in Quebec until 1969.

60 Ellen Fairclough quoted in Richard H. Bartlett, "Citizens Minus: Indians and the Right to Vote," *Saskatchewan Law Review* 44 (1979–1980): 191–92.

61 Hall, *American Empire*, 256.

62 Ibid., 255, 496.

63 Howard Ramos, "Divergent Paths: Aboriginal Mobilization in Canada, 1951–2000" (PhD diss., McGill University, 2004).

64 Jane Jenson and Martin Papillon, "Challenging the Citizenship Regime: The James Bay Cree and Transnational Action," *Politics & Society* 28, no. 2 (2000): 260 [245–64].

65 Coates, *A Global History*, 243.

66 Muckle, *Indigenous Peoples*, 18.

67 See, for example, Howard Adams, *Prison of Grass: Canada from a Native Point of View*, rev. ed. (Saskatoon: Fifth House Publishers, 1989 [1975]); Lee Maracle, *Bobbi Lee: Indian Rebel* (Toronto: Women's Press Literary, 1990 [1975]).

68 The Kino-nda-niimi Collective, "Idle No More: The Winter We Danced," in *The Winter We Danced: Voices from the Past, the Future, and the Idle No More Movement*, ed. The Kino-nda-niimi Collective (Winnipeg: Arp Books, 2014), 25.

69 The Kino-nda-niimi Collective, "Timeline of Major Events Spanning *The Winter We Danced*," in *The Winter We Danced*, 389.

70 Much of this information is taken from ibid., 389–409.

71 Yasmin Jiwani and Mary Lynn Young, "Missing and Murdered Women: Reproducing Marginality in News Discourse," *Canadian Journal of Communication* 31 (2006): 895–917.

72 Kathryn Blaze Baum, "Two Men Charged with Attempted Murder of Rinelle Harper," *The Globe and Mail*, November 12, 2014, http://www.theglobeandmail.com/news/national/two-men-charged-with-attempted-murder-after-attack-on-winnipeg-teen/article2155030.

73 Adele Perry, "This History Is Not Over," *Winnipeg Free Press*, June 9, 2015, http://www.winnipegfreepress.com/special/featured/This-history-is-not-over-306659721.html.

2

Immigration Policy, Colonization, and the Development of a White Canada[1]

BARRINGTON WALKER

Introduction

Immigration has played a central role in the making of modern Canada. This chapter provides a brief overview of Canadian immigration policy and the development of Canada, more specifically the development of a "white" Canada. It charts a long story of race in Canada, through which we can view some of the broad historical contours of what I am terming the "Canadian racial state." How have "race" and the immigrant experience affected the creation of the modern Canadian state? What impact have Canada's histories of race and immigration had upon its history as a colonizing nation, a nation that has displaced and dehumanized its First Nations' peoples to an appalling degree? What is the relationship between the newer and covertly racial "economic apartheid" that informs the reality of Canada's (mostly) urban racialized populations and the older, balder assertions of apartheid that were crystallized in the creation of the reserve system in Canada? What role has racism and perceptions of racial difference played in laying the foundations of the country? How might one consider this history alongside and in concert with the more conventional frameworks we have for understanding the development of Canada, such as geography, politics, class conflict, and perhaps gender?

These are huge, daunting questions. Perhaps the most fundamental difficulty that confronts those interested in thinking about race and racism in Canada is, to cite Dionne Brand's well-known phrase (cited in Constance Backhouse's celebrated work *Colour-Coded*), the "stupefying innocence" about racism so prevalent in this country.[2] Here I will argue that race should be considered central to Canada's past, embedded in the very DNA of the nation. "Race" has a polyvalent quality that manifests itself across time and space, making it a fount of endless inquiry, maddeningly difficult to pin down, and a moving target across space and time. At the same time, many thinkers have attempted to identify its foundational moment. Was it found in the formative era of Native–non-Native contact? Was it in the history of slavery in New France and British North America? Was it the federal government's policy toward the Chinese in nineteenth-century British

Columbia?[3] Or do we find the defining moment of Canadian racism in immigration policy, more specifically the racially exclusionary and preferential immigration acts of 1906 and 1910, as well as the racially driven deportation policies that emerged during this era? The fact is that virtually all of these moments in the history of Canada's racial state were pivotal. Taken together, these instances—alongside many others—point to a broad web of interlocking attitudes, outlooks, techniques, and modes of racial governance in the colonial and early Confederation eras that created much of the foundation of modern Canada. The most intensive period of migration in human history took place between 1850 and 1930, when about 130 million people left Europe, China, and India and travelled to North and South America, Southeast Asia, the East Indies, the West Indies, and the Pacific. Canada was of course part of this: it is not only a cliché that Canada is a "nation of immigrants." This formulation of Canadian history ignores the territory's original Indigenous inhabitants and also avoids the thorny question, "Which immigrants?" Why have so many Canadians come from European backgrounds, in comparison to Asia, Africa, the Caribbean, and Latin America? In this chapter, we will learn how the Canadian racial state helped to shape the labour, family, and kinship ties that were deemed permissible and appropriate to the sort of "Canada" brought into being through immigration.[4]

American racial theorist David Theo Goldberg writes that racial states have been oriented toward racial naturalism (i.e., the idea of race as being characterized by fixed biological essences) and racial historicism (the idea that various—invariably inferior—races can ascend to the level of superior races through the guiding hand of paternalism or tutelage—coercive or otherwise).[5] There is also a vast and growing historiography on the history of race and immigration in Canada exploring the pillars of racial hierarchy and national belonging that framed much of Canada's nation building project. How were ideas of race, racial hierarchy, and national belonging articulated in the language of naturalism in early Canadian history? How has this continued in the culturally inflected neoliberal racisms of the later twentieth century and our present moment?

The first part of this chapter will explore the origins of the Canadian racial state by grounding it in several historical moments in pre- and post-Confederation Canada. These moments are not individually foundational nor singularly important; rather, they constitute useful moments for thinking about how Canada's racial state was shaped in law, society, and culture over the centuries. Each of these instances demonstrates its predominantly naturalist orientation in the late nineteenth century and in the twentieth century in the years prior to World War II. First, we will discuss race, colonialism and the state, and the *Indian Act* of 1876. Next, this chapter discusses the contours of the Canadian racial state through the prism of immigration restrictions against Chinese and South Asian people. Our discussion will then turn to a consideration of work that I have done previously on the history of black Canadians and "Jim Crow," followed by the theme of race and national belonging in the work of Canadian politician J.S. Woodsworth, specifically his important book *Strangers Within Our Gates*.[6] It would be an error, as Ian McKay has pointed out, to crudely and simply paint Woodsworth with the brush of nativism and racism.[7] Rather, the task here will be to look at how his work is demonstrative of the racial anxieties, tensions, and paradoxes of liberal/historicist racism at a time of rapid demographic change in Canada. Each of these case studies reveals the strong current of what Goldberg has identified as racial historicism: that inferior races needed the guidance of superior races to help them ascend or "evolve" to a higher order of humanity.

The 1876 *Indian Act*

In 1876 the federal government passed an act with the innocuous-sounding title "An Act to amend and consolidate the laws respecting Indians." In a sense the *Indian Act*, which was assented on April 12, 1876, did just that. It tidied up the legal framework concerning First Nations in Canada by consolidating laws that had been passed in the pre-Confederation era and applied them to all the provinces as well as the North West Territories and the Territory of Keewatin. Much has been written about the *Indian Act*. It has been (rightly) called a paternalistic, assimilationist, colonialist, and even genocidal piece of legislation by many First Nations; such charges, while they may smack of hyperbole to some, are in fact quite justified. What is striking about the original *Indian Act*, as many scholars of Native and non-Native history have pointed out, is that it was a foundational moment in how race was legally produced by the state in late nineteenth-century Canada. The 1876 *Indian Act* was very much a product of its time. It emerged from the liberal racialist sentiments that existed in the earlier part of the nineteenth century; these sentiments were all the more pronounced after the threat that First Nations' peoples presented to non-First Nations' settlement had been subdued. At the same time, it was produced on the cusp of the doctrine of scientific racism that would reach its high-water mark at the turn of the century. The *Indian Act* is a curious mixture of both of these modes of racial thought. Two examples stand out in its text. One is the creation of the category of the "Indian" (sometimes referred to in the act as persons and sometimes not). The second is the provision for enfranchisement (about which I will say more later). According to the act, an Indian was defined by blood. Section 3 of the act defines an Indian as "Any male person of Indian blood reputed to belong to a particular band," as well as the children or wife of a such person. But Indians were also defined not only by strictly blood or biological criteria but also by ideas of Indian culture, namely, those who engaged in the "Indian mode of life." The legal category of the Indian, in essence, was to some extent flexible and performative. And if an Indian was a product of cultural markers, the idea of enfranchisement took this logic a step further, for one could perform whiteness as well. Enfranchisement was not merely the acquisition of the vote but much more profound. It was the acquisition of full citizenship rights. Voluntary enfranchisement was one of the most important aspects of Canadian Indian policy. At the age of 21 all Indians were eligible to apply to the Superintendent General for enfranchised status. The Superintendent would then judge "the degree of civilization to which he or she has attained, and the character for integrity, morality and sobriety which he or she bears" (*Indian Act*, S. 86). After the successful conclusion of a probationary period, the Indians would hence "no longer be deemed Indians, except in so far as their right to participate in the annuities and interest moneys, and rents and councils of the band of Indians to which they belonged." Involuntary enfranchisement occurred when First Nations women married non-Natives or when Indians acquired university degrees or became ordained ministers. Enfranchisement was the embodiment of racial historicist colonial governance. It was the legal animation of the assimilationist thrust of the government's Indian policy.

Early Immigration: Laying the Foundations of White Canada

The Canadian state's desire to assimilate its First Nations peoples, to incorporate them into the national body according to normative ideas of Canadianness and whiteness, was mirrored in the emergence of Canada's immigration policy. Canadian immigration policy has always been concerned with preserving that fundamental "character" of the nation while balancing the needs and desires of industrialists, who often pushed for immigration out of desire for cheap and compliant (at least, that was the stereotype) labour, and nativists, who wanted to guard the country's gates against newcomers. The late nineteenth and early twentieth centuries have been described as the era of "immigration and the consolidation of the Dominion."[8] In the early post-Confederation period, roughly between 1867 and 1892, immigration was a key feature of the young federal government's national building aspirations. Immigrants, in short, were to provide the new confederation with both a labour and a consumer market. During this period the general contours of the government's immigration policy were quite clear: the procurement of homesteads for prospective immigrants, various forms of assisted settlement (e.g., advertising, assisted passage, or group settlements), and western expansion that both facilitated and was facilitated by immigration and early industrialization.[9]

The control of Canada's borders is the most significant area where white supremacy was positively expressed in and through the law. The history of Canadian immigration is long and complex, but some general patterns in its evolution are clear. In the colonial era, immigration policy was in essence a recruitment and settlement policy designed to fill the empty lands that had been surrendered by First Nations people who had now fallen from being allies of the Crown to Crown wards. The era of "coercive tutelage," which was tied to the drive to create and entrench white settler colonies in British North America, quickly followed.[10] The Immigration Acts that were passed in 1906 and 1910 created a framework for immigration policy based on "the principle that the absolute right of the state [was] to admit and exclude new members. . . ."[11] In the early twentieth century Canadian immigration policy, the decision about inclusion and exclusion, was based on explicit racial hierarchies. Citizens of the British Isles were preferred over Central Europeans, who were in turn favoured over those from Southern Europe. Asians, Africans, and South Asians were either barred outright or kept out of the country through a range of ingenious devices, such as the continuous journey immigration requirement that was passed in 1910.[12] However, exceptions were made when cheap, exploitable labour power of racialized others were required to build the nation.

The Canadian State and Immigration Restrictions: Chinese and South Asians

The stories of Chinese and South Asian immigration to Canada from the mid-nineteenth to the early twentieth century exemplify a central tension in Canadian immigration history. On one side were powerful economic interests—mine owners and railway company executives, for example—who appealed to the state to serve their business interests. On the other side were those who wanted to preserve and promote a "White Canada." The Chinese first came to Canada—British Columbia in particular—in the mid-nineteenth century in search of gold.[13] The Chinese sojourn to Canada was part of a larger exodus of young men out of Guangdong province. Pushed from home by economic hardship and social dislocation and pulled by the promise of economic prosperity, many went in search of the mythical "Gold Mountain" in British Columbia.[14] The Chinese presence in British Columbia was, almost from the beginning, accompanied by negative racial baggage. Peter Ward has described the constellation of attitudes that were projected upon the Chinese which, he argues, were crystallized in the archetype of "John Chinaman."[15] John Chinaman was an expression of pervasive white supremacist anxieties that existed toward the Chinese in the nineteenth century. These anxieties emerged out of both the class and psychosocial worries that Chinese bodies produced in white people. In a variety of formal and informal settings, whites routinely described the Chinese as inscrutable, cunning, sexually perverse, filthy, and prone to vice and criminality, including gambling and illegal drugs.[16]

This ideological milieu produced the legislative and public policy climate that sought to regulate and ultimately halt the presence of the Chinese in Canada. The end of the gold rush in the 1860s gave rise to hardened racial attitudes toward the Chinese. In the period between 1863 and 1871, racial antipathy toward the Chinese—though far from uniform—began to steadily, if unevenly, grow and to manifest in public policies. The province of British Columbia began to articulate the racial parameters of citizenship. During this time governments began to curtail the Chinese right to vote: by 1865 one member of the Vancouver Island Assembly pushed the House to apply a $10 head tax; a $50 poll tax was considered by the Assembly in 1871 as well. While neither proposal received sufficient support, they set the stage for the legislative climate that would emerge in the post-Confederation era.[17] By 1878, legislative mechanisms began to take on more urgency in British Columbia as Chinese immigration increased noticeably.[18] The *Chinese Tax Act* imposed a $10 fine on the Chinese to stem the flow of migrants. The act was later struck down by the Supreme Court of British Columbia on the basis that it was outside the bounds of the province's legislative reach.[19] Workers under the auspices of the Workingman's Protection Association in British Columbia also began to mobilize against the Chinese.[20]

Up to this point and until 1884, the Canadian government had adeptly avoided the growing cries from British Columbia to limit Chinese immigration. After all, their labour power was needed to complete the Canadian Pacific Railroad (CPR)—the steel ribbon that was to tie the country together and launch Canada into the modern era. When anti-Asian activists in the provincial legislature successfully swayed the house to pass an anti-Chinese *Immigration Act* in 1884, it was overturned by the federal government, which at this time was vehemently opposed to stemming Chinese immigration, as the CPR was not yet finished. This view was echoed by Sir John A. Macdonald's commissioners on the Royal Commission on Chinese Immigration.[21]

Once the CPR was complete, the question then arose: Given that Chinese labour would soon no longer be required to serve the ends of Canadian nation building, what was to be done with the Chinese? Predictably, in 1885 the federal government became more open to the voices of opposition coming from British Columbia, a case of "labour used, labour discarded."[22] In 1885, in the face of vehement anti-Chinese agitation that had reached its peak and a surplus of idle Chinese labourers, the federal government finally capitulated to the desires of BC's nativists and racists by passing a *Chinese*

Immigration Act. The 1885 act imposed a head tax of $50 on all prospective Chinese immigrants. The tax was raised to $100 in 1900 and to $500 in 1903. Through the passage of the *Electoral Franchise Act*, the Chinese were also denied the right to vote. In 1923, the federal government passed the *Chinese Exclusion Act*, which effectively banned all Chinese immigrants from Canada with a few rare exceptions (diplomats, foreign students, or under special circumstances at the discretion of the Minister of Immigration).[23]

Anti-Chinese sentiment in Canada was thus enshrined in Canadian law. Timothy Stanley argues that various provincial and federal legal prohibitions against Chinese participation in Canadian civic life were the first instance in which race was enshrined in Canadian law.[24] In this respect, the story of the Chinese is unique. It was more common that the Canadian state used surreptitious means to exclude unwanted racial groups. South Asians, and the well-known story of the *Komagata Maru*, was a case in point.

South Asians had been a fixture in British Columbia since the late nineteenth century. Most were Sikhs from the Punjab region of India. Like the Chinese and other groups of nineteenth-century bachelor workers, Sikh men came in search of waged work and the opportunity to send remittances back home. The arrival of these newcomers—which reached its peak in 1907 when the population grew to some 4,000 people[25]—sparked immediate opposition in British Columbia, accompanied by a plethora of negative racialized images of this group and sparking a concerted effort, including diplomatic efforts and landing fees, to curtail further South Asian immigration.[26]

As it was in the case of the Chinese, the Canadian state was committed to maintaining a white Canada in the face of this unsettling wave of nonwhite migration. But the Canadian government was not able to use the same mechanisms that it had used to bar the former group. While racial discourse in British Columbia baldly asserted the innate inferiority and undesirability of the "Hindoo" in Canadian life, such overt formal racism had to be studiously avoided by the Canadian government. As historian Peter Ward has explained:

> While Oriental immigration had long troubled Ottawa, that of East Indians caused particular embarrassment. Most British Columbians objected to Indians as much as they did other Asiatics and in the wake of the Vancouver riot further immigration restrictions seemed necessary, if only to prevent renewed violence. Yet Canadians and East Indians were both British subjects and, in order to prevent unrest in India, overt racial discrimination was to be avoided. Canadian, British, and Indian officials shared this desire equally.[27]

Faced with the need to avoid stirring up unrest in India and creating discord within the British Empire, the Canadian government passed the "continuous passage" rule in 1908. The act stipulated that East Indian immigrants to Canada would not be permitted to enter unless they arrived in Canada from their country of origin "by a continuous journey on through tickets purchased before leaving the country."[28] This provision was effective because during this era it was impossible to acquire direct passage to Canada from India. By 1913, the continuous journey provision, which had been briefly struck down by legal challenge when it was first introduced, had been enshrined (and slightly amended to discourage legal challenges) into the 1910 *Immigration Act*. It dramatically slowed South Asian immigration.[29]

In 1913 members of the Indian community, spearheaded by a wealthy entrepreneur named Gurdit Singh, sponsored the arrival of 376 East Indian residents of Hong Kong, China, and Japan.[30] Vancouver authorities did not allow the ship, the *Komagata Maru*, to come in to port and its passengers were not allowed to disembark. Amidst a heated public debate that took place in the media and in parliament, the passengers languished aboard the ship for two months. Immigration officials prolonged inquiries on the issue of individual passengers' admissibility, stalled the provision of food and medical care, and allowed the conditions aboard the ship to steadily worsen to an intolerable degree. In the end, one of the *Komagata Maru*'s passengers, whose case served as a "test case," lost an appeal in the British Columbia Court of Appeals, which ruled that "he had violated three orders-in-council. In particular he had not come to Canada on a continuous journey, he could not meet the $200 landing-money requirement, and, as an unskilled labourer in Canada (although not in India), he was not permitted to enter British Columbia."[31] Shortly after the court's decision, the *Komagata Maru* lifted its anchor and was escorted away by the navy while onlookers cheered wildly.[32] The stories of both Chinese and South Asian exclusion show how national belonging was closely aligned to ideas about race and racial hierarchy in Canada. They also illustrate the plethora of tools—direct and indirect—that the state had at its disposal to create a white Canada.

Strangers

Let us now turn to another moment in the shaping of Canadian racial hierarchies: J.S. Woodsworth's publication of *Strangers Within Our Gates* in 1908. During the time he wrote *Strangers*, Woodsworth was one of Canada's leading socialist politicians. Born in 1874, the son of a conservative Methodist minister was one of the founding members of the Canadian Commonwealth Federation (CCF). The CCF, precursor to today's New Democratic Party (NDP), believed that it had a progressive, open-minded commitment to social justice, particularly for the Canadian working class.

Figure 2.1 J.S. Woodsworth's *Strangers Within Our Gates* (1908). Even among socially progressive thinkers such as CCF founder J.S. Woodsworth, a distinct racial hierarchy and immigration preference was obvious.

The turn of the century was a watershed period in the history of immigration in Canada. During this time the country was undergoing a rapid demographic transformation, brought on by the country's emergence as an exporter of natural resources and the maturation of its manufacturing sector. As we saw in the case of railway building, the country was in need of workers willing to do the heavy lifting to support the emergence of Canada's industrial capitalist sector. Because of this, wealthy industrialists pushed the government to consider the "non-preferred" peoples of Southern and Central Europe as well as the Chinese labour hired predominantly to build the railroad. As we have seen, it was a time of intense feelings about immigration and how "Canadianness" ought to be defined and lived. *Strangers* was Woodsworth's answer to the problem of immigration in contemporary Canadian life:

> This little book is an attempt to introduce the motley crowd of immigrants to our Canadian people and to bring before our young people some of the problems of population with which they must deal in the near future.[33]

Woodsworth's little book was not the work of a nativist nor a self-conscious racist. Indeed, as the twentieth century wore on there would emerge a hue and cry from many who wanted to shut Canada's doors tightly. This included, most alarmingly, proponents of eugenic thought who believed that new strains of racial and inferior non-British and non-Celtic blood would have an inexorably deleterious effect on the health of the nation, infecting its generous host. Unlike many of his contemporaries, Woodsworth was not an exclusionary nationalist. Rather, *Strangers* sought to provide a forum to foster debate about how Canada would solve the problem of the rapid influx of so many different racial/national groups to Canada's shores. In Chapter 3, titled "With the Immigrants," Woodsworth made the case for why he believed that Canada should care for its newcomers, comparing the story of a striving Russian Jewish immigrant with his more lacklustre native Canadian counterpart:

> Such stories give us hope for the future. Such courage—such endurance—such struggles cannot but develop a high type of character. Compare the experiences with the easy going, self satisfied, narrow, unprogressive lives of many who are hardly holding what their fathers gained! The latter, with their little round of petty pleasures, despise the poorly clad "foreigner" with his broken English and strange ways; but the odds are largely on the side of the new immigrant.[34]

Woodsworth saw such stories as indicative of the boundless promise of the immigrant. Where others saw dangerous foreigners who threatened the very fabric of British Canada, he saw the human capital of new immigrants, a resource that the country could tap for its national development, its maturation from a British colony to an independent nation. Woodsworth's attitudes toward the immigrant were liberal (particularly considering his time). Yet, as many have pointed out, he was also very much a product of an era defined by overt notions of racial hierarchy and concerns about immigrant assimilability. While *Strangers* was not a nativist project (to be sure, he did not advocate that Canada should throw its borders wide open—far from it), it was still forged in the crucible of racial historicism. The point of the book was to highlight the fact that among the seemingly strange new immigrants there existed many excellent candidates for absorption into Canadian life. Indeed, it could be argued that this text is a progenitor of the post–World War II multiculturalist Canadian (racial) state.

As many have pointed out, Woodsworth's book is organized by chapters that highlight a particular group. A distinct hierarchy of racial preferences is evident. The first dedicated chapters highlight the British, Americans, the Scandinavians, the Germans and the French; the next group of chapters deal with immigrants from southeastern Europe (whom he defined as Russians, Doukhobors, and Lithuanians). The next are about immigrants from Austria-Hungary and the Balkan States, the Hebrews, the Italians, and the "Levantine Races" (Woodsworth defined them as Greeks, Turks, Armenians, Syrians, and Persians). He rounded out his chapters by ending with those he deemed least assimilable: "The Orientals" (Chinese, Japanese, and Hindus) and, curiously, "The Negro and the Indian." This is perhaps the strangest and most underdeveloped, confused, and contradictory chapter in this book.

What was curious about Woodsworth's chapter on the Negro and the Indian was that he did not consider either of these groups to be immigrants qua immigrants. Blacks did not qualify for this designation in Woodsworth's schema since, in his words, "[c]ontiguity to the United States is accountable largely for our negro population. We group them because both stand out entirely by themselves."[35] Woodsworth's rationale for grouping blacks and Indians together was simply their distance from the "ordinary." "Neither the negro nor the Indian are immigrants and yet they are so entirely different from the ordinary white population that some mention of them is necessary if we would understand the complexity of our problems."[36]

Woodsworth went on to discuss at length the peculiar history of the Negro in America by quoting at length from John R. Commons, a self-styled expert on this history. What distinguished the Negro was that he was descended from people in Africa who were "unstable" and "easily aroused to fear." Moreover, said Woodsworth, still citing Commons's work, blacks experienced a "momentous change [being] shifted from equatorial Africa to the temperate regions of America." And the very qualities of "manliness" and "intelligence" needed for citizenship were "systematically expunged from the Negro race through two hundred years of slavery." Woodsworth then curiously stated that whether "we" agree with these conclusions or not "we may be thankful we have no negro problem in Canada." With regard to Indians, Woodsworth similarly drew heavily from the work of another author, Rev. Thompson Ferier. Ferier wrote that although some Indians had experienced success by becoming as prosperous as their white neighbours, others had succumbed to the "vices of the white man." But even these two groups, farthest removed from the "ordinary white Canadian," were not irredeemable. Despite their history of African savagery and enslavement, according to Woodsworth, "many Negroes are members of various Protestant churches and are consistent Christians." He also noted that "the Indian of today is very much nearer to the civilized white man than to his pagan ancestor."

In sum, *Strangers* shows us the complexities of racial liberalism in turn-of-the-century Canada. It is worth repeating that Woodsworth was considered, on many issues, socially progressive. His fondness for racial hierarchy and racial assimilation has fallen out of favour in the years since the publication of his book (at least for the most part). Racial liberalism has moved beyond this particular articulation of racial difference in recent years. Nonetheless, his view that "Indians" and "Negroes" presented the greatest challenge to Canada's racial state has been rather prescient.

Jim Crow in Canada

"Jim Crow" is the informal name for the various systems of racial segregation and inequality most associated with—but not exclusive to—the southern states of the United States. In Canada, as elsewhere, the system lies at the nexus of law and social custom. But the latter—save a few notable exceptions—was prevalent in Canada. It is here, in areas like religion, social attitudes, and socioeconomic status and the forms of racial violence most commonly associated with the South—the realms of "custom" and "popular prejudice"—that the continental dimensions of Jim Crow get thrown into sharp relief. The similarities between de facto, extralegal manifestations of Jim Crow in the United States and Jim Crow in Canada are a result of the naturalist racial presumptions that structure them. As Goldberg argues, mob violence in the American South—typified in the alarming number of lynchings that took place between the 1880s and 1920s—was racial naturalism's reassertion in the face of the challenges posed by the rule of law.[37] The opposite was true in Canada, where vigilante justice was a naturalist challenge to the dominant historicist legalism that simply was too inadequate to police the colour line or, more pointedly, interracial sex. Mob violence in Canada was an expression of racists' frustration at the law's inability to maintain a proper, natural racial hierarchy.

A Liberal Racial Order?

In one of the most influential articles ever published in Canadian historiography, Ian McKay makes the argument for what he terms a "liberal order framework" for understanding Canadian history. Canada, says McKay, should be rethought as a "historically specific project of rule"—a liberal order—in which individual rights are considered paramount.[38] Canada's liberal order framework excluded the racially subaltern from its conception of the subject, as these individuals were deemed too deficient to be worthy of full citizenship rights, including the franchise.[39] This is why governments denied Chinese and South Asians the vote in British Columbia and why Aboriginals were constituted as noncitizens. For Aboriginal people, enfranchisement meant relinquishing their Indian status.[40] It is certainly true that the Canadian state's project of building a modern Canada based upon liberal principles often placed the racial Other outside of its purview, deeming them objects rather than subjects. However, the story is complicated, and perhaps McKay has been too hasty in placing the racially marginalized outside of the reach of liberal order governance.[41] Rather, racialized peoples' relationship to Canada's liberal order was uneven and often ambivalent. The laws of Canada constituted unassimilated Aboriginal peoples as noncitizens and even nonpersons until the mid-twentieth century. Nonetheless, the state was willing to grant the assimilated Indian—who was, of course, the opposite of the figure excluded from McKay's liberal order schema—the fruits of full citizenship, albeit at the high cost of his or her Indian status. Goldberg argues that colonial policies of assimilation were quintessentially historicist: "Colonial assimilationists were confident of their possession of universally just laws, building the policy on the assumption that natives should become civilized through their acquisition of the rule of law and the custom of the colonizers, by ceasing, that is, to be native."[42]

Like Aboriginal peoples, black Canadians were by no means fully outside of the purview of Canada's liberal order framework. This had much to do with the dominance of a historicist attitude toward race in the British Empire, particularly with the dawn of the Age of Reform at the late eighteenth to the early nineteenth century.[43] The end of slavery in British North America began in Upper Canada in 1793, when Governor John Graves Simcoe—who many scholars argue was affronted by the violent spectacle of the sale and forced removal of a female slave named Chloe Coolie in Upper Canada—engineered slavery's gradual demise, and was complete with the *Imperial Act* of 1833 that abolished slavery across the British Empire.[44] The abolition of slavery in the British Empire created a frontier of legal freedom for blacks in Britain's North American possessions. The British were also willing to flex their muscle to provide legal protections for runaway American slaves who were threatened with extradition to the United States between the 1820s and the American Civil War. During this period US officials made several attempts to criminally extradite runaway slaves; in the vast majority of cases, Canadian officials refused to grant these requests. Their actions were informed by a British colonial policy and an international treaty (the Webster-Ashburton Treaty) hammered out with the United States. British Canadian authorities held firm in their conviction that only slaves who had committed offences deemed crimes on both sides of the border were candidates for extradition. Therefore the American slave owners' charge of "theft of a slave" fell upon deaf ears in British North America, where slavery had been abolished. Moreover, the colonial and imperial governments north of the forty-ninth parallel also refused to extradite slaves for crimes such as theft of horses, which were used to aid their transit to freedom.[45]

Colonization experiments in the late eighteenth and nineteenth centuries are also evidence of the British Empire's prevalently historicist conception of race and blackness, as it was also evidence of blacks' desire for freedom and coveted land in the context of the British Empire. The founding and settlement of Sierra Leone on the west coast of Africa was an opportunity for black Nova Scotians who were bitterly disappointed by the province's unfulfilled promise of social and economic equality.[46] Many of slavery's opponents looked at Sierra Leone, a company/colony chartered by the British government, as an "experiment in social change" in the all-important transition from slavery to freedom.[47] By the early twentieth century on the other side of the Atlantic, a number of all-black settlements were founded in Upper Canada and Canada West. These settlements, which bore names such as Oro, Wilberforce, Dawn, The Refugee Home Society, and Elgin/Buxton Mission, were also conceived of as sites where blacks could overcome their backward historical development and gain the necessary social, cultural, and economic tools to make the transition to freedom.[48]

Finding Jim Crow in a Liberal Racial Order

Jim Crow in Canada must be considered within the broader contexts of a British Empire that was generally committed to a brand of white supremacy in support of evolutionary and historicist racial ideas (though not racial equality) and a Canadian state that, in stark contrast to the United States, granted black citizens the franchise and "full legal protections."[49] These legal protections did not reflect the reality of the lowly social and economic status of black Canadians.[50] The term Jim Crow was often invoked by African-Canadians and sympathetic whites to describe attitudes, values and outlooks, and social practices in Canada that strongly resembled the racial cultures of the US's Jim Crow regime. In Canada, Jim Crow frequently reared its ugly head when the liberal racial order could not seamlessly accommodate powerful biologist assumptions about blacks' racial inferiority.

Allen P. Stouffer has written that after the end of the American Civil War, many Ontario newspapers commented upon the freed slave's bleak prospects for making the transition to a post-emancipation society. One Ontario editorial stated:

> [Blacks] are savage by nature, and utterly incapable of self-sustained civilization. Four thousand years ago, they lived side by side with Egyptian and Arab civilization, and were just as savage then in Africa as they are now. More pains have been taken, more money and labour extended to civilize the Negro than any other race. Yet, in his native wilds, he is still a savage, and is reverting rapidly to the savage state wherever relieved from slavery and left to cultivate a civilization of his own. There was never found a nation, tribe, or society, however small, of white savages. The civilization of whites is indigenous—part of their natures congenial with their race. The savage state is natural to the Negro. He never was found with an indigenous civilization, nor any civilization at all, after he had lived in a society composed on Negroes for five generations.[51]

These kinds of biologically driven explanations of black racial inferiority and a rejection of evolutionary or historicist explanations for blacks' low status were quite common in Canada, and they tell us a lot about the power of the naturalist racial commitment in Canada, even if it was not constituted through positive law as it was elsewhere.

The spectre of interracial rape also reflected naturalist racial anxieties. In a 1920s' rape case in which an itinerant black Canadian labourer was found guilty of the horrible assault of an 80-year-old white woman, the presiding judge congratulated the jurors for respecting the law, maintaining their faith in British justice, and resisting the urge to lynch the accused. In another case, the defence counsel of a black man charged with raping a white farmwoman contended that the victim died "of shock" rather than physical violence. Crown counsel argued that the shock produced by merely seeing a Negro was enough to kill the victim.[52]

In Saint John, New Brunswick, a black man named John Paris was accused of the sex-murder of an eight-year-old white girl in the 1920s. The key eyewitness was the little girl's companion, who could only say that the man who had abducted her friend wore a hat similar to Paris's. Blacks from Truro, Nova Scotia, Paris's home town, travelled en masse to Saint John to testify on his behalf. Several witnesses maintained that Paris was seen in and around Saint John on the day that he was alleged to have committed the murder. The Crown tried Paris a total of five times. The first trial resulted in a hung jury. In the second trial, the Attorney General of the Province of New Brunswick personally took over the case; he won a decision against Paris (which included a mandatory sentence of death), but the decision was overturned upon appeal. The third, fourth, and fifth trials all ended in the same result as the first. After his last trial Paris was finally released, but only on the condition that a recognizance be placed over his head in case the court found any more evidence against him for a sixth trial. The John Paris case stands as one of the least-known and most unsettling events in the history of Canadian jurisprudence.[53]

It is in this historical context that African-Canadians and others began to defiantly make a case for the existence of Jim Crow in Canada despite the absence of legislated segregation. Carrie Best, a black Nova Scotian and editor of the *Clarion* newspaper in the 1940s, frequently argued for the existence of Jim Crow in Nova Scotia. In 1942, Best wrote a letter to the owner of a New Glasgow movie house called the Roseland Theatre, expressing her dismay and outrage at its policy of racial segregation:

> ... I have spent the entire afternoon conducting a personal Gallup poll to see if this rule is the carry over from the faraway days of slavery or if this is the rule of the Board of Directors and Shareholders of the Roseland Theatre Company. ... Scores of respected citizens were amazed to believe that such Jim-crow tactics are practiced on such law abiding citizens and when the time comes have said they will not hesitate to speak against it.[54]

Through the *Clarion's* editorial pages, Best declared New Glasgow "the centre of Jim Crowism in Canada." New Glasgow, said Best, "stands for Jim Crowism, at its basest, over the entire globe."[55]

A few years later when Viola Desmond, sometimes referred to as the "Rosa Parks of Canada," appeared before a judge to combat discriminatory treatment in the very same Nova Scotia movie theatre, one judge wondered aloud whether "a surreptitious endeavour to enforce Jim Crow by misuse of a public statute" had occurred.[56] In 1960s Nova Scotia the black freedom struggle was waged in the arena of Jim Crow. In the late 1960s, essayist Nancy Lubka wrote a short piece for the *Queen's Quarterly* comparing aspects of Nova Scotian society and culture to the American South:

> Last October the whole nation read about the burial incident, when a Negro child was refused burial in the cemetery.... It was a sort of anachronism, a slipping of yesterday into the present. In days gone by there were many such barriers, echoing the traditions of Jim Crow in the US. In nearly every sizable town in Nova Scotia black people live, and in most of these places there were colour bars.[57]

This "echoing of the traditions of Jim Crow" haunts the memories of black Canadians, whose bodies undermine the narration of a white Canada. Black Canadians and their allies had no difficulty pointing out similarities between patterns of racial discrimination in Canada and the southern United States. But these observable patterns were the result of the terrible legacy of racial naturalism on both sides of the border. Blacks fought hard against these discriminatory practices; their struggle for civil rights in Canada, from the mid-nineteenth century until the late 1960s, was primarily waged in the courts.

Fighting "Jim Crow" and Racial Discrimination in a Liberal Racial Order

Throughout the nineteenth and twentieth centuries, black Canadians turned to the courts to combat racism. The central irony of Canada's civil rights struggle, one that plagues the antiracist struggle in Canada to this day, is that the liberal racial order that characterized Canada often made racism quite difficult to fight in the courts. Canada's liberal racial order meant that, particularly early on, the strategy met with only a modicum of success. After enduring three trials in 1855, a black Canadian man won damages against the school board trustees in Simcoe for their refusal to allow his child to attend school through the gerrymandering of the school district. Unfortunately, this turned out to be a pyrrhic victory, as he had to sell his own farm to cover the court costs (the defendant had no such assets).[58] The prohibition of gerrymandering of school districts to exclude African-Canadian children was a welcomed development for blacks and their supporters, but ultimately it proved insufficient to stem the tide of racist feeling in Canada West. By 1859 separate schools were given formal status through an act that "provided that twelve or more heads of families, could open their own institutions and receive appointments from the common school funds." Canada West's Superintendent of Education, Egerton Ryerson, advised that where there was strong opposition to the Negroes, separate schools should be created. As a result, they were often imposed by racist whites.[59]

Through the courts black Canadians fought unequal access to theatres in 1899 and 1914. Evocative of the earlier pattern in education, both cases resulted in victories.[60] In the long run, however, these cases turned out to be aberrant rather than typical. In 1924, for example, in the case of *Franklin v. Evans*, a black Canadian man was denied service in a restaurant on the basis that the establishment did not serve "coloured people."[61] At trial, Justice Lennox decried the restaurateurs for behaving in a manner that was "unpardonably offensive." He was moved by the plaintiff's appeal for "recognition as a human being, of common origin with ourselves." Nonetheless, the court found in favour of the defendant. The now-legendary Viola Desmond and Fred Christie witnessed similar defeats in the 1930s and 1940s when they tried to fight the colour bar in a New Glasgow, Nova Scotia, movie theatre and a Montreal tavern, respectively.[62]

Ultimately, African-Canadians would have much more success in combating discriminatory treatment in public accommodations via the legislative route, through forming alliances with labour unions and ethnic leaders outside of the black community to press for change. Robin Winks argues that a sea change in racial attitudes "was punctuated, and perhaps hastened, by World War II."[63] James Walker, who wrote after Winks, presents a more nuanced argument, agreeing that there might have been a change in racial sensibilities, but cautioning against assuming that a complete paradigm shift took place in the aftermath of the war.[64]

The Jewish community in particular, which long felt the sting of virulent anti–Semitism, took an active leadership role in shaping the human rights agenda in Canada. In cities such as Toronto, Calgary, Oshawa, and Dresden, social activists demanded that municipal governments take action against racial discrimination.[65] Dresden, popularly known as the "Alabama of the north," had a large black population that was subject to virulent racism. A local organization called the National Unity Association focused attention on restaurants and barbershops that discriminated against blacks, launching a public awareness campaign that received a lot of attention (much of it negative) in the press. In 1944, Ontario passed the *Racial Discrimination Act* and in 1954 the *Fair Accommodations Practices Act*, forbidding racial discrimination in public places. In 1963 a similar *Hotel Act* was passed in Quebec. In 1962, the Ontario Human Rights Commission was created.[66] The struggles waged by Christie and Desmond were vindicated in the long run, and perhaps indirectly they had a role in shaping public consciousness.

The struggle for civil rights that took place in the realm of immigration policy was an extension of the human rights gains in the other areas mentioned above. Historian Sheldon Taylor has skillfully studied these themes in some detail.[67] In the 1950s the Negro Citizenship Committee, later renamed the Negro Citizenship Association (NCA), lobbied the Canadian government to "enlarge the section of the Immigration Act, in order to permit freer entry of Negroes into the Dominion of Canada."[68] Though a new *Immigration Act* was passed in 1952, it did not address this issue. The government obstinately refused to allow sizeable numbers of black immigrants into the country. However, under pressure from the NCA and Caribbean governments, in 1955 the Canadian government agreed to allow a limited number of domestics into the country from Jamaica and Barbados. A few years prior to this, in 1950, a small number of black Caribbean nurses of "exceptional merit were granted entry into Canada." As Madokoro explores in Chapter 8 of this volume, an amendment to the *Immigration Act* in 1962 dropped all overt references to racial preference. By 1967, the points system was implemented, ostensibly affirming the government's commitment to a colour-blind admissions policy in immigration. This did not trumpet the emergence of a new social order devoid of white supremacy, and we must be wary of rushing to embrace a too positive interpretation of this history. For, as Theo Goldberg argues, the "raceless" states that emerged in the late twentieth century are nonetheless characterized by racist practices. As we have seen, this racelessness in Canada was not "colour blind," but it was in fact "the raceless absorption and transmogrification of the racially differentiated into a state of values and rationality defined by white standards and norms, ways of knowing, thinking and doing."[69]

Conclusion

Ideas about race were integral to the making of modern Canada. Canada's emergence as a racial state was achieved through its territorial dispossession of First Nations peoples and racially preferential settlement, immigration, and citizenship policies. Due to the tireless work of civil rights and human activists in the post–World War II era, overt manifestations of racism became both socially taboo and illegal. Nonetheless, as this chapter has attempted to show, subtle forms of racism have always been an aspect of Canada's racial landscape. These subtler forms of racism remain hard to identify and combat.

Discussion Questions

1) Are the concepts of racial naturalism (the idea that race is a fixed biological essence) and/or racial historicism (the idea that "inferior" races

can ascend to the level of "superior" races through tutelage) useful for studying ideas of race in Canadian history?

2) Why was the *Indian Act* of 1876 such a foundational moment in how race was legally produced by the state in late-nineteenth-century Canada?

3) How does the history of Chinese and South Asian immigration illustrate some of the tensions and contradictions within Canadian immigration policy?

4) How does the story told in this chapter change conventional under-standings of Canada as a harmonious, multicultural country?

Further Readings

Kelley, Ninette, and Michael Trebilcock. *The Making of the Mosaic: A History of Canadian Immigration Policy.* Toronto: University of Toronto Press, 2000.

Stanley, Tim. *Contesting White Supremacy: School Segregation, Anti-Racism, and the Making of Chinese Canadians.* Vancouver: University of British Columbia Press, 2011.

Walker, Barrington. "Finding Jim Crow in Canada 1789–1967." In *A History of Human Rights in Canada: Essential Issues*, edited by Janet Miron. Toronto: Canadian Scholars' Press, 2009.

Ward, Peter. *White Canada Forever: Popular Attitudes and Public Policy Toward Orientals in British Columbia.* Montreal: McGill-Queen's University Press, 2002.

Woodsworth, J.S. *Strangers Within Our Gates: Or Coming Canadians.* Toronto: Frederick Clarke Stephenson, 1909.

Notes

1 Parts of this article are revised and adapted from Barrington Walker, "Finding Jim Crow in Canada 1789–1967," in *A History of Human Rights in Canada: Essential Issues*, ed. Janet Miron (Toronto: Canadian Scholars' Press, 2009), 81–96.

2 Constance Backhouse, *Colour-Coded: A Legal History of Racism in Canada* (Toronto: University of Toronto Press and the Osgoode Society for Canadian Legal History, 1999), 14.

3 Tim Stanley, *Contesting White Supremacy: School Segregation, Anti-Racism, and the Making of Chinese Canadians* (Vancouver: University of British Columbia Press, 2011).

4 Figures from Marillyn Lake and Henry Reynolds, *Drawing the Global Colour Line: White Men's Countries and the International Challenge of Racial Equality* (Cambridge: Cambridge University Press, 2008), 23.

5 David Theo Goldberg, *The Racial State* (Malden, MA: Blackwell, 2002).

6 J.S. Woodsworth, *Strangers Within Our Gates: Or Coming Canadians* (Toronto: Missionary Society of the Methodist Church, Canada, 1909).

7 Ian McKay, *Reasoning Otherwise: Leftists and the People's Enlightenment in Canada 1890–1920* (Toronto: Between the Lines, 2008).

8 Ninette Kelley and Michael Trebilcock, *The Making of the Mosaic: A History of Canadian Immigration Policy* (Toronto: University of Toronto Press, 2000), Chapter 3.

9 Ibid., 63–100.

10 J.R. Miller, *Skyscrapers Hide the Heavens: A History of Indian White Relations in Canada*, 3rd ed. (Toronto: University of Toronto Press, 2000), Chapter 5.

11 Kelley and Trebilcock, *Making of the Mosaic*, 113.

12 As a result of orders in council passed by the federal government that year, South Asians who journeyed to Canada could only do so "by continuous journey from the country of which they are natives or citizens, and upon through tickets purchased in that country or prepaid in Canada." See James W. St. G. Walker, *"Race," Rights and the Law in the Supreme Court of Canada: Historical Case Studies* (Waterloo, ON: Wilfrid Laurier Press and the Osgoode Society for the Study of Canadian Legal History, 1997), 257.

13 W. Peter Ward, *White Canada Forever: Popular Attitudes and Public Policy Toward Orientals in British Columbia* (Montreal: McGill-Queen's University Press, 2002), 22.

14 See Anthony B. Chan, "Bachelor Workers," in *A Nation of Immigrants: Women, Workers, and Communities in Canadian History, 1840s–1860s*, ed. Franca Iacovetta et al. (Toronto: University of Toronto Press, 1998).

15 Ward, *White Canada Forever*, Chapter 1.

16 Ibid., 4–22.

17 Ibid., 29–31.

18 Ibid., 32–33.

19 Ibid., 33.

20 Ibid., 34.

21 Ibid., 38. The *Chinese Immigration Act* was one of three that was passed during this time. The other two were the $10 poll tax and another preventing the Chinese from acquiring Crown lands. The federal government allowed only the third to stand.

22 Chan, "Bachelor Workers," 243.

23 Ward, *White Canada Forever*, 42; Kelley and Trebilcock, *Making of the Mosaic*, 98–99, 207.

24 Stanley, *Contesting White Supremacy*, 77, 82–83.

25 Ward, *White Canada Forever*, 79.

26 Ibid., 86.

27 Ibid.

28 Kelley and Trebilcock, *Making of the Mosaic*, 150.

29 Ibid., 151.

30 Ibid., 152.

31 Ibid., 154.

32 Ibid.

33 Woodsworth, *Strangers Within Our Gates*, 5.

34 Ibid., 48.

35 Ibid., 190.

36 Ibid.

37 Goldberg, *Racial State*, 147.

38 Ian McKay, "The Liberal Order Framework: A Prospectus for a Reconnaissance of Canadian History," *The Canadian Historical Review* 81, no. 4 (2000): 620, 623.

39 Ibid., 625.

40 The British colonial government passed laws in the mid-nineteenth century to assist Aboriginal peoples in making their transition to "civilization": *The Act*

for the Gradual Civilization of the Indian Tribes. Among its stipulations was the "gradual removal of all legal distinctions between [Indians]" and whites and the encouragement of Indians' acquisition of property. The act spelled out the conditions under which Aboriginal peoples could become citizens and drop their Indian status (enfranchised), such as acquiring education, Christian habits, and evidence of high moral character. Enfranchisement was again enshrined as a legal principle in the 1876 *Indian Act*, Sections 86–94. See Miller, *Skyscrapers Hide the Heavens*, 139–47.

41 McKay, "Liberal Order Framework," 637.

42 Goldberg, *Racial State*, 82. For an example of French colonial Amerindian policy in New France and the links between racial ideas and assimilation, see Sahila Belmessous, "Assimilation and Racialism in Seventeenth and Eighteenth-Century French Colonial Policy," *American Historical Review* 110, no. 2 (April 2005): 322–49.

43 I am well aware that sex between white men and black women as means to assimilate blacks was never seriously considered by whites in the pre- or post-Confederation periods in Canada, despite the widespread phenomenon of blacks "passing" for whites throughout North American history. In this context, the experiences of blacks and Aboriginals is quite distinct. For a discussion of the Age of Reform in the British Empire, see Jane Sampson, ed., *The British Empire* (Oxford: Oxford University Press, 2001), 121–38.

44 Maureen Elgersman, *Unyielding Spirits: Black Women and Slavery in Early Canada and Jamaica* (New York: Garland, 1999).

45 See Robin Winks, *The Blacks in Canada* (Montreal: McGill-Queen's University Press, 1997), 168–77.

46 The foundational text on this history is, of course, James W. St. G. Walker's *The Black Loyalists: The Search for a Promised Land in Nova Scotia and Sierra Leone 1776–1893* (Toronto: University of Toronto Press, 1992).

47 Seymour Drescher, *The Mighty Experiment: Free Labor versus Slavery in British Emancipation* (New York: Oxford University Press, 2004), Chapter 6.

48 See, for example, Winks, *Blacks in Canada*, Chapter 7, and William Pease and Jane Pease, *Black Utopia: Negro Communal Experiments in America* (Madison: State Historical Society of Wisconsin, 1963).

49 Winks, *Blacks in Canada*, 251–52.

50 Ibid.

51 Allen P. Stouffer, "A Restless Child of Change and Accident: The Black Image in Nineteenth Century Ontario," *Ontario Historical Society* 76, no. 2 (1984): 128–50.

52 See Barrington Walker, "The Gavel and the Veil: Blackness in Ontario's Criminal Courts, 1858–1958" (PhD diss., University of Toronto, 2003), Chapter 5.

53 See Barrington Walker, "John Paris' Journey: A Scottsboro Trial in 1920s Canada?" (unpublished manuscript).

54 Constance Backhouse, "'I Was Unable to Identify with Topsy': Carrie M. Best's Struggle against Racial Segregation in Nova Scotia, 1942," *Atlantis* 22, no. 2 (Spring/Summer 1998): 18.

55 Backhouse, *Colour-Coded*, 248.

56 Ibid., 266.

57 Nancy Lubka, "Ferment in Nova Scotia," *Queen's Quarterly* 76 (1969): 213–28.

58 Winks, *Blacks in Canada*, 369.

59 Ibid., 370.

60 Backhouse, *Colour-Coded*, 253–54.

61 Walter S. Tarnopolsky, *Discrimination and the Law in Canada* (Toronto: Richard De Boo, 1982), 20–21.

62 See once again Backhouse, *Colour-Coded*, Chapter 7, and James Walker, *"Race," Rights, and the Law*, Chapter 3.

63 Winks, *Blacks in Canada*, 420.

64 Walker, *"Race," Rights, and the Law*, 309.

65 Ibid., 173; Sheldon Taylor and Bromley Armstrong, *Bromley: Tireless Champion for Just Causes* (Pickering, ON: Vitabu Publications, 2000), Chapter 4.

66 Walker, *"Race," Rights, and the Law*, 173.

67 Sheldon Taylor, "'Darkening the Complexion of Canadian Society'": Black Activism, Policy-making and Black Immigration from the Caribbean to Canada, 1940s–1960s" (PhD thesis, University of Toronto, 1994).

68 Cited in Taylor and Armstrong, *Bromley*, 102.

69 Goldberg, *Racial State*, 206.

3

Canadian Businesses and the Business of Development in the "Third World"

KAREN DUBINSKY AND MARC EPPRECHT

Introduction

The "Third World" is closer than we think.[1] The introduction to this volume reminds us that Third World labour and resources are present in countless everyday consumer items that Canadians take for granted: cellphones, T-shirts, the food we eat. Most of the labour and resources that produce such goods are, to the consumer at least, invisible. Every once in a while, something—usually a catastrophe—puts the spotlight on labour or environmental conditions in the factories of the developing world. Canadian consumers are then forcefully and dramatically reminded of the conditions under which many of our daily goods are produced. For example, when the Rana Plaza garment factory in Dhaka, Bangladesh, collapsed in April 2013, killing 1,135 workers, there was a flurry of concern about the fact that a popular Canadian retail outlet, Loblaw, sold Joe Fresh-brand clothes that had been made at that factory. Talk ensued of consumer boycotts, not just of Joe Fresh, but of Bangladeshi products as a whole on account of evident, endemic corruption and abusive labour practices in that country. How could we be complicit in such things? Loblaw had to scramble to assure its customers that reforms would be made and that investment in developing countries like Bangladesh was inherently risky but was ultimately for the best. To place restraints on foreign direct investment there would only hurt the people of Bangladesh, above all young women.[2]

Reflecting on our role as consumers in the complex global supply chain is important—and shouldn't take a disaster the scope of this one to raise consciousness. Nor should it be an excuse to pat ourselves on the back for being better than the worst. The economic ties between Canada and the developing world are in fact extensive and varied. Meanwhile, the impact of our economic presence is hotly debated in the societies that supposedly benefit from our business. Moreover, Canadians are not only consumers of Third World–made products and services. Sometimes we own and run the whole operation and, if successful, directly enrich ourselves from the resources, ingenuity, sweat, and skills of the people of the developing world. They do not always express gratitude for the exchange.

This chapter examines a topic about which many Canadians are unaware: the complex, long-lasting, and often extremely lucrative ties between Canadian businesses and the countries of the Third World, and the mixed responses those ties evoke in the recipient countries. We will also raise the question of whether Canadian corporate activities and our governments' support for them are "sustainable" even in those cases where they can be shown to be relatively ethical or socially and environmentally responsible. To that end let us recall the wider context, where even the avatars of neoliberal economic theory are now beginning to express anxiety. It is a sobering thought that the government of Canada, as of 2015, positioned itself to the right of the International Monetary Fund in its opposition to a carbon tax that might impede the profitability of Canadian corporations.[3] A recent report by the Economics Department of the Organisation for Economic Co-operation and Development (OECD), not known for radical, left-leaning analysis, makes even more chilling reading. Among other trends to the year 2060, it foresees gross income inequality in Canada increasing to surpass current levels of inequality in the worst OECD performer today, the United States (which will by then be much more unequal, as will all OECD and most G-20 countries). Looking on the bright side, the report does predict considerable growth in the developing world with the caveat of "soaring health costs and productivity losses related to local pollution. . . . Risks of catastrophic environmental events will rise, and the [anticipated 100%] increase in concentration of greenhouse-gases in the atmosphere up to 2060 will lock-in further, and potentially more serious, environmental damages beyond the 2060 horizon."[4] If nothing else, it gives us pause to wonder: how much more stuff do we need?

So Why *Don't* Mexicans Drink Molson?

The topic of Canadian business relations with the countries of the Global South is almost counterintuitive. The vast majority of Canada's trade relations are within the First World. Over 70 per cent of our exports go to one country, the United States, which supplies almost half of our imports as well.[5] In terms of international corporate holdings, Canada is not a global economic superpower. Many commentators—journalists, academics, other experts—believe that Canadian businesses have held themselves back from realizing their potential in the world market. Canadian journalist Andrea Mandel-Campbell's cleverly titled book *Why Mexicans Don't Drink Molson* sums up this perspective well. For Mandel-Campbell, as well as many of the Canadian business leaders she interviews, the problem is that Canadians lack the nerve (actually she uses the word *cojones*) to compete on the global business stage, consistently preferring the domestic or the easy-to-access US market. For over a century, Canadians have had what she terms a "sailboat" mentality: why compete internationally when we can just live off the taxes from our natural resources, work nine to five, and go sailing at the cottage every weekend?[6]

If this description doesn't quite match the reality of most Canadians' lives, it does at least reflect a sentiment that is widely held. Canada was once a collection of colonies. It was an important resource hinterland for two of the world's great empires, France and Britain, who often explicitly forbade the development of industry or other autonomous Canadian enterprise. How, then, do colonies with vast natural resource wealth move past the status that Canadian economist Harold Innis pejoratively termed "hewers of wood, drawers of water"? To the extent the Canadian economy diversified and industrialized, it did so under the protective shelter of various tariffs and other government policies known since 1878 as the National Policy. This was designed to nurture Canadian manufacturing by shielding it from our more economically powerful neighbour. Canadians have been fighting about this economic strategy for over a century. The battle between National Policy "protectionism" and free trade liberalism has helped to determine the outcomes of federal elections and the fortunes of any number of prime ministers since the late nineteenth century. Some Canadians, like Mandel-Campbell, believe the National Policy "encouraged the creation of coddled state sanctioned monopolies while entrenching a clique of well-connected businessmen trained to seek government favour."[7] Others are more sanguine about its impact in Canada. Whatever one's perspective, the debate is completely national: both sides believe that when it comes to business, Canadians do not stray far from their own borders. "Risk averse" and "inward looking" are two phrases that come up repeatedly in discussions of Canadian business interests abroad. Canada has, according to economic historian Graham D. Taylor, "produced few famous global performers."[8]

There are exceptions, of course. World War II–era restraints on the use of grain for alcohol caused Canada's Seagram's distillery to use Jamaican molasses for its products; it then purchased a number of Jamaican sugar mills and distilleries which launched, for a time, a recognized global brand. The Cold War helped, too, as US military bases spread around Europe, East Asia, and other parts of the world, providing a captive market for recognized brands such as Seagram's.[9] In recent years the rise of a select number of Canadian multinationals such as Bombardier and Blackberry (the most popular smart phone in Nigeria and Indonesia) and the global reach of Canadian mining capital have gained notice. There has been a strong tendency to praise this in patriotic terms and to highlight the rise of a new, bolder spirit of nationalism within Canada as well as the benefits of "Team Canada" capitalism to the rest of the world. "Our" captains of industry are obviously ethical (liberal, socially conscious, human rights–loving, gender sensitive, or just plain "good" and "clearly polite") compared to the robber barons, looters, sexists, and exploiters coming from the United States, France, China, Malaysia, and the like.[10] All the major political parties support this basic view, and it has even attracted fans internationally. As Bono famously said in his endorsement of Paul Martin for prime minister in 2003, "I believe the world needs more Canada."[11]

Imperial Canada?

Another perspective on this topic presents a decidedly different version of Canadian business activities in the world. Depending on when and where one looks, Canadian businesses have plenty of interests, relationships, and a long history in the developing world, in some cases enjoying commercial advantage from wars of aggression by our friends and allies. The American wars in Southeast Asia in the 1960s and 1970s are perhaps the best-known case, as they belatedly attracted popular protest when uncomfortable facts began to emerge. Yet, in the build-up years of the US assault on Vietnam, Laos, and Cambodia, the mainstream press reported a boom in Canadian exports of military hardware, minerals, and chemicals to the United States in glowing, enthusiastic terms. The government of the day (a Liberal minority under Lester B. Pearson) actively supported such exports, including the infamous napalm and Agent Orange used against civilians and forests.[12] To give a less well-known example, Canada's trade with apartheid South Africa actually increased in value in the mid-1970s and 1980s, the years of South Africa's fiercest repression of its own black majority population and its most blatant aggression against its neighbours.[13] Canadian businesses such as Alcan, Massey-Ferguson, Bata Shoes, and Space Research Corporation (which developed a "supergun" for South Africa to use in its invasion of Angola) remained unmoved by the growing international condemnation of the racist regime, as likewise did our most powerful trade officials. Indeed, the memoir of long-serving international trade bureaucrat and president of the Canadian Exporters Association during that period, Frank Petrie, shows a strikingly amoral position on this question that confirms Linda Freeman's interpretation of Canada's "ambiguous" support for the anti-apartheid movement: "I had always maintained that Canada, with a third of its income and employment coming from exports, should never adopt a policy of turning down customers for political reasons . . . [it] would merely pass business to the French and others if we were to implement sanctions unilaterally."[14]

Political science professor Todd Gordon develops this perspective in his 2010 book *Imperialist Canada*. Gordon avoids the psychological or personality-based arguments favoured by many who write on Canadian global business activities. Rather than seeing timidity or even lack of "cojones," Gordon sees the steely-eyed pursuit of profits, in some cases with gross abuses of human rights against employees or people whose land was needed for the profit-making activity. In a study laden with statistics, one of Gordon's points about Canadian–Third World business relations stands out. In 1980, after-tax profits from Canadian Third World investments were $3.7 billion. By 2007, they had risen to $23.6 billion.[15] By 2012, Canadian mining assets in Africa alone exceeded that amount.[16] Trade is another indicator of Canada's diversifying interests. Imports and exports with sub-Saharan Africa roughly quadrupled between 2002 and 2011 to $16.5 billion, a trend that is widely expected to pick up speed.[17] From this perspective, Canada is no longer a nation cowering from foreign enterprises behind tariff-protected walls (if that picture ever was accurate). Now the balance is evening out. Between 1992 and 2009, the value of Canadian acquisitions of foreign assets actually matched the value of foreign purchases of Canadian assets. There were years in the 2000s when more Canadian companies purchased foreign companies than the reverse.[18] As we will explore in this chapter, Canada's global business interests extend as far as central Asia, Africa, and Asia Pacific, but they are most pronounced in Latin America and the Caribbean, where Canada ranks as the third largest investor.

Gordon is not alone in arguing that these increasingly lucrative economic ties between Canada and the developing world have been facilitated—even motored—by an aggressive, business-friendly foreign policy. Gordon's 2010 claim that Canadian foreign policy is driven by the goal of "creating conditions for successful international expansion of Canadian corporations, opening markets and resources of the Global South" has in fact long been proudly confirmed by none other than the Canadian government itself.[19] Canadian governments of all stripes have boasted of their commitment to creating jobs for Canadians by assisting Canadian corporations to find new markets and sources. It was the Liberals under Pearson who established the Canadian International Development Agency (CIDA) in 1966 with a "business cooperation" element that grew dramatically under Trudeau in the late 1970s. "Tied aid" directed taxpayer money to some of the biggest corporations in the country, including SNC-Lavalin and Bombardier.[20] Since the onset of Conservative governance in 2006, there was blurring of distinctions between profit-seeking, development assistance, and foreign policy. One of the Harper government's first acts was to merge the old Departments of External Affairs and International Trade, explicitly linking our national foreign policy goals with the expansion of Canadian business interests globally. Then, in 2013, CIDA was folded into the newly created Department of Foreign Affairs, Trade and Development. The new ministry released its Global Markets Action Plan soon after to serve as an unambiguous statement of its new priorities: "all diplomatic assets of the Government of Canada will be marshaled on behalf of the private sector" in order to fulfill an ambitious agenda of opening new markets to Canadian goods and services. "Economic diplomacy" is now the order of the day. As one official expressed it, the new message to diplomats is "take off your tweed jacket, buy a business suit and land us a deal."[21]

As McKay and Swift explore in Chapter 7 of this volume, the Pearsonian emphasis on humanitarian or peacekeeping initiatives, however honoured in the breach that may have been, has effectively been renounced. Reflective of the shift in Africa, the Global Markets Action Plan identifies only one country on that continent—South Africa, the richest one—as having "broad Canadian interests."[22] Others on the "specific opportunities" list, including some with notorious levels of corruption and human rights abuses, are primarily destinations for Canadian mining capital. Democracy and development will follow in a presumably natural process, Ed Fast, Minister of International Trade, informs us.[23] The instrumentalization of development assistance to serve the pursuit of profit was put even more baldly by the Minister for International Cooperation, Julian Fantino. Fantino defended CIDA's partnership with IAMGOLD, Rio Tinto Alcan, and Barrick Gold to deliver development aid in Burkina Faso, Peru, and Ghana, respectively: "CIDA's work with mining companies would help them compete on the international stage" and "This is Canadian money. . . . And Canadians are entitled to derive a benefit. And at the very same time . . . we're helping elevate these countries out of poverty."[24]

Here we will look in more detail at the activities of Canadian enterprises in the developing world, and we will weigh the arguments of the proponents and opponents of this emphasis on private, business-led development strategies. But it is worth pursuing the debate about Canada's place in the world of global enterprise. Have Canadian businesses always been homebodies? Do Canadian corporations abroad behave differently than those of other countries? Are Canadian taxpayers and citizens in the Third World well served by our government's promotion of corporate expansion?

Tropics of Capitalism: Latin American and Caribbean Enterprises in the Nineteenth and Twentieth Centuries

Historically, the answer to the above questions depends on where one looks and how one defines "Canadian" and "corporations." By a narrow definition, for example, Canadians have certainly had very little direct business interests or trade in Africa until very recently. Long before they became provinces, however, the economies of the Atlantic colonies were indirectly enriched by the export of slaves from West Africa as dried cod was crucial to powering the slave-dependent sugar industry. A number of well-connected, pre-Confederation Canadians had direct investments in or inheritances from Caribbean slave holdings, including the governor of Newfoundland, Sir Thomas John Cochrane, and the first prime minister of Canada, Sir John A. Macdonald.[25] It was a Canadian, meanwhile, William Stairs, a wholesome graduate of Kingston's Royal Military College, who led the expedition to conquer resource-rich Katanga as a mercenary for the most notorious capitalist enterprise of the late nineteenth century, the Congo Free State.[26] Canada's first overseas war as a nation also took place in Africa. Under British command, the presence of Canadian troops and military police in South Africa from 1899 to 1905 was justified as defending the British empire and the Christian faith against brutal Boer attacks. Yet the war was also widely regarded at the time as a barely disguised resource grab, securing the vast goldfields of the Rand for the benefit of British mining capital.[27]

In another part of the world—the Caribbean, Central and South America—an early moment of uniquely Canadian enterprise occurred at the end of the nineteenth century. For a brief period, roughly from 1896 to 1913, there was a tremendous wave to be caught and ridden by enterprising Canadian capitalists. This outbreak of what historians Christopher Armstrong and H. V. Nelles have called "tropical capitalism"[28] occurred at a unique juncture in Canadian, Latin American, and European history. Great Britain had long-standing commercial and political connections with the Caribbean and Latin America, and Canadians took advantage of their imperial connections. Since the eighteenth century Canada's trade with the region—particularly the Caribbean—was rooted in the triangular colonial system: the British New World colonies exchanged fish, lumber, and other staples for West Indian sugar, rum, molasses, and spices produced by slaves imported from Africa. A long period of transition away from that slave-based system was sped up by the emergence of the United States as an expansionary industrial power following the abolition of slavery in its southern states. The first Canadian commercial mission to the Caribbean (1865) was sent in that fraught period. It aimed to promote so-called legitimate intercolonial trade and to aid Canadian trading companies threatened by the rising power of the United States.

These ties remained strong after Canadian confederation, which gave Canadian entrepreneurs access to British capital in support of their undertakings. The Bank of Nova Scotia was a pioneer in that respect, setting up a branch in Kingston, Jamaica, in 1889. The Royal Bank followed, opening its

Havana branch in 1899. As historians Armstrong and Nelles explain it, "The early twentieth century financial community was very strategically positioned atop a small but extremely rapidly growing Canadian industrializing economy, poised alongside British capital during a peak expansionist phase, and not yet dominated by US finance."[29]

This latter point—"not yet dominated by US finance"—is key. Americans were certainly no strangers to Latin American investments, but Canada had cornered a particular part of the market. Canadian businessmen concentrated their efforts in the utility, insurance, and transportation fields. Having just created major railroad and public utility projects at home, Canadian businessmen looked abroad for the same opportunities. And so Canadian entrepreneurs financed light and power utilities and rail and tramway companies in Cuba, Puerto Rico, Brazil, Bermuda, Jamaica, Guyana, and Trinidad. As Armstrong and Nelles note, "such a political, economic and technological moment would not recur later as the US rose to hemispheric dominance in almost every field."[30]

The US rise, it should be emphasized, was backed by a willingness to deploy military power and skullduggery that Canadian governments were reluctant to imitate, indeed incapable of doing so. As Canadian participation in the South African war later dramatically illustrates (where opposition in Quebec nearly sparked a constitutional crisis), the peaceful promotion of trade and investment was the only realistic political option for Canadian governments to get involved in essentially colonial disputes.

This history set up a pattern that continued for decades. Canadian economic activities in the Third World are often eclipsed by the much more prominent presence of US economic players and the assertive use of American "hard power." Journalist Peter McFarlane called his book about Canadian political and economic relationships in Central America *Northern Shadows* for this very reason. To take one example: most Canadians know about William Van Horne, former president of the Canadian Pacific Railway. He was present at the driving of the last spike that completed Canada's railway in 1885. (In the famous photo he's the one with the top hat, who looks like the Monopoly game caricature of the capitalist. He is claimed as a Canadian icon, though he was born and raised in Illinois.) Few know that Van Horne went on to help finance and run the Cuban Railroad Company, which connected Havana to the rest of the country, and then moved on to Guatemala to do the same there. When Canadians enjoy Chiquita bananas on their morning cereal, it is because of the railway links constructed in the late nineteenth century that connected Guatemala's banana plantations to the port town of Puerto Barrios, from which have sailed millions of tonnes of produce (to this day).[31]

Canadian entrepreneurs have operated in the shadows in their business dealings in the Third World, but for them, the shadows aren't necessarily a bad place to be. In fact, the shadows can be really strategically useful. Certainly the shadows were highly sought after by the industrialists who owned a lucrative Canadian company based in Brazil, the Sao Paulo Tramway, Light and Power Company. The Toronto head office constantly tried to encourage the company's financial success while avoiding the pitfall of Brazilian nationalism and local concerns about foreign exploitation. The company's archives include directives such as a candid 1903 missive, in which the Toronto office urged the corporate secretary in Brazil "to conceal as much as possible from the public the facts concerning our business in Sao Paulo, particularly from the Brazilian public, and I would suggest that you make your reports containing the most meager details. . . . Any public report that we make up here is sure to go back to Brazil, and both on account of the question of taxes and for other reasons we should see that no information is made available in a printed form which we do not care to have the Brazilian officials know."[32]

Dark Threats and White Knights

Many of McFarlane's examples illustrate that Canadian monopoly practices could bring public benefits, such as cutting-edge technology transfer, infrastructure development, and jobs, to the recipient countries. Canadian companies on the whole tended to prefer negotiation rather than dictation of terms. Over time, both management and ownership became localized. In that sense, Canadian companies avoided the bad reputation that accrued to "Yanqui imperialists." The exception to this convenient shadow location would be the extensive, profitable network of Canadian banking interests in the Caribbean and Latin America. As historian Peter Hudson notes, banks tried to present themselves as national, not private, institutions, "representing Canada, not capital." This didn't always soften their image, and their presence, their role in facilitating the hold of foreign control over local economies, and their explicitly racist hiring practices occasionally brought them to the forefront of protests.[33] There is no escaping the fact that Canadian investment facilitated the broader entrapment of parts of Latin America as "banana republics" within the increasingly US-dominated global capital market.

A similar story, albeit with a modern twist, may be told in more recent cases of "good" Canadian companies such as Talisman Energy. Talisman took over the shares of a nonperforming oil field in a war zone in southern Sudan in 1998. Over the next five years it attempted to apply corporate social responsibility around its field, including building a state-of-the-art health clinic. As a publicly traded company, it allowed a relatively high degree of shareholder activism, all the while applying its expertise to bring the field into full production. Royalties from that production then fuelled the government of Sudan's genocidal wars in the south and subsequently in Darfur. When Talisman finally decided to get out from the gathering scandal, it sold its share and handed its technology to an Indian company in a consortium that also included the aggressively expansionist Chinese National Petroleum Company.[34]

These disparate examples reveal a strand in Canadians' engagements in the Third World—naivety about our role in facilitating if not justifying imperialism by others. Sherene Razack's study of Canada's disastrous peace-keeping mission in Somalia in 1992 makes the charge even harsher, and is as pertinent to the history of business as to the military. She detects a pattern of overt racism underlying our (cultivated) naivety.[35] In the past as much as in the present, Canadian business people invested in Cuban railroads or Sudanese oil or Mexican electric companies for one main reason: foreign investments were profitable. Canadian business people—or at least the successful ones—entered into financial relationships in developing world countries with several comparative advantages: access to investment capital (originally through British banks), superior technology (particularly in the fields of transportation and utilities), and the knowledge that came with the experience of having already overseen these sorts of projects in Canada. Yet these relations between Canadian entrepreneurs and the countries of the Global South took place in an asymmetrical colonial world, in which it was generally considered that those who *had* more *knew* more.[36] Furthermore, the racial order that sustained this world paid little attention to how global economic disparities were formed in the first place. Why was it, for example, that Britain was sitting on all this capital? Rather than asking such questions, the economic and technological advantages possessed by Canadian entrepreneurs were understood in familiar racial terms. Canadians doing business abroad became part of the "civilizing mission," much as, Razack argues, our peacekeeping forays against dark-skinned peoples help us to see ourselves as moral people.

From thinkers such as Edward Said we have a rich vocabulary of concepts from which to draw in order to understand why and how Europeans and North Americans understood their place in the world. Canadians were part of a global colonial world, in which they, as white British subjects, lined up on the side of civilization (not to mention evolution, progress, advancement, scientific enlightenment, and development) against barbarism. This gave Canadian explorers and military men like William Stairs a sense of mission that imbued their most inhumane acts—they were ordained by biology as much as God. Captain Stairs, an honoured graduate of the Royal Military College in Kingston, was actively involved in several important African military campaigns during the notorious "scramble for Africa." Having ordered savage reprisals against villages that did not supply his column with free labour and food ("Three natives were shot and their hands brought in"), and holding both blacks and "yellow-bellied Egyptians" in utter contempt ("what a lazy, aimless life these savages live"), Stairs waxed eloquently upon his mandate: "Have we [the whites] the right to divide among ourselves this vast continent, to throw out the local chiefs and impose our own ideas? To that there can be only one answer: yes! What value would it have in the hands of the blacks, who in their natural state, are crueler to each other than the worst Arabs. . . ."[37] Applauding the movement of industrialists from Canada to Latin America and the Caribbean in slightly less crude terms, the Canadian *Journal of Commerce* put it like this in 1901: "Sir William Van Horne and his associates seek fresh fields and pastures to prove that neither snows nor tropical suns could check the onward march of well-directed energy. . . . Canadian capital and clearer northern brains are fast turning the island of Cuba into a modern hive of industry." Similarly, from Mexico City the British ambassador saw a bright future for Canadian enterprise in the region because Canadian industrialists "seem to combine the push of the Yankee with the recognized integrity of the Englishman."[38]

It seems that Canadians understood their colleagues and employees in the developing world in a similarly one-dimensional, racialized colonial manner. Some investors and industrialists could barely conceal their contempt for the countries that were making them rich. A rare historical study of the day-to-day operations of a Canadian-owned enterprise, the Ozama sugar mill in the Dominican Republic (which was owned by the British Columbia Sugar Refining Company for a period between 1944 and 1955), reveals that Canadian owners and managers shared all of the prevalent stereotypes of their day. Canadian administrators refused to implement some of the reforms and advances suggested by the headquarters in Vancouver because they believed that Dominican workers were simply too backward to understand new technologies, such as radios. Workers who resisted the generally low wages (and extremely difficult labour) by, for example, occasionally moving to work in higher-paying sugar mills were seen by the Ozama administrators as lazy. In 1956 a Canadian administrator at Ozama summed up the experience of managing Dominican workers: "We had the normal difficulties of working with an indolent, insolent, and ignorant working force."[39] Despite all such frustrations, Canadian industrialists continued to seek out opportunities in the Global South. Something was drawing them or keeping them there.

From the Shadows to the Spotlight: Canadian Extractive and Engineering Industries around the World Today

Today, the "shadow" metaphor is starting to wear a bit thin, particularly if we look at the activities of Canadian extractive and engineering industries in the developing world. Canadian mining and engineering companies, particularly in Latin America and Africa, have emerged from the shadows, and these days are drawing an immense amount of attention. Much of it is not flattering. In a country infamous for the brutality of its particular form of racial capitalism (South Africa), for one example, it says something very disturbing when workers there voted Canada's Placer Dome as the second worst employer in the country in 2001.[40] For different reasons, Canada's Barrick Gold is also not especially welcomed by the local population of North Mara, Tanzania. "The Killing Continues at a Canadian-Owned Mine in Tanzania" is not the kind of headline that stirs Canadian national pride.[41] Toronto-listed Acres International earned other dubious firsts through its engineering work on a massive dam in Lesotho. It was the first international company to be found guilty of bribery of a state official there, and the first to be debarred from World Bank contracts for corrupt practices.[42]

To get a sense of the debate about Canadian mining companies in the world, here are two perspectives voiced in February 2013 in the *Globe and Mail*. Reporting on the enormous scale of Canadian mining holdings in different African countries as well as several high-profile corruption scandals involving Canadian companies in Chad, Eritrea, and Libya, veteran reporter Doug Saunders made a startling historical comparison. In a story headlined "Canada's African Adventure Takes a Colonial Turn," Saunders declared: "Canada is no longer simply 'doing business' or 'providing aid' in Africa. What we're doing is something that bears a striking resemblance to the things Britain and France were doing in Canada two centuries ago."[43] A few weeks after Saunders's article appeared, Julian Fantino, who was then Minister of International Cooperation, attended a meeting of the Canadian Mining Industry and had this to say about Canadian mines overseas:

> The mining, oil and gas sector's ... involvement in development is helping to lift millions of people out of poverty. We are committed to assisting our partners in the developing world get it right. We also do this work because it creates relationships based on mutual prosperity in the long run. Moreover, this work represents Canadians['] generosity and our fundamental values of freedom, democracy, human rights, and the rule of law.[44]

It's hard to imagine two more different perspectives than Saunders's and Fantino's. Yet both were written by well-known public figures, and published in leading mainstream Canadian newspapers. What is behind these powerful, and powerfully conflicting, opinions about Canadian mining companies overseas?

The activities of Canadian mining industries in the developing world are generating massive commentary for a number of different reasons. One is the sheer scope of the operations. Three-quarters of the world's mining companies are Canadian. Nearly half of all mining companies whose shares are traded on the Toronto Stock Exchange were engaged in operations outside Canada in 2012. Of the 4,322 projects carried out by those companies outside Canada, 1,526 were in Latin America, 1,197 in the United States, 652 in Africa, 339 in Australia, 313 in Asia, and 295 in Europe.[45] Canadian companies control almost 70 per cent of mining operations in Latin America. The presence of Canadian companies in Latin America has increased significantly: there have been 1,200 to 1,500 projects in any given year recently.[46] Thus in 2012 there were 67 Canadian mining companies operating in Argentina, 50 in Brazil, 55 in Chile, 39 in Colombia, 17 in Brazil, 201 in Mexico, and 89 in Peru. The volume of mining projects in each country has increased as well. In 2012, Canadian companies undertook 228 mining projects in Argentina, 154 in Brazil, 145 in Chile, 86 in Colombia, 585 in Mexico, and 231 in Peru.[47]

Two outspoken commentators on Canadian mining companies, Professors Alain Denault and William Sacher, note that the activities of Canadian companies "are experienced generally not by Canadians but by citizens of other countries."[48] Why is Canada such a global mining powerhouse? Some say it is a logical conclusion of our history. Peter Munk, former chairman of Barrick Gold, the world's largest gold mining company, puts it like this: "Mining is a very Canadian business, after fur trading, the second activity for which we were known. . . . We had the biggest mining schools, we had the biggest mining companies, more discoveries than anybody else. We produced the best miners. We had world-class companies."[49] Other commentators also point out that Canada has extremely lax mining regulations, the most permissive in the developed world, some say. Professors Denault and Sacher are two who make the argument that Canada has become a refuge for an extremely dangerous industry. The Canadian legal jurisdiction is used, they argue, "as a base and launch facility for questionable projects overseas. Canada is a judicial and financial haven that shelters its mining industry from the political or legal consequences of its extraterritorial activities by providing lax domestic regulation."[50]

Legal and reputational risk is further minimized by the common practice of outsourcing the riskiest tasks—such as mine security—to local providers. Can you then blame Barrick for all those deaths at its North Mara mine when the actual shooting was not done by Canadians but by Tanzanian police or contract employees of a Tanzanian company? How can Barrick be blamed for widespread sexual assaults by its contract personnel at Pogera mine in Papua New Guinea when gang rape is, according to owner Peter Munk, a local "cultural habit"?[51]

Mining industry proponents such as Julian Fantino argue that mining projects bring "development": taxes, employment, and a higher quality of life. Fantino is praising not only mining companies, of course, but also his government, which provides millions of dollars to support the activities of private companies abroad and also a controversial new development aid program that supports partnerships between NGOs and mining companies. Here Fantino is echoing three commonly held beliefs: that private sector investment eradicates poverty, that the private sector is inherently more "efficient" than government or NGOs, and that Canadians have something to teach the Third World about this. Mining industry spokespeople make the same arguments. Speaking to his company's shareholders, Barrick Gold's Peter Munk elaborated on the benefits he believes his company provides: "By moving into these countries and developing their mines, and most of these countries now are developing countries, we provide, way beyond the importance of money, we provide human dignity. We provide an opportunity for those people to earn their money, rather than hold out their hands."[52]

A vast scholarly literature and a rich tradition of journalistic observation, in print media and in a number of new documentary films, challenge these accounts of the benefits of mining. One could start with the people of North Mara, where literally thousands of intruders risk their lives every night (and pay bribes for the privilege) to earn their human dignity by picking through waste rock produced at Barrick's mine in pursuit of crumbs of gold the company could not retrieve. A wide range of commentators, from local communities affected by mining operations as well as Canadians who study the situation, have compiled a long list of other charges about the damage caused by mining.[53] The common denominator is conflict and loss. Mining activities have contributed to conflicts that have led to deaths, rape, child soldier recruitment, and refugees. Their presence sometimes results in net losses to public treasuries (in host countries) because of corruption or smuggling. Mining companies themselves have assisted in rewriting the mining codes in several countries in such a way as to strengthen their position and provide minimal tax benefits to host governments. In Guatemala, for example, the mining code was changed to become more open to foreign investment in 1965. Canadian scholar Catherine Nolin notes that there were "strong links" between the executives of INCO (then an active mining company in Guatemala) and Guatemalan officials as the new mining code was being drafted. Allegations continue to this day that the Guatemalan mining code was drafted in English first, based on discussions with INCO representatives.[54]

Claims of job creation can also be highly misleading. Why did South African workers identify Placer Dome as that country's second worst employer? Far from creating jobs and dignity, it won a reputation for ruthlessness precisely for eliminating thousands of jobs—a third of the work force—in the name of modernization.[55] Many countries have also seen violent evictions of entire populations (e.g., Talisman in Sudan), and people are experiencing loss of traditional farming, employment-rich artisanal mining, and other means of making a living as mining irreparably changes the surrounding environment. Indeed, the environmental damages almost defy calculation. Mines can create long-lasting pollution of huge land and water masses, tremendous health damage to both humans and livestock, and major public health problems. Mines also divert much-needed resources, such as rivers, for their own purposes. The average rural Guatemalan family uses 60 litres of water per day. The Canadian-owned Marlin Mine, owned by Canada's Goldcorp, requires 250,000 litres per hour.[56] Clearly, Denault and Sachar are not alone in their conclusion that such investments "often leave host countries worse and not better off than they were before."[57]

Plenty of economic activities bring with them a mix of positive and negative effects. Even in financial terms alone, however, there is plenty of evidence to question how much economic advantage accrues to developing countries from the mining industry. About two-thirds of the people living below the poverty line reside in nations rich with extractive resources, yet they rarely receive any meaningful benefits from their country's resource wealth.[58] The Democratic Republic of the Congo is arguably the world's richest country in terms of natural resources, holding an estimated $24 trillion in untapped mineral reserves (and $3 billion in Canadian mining company investments). In terms of income it is instead one of the poorest: the International Monetary Fund (IMF) estimates that the average Congolese person makes about a dollar a day.[59] Zambia is a country rich in copper reserves. It is home to 20 per cent of Canadian mining assets in Africa, worth approximately $6 billion. In March 2013, Canada completed a foreign investment promotion and protection agreement (FIPA) deal, designed, in the words of the Canadian government, to provide greater confidence to Canadian investors.[60] Yet in December 2012, the NGO Global Financial Integrity released a report that indicated that Zambia lost approximately $8.8 billion between 2001 and 2010 to illicit financial outflows (IFFs). This figure is twice the annual revenue of the Zambian government. Zambia privatized its copper mining industry over a decade ago, a condition imposed on developing countries around the world by international lending institutions. Since then, Zambia has found it difficult to prevent money escaping from the country. Multinational companies operating in Zambia, especially in copper mining, have moved capital through Western banks and tax havens in an effort to protect their profits from taxation.[61] As for Nigeria, one of Canada's two "strategic partners" in Africa and our largest bilateral trading partner on the continent (dominated by oil and gas), scholar George B.N. Ayittey draws on its government's own estimates that report at least US$412 billion has been stolen by government officials from public coffers from independence to 2005, a trend that has allegedly been "institutionalized" with another $20 billion stolen under former President Muhammadu Buhari, who lost power in 2015.[62]

Those are examples of why some have termed this situation the "resource curse." Mining-dependent developing countries are kept poor, by this argument, because of endemic corruption, inflated currencies, loss of competitiveness, a loss of development of other economic sectors, and unequal distribution of benefits such as employment and profits.

The conflicts in local communities generated by the presence of mines have also resulted in tremendous loss and strife. A close-up look at some of these conflicts can be found in a comprehensive report released in 2014 by the Working Group on Mining and Human Rights in Latin America. The product of an international consortium of seven Latin American non-governmental organizations, underwritten by the development agency of the Catholic Church in Germany, the project studied 22 mining conflicts in 9 Latin American countries, in order to identify trends and patterns and to explore Canadian policies that encourage human rights violations. The report selected the 22 conflicts from an astounding 198 mining-related conflicts in Latin America contained in the database of the Observatory of Mining Conflicts in Latin America (OCMAL), another NGO.[63] The report, *The Impact of Canadian Mining in Latin America and Canada's Responsibility*, makes harrowing reading. As well as cataloguing what are by now fairly well-documented and familiar stories of forced displacement, environmental damage, and adverse health effects of mining, this report also examines the extent of community breakdown, typically created as mines fail to recognize traditional authorities of collective representation in local communities. As a result, there has been a trend toward what the report terms the criminalization of social protest. As the report puts it, "given the absence of prior consultation, lack of response to complaints, and the failed attempts at dialogue, communities opposing large-scale mining have found a more effective way to express themselves and raise their profile: roadblocks, obstruction of mining activities, and social protest."[64] When people are not heard or given the opportunity to be heard at the local level, their attempts to find means to express themselves through such measures are often deemed criminal, and suppressed violently. The report also highlights a long list of Canadian policies that contribute to the problems. This issue returns us to the reason why three-quarters of the world's mines find Canada a congenial home—the "haven" theory expressed by Denault and Sacher. The Working Group's report comes to a simple, damning conclusion:

> It follows from the information compiled in the report that the Canadian government provides broad support to the extractive sector without requiring sufficient guarantees from Canadian companies that they will not harm the environment or cause human rights violations abroad. In some cases, the Canadian government has supported extractive projects even after it became aware of amply documented environmental abuses and human rights violations. Canada offers its mining companies political, economic, and legal privileges that have extremely negative consequences for the protection of the human rights of the populations of the countries in which the projects are developed.[65]

Canadians who have been involved in investigating and publicizing human rights violations, environmental damages, and labour abuses by Canadian mining companies across the world are increasingly focusing their energy on the Canadian roots of the issue. As Grahame Russell, a Canadian lawyer who works for the NGO *Rights Action* in Guatemala, puts it, "this is not narrowly a 'Guatemalan' problem; it is profoundly a 'Canadian' problem."[66] In 2011 the Canadian mining industry received more than $17 billion in financing and insurance from Export Development Canada, the government body that promotes foreign investment. All Canadians are investors—to the tune of $2.5 billion—in various mining projects through the investments of the Canada Pension Plan.[67]

This is one reason why Canadians travelling in countries with active disputes between Canadian mines and local populations are now advised to remove Canadian flags from their backpacks, a tremendous reversal of the usual stereotype of the internationally revered Canadian. But there are

Canadian solutions to at least some of these problems. In 2010, Liberal MP John McKay introduced Bill C-300, the "Responsible Mining Act," designed to provide a modest amount of regulation, oversight, and dispute resolution for the activities of Canadian mining companies overseas. Bill C-300 proposed that mining companies must comply with certain international human rights and environmental standards widely accepted by the industry as best practice. There were also proposed consequences. Mining companies in contravention of these standards would lose financial support from Export Development Canada, and also lose the support of Canadian trade commissions and embassies. The mining industry went into overdrive and lobbied hard for the defeat of the bill. It was defeated, by a narrow vote: 140–134.[68] In response to the publicity generated by this initiative, the Conservative government introduced an Office of the Extractive Sector Corporate Social Responsibility Counsellor, as a central pillar in the government's "Corporate Social Responsibility strategy" for Canada's extractive sector. The CSR Counsellor was to provide remedy for people who had been harmed by the overseas operations of Canadian extractive companies by mediating disputes. Four years later, in 2013, the counsellor resigned. During her term in office, the counsellor did not mediate any of the cases brought before her, and none of the complainants received remedy. The deck was stacked against her, as dispute mediation was contingent on voluntary participation of the companies in question. As widely predicted, all companies on the receiving end of complaints made use of the voluntary nature of the office to walk away from offers of mediation with no consequences.[69]

Lax oversight in Canada means that in a surprising number of cases Canadian corporations are instead being held accountable by courts, shareholder activism, and public opinion internationally. Talisman Energy, notably, quit Sudan not primarily because of fear of pressure within Canada but to avert further sanctions and lawsuits filed against it in the United States.[70] In another recent case, Canadians may remember our involvement in the war to overthrow Libyan dictator Muammar Gaddafi. Less well-known is that Montreal-listed SNC-Lavalin was building a gigantic prison in Libya at the time of the war, and that the company was accused of paying massive bribes to get that contract. Justice is currently being pursued in the Swiss courts.[71]

Campaigns to provide effective mining oversight and a CSR office with the power to actually enforce change continue at the federal level in Ottawa. But another novel and tremendously significant initiative has brought the issue of the behaviour and responsibility of Canadian corporations abroad right back home, to the gleaming office towers of Toronto where so many

Figure 3.1 Community members from La Union, El Estor, Guatemala, looking at the October 2009 issue of *Ryerson Free Press*, which featured the ongoing conflicts with Canadian mining companies there.

Photo by James Rodríguez, MiMundo.org

mining companies are headquartered. In March 2013, a group of Indigenous Guatemalans successfully attempted to have their day in court in Canada. The dispute was about whether a Canadian mining company, HudBay Minerals Inc., can be held liable for alleged violence at a Guatemalan mine owned by a subsidiary. The Guatemalan women told their stories of gang rape by security forces hired by the company; in another case, Angelica Choc told her story of losing her husband, an activist against the mine, who was shot by security forces in the mine's employ, near the town of El Estor in Guatemala. A few months later, on July 22, 2013, a judge ruled that Canada is the appropriate jurisdiction for Mayan plaintiffs from Guatemala to sue HudBay Minerals for the events that occurred in Guatemala, and that HudBay can be held legally accountable for the actions or omissions of its Guatemalan subsidiary company CGN (Guatemalan Nickel Company). The case is years away from trial. But the fact that it is proceeding to trial at all is a remarkable, possibly precedent-setting reminder to everyone—Canadian businesses especially—that the distance between Canada and the Third World is not as far as might be imagined.[72]

Conclusion

As we look critically at the activities of Canadian businesses in the Third World, we have tried to avoid romanticizing the lives of people most directly affected. For example, artisanal mining—as distinct from highly industrialized mining—may employ many people, but it can be extremely dangerous and devastating to local environments. We also must not ignore the overwhelming need for employment that faces people in the developing world. Enterprises such as gold mines—just to name one example—generate tremendous conflict because they arrive with promise and hope for a just distribution of economic benefits. That is exactly the point at which conflicts arise, but it is also the pressing economic need of developing countries that makes these stories so complicated.

It is also critical, as we hope we have shown, to disabuse ourselves of mythology about an inherent Canadian goodness, in business as in any other sphere of national identity. We have shed some light on the history of corporate activities in the Third World that seriously contradict that mythology. In some noteworthy cases Canadian malpractices have been held to account only by pressure or shaming from the United States, Switzerland, and Lesotho. However, it bears remembering the reports cited earlier from the OECD and the IMF, whose warnings ultimately derive from the scientific consensus on human-caused global climate change.[73] In the context of very sober predictions of global calamity related to untrammeled capitalism, does it really matter if Canadian corporations are "worse" than, say, Swedish ones but better than Saudi? Should the arrogance, bad judgement, greed, or callousness that Canadian business leaders have so often shown surprise us? Surely that is what they are paid for. Perhaps the more pertinent issue is this: Is the model of global capitalism by which Canadians have on the whole so handsomely benefited and which is predicated on a deadly illusion of perpetual economic growth really sustainable? Rather than asking if Canadian oil or Canadian corporations are ethical, should we not be asking if oil and corporations as currently in play are ethical, full stop? If not, what can shareholders, pension fund contributors, consumers, and concerned citizens do?

There are provocative answers to this question coming from many sources, including the postdevelopment, environmental justice, and degrowth movements. Wherever these may lead, it is important to enter the discussion with evidence rather than wishful thinking.

Box 3.1

This is a brief excerpt from a report written by Cathy Gerrior, a Mi'kmaq Elder, after visiting Guatemala from Canada to learn about the activities of Canadian mining companies there.

A Native Perspective of Gold Mining in Guatemala and Its Devastating Impacts on Our Brothers and Sisters, the Mayans

It is majestic and deceptive to drive through the countryside of Guatemala with its volcanoes, and seemingly endless food and natural resources. It is shocking to learn that the Native people of Guatemala were forcibly evicted from their traditional lands so that all this could be produced for the sole benefit of Canada and the United States, and that the Mayan People are forced to work the fields during harvest for about $2 per day.

From my conversations with these amazing people, they too believe that the taking of these metals that belong in the Earth creates an imbalance that negatively impacts all life on earth. They are deep in Mother Earth for a reason, and ravaging the earth for these metals unleashes things that we do not understand but are all negatively impacted by.

Is mining for precious metals evil? That answer has not been revealed to me. I believe, though, that mining in the way that these Canadian gold mining companies choose to mine, with total disregard to human life, rights and responsibilities, and at the expense of Mother Earth and all who dwell on her, for mere profits is, at the very least, blind greed. You judge the rest. Please educate yourself. Then do something. It is all very devastatingly familiar.

For the full report see:
http://www.rightsaction.org/action-content/native-perspective-gold-mining-guatemala-and-its-devastating-impacts-our-brothers-and.

Discussion Questions

1) If the vast majority of Canadian trade relations remain with First World countries, why are Canadian economic relations with the countries of the Global South worthy of attention?
2) Is the metaphor of operating "in the shadow" appropriate to describe Canadian businesses in the Third World historically? Is it still appropriate today?
3) Why are Canadian mining companies in Africa and South/Central America drawing so much attention?
4) Some of the fundamental truths that neoliberal First World governments believe about economic activity are: a) that private-sector investment eradicates poverty, b) that the private sector is inherently more efficient than government, and c) that First World countries have something to teach the Third World about this. What are the arguments for or against this position?
5) Imagine a conversation between a Canadian mining industry executive and a Guatemalan farmer who lives near a proposed mine site. What do they have to say to each other, and is common ground or consensus possible?

Further Readings

Armstrong, Christopher, and H. V. Nelles. *Southern Exposure: Canadian Promoters in Latin America and the Caribbean, 1896–1930.* Toronto: University of Toronto Press, 1988.

Butler, Paula. *Colonial Extractions: Race and Canadian Mining in Contemporary Africa.* Toronto: University of Toronto Press, 2015.

Clark, Timothy David, and Viviana Patroni. *Community Rights and Corporate Responsibility: Canadian Mining and Oil Companies in Latin America.* Toronto: Between the Lines, 2006.

Denault, Alain, and William Sacher. *Imperial Canada Inc.: Legal Haven of Choice for the World's Mining Industries.* Vancouver: Talonbooks, 2012.

Gordon, Todd. *Imperialist Canada.* Winnipeg: Arbeiter Ring Publishing, 2010.

Mandel-Campbell, Andrea. *Why Mexicans Don't Drink Molson.* Vancouver: Douglas and McIntyre, 2007.

Pederson, Alexandra. "Power, Violence and Mining in Guatemala" *ReVista: Harvard Review of Latin America,* Winter, 2014. http://revista.drclas.harvard.edu/book/power-violence-and-mining-guatemala.

Suggested Documentaries

Defensora. Rachel Schmidt, 2013. http://www.defensorathefilm.com.
Gold Fever. Northland Films, 2012. http://www.goldfevermovie.com.

Marmato. Marc Greico, 2014. http://www.marmatomovie.com.

Mirages of Eldorado. Multi-Monde Productions, 2008. http://pmm.qc.ca/eldorado/ en/home.php.

Silence Is Gold. NFB, 2012. https://www.nfb.ca/film/silence_is_gold/.

Under Rich Earth. Malcolm Rogge, 2008. http://underrichearth.ryecinema.com.

Website Resources

Mining Watch Canada. www.miningwatch.ca/.

Notes

1   We share the general scholarly consensus that the Third World does not exist as a place. See, for example, Vijay Prashad, *The Darker Nations: A People's History of the Third World* (New York: New Press, 2007); Nigel Harris, *The End of the Third World: Newly Industrializing Countries and the Decline of an Ideology* (London: I.B. Taurus, 1986); Guy Arnold, *The End of the Third World* (New York: St. Martin's Press, 1993). We hold, however, that the phrase still has traction as a metaphor for global inequality linked to the hegemonic capitalist system that is better than any of the commonplace alternatives (Global South, emerging markets, LDCs, and so forth).

2   "There was a huge outpouring of concern and even anger about what happened and how it could possibly happen," said Bob Jeffcott, a policy analyst with the Toronto-based Maquila Solidarity Network, which has worked for years with global groups on factory safety. Amber Hildebrandt, "Bangladesh's Rana Plaza Factory Collapse Spurs Change, Finger-pointing. Only $15 Million of a Promised $40-Million Fund Committed," *CBC News*, April 24, 2014, http://www.cbc.ca/news/canada/bangladesh-s-rana-plaza-factory-collapse-spurs-change-finger-pointing-1.2619524.

3   Julian Beltrame, "IMF Calls on Canada to Raise Carbon Taxes, Cut Income Taxes," *Globe and Mail*, July 31, 2014, http://www.theglobeandmail.com/report-on-business/industry-news/energy-and-resources/imf-calls-on-canada-to-raise-carbon-taxes-cut-income-taxes/article19872600/.

4   OECD (Organisation for Economic Co-operation and Development), "Shifting Gear: Policy Challenges for the Next 50 Years," *OECD Economics Department Policy Notes*, no. 24 (July 2014).

5   "Canada's State of Trade: Trade and Investment Update 2012," Government of Canada, Foreign Affairs Trade and Development Canada, http://www.international.gc.ca/economist-economiste/performance/state-point/state_2012_point/2012_5.aspx?lang=eng.

6   Andrea Mandel-Campbell, *Why Mexicans Don't Drink Molson* (Vancouver: Douglas and McIntyre, 2007), 35.

7   Ibid., 77.

8   Graham D. Taylor, *The Rise of Canadian Business* (Toronto: Oxford University Press, 2009), 197.

9   Graham D. Taylor, "The Whisky Kings: The International Expansion of the Seagram Company, 1933–95," in Andrew Smith and Dimitry Anastakis, eds.,

Smart Globalization: The Canadian Business and Economic History Experience (Toronto: University of Toronto Press, 2014), 193.

10 For a highly polemical example of this argument, see Ezra Levant, *Ethical Oil: The Case for Canada's Oil Sands* (Toronto: McClelland and Stewart, 2010). In more scholarly language, see Victoria Schorr and Paul Hitschfield, "Canadian Trade and Investment in Africa," *Canada-Africa Relations: Looking Back, Looking Ahead*, ed. Rohinton Medhora and Yiagadeesen Samy (Waterloo, ON: Centre for International Governance Innovation in partnership with Carleton University, 2013), 147.

11 "Bono Endorses Martin, Canada in Helping Third World," *Globe and Mail*, November 16, 2003, http://www.theglobeandmail.com/news/national/bono-endorses-martin-canada-in-helping-third-world/article1169121/.

12 Victor Levant, *Quiet Complicity: Canadian Involvement in the Vietnam War* (Toronto: Between the Lines, 1986).

13 Linda Freeman, *The Ambiguous Champion: Canada and South Africa in the Trudeau and Mulroney Years* (Toronto: University of Toronto Press, 1997).

14 Frank Petrie, *As Far as Ever the Puffin Flew* (New York: Vantage, 1997), 309.

15 Todd Gordon, *Imperialist Canada* (Winnipeg: Arbeiter Ring, 2010), 11. See also Yves Engler, *The Black Book of Canadian Foreign Policy* (Vancouver: RED and Fernwood Press, 2009), a kind of catalogue of nefarious activities by Canadians in the world generally.

16 Schorr and Hitschfield, "Canadian Trade," 144.

17 Ibid., 138–39.

18 Gordon, *Imperialist Canada*, 21.

19 Ibid., 10.

20 David R. Morrison, *Aids and Ebb Tide: A History of CIDA and Canadian Development Assistance* (Waterloo, ON: Wilfrid Laurier University Press in association with The North-South Institute, 1998); David Gillies, "Export Promotion and Canadian Development Assistance," in *Canadian International Development Assistance Policies: An Appraisal*, ed. Cranford Pratt (Montreal: McGill-Queen's University Press, 1994), 186–209.

21 John Ibbitson, "Tories' New Foreign Affairs Vision Shifts Focus to 'Economic Diplomacy,'" *Globe and Mail*, November 27, 2013.

22 "The Global Markets Action Plan," accessed July 15, 2014, http://international.gc.ca/global-markets-marches-mondiaux/markets-marches/index.aspx#tab2.

23 According to his press release of June 20, 2014, Ed Fast visited Madagascar, Burkina Faso, and Tanzania "to foster a peaceful, democratic and prosperous future" through the protection of foreign investment in the extractive and renewable energy sectors. http://www.international.gc.ca/media/comm/news-communiques/2014/06/21a.aspx?lang=eng.

24 Kim Mackrael, "Fantino Defends CIDA's Corporate Shift," *Globe and Mail*, December 3, 2012, http://www.theglobeandmail.com/news/politics/fantino-defends-cidas-corporate-shift/article5950443/. For a critical assessment of these projects see Stephen Brown, "Undermining Foreign Aid: The Extractive Sector and the Recommercialization of Canadian Development Assistance," in *Rethinking Canadian Aid*, ed. Stephen Brown, Molly den Heyer, and David R. Black (Ottawa: University of Ottawa Press, 2015); and Elizabeth Blackwood and Veronika Stewart, "CIDA and the Mining Sector: Extractive Industries as

an Overseas Development Strategy," in *Struggling for Effectiveness: CIDA and Canadian Foreign Aid*, ed. Stephen Brown (Montreal: McGill-Queen's University Press, 2012), 217–45.

25 According to Nick Draper, one of the researchers who tracked compensation to slave owners, Macdonald married into Jamaican plantation money through his second wife. "Canada's" biggest direct slave holder appears to have been Robert Neilson of Hamilton, who won compensation of £28,763 for liberating his 568 slaves in Trinidad, that is, roughly 500 times the average annual earnings of a skilled worker. Paul Waldie, "Sir John A. Macdonald Had Family Ties to Slave Trade," *Globe and Mail*, March 2, 2013, http://www.theglobeandmail.com/news/world/sir-john-a-macdonald-had-family-ties-to-slave-trade/article9242022/.

26 Roy MacLaren, ed., *African Exploits: The Diaries of William Stairs, 1887–1892* (Montreal: McGill-Queen's University Press, 1998).

27 Carman Millar, *Canada's Little War: Fighting for the British Empire in Southern Africa, 1899–1902* (Toronto: James Lorimer, 2003).

28 Christopher Armstrong and H.V. Nelles, *Southern Exposure: Canadian Promoters in Latin America and the Caribbean, 1896–1930* (Toronto: University of Toronto Press, 1988).

29 Ibid., x–xi.

30 Ibid., xi.

31 Peter McFarlane, *Northern Shadows: Canadians and Central America* (Toronto: Between the Lines, 1989), 25–38.

32 Armstrong and Nelles, *Southern Exposure*, 60.

33 Peter James Hudson, "Imperial Designs: The Royal Bank of Canada in the Caribbean," *Race and Class* 52, no. 1 (Winter 2010): 36.

34 This controversy generated extremely polarized opinions but the Canadian ambassadorial representative at the time provides a nimbly balanced account. See Nicholas Coghlan, *Far in the Waste Sudan: On Assignment in Africa* (Montreal: McGill-Queen's University Press, 2005), and, for a scholarly assessment, Penelope Simons and Audrey Macklin, *The Governance Gap: Extractive Industries, Human Rights, and the Home State Advantage* (New York: Routledge, 2014).

35 Sherene Razack, *Dark Threats and White Knights: The Somalia Affair, Peacekeeping and the New Imperialism* (Toronto: University of Toronto Press, 2004).

36 Molly Kane, "International NGOs and the Aid Industry: Constraints on International Solidarity," *Third World Quarterly* 34, no. 8 (2013): 1505–15.

37 MacLaren, *African Exploits*, 247. Stairs's diary is a fascinating document that reveals both the casual brutality of the ivory business and a hint of self-awareness that his actions would not pass muster with public opinion even in Britain, let alone back home in Canada. "I often wonder what English people would say if they knew of the way in which we 'go for' these natives. Friendship we don't want as then we should get very little meat and probably have to pay for the bananas."

38 Armstrong and Nelles, *Southern Exposure*, pp. 38, 85.

39 Catherine C. LeGrand, "Informal Resistance on a Dominican Sugar Plantation during the Trujillo Dictatorship," *Hispanic American Historical Review* 75, no. 4 (1995): 597.

40 Bernard Simon, "The Big Dig: Placer Dome Is Drilling the World's Longest Mineshaft in South Africa," *Report on Business Magazine*, March 30, 2001, 50–58.

41 This comes from an unabashedly hostile activist group, which estimates 89 deaths of intruders onto company property since 2012. Accessed July 16, 2014, protestbarrick.net. However, similar accusations are made in *Report on Business*: Geoffrey York, "Barrick's Tanzanian Project Tests Ethical Mining Policies," *Report on Business Magazine*, September 29, 2011.

42 "Corruption in Lesotho: Small Place, Big Wave. A Conviction for Bribery Could Have a Wide Impact," *Economist*, September 19, 2002, http://www.economist. com/node/1338833; Bretton Woods Project, "Landmark Decision: Canadian Company Debarred," July 26, 2004, http://www.brettonwoodsproject. org/2004/07/art-62691/.

43 Doug Saunders, "Canada's African Adventure Takes a Colonial Turn," *Globe and Mail*, February 2, 2013.

44 Julian Fantino, "Extraction for Development," *Financial Post*, February 28, 2013, http://business.financialpost.com/2013/02/28/extraction-for-development/ ?__lsa=6cd4-6c6b.

45 Working Group on Mining and Human Rights in Latin America, *The Impact of Canadian Mining in Latin America and Canada's Responsibility*, Due Process of Law Foundation, April 3, 2014, http://www.dplf.org/en/news/ report-impact-canadian-mining-latin-america-and-responsibilities-canada.

46 McGill Research Group Investigating Canadian Mining in Latin America, accessed July 10, 2014, http://micla.ca/.

47 Working Group on Mining and Human Rights, *Impact of Canadian Mining*, 4.

48 Alain Denault and William Sacher, *Imperial Canada Inc.: Legal Haven of Choice for the World's Mining Industries* (Vancouver: Talonbooks, 2012), 1.

49 "An Interview with Peter Munk," *Economist*, April 29, 2014.

50 Deneault and Sacher, *Imperial Canada Inc.*, 3.

51 Michael Posner, "Peter Munk's Reflections on Being a Winner," *Globe and Mail*, February 18, 2011.

52 Peter Munk, "Speech to Shareholders Barrick Gold," April 2010. Papua New Guineau Mine Watch. https://ramumine.wordpress.com/2013/03/31/ fallacies-of-neoliberalism-peter-munk-of-barrick-gold-in-his-own-words/.

53 As well as the numerous references in these notes, see also Liisa North, Timothy David Clark, and Viviana Patroni, eds., *Community Rights and Corporate Responsibility: Canadian Mining and Oil Companies in Latin America* (Toronto: Between the Lines, 2006); Alain Deneault, Delphine Abadie, and William Sacher, *Noir Canada: Pillage, corruption et criminalité en Afrique* (Montreal: Les Éditions Écosociété, 2008); and Bonnie Campbell, ed., *Mining in Africa: Regulation and Development* (London: Pluto Press, 2009).

54 Catherine Nolin and Jaquie Stephens, "'We Have to Protect the Investors': Development & Canadian Mining Companies in Guatemala," *Journal of Rural and Community Development* 5, no. 3 (2010): 37–70, 50.

55 The business press interpreted this positively. As reporter Bernard Simon put it, "Placer may not have endeared itself to the union, but there is no denying the impact of the layoffs and other cost-cutting measures on the bottom line. When Harris and his team took over, South Deep ranked 19th out of 19 South African gold mines in a quarterly survey for productivity, cost control and ore-body development by Johannesburg-based BoE. In BoE's latest rankings, South Deep is the star performer, surging to No. 7. Ranked by total working costs,

South Deep stands at No. 5. The mine is 'slowly clawing [its] way towards being internationally competitive,' the survey concludes." Bernard Simon, "The Big Dig," *Globe and Mail*, March 30, 2001, http://www.theglobeandmail.com/report-on-business/rob-magazine/the-big-dig/article18291711/?page=all.

56 Guatemala Human Rights Commission/USA, "Goldcorp's Mining in San Miguel Ixtahuacán," accessed July 5, 2014, http://www.ghrc-usa.org/AboutGuatemala/Goldcorp.htm.

57 Denault and Sacher, *Imperial Canada Inc.*, 2.

58 Ibid., 34.

59 Colin Kinniburgh, "Beyond 'Conflict Minerals': The Congo's Resource Curse Lives On," *Dissent: A Quarterly on Politics and Culture* (Spring 2014).

60 DFAIT news release, "Harper Government Concludes Investment Agreements with Cameroon and Zambia," *Protecting Canadian Investments in High-Growth Markets around the World Creates Jobs, Growth and Prosperity for Canadians*, March 4, 2013.

61 Sarah Freitas, "What Billions in Illicit and Licit Capital Flight Means for the People of Zambia," Financial Transparency.org, December 13, 2012, https://financialtransparency.org/what-billions-in-illicit-and-licit-capital-flight-means-for-the-people-of-zambia/. See also Jamie Pickering, "Zambia's Tangled Webs and Flows," *Think Africa Press*, September 6, 2013; and Travis Lupick, "Canada at the Forefront of a Controversial Mining Boom in Africa," Straight.com, April 18, 2013.

62 George B.N. Ayittey, "The Smart Way to Fight Corruption (Part I)," April 27, 2012, https://seunfakze.wordpress.com/2012/04/27/the-smart-way-to-fight-corruption-part-i-by-ayittey/; and Festus Owete, "Jonathan Has Institutionalised Corruption in Nigeria, says Amaechi," *Premium Times*, March 6, 2014, https://www.premiumtimesng.com/news/156297-jonathan-institutionalised-corruption-nigeria-says-amaechi.html#sthash.h2f5WSRD.dpbs.

63 Working Group on Mining and Human Rights, *Impact of Canadian Mining*. Another source, the McGill Research Group Investigating Mining in Latin America, discovered 85 cases of community/Canadian mining company conflict since the Canadian mining boom began in the 1990s, "McGill Research Group Investigating Canadian Mining in Latin America," accessed July 10, 2014, http://micla.ca/. A further important study of Canadian mining in Guatemala is Alexandra Pederson, *Landscapes of Fear: Community Resistance to Neoliberal Development in Guatemala* (PhD diss., Queen's University, in progress).

64 Working Group on Mining and Human Rights, *Impact of Canadian Mining*, 12, 14.

65 Ibid., 25.

66 Grahame Russell, "Mining, Repression and the Rhetoric of Democracy and the Rule of Law in Guatemala," Rabble.ca, August 13, 2012.

67 Working Group on Mining and Human Rights, *Impact of Canadian Mining*, 25.

68 Penelope Simons and Audrey Macklin, "Defeat of Responsible Mining Bill Is Missed Opportunity," *Globe and Mail*, November 3, 2010. The bill could have passed had all Liberal and NDP MPs shown up to vote.

69 Catherine Coumans, "Op-Ed: Canada Needs Effective Mining Oversight," *Ottawa Citizen*, October 31, 2013.

70 Coghlan, *Far in the Waste Sudan*, 54–58.

71 Dave Seglins and John Nicol, "Riadh Ben Aïssa, ex-SNC-Lavalin Executive, Agrees to Settlement Plan," *CBC News*, August 18, 2014, http://www.cbc.

ca/news/canada/riadh-ben-a%C3%AFssa-ex-snc-lavalin-executive-agrees-to-settlement-plan-1.2739464. To be fair, this may be a case of the Swiss simply moving faster than the Canadians as Ben Aïssa also faces extradition charges in Canada.

72 The story of this lawsuit is well told in *La Defensora*, directed by Rachel Schmidt (Guatemala: Earth and Sky Films, 2014).

73 IPCC (Intergovernmental Panel on Climate Change), "Climate Change 2014. Impacts, Vulnerability, and Adaptation," 2014, http://ipcc-wg2.gov/AR5/images/uploads/WGIIAR5-Chap22_FGDall.pdf.

4

Canada and the Third World:
Development Aid

MOLLY KANE

Introduction

Public support for development aid is often used to measure the extent to which Canadians want to make a contribution to bringing about a more just, healthy, and peaceful world. However, assessments of the impact of development aid on the Third World rarely lead to the conclusion that it has significantly advanced that vision. In fact many have argued that aid more often causes harm than good.[1] Alternative approaches to Canadian international cooperation are both necessary and possible. To pursue viable alternatives we need to appreciate that development aid is, and has always been, an instrument of foreign policy. Its primary purpose has been to serve the interests of Canada, however complex and contradictory those interests may be.

This chapter will explore some of the ways in which development aid has been an instrument of Canadian foreign policy since the end of World War II. We will present in brief how aid has been used to leverage influence among other industrialized countries for the advancement of Canadian economic and security interests; how it has been used to manage domestic political tensions and demands, including the aspirations of Canadians for a better world; and how it has been used to pressure Third World governments to align their national policies—and their positions within international governance institutions—with Canadian interests, notably those of Canadian corporations. The chapter will conclude with propositions for how alternative approaches to international cooperation might be envisioned, reflecting an evolution in the understanding of Canada's historical relationship with the Third World and a more democratically determined foreign policy framework to meet the interests of Canadian citizens for the future. (See Table 4.1 for a timeline of selected global events and the evolution of Canada's development program.)

Setting the Scene

In early 2012 the Canadian International Development Agency (CIDA) announced its support for a partnership project with Toronto-based

IAMGOLD Corporation and the international development aid organization Plan Canada, to provide job-skills training for youth in Burkina Faso, the West African country where IAMGOLD has extensive mining operations. The project was one of several similar contracts announced over the previous months with Canadian mining companies and Canadian development NGOs in Ghana, Peru, Mali, and Senegal.

The partnership triad of a public agency funded by taxpayers, a profitable mining company, and a Canadian charity made the news as yet another example of the government's increasingly explicit alignment of Canadian aid priorities with the financial interests of Canadian resource extraction companies, a topic elaborated upon by Dubinsky and Epprecht in this volume. Advocates for development aid as a means to combat poverty in the Third World criticized both the government and Plan Canada for entering into such an arrangement with IAMGOLD, asserting that it was not appropriate to use public funds allocated for development assistance to subsidize shareholder profits, nor to meet the needs of private corporations seeking social acceptance for their often destructive operations, especially to advance a development model of dubious value to developing countries. The criticism was only the latest salvo in a long-standing debate regarding the ethics of development-NGO partnerships with mining companies, and the real contribution of mining in Africa to the continent's development aspirations.[2]

IAMGOLD Corporation's president, Steve Letwin, defended the project, saying, "It's very hard to escape the cynicism that comes with programs like this. People try to look behind it for other motives. They just can't believe that there's a sincere intention by the company to try to help." In the same interview, Letwin revealed why there might be good reason for public skepticism regarding the corporation's motivation to help:

> "If youth don't have doors or windows to get out, to improve, then we're going to have problems at that mine, and we're going to have problems as a society," he said. What problems could the mine suffer if young people remain unemployed? "Over the course of time, they're going to want more of a take," he said. "And that, in turn, would mean increased taxes and royalties."[3]

The Canadian Minister for International Cooperation at the time, Julian Fantino, defended CIDA's promotion of Canada's mining and extractive industries, saying, "We're not getting into the extractive business . . . [CIDA's support for extractive industries] is trying to help the needy countries to enable them to help themselves, to develop sustainable economies such as we've seen so that we don't have to continually bail them out with their food issues, their education, their health issues and on it goes."[4] As crude as this statement is, it reveals some widely held myths regarding the ways in which the Canadian economy developed, and the extent to which it is "sustainable." It also reveals misconceptions about how Canadian aid programs have been "bailing out needy countries" with their "food, education, and health issues." These misconceptions indicate a lack of understanding of the history of the exploitation of natural resources and labour from the countries of the Third World and the often contradictory role that development aid has played in those relations of exploitation, right from the inception of the international development era in the 1950s.

Fantino's blunt rationale for using public funds to support extractive industries may appear to reflect radical changes in Canadian aid policy. His position certainly diverges from most of the current professional and scholarly discourse regarding the proper use of aid for development effectiveness.[5] However, the underlying belief that public subsidy of private investment in extractive industries may be justified in the name of Third World development is not really new. Nor is the assertion that Canada's foreign aid budget should aim (also) to serve the interests of Canadian corporations. Both are among the often-contested principles that have determined how Canada has rationalized and delivered development aid within its foreign policy objectives over the past six decades. The Canadian scholar Cranford Pratt has pointed out that the relationship between the public sector and the corporate sector is not unique to foreign policy:

> Ours has never been a laissez-faire government. The federal government and most provincial governments have always regarded the tender care of the health, profitability, and development of the private sector as a central responsibility. The relationship between the public sector and the private has been reinforcing and supportive, with government policies promoting in a wide variety of ways the interests of capitalism in Canada. Moreover, historically, the relations between business and government have been anything but at arm's length. It is not therefore novel or iconoclastic to presume that this close relationship will have its impact as well upon Canadian foreign policy.[6]

What have evolved over the years are the nature and agenda of foreign policy as a whole, the vision of Canada's place in the world, and the approaches used to engage in international relations in keeping with that vision. To better understand some of the tensions related to how development aid has been an instrument of foreign policy, we will take a look in the next section at the origins of the development aid "project" of the industrialized countries, and Canada's positioning as an emerging economic power following the devastation of World War II.

The Post–World War II Context and the Development Project

In the aftermath of World War II, popular campaigns in industrialized countries for social welfare and better working conditions were transforming the social contract between governments and citizens, and between labour and capital. Canada was no exception to these trends. The idealism of a world without want and a new era of human progress that could emerge from the ruins of war inspired the founding of the United Nations in 1945 and the Universal Declaration of Human Rights three years later.

For the peoples of the Third World, and for the disenfranchised of Europe and North America, notably Indigenous peoples and the African diaspora, it was a time of great promise. Social upheaval indicated tremendous momentum, a decisive rupture with the colonial past. It was a time to invent futures of freedom and self-determination, futures that were claimed and asserted by the Third World through cultural expression and political action. After decades of resistance to imperial rule, India gained its independence from Britain in 1947, and the sun began to set on the British empire as movements for independence swelled in Africa as well. The peasant revolution of China, culminating in the founding of the People's Republic of China in 1949, and the rising influence of the Soviet Union in many parts of the world signalled seismic shifts in relations within nations, among peoples, and among states.

Within a decade after World War II, in April 1955, 29 countries of Asia and Africa gathered in Bandung, Indonesia, for a conference to build cooperation between the two continents and to assert their adherence to a nonaligned movement in resistance to the polarization of the deadly rivalry between the Soviet Union and the United States. The Bandung Declaration, also explored in the chapter by Webster, captured a collaborative spirit of independence movements and the aspirations of the participating countries to make great strides in economic development of their societies within a new international order. The development they envisioned recognized the economic legacies of colonialism and included plans for economic diversification and industrialization, including processing of raw materials before export, and investment in transportation and financial infrastructure to encourage regional trade and cooperation. The final communiqué of the Bandung Conference also emphasized the importance of cultural cooperation among African and Asian countries, human rights and self-determination, the urgent problems of "dependent peoples" still subjected to colonialism, and the promotion of world peace and cooperation.[7]

Throughout those early years of the postcolonial period, the aspirations of Third World societies were expressed as demands for democratization and transformation of international relations, systems, and structures. Financial assistance, as working capital in such a transformation, was sought to address the failures of colonial economies—that had been shaped by relations of wealth extraction and domination—to meet the needs and aspirations of the majority. A new international order would require adjustments that would not necessarily deliver financial benefit to the industrialized countries in the short term, but would be supported because of the recognition that in the longer term all peoples would benefit from greater equality and shared prosperity and human security. This vision of the changes required was premised on attributing the scourges of impoverishment and human suffering in the Third World to the social, political, and economic legacies of colonialism. In scope and scale the visions for change were a far cry from the limited goals of poverty reduction that have now come to be associated with development aid.

While the Third World was confronting the needs of reconstruction following colonialism, the European powers, which had benefited from the extraction of wealth from their colonies over centuries, required a massive mobilization of external investment for their own reconstruction following the war. A European Economic Recovery Program, better known as the Marshall Plan (after the US Secretary of State George Marshall) was financed and directed by the United States from 1948 to 1952. During those four years the United States provided $13 billion in economic and technical assistance to the European countries that had joined the Organisation for European Economic Co-operation (OEEC), forerunner to the Organisation for Economic Co-operation and Development (OECD), which was formed in 1961. Much of the Marshall Plan resources were used to buy raw materials and manufactured goods from the United States and Canada, the other allied country that had emerged from the war without damage to its economic infrastructure. The allowance by the United States for the purchase of goods from Canada is an indicator of the integration and subordination of the Canadian economy to that of the United States in the post-War period.[8]

The contributions of the United States and Canada to the reconstruction of Europe were critical to the global realignment of economic and military power. The unprecedented financial investments of the Marshall Plan were mobilized, not only for the direct benefit of Europe, but as a bulwark against the perceived threat of Soviet antagonism to capital and expansion of influence in the rest of the world. The resources and labour of the colonies had made the industrialization of Europe possible, and they were still required for the massive reconstruction of public and private infrastructure needed at the end of the war. They were also required for the continued growth and profitability of the corporate and financial sectors in Europe and the emerging empire of the United States. Through its financing of the Marshall Plan, the United States gained access to the resources and markets of Asia and Africa that had been off-limits during European colonial rule, as the opening of colonial markets to the United States was a condition for the European powers to have access to funds from the Marshall Plan.[9]

An important aspect of the global social, political, and economic restructuring being worked out among the industrialized countries at that time was reckoning with the social mobilizations for rights and freedoms going on in the colonies. The ambition and rationale for the establishment of global institutions for cooperation in the delivery of development aid was spelled out first by US President Harry Truman in his inaugural address in January 1949. In his Four Point Speech, Truman proclaimed the determination of the United States to "provide good will, strength, and leadership" to bring about "a major turning point in the long history of the human race." Truman charged that the biggest threat to achieving that turning point was communism:

> The American people desire, and are determined to work for, a world in which all nations and all peoples are free to govern themselves as they see fit, and to achieve a decent and satisfying life. Above all, our people desire, and are determined to work for, peace on earth—a just and lasting peace—based on genuine agreement fully arrived at by equals.
>
> In the pursuit of these aims, the United States and other like-minded nations find themselves directly opposed by a regime with contrary aims and a totally different concept of life.[10]

Claiming the initiative to "build an even stronger structure of international order and justice," the United States would have as its "partners" countries that, "no longer solely concerned with the problem of national survival, are now working to improve the standards of living of all their people. We are ready to undertake new projects to strengthen the free world." Truman presented four courses of action for the coming years, for "our program for peace and freedom." The four included support for the United Nations and its expansion through the addition of "new nations which are being formed in lands now advancing toward self-government under democratic principles," "continuation" of programs for world economic recovery, and strengthening "freedom-loving nations against the dangers of aggression." The fourth course of action was concerned with development aid:

> Fourth, we must embark on a bold new program for making the benefits of our scientific advances and industrial progress available for the improvement and growth of underdeveloped areas.

> More than half the people in the world are living in conditions approaching misery. Their food is inadequate. They are victims of disease. Their economic life is primitive and stagnant. Their poverty is a handicap and a threat both to them and to more prosperous areas.

The world powers, including Canada, that went on to establish and finance the institutions to implement the "bold new program" of development, while upholding humanitarian objectives, were not engaged in supporting processes of decolonization. International aid was provided not—as it was to postwar Europe—in order to rebuild what was understood to be a civilization worth conserving and necessary for the prosperity of capitalism. Rather, colonial assumptions about the inferiority and backwardness of the "natives" were perpetuated in the continuation of forms of tutelage and indirect rule though aid. More importantly, the project of post-independence development sought to modernize, not arrest, the extraction of wealth from the former colonies to the industrialized North. Even with its promise of a better future, the development project was constructed on the shaken foundations—rather than the ruins—of colonialism.[11]

Canada Joins the Development Project

With the advent of the diagnosis of "underdevelopment" as the problem facing the peoples of Africa, Asia, and Latin America, the countries that had benefited from colonial relations of wealth extraction took on the "white man's burden"[12] of development assistance, as the self-appointed arbiters and architects of future progress for the rest of the world. Canada's leadership and commitment to this emerging development aid regime strengthened its position as a player among industrialized countries within the various institutions that were setting the terms of regional and global political and economic relations. A significant commitment to development aid coordinated within the OECD assured Canada a place at the table of the post-independence restructuring of relations among nations as a "developed country donor," and therefore one of those countries directing the terms of engagement between global capital and the former colonies, now called "developing countries."

Canada engaged initially in development cooperation through its membership in the Commonwealth. Following a meeting of the Commonwealth Conference of Foreign Ministers held in Colombo, Sri Lanka, the Colombo Plan was launched in 1950 to provide a framework for cooperation around specific bilateral (country-to-country) projects in Asia and the Pacific. Cooperation continued with participation in the Commonwealth

Caribbean Aid Program in 1958, the Commonwealth Africa program in 1960, and Francophone Africa in 1961. In 1961 Canada was a founding member of the Development Assistance Committee (DAC) of the OECD.

The anticommunist rationale for aid, expressed by President Truman, resonated with the Canadian government at the time:

> The Canadian government's initial justification for joining the Colombo Plan was couched unequivocally in the rhetoric of Cold War security and support for the American-led Western alliance. . . . Lester Pearson, Canada's secretary of state for External Affairs, told the House of Commons in February 1950: "If South–East Asia and South Asia are not to be conquered by communism, we of the free democratic world . . . must demonstrate that it is we and not the Russians who stand for national liberation and economic progress."[13]

Over time, the explicit Cold War rhetoric gave way to expressions of what would come to be appreciated as Canadian "humane internationalism." Even by 1955, Pearson spoke of the "genuine desire of Canadians to help others less fortunate, the recognition that the more quickly other people's standards of living rise the better off we shall all be, the conviction that economic and social progress are essential to a durable peace . . . all of these seem to be more solid and more fundamentally significant reasons for providing assistance. . . . It is a sorry commentary . . . that without (the communists) and the threat which they represent we might not so readily have done what we should have been doing anyway."[14]

The "genuine desire of Canadians to help others less fortunate" inspired the engagement of government and citizens in the creation of new institutions, programs, and organizations (NGOs) dedicated to Third World development and international cooperation. Pearson's leadership was recognized in 1967, shortly after he stepped down as prime minister, when he became the chair of the Commission on International Development with a mandate from the World Bank to assess the record of development aid and to "clarify the errors and propose the policies which will work better in the future."[15] The Pearson Commission report, *Partners in Development*, contributed to strengthening Canada's reputation as a keen player in international cooperation for development, urging reform in aid delivery as well as increases in aid volume.

> Pearson's report, submitted in September 1969, supported many trade reforms that industrial countries had been resisting—such as a non-reciprocal preference scheme for developing country exports, supplementary financing for temporary loss of export earnings, and buffer stocks to stabilize commodity prices. It urged developing countries to be more open

to private investment, and developed countries to offer better incentives to encourage such investment. On the aid front, the commission called for softer loans, recognition of debt relief as a legitimate form of aid, greater untying of bilateral ODA to cover local costs and procurement in developing countries, and an increase in the proportion of aid flowing to multilateral institutions to at least 20 percent by 1975. . . . Pearson added a new target to the lexicon: each donor's net disbursements of ODA (official development assistance as defined by the OECD-DAC) "should . . . reach 0.7 percent of its GNP by 1975 or shortly thereafter, but in no case later than 1980."[16]

Canada's commitment to development aid took on a more substantial form just prior to the release of the Pearson report with the creation of the Canadian International Development Agency (CIDA) in 1968 by the Canadian government under Pierre Trudeau. The establishment of CIDA, and the appointment of a strong leader in its first president, Maurice Strong, signalled a more sophisticated, robust, and enduring approach to international cooperation for development. With the creation of CIDA, Canada set in place the means to develop policies, programs, and expertise in development cooperation with greater autonomy and clarity of mandate than had been possible when aid had been delivered through CIDA's forerunner, the External Aid Office of the Department of Foreign Affairs.

Canada's commitment to international development on the global scene was further buttressed with the creation of the International Development Research Centre (IDRC) in 1970 by an act of parliament that received unanimous support. IDRC was set up as a Crown corporation financed by appropriations made annually by parliament and governed by a board of 21 members, of whom only 11 needed to be Canadians; the remaining 10 positions were intended to bring perspectives and experience from developing countries.

A New International Economic Order?

The first half of the 1970s was arguably a zenith in the mobilization of global efforts for Third World development articulated as demands for a new international order, rather than specific targets or goals to be delivered by existing economic systems and institutions. On May 1, 1974, the General Assembly of the United Nations passed a Declaration on the Establishment of a New International Economic Order (NIEO) in which the members of the United Nations:

> *Bearing in mind* the spirit, purposes and principles of the *Charter of the United Nations* to promote the economic advancement and social progress

of all peoples, *Solemnly proclaim* our united determination to work urgently for the Establishment of a New International Economic Order based on equity, sovereign equality, interdependence, common interest and cooperation among all States, irrespective of their economic and social systems which shall correct inequalities and redress existing injustices, make it possible to eliminate the widening gap between the developed and the developing countries and ensure steadily accelerating economic and social development and peace and justice for present and future generations.[17]

The Declaration set out

the basic principles on which such a new and viable system of international economic co-operation might be progressively constructed. Its main focus was on redressing the imbalances in the relations of developing and developed countries and on promoting the accelerated development of developing countries on the basis of collective self-reliance. Accordingly, the principles set forth in the Declaration for conduct of international economic relations cover a number of key areas in which fundamental imbalances exist, including the following: *(a) effective control over natural resources, (b) regulation of the activities of transnational corporations, (c) just and equitable prices for primary commodity and other exports of developing countries, (d) reforms in the realm of money and development finance, (e) access to markets by products of developing countries, and (f) strengthening the science and technology capacities of developing countries.*[18]

Structural Adjustment, the Berg Report, and the Privatization of Social Welfare

In the early years of the post-independence period remarkable gains were made in economic development and improved social welfare. These gains of independence are often forgotten today.[19] However, by the end of the 1970s, the pressures of the contesting interests of capital to deal with crises in the global financial system, and the subsequent rise and eventual domination of neoliberal ideology and institutions began the long siege of "humane internationalism" and the ascendance of a model of development that was less about moving to a new order of cooperation for mutual benefit and more about the further subordination of Third World economies and societies to the needs of the financial sectors and corporations based in Europe, North America, and Japan. The crises of growth of the economies of Europe, the United States, and Japan translated to devastation for the peoples of the Third World.[20]

The international economic order that emerged in the 1980s and gained in legitimacy over the following three decades did not bring forward the aspirations of the 1974 UN Declaration. On the contrary, countries in the Global South experienced reversals of the gains of independence in the context of the worldwide recession of the 1970s. As Firoze Manji explains:

> Almost without exception, the same set of social and economic policies were implemented under pressure from the IFIs (international financial institutions) across the African continent—the so-called structural adjustment programmes (later rebranded as Poverty Reduction Strategy Programmes—PRSPs), all to ensure that African countries serviced the growing debt. But the agenda of the creditors was also to use the debt "crisis" to open avenues for capital expansion, through extreme privatization and liberalization of African economies.[21]

An influential World Bank document of 1981, known as the Berg Report, set the course of structural adjustment as a remedy for "underdevelopment" and therefore a framework for debt relief and international development assistance going forward:

> (The Berg Report's) assessment of the causes of the African crisis was highly "internalist," sharply critical of the policies of African governments for having undermined the process of development by destroying agricultural producers' incentives to increase output and exports. Overvalued national currencies, neglect of peasant agriculture, heavily protected manufacturing industries and excessive state intervention were singled out as the "bad" policies most responsible for the African crisis. Substantial currency devaluations, dismantling industrial protection, price incentives for agricultural production and exports, and substitution of private for public enterprise—not just in industry but also in the provision of social services—were singled out as the contrasting "good" policies that would rescue Sub-Saharan Africa from its woes.[22]

The World Bank and OECD donors operated within a consensus that acknowledged in theory the importance of developing country "ownership" for effective development strategies. However, in practice, the actual permissible policy space for those strategies continued to shrink and Third World governments imposed the macroeconomic orthodoxies of the international financial institutions on their countries, overruling not only the demands of social sectors resisting the required austerity, but even, in many cases, the elected officials and governance institutions that sought alternative paths to resolve the crises of public revenue generation and debt servicing.[23]

There is no lack of evidence of the devastating impact on developing countries of the measures imposed through structural adjustment, nor of the effects of the interference of aid donors and debt creditors in local governance, inhibiting the functioning of legislative bodies and the accountability of governments to citizens. The Structural Adjustment Participatory Review Initiative (SAPRI), an extensive five-year collaborative project carried out by citizen groups, developing country governments, and the World Bank, assessed the impact of the measures that constituted structural adjustment. The report on the SAPRI process, published by the members of the SAP-RIN civil society network in 2004, arrived at the conclusion that "if there is to be any hope for meaningful development for countries of the South, and for the sustained reduction of poverty and inequality, the Western-inspired and imposed doctrines of structural adjustment and neo-liberal economics must go."[24]

That conclusion has yet to win the day in official development aid policy. By the 1990s, the alignment of development aid thinking with neoliberal economic orthodoxy was so thorough that it had become "common sense," permeating many aspects of aid research and development programs, from high-level government negotiations to local initiatives of both governments and civil society. Canada endorsed this alignment and promoted liberalization by making its official aid to debt-burdened countries conditional on their adherence to an IMF-approved Poverty Reduction Strategy, which set the terms for development financing, including foreign aid, and the priorities for national budget expenditure. The IMF-sanctioned poverty reduction strategies often included conditions that prevented developing countries from using the very measures that industrialized countries had employed for their own industrialization, such as tariffs to protect agricultural producers and strengthen local markets. By tying aid to conformity with these IMF-imposed conditions, OECD donors reinforced measures that were detrimental to the development of Third World industries and agricultural production for domestic and regional markets. The donor/creditors were thus effectively "kicking away the ladder" they had used for the development of their own economies.[25]

Canadian ODA was also used to provide "technical assistance" to Third World governments to improve incentives for foreign investment, especially in the mining sector through the "reform" of mining codes. Under the guise of "technical assistance," Canadian aid was used to encourage alignment of Third World trade policy with the interests and objectives of industrialized countries in global negotiations within the Global

Agreement on Tariffs and Trade (GATT) and, later, the World Trade Organization (WTO).

There were many voices in Canada who shared the critique of structural adjustment coming from the Third World and expressed their own opposition to the policies of liberalization and austerity. Canadian NGOs and development researchers formulated critiques of the neoliberal approaches to development—often with financial support from CIDA—and engaged in dialogue and debate with government officials around improving development policies related to human rights, gender equality, the environment, humanitarian assistance, and reform of food aid, among other issues. CIDA also provided funding to environmental organizations and NGOs who were engaged in the growing critique of the impact on ecosystems of the growth-based model of development at the foundation of neoliberal policies.

However, the privatization of social welfare in developing countries due to structural adjustment, as well as rising public pressure to respond to deepening Third World inequality and poverty, contributed to building an aid industry in which NGOs played in integral role:

> The integration of INGOs (International NGOs) into the logic and institutions of the development industry intensified during the structural adjustment period of the 1980s, when funding for INGOs from official donors increased at the same time that governments of debt-burdened countries were instructed to strip the public sector and implement macroeconomic policies that resulted in increased inequality and loss of livelihoods and basic services for the impoverished. The official aid donors, when confronted with the critique of the adjustment policies and the resistance of affected sectors of society, provided funding to INGOs, the "human face of structural adjustment," to alleviate poverty and, ostensibly, to replace the services and functions of increasingly under-resourced and disempowered African states. During the structural adjustment period, known as the "lost decade of development for Africa" (as elsewhere in the global South), austerity might have been the rule for the public sector, but it was not the operating principle for the industry of development agencies and professionals taking advantage of the privatisation of social welfare.[26]

Over time most NGOs, though critiquing specific policies, still made the case to the Canadian public for development aid as the primary tool for poverty alleviation, in spite of the constraints of the larger political and economic context in which it was being delivered. Public support in Canada for development aid reached a high point during the 1980s when reports of suffering due to famine, most especially in Ethiopia in 1984, reached

Canadian homes through the television news. An unprecedented surge in charitable donations and NGO mobilization indicated that Canadians were indeed watching and concerned about the action that Canada would take in a global response to the humanitarian crisis.[27] The government of the time, under the leadership of Prime Minister Joe Clark, named former minister David MacDonald as Canadian Emergency Coordinator/African Famine to "assess the gravity of the crisis, propose concrete steps for government assistance, work with Canadian NGOs in mobilizing Canadian support, seek help from the provinces, and cooperate with other donors and agencies."[28]

The momentum to give greater importance to Canada's aid program, to collaborate with Canadian NGOs, and to give more priority to the needs of Africa resulted in the creation in 1986 of Partnership Africa Canada, an innovative funding model jointly governed by Canadian and African NGOs. Parliamentary interest in Canada's aid program also focused on renewal and reform following recommendations made in a milestone report of the House of Commons Standing Committee on External Affairs and International Trade (SCEAIT) tabled in 1987. Known as the Winegard Report (after the Committee's chair, William Winegard), the report argued that Canada's aid program was "beset by 'confusion of purpose' [and] needed a clear concentrated mandate and a streamlined, decentralized delivery system." On the policy side, the government's response to Winegard affirmed that "[t]he primary purpose of our development effort is to help the world's poorest countries and people." Another guiding principle was to "strengthen the links between Canadian citizens and institutions, and those in the Third World—in short, partnership."[29]

Over the following decade, Canada increased its investment in strengthening the links between Canadian citizens and those in the Third World through CIDA's support for Canadian NGOs to "partner" with Third World NGOs and social movements in a wide range of programs from health, education, and social service delivery; to training and technical cooperation; to research and advocacy for human rights and democratization. CIDA made provision for "responsive" funding mechanisms that fostered collaboration and longer-term relationships among NGOs, enhancing the learning of Canadians about the ways in which their lives and societies were connected. CIDA provided support to coalitions of NGOs to focus on specific countries or regions as well as collaborative interventions around specific areas of work, such as the Reconstruction and Rehabilitation Fund.[30] Funding for Canadian NGOs included efforts to educate Canadians about development issues and build a local constituency of support for development aid.

A large number of civil servants within CIDA, many of whom had spent time in the Third World as volunteers, championed the NGOs' partnership approach, recognizing the possibility of innovation of development programs "on the ground" that benefited from the flexibility that would not have been possible for large-scale projects carried out by governments or multilateral institutions. At the same time, the choice of countries of focus did not escape being determined by larger political, if not partisan, pressures, including concerns about catering to the interests of specific key commercial sectors (such as agriculture and mining) as well as specific communities of voters within Canada, such as, for example, Haiti, the Philippines, and Sri Lanka (at different historical moments).

Canadian development assistance has also been used to manage the ongoing political dynamics regarding the place of Quebec within the federal system and Quebec's own aspirations for a distinct approach to international relations. This distinctiveness has been expressed and promoted by Quebec governments (of all political parties) and by Quebec civil society organizations. Not surprisingly, the specific history of Quebec within Canada, its distinct political culture and *contrat social*, its special links with the **francophonie**, and its specific communities of immigrants from francophone countries, have shaped the unique ways in which Quebec-based organizations have engaged in Third World solidarity and international cooperation for development. It is not within the scope of this chapter to give adequate treatment to that history, nor to the nature of some of the qualities of international engagement that are specific to Quebec. However, it is important to recognize that the differences exist and that development aid has been used by both the Canadian and the Quebec governments to assert influence in the francophone world, and to demonstrate their legitimacy at home in representing the perspectives and priorities of Quebeckers abroad, from the launch of the first aid program for francophone Africa in the late 1950s until today.[31]

Development Aid—Special Project or Part of a Coherent Whole?

Canada's foreign policy encompasses more than narrowly defined commercial interests. It covers a full range of concerns including finance, defence, diplomacy, the environment, health, human rights, agriculture, culture, and education. In the various foreign policy reviews undertaken by Canadian governments since the launch of development aid, there have been many debates as to whether policy "coherence" among the various elements of foreign policy is beneficial or detrimental to the achievement of Third World development goals. Coherence as an objective does not necessarily imply any one ideological approach or framework. In other words, a government can have a coherent approach to promoting the interests of Canadian corporations and industrial agriculture through its diplomatic missions and representation at the UN and other global negotiations, just as it could have a coherent approach to promoting environmental protection, healthy food systems, and democratic economies through the same vehicles. Some advocates for development aid have argued against policy coherence where aid is concerned for fear that its mandate for poverty reduction will inevitably be trumped by more "strategic" interests of other, more powerful ministries. Others have argued that without policy coherence, development aid remains an ineffective "sideshow" to the policies of the ministries that really count in terms of consequences for the Third World—such as trade, finance, agriculture, immigration, and defence.

From the early years of the Cold War, aid policy has been inextricably linked, and subservient to, the defence policies and security interests of donor countries. Changes in Canada's military role in the world have had an impact on aid priorities and aid delivery. The places where people are living in times of war are characterized by aid agencies in a variety of ways—as "failed states," "conflict situations," "postconflict situations," "humanitarian crises"—in which aid is advanced as a means to save lives and, in some situations, attempt to address problems underlying the conflict. However, the appropriate use of development aid in situations of war remains deeply problematic.

The rapid growth in the development aid program to Afghanistan following Canada's entry into the war is a stark example of the ways in which development aid is easily instrumentalized by foreign policy objectives that are geopolitical in nature, at the expense of the integrity of the stated goals and priorities of international development aid efforts. Canadian scholars have argued that it is very difficult to have an accurate assessment of the actual impact of the aid program to Afghanistan, despite the fact that it was the largest bilateral aid program ever carried out by Canada.[32] However, there is ample evidence that "many Canadian development projects were components of ISAF's [NATO's International Security Assistance Force] counter-insurgency strategy, aiming to win the hearts and minds of ordinary Afghans."[33]

In light of the increasing tendencies of the Canadian government to divert the limited resources of ever-decreasing aid budgets to military and commercial objectives of questionable value to developing countries, advocates for development aid within Canadian civil society and Liberal and NDP Members of Parliament made a concerted effort to protect the mandate and purpose of aid through legislation. Working closely with NGO aid advocates, Liberal MP John McKay shepherded a private member's bill through parliament, establishing a legal framework for government accountability in aid spending. Bill C-293, also known as the *Official Development Assistance Accountability Act*, received Royal Assent in 2008:

> Its purpose is to ensure that all Canadian official development assistance (ODA) is focused on poverty reduction and is consistent with aid effectiveness principles and Canadian values. It applies to all federal departments and agencies that provide ODA.
>
> For activities to be reported to Parliament as ODA, the Minister must be of the opinion that they meet three criteria set out in section 4.1 of the Act:
>
> - contribute to poverty reduction;
> - take into account the perspectives of the poor; and
> - be consistent with international human rights standards.[34]

The act provides exemption from the three criteria for emergency or disaster assistance in ODA-eligible countries. It stipulates that consultations on ODA with governments, international organizations, and Canadian civil society organizations must take place at least once every two years. The act also requires the Minister of International Development to table a report to parliament each autumn on behalf of the government to provide a summary of the activities undertaken under the act.

Legislation alone cannot ensure the overall coherence in Canada's foreign policy that is required to make a significant contribution to the eradication of poverty and fulfillment of global human rights. However, proponents of the legislation hoped that it would set the terms and conditions for greater transparency and accountability to the Canadian public regarding aid spending, and would succeed in ensuring some protection of aid budgets from the increasing encroachment of other more powerful interests.

From New International Economic Order to New International Aid Order?

At the beginning of the twenty-first century, just before the unleashing of the "war against terror" in 2001, global advocates for development were advancing a renewed framework for international cooperation, the Millennium Development Goals (MDGs), based on the United Nations Millennium Declaration that called for reaffirmation of "our commitment to the purposes and principles of the Charter of the United Nations, which have proved timeless and universal." The member states made ambitious pledges to "spare no effort to free our fellow men, women and children from the abject and dehumanizing conditions of extreme poverty, to which more than a billion of them are currently subjected."[35] All member states and 23 international organizations pledged to meet eight goals by the year 2015:

- To halve the number of undernourished people
- To achieve universal primary education
- To promote gender equality and empower women
- To reduce child mortality
- To improve maternal health
- To combat HIV/AIDS, malaria, and other diseases
- To ensure environmental sustainability
- To develop a global partnership for development

In spite of the formalities of a global agreement, the Millennium Development Goals established more of a catalogue for a global aid marketplace than a concerted international strategy for transformation. The MDGs provided a framework and common discourse around which development aid programs could be rationalized, financed, and measured. Each goal was broken into specific targets of results, reinforcing a technical, reductionist approach to social change that failed to take into account the interdependency and the political nature of the problems being addressed. The neoliberal consensus that drove structural adjustment also underpinned the Millennium Development Goals, effectively reinforcing a "monoculture" of approaches to development within a paradigm established and financed by the OECD countries.

Consistent with that paradigm, the Development Assistance Committee (DAC) of the OECD launched a process of reform of aid delivery with the Paris Declaration on Aid Effectiveness in March 2005. The declaration set out the following five principles:

1. **Ownership**: Partner countries exercise effective leadership over their development policies and strategies, and coordinate development actions.
2. **Alignment**: Donors base their overall support on partner countries' national development strategies, institutions, and procedures.
3. **Harmonization**: Donors' actions are more harmonized, transparent, and collectively effective.
4. **Results**: Managing resources and improving decision-making for results.

5. **Mutual accountability**: Donors and partners are accountable for development results.[36]

CIDA embraced the principles of the Paris Declaration and engaged in the high-level forums to refine and monitor its implementation in Accra (2008) and Busan (2011). The Paris Declaration was criticized by international NGOs for omitting civil society organizations (CSOs) as "development actors in their own right." An international coalition of development NGOs, the Open Forum for CSO Development Effectiveness, mobilized to influence the outcomes of the high-level forums and to establish their own effectiveness principles eventually codified in the "Eight Istanbul Principles for CSO Development Effectiveness."[37]

Some international NGOs saw the aid effectiveness venue as a means to advocate for progress on specific issues or causes, using achievement of the MDGs as a reference to measure the effectiveness of aid in achieving social progress. Women's organizations, for instance, criticized the Paris Declaration for being "gender blind" and for being selective in its aims of "alignment and harmonization." They asserted that women's movements around the world have contributed to and rely on United Nations processes to advance their agendas at home, especially the Convention on the Elimination of All Forms of Discrimination against Women (CEDAW) and the Beijing Platform for Action (BPFA) of the 1995 Fourth World Conference for Women for Development and Peace and Equality. They pointed out that, unlike the Paris Declaration, these processes and agreements include an explicit analysis of women's status and of poverty. The Beijing Platform for Action declares:

> In order to eradicate poverty and achieve sustainable development, women and men must participate fully and equally in the formulation of macroeconomic and social policies and strategies for the eradication of poverty. The eradication of poverty cannot be accomplished through anti-poverty programmes alone but will require democratic participation and changes in economic structures in order to ensure access for all women to resources, opportunities and public services.[38]

The development aid paradigm of technical solutions for social needs and aspirations has an insidious effect of moving debate regarding social priorities and self-determination from the public realm into privatized programs and projects that must be marketed to aid donors. Due to political pressures within donor countries, most of the aid budget has to be disbursed quickly and efficiently and yield measurable, reportable results. The work that is likely to be funded must therefore meet those requirements and be assessed by the responsible bureaucrats as feasible and justifiable within a relatively short timeframe and a calculus that is inherently risk-averse and subject to pressures of partisan politics. Reliance on the aid regime to fund social change necessarily sets limited parameters for agendas for change and the means by which change can be pursued. Dependency on foreign aid shifts authority and accountability from the public institutions and leaders of developing countries to the donors and creditors who finance their programs and their regimes.

These constraints apply to social change dynamics domestically as well, as Canadian antipoverty and human rights groups will attest. However, the problem is exacerbated when it is part of a larger myth of the superior knowledge and capacity of the foreign "donor" and the belief that the donor's advice and preferences for intervention are to be followed even if the intervention has not been identified as a priority or desirable strategy by the people directly involved, the citizens of the recipient country. As the Colombian scholar Arturo Escobar has argued:

> Development fostered a way of conceiving of social life as a technical problem, as a matter of rational decision and management to be entrusted to that group of people—the development professionals—whose specialized knowledge allegedly qualified them for the task. Instead of seeing change as process rooted in the interpretations of each society's history and cultural tradition—as a number of intellectuals in various parts of the Third World had attempted to do in the 1920s and 1930s (Gandhi being the best known of them)—these professionals sought to devise mechanisms and procedures to make societies fit a preexisting model that embodied the structures and functions of modernity.[39]

We Make the Path by Walking: Ways Forward for the Future

Development aid has been the primary means by which industrialized countries have responded to the demands coming from their own citizens to meet the needs and aspirations of the impoverished in the Third World. The "poor" are defined by the aid relationship as being the beneficiaries of the expertise and generosity of those countries that have already "developed" themselves, rather than people struggling for emancipation from the very structures and systems that continue to make the accumulated wealth of the "donor" countries, and the dispossession of the poor, possible.

The dispossession that has been facilitated by neoliberal economic policies is well documented. In a study of 33 African countries, Boyce and Ndikumana reported that these countries had "lost a total of $814 billion (constant 2010 US$) from 1970 to 2010. This exceeds the amount of official development aid ($659 billion) and foreign direct investment ($306 billion) received by these countries. . . . While Sub-Saharan Africa is typically referred to as a heavily indebted, aid-dependent region, in reality the subcontinent appears to have transferred to the rest of the world more than it has received."[40]

Research by Global Financial Integrity recently estimated that illicit financial outflows cost African economies US$55.6 billion per year from 2002 to 2011 (the most recent decade for which comprehensive data was available), fueling crime, corruption, and tax evasion.[41] "The problem with illicit outflows from Africa is so severe that a May 2013 joint report from GFI and the African Development Bank found that, after adjusting all recorded flows of money to and from the continent (e.g., debt, investment, exports, imports, foreign aid, remittances, etc.) for illicit financial outflows, between 1980 and 2009, Africa was a net creditor to the rest of the world by up to US$1.4 trillion."[42] The July 2014 report, *Honest Accounts? The True Story of Africa's Billion Dollar Losses*, points out that this trend continues today:

> The reality is that Africa is being drained of resources by the rest of the world. It is losing far more each year than it is receiving. While $134 billion flows into the continent each year, predominantly in the form of loans, foreign investment and aid, $192 billion is taken out, mainly in profits made by foreign companies, tax dodging and the costs of adapting to climate change. The result is that Africa suffers a net loss of $58 billion a year. As such, the idea that we are aiding Africa is flawed; it is Africa that is aiding the rest of the world.[43]

Official development assistance has never exceeded the net flow of resources out of developing countries to the so-called donor countries, in spite of common perceptions that it is the "rich" countries that help the poor. Development aid flows depend on and reinforce an assumption that what is beneficial for the "donor" economies—economic growth—will benefit the world at large. Development aid budgets are promoted as a responsible redistribution to the poor of a small portion of the surplus of that growth. The conventional rationale for official development aid has been that it assists those who have been "marginalized" or "left behind" by social and technological progress in the West to "catch up," to have the "capacity" to join a "level playing field" of global capitalism and reap the rewards of "modern" life. It helps people to help themselves. However, public debates in donor countries about the appropriate amount that should be allocated to development aid often obscure the ways in which the economic model generating the surplus to be "shared" creates the very social and environmental problems that aid is supposed to "fix."

So, what happened to the agenda of a new world order? What happened to the understanding that no amount of aid will ever be as significant for the beneficial transformation of postcolonial economies as the reform of taxation, regulation of corporations, and equitable trade agreements? That the well-being of the majority of people living in "developing countries," as in other parts of the world, depends on democratic freedoms and global, binding, and effective agreements for disarmament and demilitarization, and the protection of biodiversity, land, forests, oceans, lakes, and rivers—not as commodities to be monetized, but as living systems on which all life depends.

Canadians will rightly point to decades of inspiring and effective initiatives to which Canada has contributed in the pursuit of the reduction of poverty, the relief of suffering, and the affirmation of human dignity. It is important to celebrate and learn from that history and to assess under what conditions such interventions may make a positive difference. At the same time, given the causes of impoverishment in the Third World today—resource grabbing, low-wage jobs and unemployment, volatility in commodities (and commodity dependency), impunity, corruption and state violence of postcolonial governments,[44] militarization and arms proliferation, and environmental collapse—the track record of development aid to address those problems does not provide grounds to have confidence in its relevance for the future. There is no reason to believe that more of the same, even in greater amounts, will bring anything other than more of the same. As the Canadian development expert Ian Smillie has said,

> [The] development problems of the poorest countries cannot be solved by aid alone, much less by NGO projects. Moreover by dealing exclusively in development as feel-good opportunities for Canadians who want to "adopt" a child or dig a well, some of Canada's most prominent CSOs miss the bigger picture and present a misleading image to Canadians. It is not only, or even mostly, about "showcasing best practices in international development." It is about fixing what's broken all around the showcase. It is not about building a more efficient underground railway with "exit strategies" and "sustainable results"; it is about ending slavery.[45]

We need an understanding of history that fully acknowledges that today the richest 1 per cent of the world's people own more than 48 per cent of global wealth.[46] Ours is a world of dramatic and deepening inequality, not only of income but also of access to democratic participation in the determination of social, economic, and political life. We need a new consensus on what is at stake for the future. What is at stake is not the sustainability of *development*, which under neoliberal corporate hegemony has come to be equated with the sustainability of economic *growth*—albeit "inclusive," "gender-sensitive," or "green." What is at stake is the irreparable devastation that the current international economic order is generating for humanity.

We could gain in understanding of the future of development aid by reviewing its potential in the light of its historical origins. The African-American writer Saidiaya Hartman offers helpful insight into such a review with her observations about the "afterlife" of slavery in America:

> Slavery had established a measure of man and a ranking of life and worth that has yet to be undone. If slavery persists as an issue in the political life of black America, it is not because of an antiquarian obsession with bygone days or the burden of a too-long memory, but because black lives are still imperiled and devalued by a racial calculus and a political arithmetic that were entrenched centuries ago. This is the afterlife of slavery—skewed life chances, limited access to health and education, premature death, incarceration, and impoverishment.[47]

The world that launched the institutions and programs of the aid industry was living in the afterlife of empire, the afterlife of fascism, the afterlife of nuclear war. That afterlife included the material foundations of economic relations of wealth extraction, as well as a "racial calculus and a political arithmetic" that entrenched important cultural, ideological, and psychosocial legacies. Development aid, even with its noble intentions, was launched and administered in a largely unacknowledged afterlife of colonialism that was also characterized by "skewed life chances, limited access to health and education, premature death, incarceration, and impoverishment." When the nature of this afterlife is not exposed to the light of day, when the nature of the injury done is not acknowledged, then the dominant logic of the past continues to determine the future, and development aid policies and programs remain a set of variations on a still destructive theme.

The social forces of humanitarianism that emerged following World War II made significant gains in building international solidarity for a common future. Over many decades in Canada, constituency-based groups (such as churches, trade unions, immigrants, women's organizations, scholars, professional associations, and students) built alliances of common cause that defined the goals of Third World development in terms of empowerment, democratization, and the promotion of human rights and civil liberties. They recognized the value of shared stewardship of the global commons and protection of the environment; resistance against racism, impunity, militarism, and repression; and affirmation of the dignity of labour, the emancipation of women, and freedom of expression. This solidarity has been anchored in the ethics and politics of justice and the need for repair of harm done. The case for such repair, for *reparations*, is made not as a mechanism for blame or demand for monetary compensation, but rather as a means to recognize the nature of the injury done in order to nurture the possibilities of a more healthy, life-sustaining future.

For the past 30 years Canadian foreign policy, and therefore Canadian aid policy, has been carried out under the triumphalism of neoliberalism, creating an increasingly hostile environment for such alliances for transformative change to thrive. Forces for social and political reform have been instructed to accommodate an implicit social contract that recognizes "stakeholders" in negotiations among three sectors of society: government, the "private sector" (corporations), and "civil society." It assumes that, working together, these actors will arrive at "win-win" arrangements for the common good. And yet, the age of the unfettered rule of corporations has turned out to be unprecedented in human history for the widening of economic inequality; the proliferation of ever-more horrific technologies of war, surveillance, and repression of dissent; the loss of knowledge through loss of language and historical memory; the loss of biodiversity and healthy ecosystems; and ultimately for changes in climate and weather that "change everything," as Naomi Klein has so forcefully argued.[48] Without radical and urgent changes in how we live as peoples who share the earth, the consequences for humanity will be catastrophic and irreversible.

What would the majority of Canadians who are young adults today say about the foreign policy their country should have in light of the afterlife of the past 60 years of the development era? What would they want their government to do on their behalf to ensure their chances for a healthy future? Would they view the countries of origin of their parents and grandparents as far-away objects of charity in need of "bail-outs"? Would they place the profitability of Canadian mining companies over Canada's responsibility for taking leadership in global action to combat climate change?

What impact will the rising resistance of Canada's Indigenous peoples— who are seeking justice, healing, and repair in the afterlife of their own colonization—have on how other Canadians view the struggles of Indigenous peoples around the world who are resisting "development" with its concomitant dispossession of resources, livelihoods, and freedoms? Rather than asking how to make development aid more effective, should we not be asking, "In the face of increasing environmental destruction, war, impoverishment, and hunger, what role should Canada play in the world today to nurture a life-sustaining and life-affirming future for humanity?"

Table 4.1   Timeline of selected global events and Canada's aid program

Year	Global Event	Prime Minister of Canada	Canada's Development Aid Program
1944	Bretton Woods Conference	Louis St. Laurent (1948–1957)	
1948	General Agreement on Tariffs and Trade (GATT)		
1949	Founding of United Nations		
1950	Colombo Plan		Canada joins Colombo Plan
1955	Bandung Conference		
1957	Ghana first African nation to declare independence	John Diefenbaker (1957–1963)	
1958			Commonwealth Caribbean Aid
1959			Economic and Technical Assistance Bureau (Dept. of Trade and Commerce)
1960	Indigenous people in Canada are allowed to vote		External Aid Office (Dept. of Foreign Affairs and International Trade; DFAIT)
1961	President Patrice Lumumba of the Congo assassinated		
1962	Cuban Missile Crisis Second Vatican Council begins		
1963	Vietnam War	Lester Pearson (1963–1968)	
1968		Pierre Elliott Trudeau (1968–1979)	Canadian International Development Agency (CIDA)
1969			Partners in Development (the Pearson Report)
1970			International Development Research Centre (IDRC)
1972	President Ferdinand Marcos declares martial law in the Philippines		
1973	President Salvador Allende of Chile assassinated Independence of Guinea Bissau from Portugal		

Table 4.1 (Continued)

Year	In the World	Prime Minister of Canada	Canada's Development Aid Program
1974	UNCTAD Declaration for Establishment of New International Economic Order (NIEO)		
1975			Strategy for International Development
1979		Joe Clark (1979–1980)	
1980	Lagos Plan of Action	Pierre Elliott Trudeau (1980–1984)	
1981	African Charter on Human and People's Rights Contra War in Nicaragua begins World Bank Berg Report		
1982	One million people march for global disarmament in NYC		
1984		John Turner (1984) Brian Mulroney (1984–1993)	
1986	UN Declaration on the Right to Development Our Common Future		Winegard Report Creation of Partnership Africa Canada (PAC)
1987	Report of World Commission on Environment and Development (Brundtland Report)		
1989	Fall of Berlin Wall		
1990	Arusha Charter		
1992	UN Conference on Sustainable Development (Rio)		The "Somalia Affair"
1993	World Conference on Human Rights (Vienna)	Kim Campbell (1993) Jean Chrétien (1993–2003)	
1994	Rwandan genocide End of apartheid regime in South Africa		

(continued)

Table 4.1   (Continued)

Year	In the World	Prime Minister of Canada	Canada's Development Aid Program
1995	World Trade Organization founded UN Fourth World Conference on Women First Conference of Parties of the UN Framework Convention on Climate Change (UNFCCC)		Canada in the World: Government Statement
1997	Kyoto Protocol of UNFCCC		Ottawa Land Mines Convention (international treaty to ban land mines)
2000	UN Millenium Declaration Millenium Development Goals		
2001	September 11 attacks in United States World Conference on Racism (Durban) World Social Forum in Porto Alegre, Brazil		Canada enters war in Afghanistan
2002			Canada ratifies Kyoto Protocol
2003		Paul Martin (2003–2006)	
2004	Bolivarian Alliance for the Peoples of Our America (ALBA)		
2005	Paris Declaration on Aid Effectiveness Make Poverty History campaign		
2006		Stephen Harper (2006–2015)	
2007	UN Declaration on the Rights of Indigenous Peoples		
2008			ODA Accountability Act receives Royal Assent

Table 4.1   (Continued)

Year	In the World	Prime Minister of Canada	Canada's Development Aid Program
2010	People's Agreement of Cochabamba on Climate Change and the Rights of Mother Earth African Mining Vision (Economic Commission for Africa)		
2011			Canada withdraws from Kyoto Protocol
2012	Rio+20 Conference		
2013			Canada withdraws from United Nations Convention to Combat Desertification CIDA and DFAIT amalgamated into DFADT

Discussion Questions

1) In the post–World War II era, some in Western countries framed overseas development assistance as part of a "white man's burden." What does this phrase refer to, and is it an accurate way of thinking about development aid?

2) What were some of the effects of structural adjustment policies on Third World countries and on the project of development in general?

3) According to Kane, "aid has been the primary means by which industrialized countries have responded to the demands coming from their own citizens to meet the needs and aspirations of the impoverished in the Third World. The 'poor' are defined by the aid relationship as being the beneficiaries of the expertise and generosity of those countries that have already 'developed' themselves, rather than people struggling for emancipation from the very structures and systems that continue to make the accumulated wealth of the 'donor' countries, and the dispossession of the poor, possible." Are there other ways of thinking about the relationship between "developed" and "underdeveloped" countries? Is there an obligation on the part of people in the "developed" world to participate in aid projects? If not aid, then what?

4) Is Canada a generous country? How would a panel of "ordinary" Canadians answer this?

Further Readings

Kane, Molly. "International NGOs and the Aid Industry: Constraints on International Solidarity." *Third World Quarterly* 34, no. 8 (September 20, 2013): 1505–15. http://dx.doi.org/10.1080/01436597.2013.841393.

Klein, Naomi. *This Changes Everything.* New York: Alfred A. Knopf, 2014.

Levitt, Kari Polanyi. *Silent Surrender*, rev. ed. Montreal: McGill-Queen's University Press, 2002.

Morrison, David. *Aid and Ebb Tide: A History of CIDA and Canadian Development Assistance.* Waterloo, ON: Wilfrid Laurier University Press/North South Institute, 1998.

Sogge, David. *Give and Take: What's Wrong with Foreign Aid?* London: Zed Books, 2002.

Stewart, Veronika. "CIDA and the Mining Sector: Extractive Industries as an Overseas Development Strategy." In *Struggling for Effectiveness: CIDA and Canadian Foreign Aid*, ed. Stephen Brown. Montreal: McGill-Queen's University Press, 2012.

Notes

1   See David Sogge, *Give and Take: What's Wrong with Foreign Aid?* (London: Zed Books, 2002).

2   For more on the impact of mining on development see Bonnie Campbell, *Mining in Africa: Regulation and Development* (London: Pluto Press, 2009); Elizabeth Blackwood and Veronika Stewart, "CIDA and the Mining Sector: Extractive Industries as an Overseas Development Strategy," in *Struggling for Effectiveness: CIDA and Canadian Foreign Aid*, ed. Stephen Brown (Montreal: McGill-Queen's University Press, 2012).

3   Geoffrey York, "In West Africa, a Canadian Mining Company Pioneers 'the New Humanitarianism,'" *Globe and Mail*, March 20, 2012, http://www.theglobeandmail.com/news/world/in-west-africa-a-canadian-mining-company-pioneers-the-new-humanitarianism/article535009/.

4   Laura Payton, "CIDA Not Getting into Mining, Julian Fantino Says," *CBC News*, November 28, 2012, http://www.cbc.ca/news/politics/cida-not-getting-into-mining-julian-fantino-says-1.1137076.

5   For more see *Struggling for Effectiveness: CIDA and Canadian Foreign Aid*, ed. Stephen Brown (Montreal: McGill-Queen's University Press, 2012).

6   Cranford Pratt, "Canadian Policy Toward the Third World: Basis for an Explanation," *Studies in Political Economy* 13 (1984): 27–56.

7   "Final Communiqué of the Asian-African Conference of Bandung (24 April 1955)," http://franke.uchicago.edu/Final_Communique_Bandung_1955.pdf.

8   See Kari Polanyi Levitt, *Silent Surrender*, rev. ed. (Montreal: McGill-Queen's University Press, 2002).

9   The exception to the exclusion of the United States being the Philippines, which was a formal colony of the United States from 1898 (when it purchased

the Philippines from Spain for $20 million) until 1946, when the United States recognized its independence, after a long struggle for freedom by Filipinos. The United States nevertheless retained privileges of economic exploitation and land ownership that continued for several decades and were protected by the US-supported dictatorship of Ferdinand Marcos.

10 Harry Truman, "Inauguration Speech," http://www.bartleby.com/124/pres53. html.

11 See Molly Kane, "International NGOs and the Aid Industry: Constraints on International Solidarity," *Third World Quarterly* 34, no. 8 (September 20, 2013): 1505–15.

12 See "The Black Man's Burden: A Response to Kipling," on the History Matters website: "In February 1899, British novelist and poet Rudyard Kipling wrote a poem entitled 'The White Man's Burden: The United States and The Philippine Islands.' In this poem, Kipling urged the US to take up the 'burden' of empire, as had Britain and other European nations. Theodore Roosevelt, soon to become vice-president and then president, described it as 'rather poor poetry, but good sense from the expansion point of view.' Among the dozens of replies to Kipling's poem was 'The Black Man's Burden,' written by African-American clergyman and editor H.T. Johnson and published in April 1899. A 'Black Man's Burden Association' was even organized with the goal of demonstrating that mistreatment of brown people in the Philippines was an extension of the mistreatment of black Americans at home." http://historymatters.gmu.edu/d/5476/.

13 David Morrison, *Aid and Ebb Tide: A History of CIDA and Canadian Development Assistance* (Waterloo, ON: Wilfrid Laurier University Press/North South Institute 1998), 12.

14 Morrison, *Aid and Ebb Tide*, 12.

15 Lester B. Pearson, *Partners in Development: Report of the Commission on International Development* (New York: Praeger, 1969), vii, cited in Morrison, *Aid and Ebb Tide*, 84.

16 Morrison, *Aid and Ebb Tide*, 85.

17 United Nations resolution adopted by the General Assembly, "Declaration on the Establishment of a New International Economic Order," May 1, 1974, http://www.un-documents.net/s6r3201.htm.

18 "Towards the New International Economic Order, Analytical Report on Developments in the Field of International Economic Cooperation since the Sixth Special Session of the General Assembly," article 15, 3; A/S-11/5, The Director-General for Development and International Economic Co-operation (New York: United Nations, 1982). https://searchworks.stanford.edu/view/1764753.

19 See Surendra Patel, ed., *The Historical Process*, vol. V of *Technological Transformation in the Third World* (UNU/WIDER, 1995).

20 See Susan George, *A Fate Worse Than Debt: The World Financial Crisis and the Poor* (New York: Grove Press, 1988); and Structural Adjustment Participatory Review International Network (SAPRIN), *Structural Adjustment: The SAPRI Report—Policy Roots of Economic Crisis, Poverty and Inequality* (London: Zed Books, 2004).

21 "African Awakening: The Courage to Invent the Future," in *African Awakening: The Emerging Revolution*, ed. Firoze Manji and Sokari Ekine (Oxford: Pambazuka Press, 2011), 4–5.

22 Giovanni Arrighi, "The African Crisis: World Systemic and Regional Aspects," *New Left Review* 15 (May/June 2002): 7.

23 For an illustrative example see Linus Attarah, "Playing Chicken: Ghana vs the IMF," *Corpwatch*, last modified June 14, 2005, http://www.corpwatch. org/article.php?id=12394. Also see Rita Abrahamsen, *Disciplining Democracy: Development Discourse and Good Governance in Africa* (London: Zed Books, 2000).

24 *Structural Adjustment: The SAPRI Report—Policy Roots of Economic Crisis, Poverty and Inequality* (London: Zed Books, 2004), i.

25 See Ha-Joon Chang, *Kicking Away the Ladder: Development Strategy in Historical Perspective* (London: Anthem Press, 2003).

26 Kane, "International NGOs and the Aid Industry," 1507.

27 For more on the African crisis and the government response see Morrison, *Aid and Ebb Tide*, 234–38.

28 Morrison, *Aid and Ebb Tide*, 235.

29 Gerald Schmitz, Marcus Pistor, Megan Furi, and Political and Social Affairs Division, "CIR 79–16E, Aid to Developing Countries," last modified May 2, 2003, http://publications.gc.ca/Collection-R/LoPBdP/CIR/7916-e.htm.

30 Some examples of these programs: Philippines Development Assistance Programme, Philippines Canada Human Resource Development Program, COCAMO (Mozambique), the Central America Monitoring Fund, and the Indonesia Canada Forum.

31 See the Association québécoise des organismes de coopération internationale (AQOCI), http://www.aqoci.qc.ca.

32 Stephen Baranyi and Anca Paducel, "Whither Development in Canada's Approach Toward Fragile States," in *Struggling for Effectiveness*, ed. Stephen Brown, 114–15.

33 Ibid., 114; also see Tom Blackwell, "Canada's $1.5B Afghanistan Aid Effort 'Divorced from Reality,' According to Damning, Previously Unreleased Documents," *National Post*, October 12, 2012, http://news.nationalpost. com/2012/10/12/canadas-1-5b-afghanistan-aid-effort-divorced-from-reality-according-to-damning-previously-unreleased-documents/.

34 "Official Development Assistance Accountability Act," http://www. international.gc.ca/development-developpement/partners-partenaires/bt-oa/ odaaa-lrmado.aspx?lang=eng.

35 "Resolution Adopted by General Assembly," http://www.un.org/millennium/ declaration/ares552e.htm.

36 "Paris Declaration and Accra Agenda for Action," http://www.oecd.org/docu ment/18/0,2340,en_2649_3236398_35401554_1_1_1_1,00.html.

37 "Istanbul Principles," http://www.ccic.ca/_files/en/what_we_do/2010_09_ istanbul_principles.pdf.

38 "Platform for Action," http://www.un.org/womenwatch/daw/beijing/platform/.

39 Arturo Escobar, *Encountering Development: The Making and Unmaking of the Third World* (Princeton, NJ: Princeton University Press, 1995), 52. Cited in Kane, "International NGOs and the Aid Industry," 1515.

40 James K. Boyce and Léonce Ndikumana, *Capital Flight from Sub-Saharan African Countries: Updated Estimates, 1970—2010* (Amherst: University of Massachusetts, 2012), 1.

41 Dev Kar and Brian LeBlanc, "Illicit Financial Flows from Developing Countries: 2002–2011," *Global Financial Integrity*, last modified December 11, 2013, http://www.gfintegrity.org/?s-Illicit+Financial+Flows+from+Developing+ Countries, 7–16.

42 Kar and LeBlanc, "Illicit Financial Flows from Developing Countries: 2002– 2011," *Global Financial Integrity*, last modified December 11, 2013, http://www. gfintegrity.org/press-release/.

43 *Honest Accounts? The True Story of Africa's Billion Dollar Losses*, Report by Health Poverty Action; Jubilee Debt Campaign; World Development Movement; African Forum and Network on Development (AFRODAD); Friends of the Earth Africa; Tax Justice Network; People's Health Movement Kenya, Zimbabwe and UK; War on Want; Community Working Group on Health Zimbabwe; Medact; Healthworkers4All Coalition; groundwork; Friends of the Earth South Africa; JA!Justica/Ambiental/Friends of the Earth Mozambique, July 2014, 5, http://www.healthpovertyaction.org/wp-content/uploads/ downloads/2014/08/Honest-Accounts-report-web-FINAL.pdf.

44 For more on despotism in Africa, see Firoze Manji, "Why Have There Been So Many Despotic Governments in Africa?" *Al Jazeera*, last modified July 29, 2014, http://www.aljazeera.com/indepth/opinion/2014/07/despotic-governments-africa-2014728125216648975.html.

45 Ian Smillie, "Tying Up the Cow," in *Struggling for Effectiveness*, ed. Stephen Brown, 283.

46 Jill Treanor, "Richest 1% of People Own Nearly Half of Global Wealth, Says Report," *Guardian*, October 14, 2014, http://www.theguardian.com/business/ 2014/oct/14/richest-1percent-half-global-wealth-credit-suisse-report.

47 Saidiaya Hartman, *Lose Your Mother: A Journey Along the Atlantic Slave Route* (New York: Farrar, Strauss and Giroux, 2007), 6.

48 Naomi Klein, *This Changes Everything* (New York: Alfred A. Knopf, 2014).

5
From Missionaries to NGOs

RUTH COMPTON BROUWER

Introduction

Decades before Canada formally existed, long before Canadian businesspeople and diplomatic representatives made their way to Third World countries, and more than a century before the Canadian International Development Agency (CIDA) began providing official development assistance and support for nongovernmental organizations (NGOs), Christian missionaries were presenting a "Canadian" face to what we now call the developing world. In 1848 when Scottish-Canadian John Geddie was sent as a missionary from Nova Scotia to the island of Aneityum in the New Hebrides (now the Republic of Vanuatu), the Presbyterian denomination that sponsored him became the first colonial church to establish its own foreign mission. Given the remoteness of Geddie's destination and the island's reputation as "the nadir of human spirituality,"[1] it might appear that his church had adopted the perverse goal of seeking souls for conversion that were as challenging as possible to reach. In reality, his destination reflected the fact that from the outset Canadian foreign missions, whether Protestant or Catholic, were associated with transnational missionary-sending enterprises. Initially, for Anglo-Protestant Canadians, these enterprises were headquartered in Britain. But from the late nineteenth century, as the missionary movement shifted into high gear and the mainstream Canadian Protestant churches began to be more significantly and systematically missions-focused, organizational ties with their denominational counterparts in the United States became increasingly important. And instead of small and thinly populated islands in the South Pacific, these Canadian churches turned their attention principally to Britain's South and Southeast Asian colonies and to densely populated countries in East Asia: China, Japan, and Korea. As for the Caribbean, Latin America, and Sub-Saharan Africa, these regions would not, even in the twentieth century, become as major a focus as Asia for their missionary activities.

By contrast, when secular NGOs like Canadian University Service Overseas (CUSO) began sending volunteers to the developing world in the 1960s—the first United Nations Development Decade—the Caribbean and, to a much greater extent, newly decolonized countries in Africa quickly became important destinations. The first two parts of this chapter provide a crucial "backstory" to the 1960s' NGO phenomenon by presenting an overview of the modern international missionary movement and Canada's place within it during the period one historian has called "Imperial High Noon, 1870–1945."[2] Necessarily brief and highly selective, the overview draws on the rich historical literature about the movement that has emerged from a generation's worth of scholarship informed by new ways of thinking about the movement's shifting character and composition and its foundational role in the West's understanding of the Global South. Focusing on the post–World War II era and highlighting the experience of the United Church of Canada (the country's largest Protestant denomination), the third part of this chapter charts transformations in the overseas outreach of the mainline churches in the 1960s, transformations that, in practice, made them faith-based NGOs. Part Three also deals with secular NGOs, and here I focus principally on CUSO, the first Canadian NGO to undertake development work from a secular stance and in a context of rapid decolonization. Secular NGOs such as CUSO had more in common with their faith-based counterparts than they initially chose to recognize. Both groups, meanwhile, sought to distance and differentiate themselves from what they viewed as the bad old days of missionary colonialism (though contemporaries and recent scholars have been alert for echoes of that earlier era). As Molly Kane elaborates in this book, in the twenty-first century NGOs continue to have a significant if sometimes contested role in Canada's aid and development work. But the mainstream missionaries who pioneered Canada's people-to-people contacts with the Global South and who once loomed large in the nation's consciousness have largely disappeared from the scene. Are missions, then, history? A brief epilogue shows otherwise by sketching conservative Canadian churches' involvement with a resurgent international missionary movement in the late twentieth and early twenty-first century, a movement now dominated by Pentecostals and other "evangelicals"[3] from the United States and, importantly, from the Global South itself.

Overseas Missions in an Imperial Age

Nova Scotia-born George Monro Grant, the principal of Queen's College (later University) from 1877 until his death in 1902, was a respected figure across Canada as a notably liberal churchman and a kind of public intellectual and moral conscience within and beyond his own denomination, the Presbyterian Church in Canada. A staunch nationalist with a broad vision of what Canada could become, Grant was also a firm imperialist. Deeply committed to the cause of foreign missions—he would serve for decades on his church's Foreign Missions Committee (FMC)—he believed that the British Empire had a providential role to play in the global spread of Christianity. Thus, writing in his church's official periodical in 1876, he endorsed the view of his missionary brother in Madras (Chennai) that the conversion of the Indian subcontinent was "the work given by God in a special sense to the whole British Empire."[4] The following year, Marjory MacMurchy, the recording secretary of the Presbyterian church's Toronto-based Woman's Foreign Missionary Society (WFMS), was even more specific about the link between Canada, missions, and empire. Writing in the same periodical as Grant about her church's newly opened mission in Indore, Central India (located in today's Madhya Pradesh state), MacMurchy said, "England has given the people of Indore an organized army, protection, wise administration of law, and education. . . . To Canada is left the distinguished honour of sending the gospel."[5]

For twenty-first-century Canadians who pride themselves on taking a "live and let live" attitude to the religious, cultural, and social practices of others, it is difficult to conceive of a time when Canadians, including those deemed liberal, thought it so important and so right to convert the non-Western world to Christianity that they gave their scarce dollars and occasionally their lives to the cause. Yet even when proselytization was still being prioritized, the missionary movement was never just about converting non-Christians. Nor, despite what Grant's and MacMurchy's statements may have seemed to imply, was it envisioned and practiced as exclusively a part of the British imperial project.

By the last part of the nineteenth century in both Europe and North America, participation in overseas missions had come to be regarded not only as a Christian obligation but also as a defining characteristic of healthy and vibrant churches. Apologists for missions spoke repeatedly about the positive reflex influence of missionary work upon the sending churches. For the mainline churches, participation also involved a kind of keeping up with the denominational Joneses in terms of contributions in finances and personnel and in the development overseas of institutional infrastructure, what one historian calls a "bricks and mortar" approach.[6] Operating in tandem with this pragmatic concern was the phenomenon known as the "romance of missions." A genre of literature developed that offered highly coloured accounts of men and women who had risked or lost their lives in the course of taking the Christian gospel to insalubrious corners of the "heathen" world. Risk-taking missionaries were their era's superheroes. Accounts of their exploits were carried in the secular press as well as in denominational publications and recounted to rural and urban audiences alike in Sunday school talks and sermons. The genre was well established from the mid-nineteenth century when England's David Livingstone became the most celebrated example of a missionary superhero, particularly with his death in "darkest Africa."[7]

While the most famous missionary heroes were men, women in Britain and North America developed and devoured narratives about self-sacrificing missionary wives and heroic female missionaries. At the home base, women were the most avid enthusiasts of missions. Moreover, by the end of the 1800s, and decades earlier in some cases, missionary wives and career women missionaries outnumbered men in mission fields.[8] Whether in their own communities as supporters of the cause or as workers in overseas fields, women were encouraged to participate so long as they remained in a subordinate relationship to their churches' male decision-making bodies and, in the case of home-base women, did not neglect their domestic responsibilities as the risibly incompetent Mrs. Jellyby so famously did in Charles Dickens's novel *Bleak House*. Given the vast number of women involved in the overseas missionary movement, the kinds of tasks they undertook as part of what they called "women's work for women," and the potential for such work to undermine Indigenous social norms and relationships, there has, not surprisingly, been considerable scholarly debate about women missionaries' role in "cultural imperialism."[9]

The increasing compulsion to missionize in the late nineteenth century coincided with the growth of ideas about white racial superiority. Such ideas were crucial to strengthening assumptions about the West's rights over, and duties to, the non-Western world in the course of the 1800s. It is worth noting that at the beginning of the century British missionizing groups in a few settings had briefly sanctioned the idea of having male missionaries marry converted Indigenous women of good families in order to have them share in and expedite the task of evangelization.[10] The experiment was abandoned, though, decades before the conceptual establishment of racial hierarchies based on what was called scientific racism—biological explanations for social differences and inequalities—took hold. Of course, if missionaries had subscribed fully to the most extreme claims of scientific racism they would not have believed in the possibility of making converts of the "lower" races much less of raising them to a "higher" level of civilization. Nevertheless, until the early twentieth century—and much longer in some cases—many of them did believe in hierarchies of racial development that in turn determined their missionary strategies for particular countries as well as their everyday dealings with the Other.

Even during the heyday of the overseas missionary movement, there were, of course, skeptics in both Britain and North America. This was not necessarily because the doubters questioned their era's assumptions about the inferiority of non-Western peoples. Indeed, some doubters thought them so inferior as to be a waste of Westerners' time and resources.[11] Other contemporary skeptics of foreign missionary activity saw such activity as no more than a hypocritical ruse for justifying and exalting imperial ambitions. Given the chronological overlap between the heyday of the missionary movement and the era of high imperialism, and mission advocates' numerous references to British imperial rule as "providential," it is unsurprising that skeptics of the two phenomena saw them as inescapably, and malignantly, intertwined. Likewise, the overlap helps to explain why, well into the late twentieth century, professional and popular historians alike tended to view secular imperialism and Christian missions as two sides of the same coin and to assume that the British Empire was an unproblematically missions-friendly zone.

The British Empire was certainly a stimulus to missions from the metropole and from "white" colonies such as Canada. Its political and military institutions created an enabling environment for the kind of cultural transformation that missionaries sought to achieve through proselytization in colonized lands such as India and Nigeria, with ancient and complex cultures of their own. Chinua Achebe's *Things Fall Apart*, set in colonial Nigeria, is a poignant rendering in fiction of the societal disruption created by missionaries in an early-stage contact zone.[12] At the same time, an abundance of recent research on missions and the missionized has done much to complicate long-held assumptions about an invariable symbiosis between Anglo-Saxon missions and the British Empire. Scholars have identified numerous sites and moments of colonial encounter in which British imperial officials were anxious to be free from the nuisance factor created by proselytizing and moralizing missionaries (who, not insignificantly, were frequently also of a lower social class). Missionaries were sometimes, for example, concerned about and at odds with particular imperial policies such as the production and sale of opium. Brian Stanley's *The Bible and the Flag* shows early-nineteenth-century spokesmen for missions tying themselves in rhetorical knots trying to explain that Britain's first opium war with China was both a sinful war of commerce *and* God's providential way of opening China to Christian missions. Late-nineteenth-century missionaries in India, where the opium was produced, were more likely to regard the trade as an outright evil, although even then they were inclined to be circumspect so as not to alienate local colonial and Indigenous officials. In the early twentieth century, imperial policy in northern Nigeria, which "seemed actively to favour Islam," was another perennial source of concern, Stanley notes. "Missionaries complained with some justification that the *pax Britannia* was doing more to advance the cause of Islam than the gospel of Christ."[13]

Some of the largest missions were built up in East Asia, where Britain and other Western nations typically had no formal imperial control, though they certainly practiced gunboat diplomacy to great effect to promote their commercial interests. Moreover, Scandinavian countries became heavily involved in missionary activity—they would later also be prominent in development work—without, for the most part, any parallel involvement in secular imperialism.[14] Most important of all, though, in terms of rethinking the links between missionary activity and specifically *British* imperialism, is the fact that even before World War I American missionaries significantly outnumbered their British counterparts. Even in India, the so-called jewel in the imperial crown, American missionaries were almost as numerous as British on the eve of the war.[15] Canadian-born historian of US foreign policy Andrew Preston calls the missionaries "the advance agents of *American* imperialism." Confident and enthusiastic, the liberal Protestants who would long dominate their ranks were committed to promoting progress through the implanting of American and Christian values. Preston labels their agenda "the imperialism of human rights" and observes that it combined "internationalism and nationalism, cosmopolitanism and parochialism, in highly combustible and unpredictable ways."[16] Rushing to assist with this agenda from 1888 and to give it youthful vigour was the Student Volunteer Movement for Foreign Missions (SVM), which would spread ecumenically from the United States to campuses in Canada and elsewhere, bearing as its watchword "the evangelization of the world in this generation."[17]

Missionaries and the missionized became involved in complex symbiotic relationships. Missionaries may have wanted to practice the most invasive form of cultural imperialism: viz., the changing of a people's religious faith and hence also their understanding of their place in the social order, the nature of family life, and much else. But depending on particular contexts, many mainstream Protestant missionary groups quickly concluded that rather than (or in addition to) conducting a frontal assault on "heathen" beliefs and practices, effective communication would require indirect strategies such as the offering of educational and medical services and other social services as a way of winning a hearing for their Christian message. Those among the missionized who wanted to adopt Western cultural offerings that met their own needs—the ability to read, for instance, in order to advance socially and economically—quickly became adept at using mission services selectively. The Bible might be a required text in mission schools, for instance, but that by no means meant that students, even when they won prizes in Bible study, thereby became Christianized. They and their families developed a level of agency in dealing selectively with mission institutions. The missionized could, at times, choose from among the messages, or adapt the tools that suited their purposes. This both frustrated their mission mentors and at the same time helped them understand—and, over time, respect—the depth of non-Western people's commitments to their own cultures.

Particularly in South Asia and East Asia (and also, though it generally did not involve Canadian denominations, the Middle East), the institutional infrastructure came to include not just elementary schools and simple dispensaries but high schools, colleges, universities, and medical facilities for training Indigenous practitioners as well as treating illnesses. Even between the two world wars, and despite much evidence to the contrary, these relatively expensive institutions were still frequently justified by mainstream missionaries to their home-base supporters as effective means for winning converts. Nevertheless, during this period there were influential voices within mainstream mission circles and among their more liberal lay supporters, particularly in the United States, calling for a wholesale rethinking of missions, a rethinking that would eschew the emphasis on making converts, or leave that task to Indigenous Christians, and instead concentrate on providing upgraded and more fully professional institutional and social-service supports in order to assist Third World people of all faiths to lead fuller, less impoverished lives. The interdenominational approach that had facilitated the establishment of many of the larger and more expensive institutions was to be continued and expanded, according to this vision, and accompanied by a new ecumenism that, mindful of new global threats from secularism, would involve a less confrontational and even a more cooperative approach to the world's other major religions. The suggested new approach was elaborated most fully, and controversially, in 1932 in *Re-Thinking Missions: A Laymen's Inquiry after One Hundred Years.* Meanwhile, the increasingly ecumenical approach had been carried forward from 1921 by the newly established International Missionary Council and its specialized subcommittees, publications, and conferences. Meanwhile, too, there was a waning of the gendered "separate-spheres" approach to mission work, particularly in contexts where such an approach was regarded as both culturally unnecessary and a barrier to upgrading missions' institutional professionalism.[18]

The modernizing and irenic approach to the missionary task struck many conservative missionaries and their home-base supporters as so wrongheaded and defeatist that it effectively ended the "papering over" of preexisting rifts between themselves and the liberals, with many conservatives now coming to be styled fundamentalist. The modernizers were essentially fraudulent, the conservatives charged, for they were selectively retaining an evangelical identity for pragmatic reasons (essentially home-base fundraising), while downplaying actual evangelization. Predictably, the rifts were earliest and most pronounced in the United States, and it was there that they would remain the strongest.[19] Eventually, the conservatives would triumph within the world of missions and the modernizers effectively withdraw, but in the interwar period the modernizers remained very much in the ascendant, their work anticipating many of the kinds of tasks that would be taken up in the post–World War II era by NGOs engaged in international development.

"Canada's Share in World Tasks": Mainstream Protestant Missions

How did Canada's churches fit into the narrative of the missionary movement outlined in the preceding pages? In proportion to their nation's population, Canadians were probably overrepresented in the international missionary movement.[20] Through their ongoing close associations with their British denominational kin as well as through the more important cooperative links they forged with their American denominational counterparts, the Canadian Protestant churches were exposed to a double dose of enthusiasm for missions. Furthermore, it was by no means unusual for Canadians seeking an appointment sooner rather than later, or in a particular mission field, actually to enlist in the ranks of a US or, less often, British sending agency. Indeed, some well-known "American" missionary heroes were Canadian-born. When in the early twentieth century Catholics from French- and English-speaking Canada became more heavily involved in the missionary movement through national as well as transnational mission-sponsoring societies, they added a significant new dimension to the roles that Canadians had begun playing in the nineteenth century as would-be proselytizers and agents of cultural change in the Third World.[21]

During the last three decades of the nineteenth century, five major Canadian Protestant denominations—Anglicans, Baptists, Congregationalists, Methodists, and Presbyterians—had established overseas missions. The Congregationalists, the smallest of these, established a mission in the Portuguese colony of Angola in southern Africa in cooperation with their US Congregationalist counterparts. For the most part, though, these denominations focused on sending workers to India and China, Japan and Korea. By 1920 when the Canadian Council of the Missionary Education Movement published an overview of their undertakings as *Canada's Share in World Tasks*, the largest of these denominations as well as the one with the largest number of missionaries and mission sites was the Presbyterian Church in Canada.[22] Established as a national church in 1875, as of 1920 it had 305 overseas personnel, including missionary wives and 106 "lady missionaries." They were concentrated in stations in north and south China, Formosa (Taiwan), Korea, and India, with a much smaller number in Trinidad and British Guiana

(Guyana). Some eight years earlier they had turned over their historic New Hebrides mission to their Australian counterparts.[23]

As seen, even before 1900 single women missionaries and missionary wives already outnumbered male workers on the foreign mission staffs of most mainstream Protestant mission societies. In the case of the mission established by Canadian Presbyterians in 1877 in Central India, a part of British India nominally ruled by native princes, the pattern of female predominance was even more pronounced: single women alone outnumbered men from the first year of the mission's existence.[24] A number of factors lay behind the preponderance of women in mainstream Protestant missions, but a crucial argument supporting it was the early claim that only women could evangelize other women. The claim was made with most validity in missions such as those of the Canadian Presbyterians in India, where high-caste Hindus and Muslims valued the practice of female seclusion in the zenana quarters of the home. Even in India, though, it was a somewhat specious argument, since the majority of the population simply could not afford the luxury of strict female segregation, whatever their beliefs. Nonetheless, the concept of the zenana served Canadian and other Western women well, since it provided a rationale for their undertaking activities that would otherwise have been regarded as unseemly for respectable Christian women. A Presbyterian student journalist who would later become managing editor of the Toronto *Globe* effectively made the case for them in 1888 following the designation of a trained nurse for the church's new mission field in North Henan (formerly spelled Honan), China:

> This appointment . . . illustrates the prominence that must be given to woman's work in the evangelization of the world. Here is a sphere less injurious to true womanhood than many into which women are clamouring for admission, more in harmony with her better nature and God's evident designs, in which her own long pent-up energies and powers may find full scope to her own advantage and the immeasurable blessing of humanity.[25]

Here one is reminded of the point made decades ago by Edward Said—amplified in this volume in Rutherford's essay—that Orientalist concepts served the West even when they were at odds with the dominant reality in Asian societies.[26] Nor was it only the women who actually went overseas who benefited from this particular Orientalist assumption. Behind the hundreds of missionary wives, whose primary role was to model an ideal image of Western monogamous family life, and the single full-time women missionaries were the thousands of women at the home base who joined women's missionary societies. Beginning, in the case of the Canadian

Presbyterians, with the formation of the WFMS in Toronto in 1876, hundreds of local societies were formed to raise money and study the work of their overseas women missionaries. Women's missionary societies of this and other denominations became, collectively, by far the largest women's organizations in nineteenth- and early twentieth-century Canada. They were led at national and regional levels by prominent middle-class women, often linked by marital relationships to their male counterparts on the FMC. Local societies across the country provided a respectable outlet for women to meet and socialize. Their members would have been especially likely to take to heart admonitions like those issued by the editor of the *Presbyterian Record* in 1877 that church members should study and discuss mission news "until the names of our missionaries and the stations they occupy become as familiar as household words."[27]

The message sent from those in charge of denominational home-base sending organizations to their early missionaries of both sexes was clear and consistent: they were to have as their priority the making of Christian converts. Nevertheless, as shown earlier, there were realities on the ground as well as interrelated concerns among the sending agencies that served early on to undermine missionaries' ability or desire to make an absolute priority of direct evangelization of the sort traditionally associated (at least in mission stereotypes) with the work of ordained male missionaries. In the case of Canadian Presbyterians, male and female home-base officials readily accepted the claims of their India missionaries that institutional work and social services were necessary indirect strategies and that, moreover, they should be run by personnel who were well trained professionally in order to attract a following and overcome the resistance of local British and "native" officials. Both sets of officials had initially been hostile to the Canadian missionaries' presence. That early period, later recalled as an era of "freezing coldness," was overcome in part by the visit of a new viceroy, Lord Dufferin, formerly Canada's governor general, but more lastingly by the "missionary . . . diplomacy" of female schooling and especially medical work by and for women under doctors with full professional training.[28]

It was widely assumed among North American Christians that the peoples of Asia, as the possessors of ancient and complex religious and cultural traditions, required mission strategies and personnel more sophisticated than those considered adequate for Christianizing Africans and North America's First Nations. This is why mainstream missionary societies emphasized what they considered to be the professional credentials of their foreign missionaries. Accordingly, female applicants without strong credentials—or over age, or in less than robust health—were told almost routinely after the early years by the Presbyterian church's foreign missions establishment that, while they could not receive an overseas appointment, they could have their applications passed along to those FMC members responsible for hiring workers for the Canadian Northwest (astonishingly, First Nations' work remained under the umbrella of *foreign* missions until 1912). The message to an enquirer in 1902, for instance, was that residential-school teachers there would require "only the ordinary public school certificate." This bias in assessing applications from women may have been strongest among Presbyterians, but it certainly extended to other mainstream denominations[29] and no doubt to the assessment of male as well as female applicants for the churches' missionary work.

By the time that *Canada's Share in World Tasks* was published, the Canadian Presbyterian mission in Central India had established an arts college affiliated with the University of Allahabad as well as a theological seminary, day schools and high schools, dispensaries, and six hospitals. Its high school for girls, established in 1909, was said to have been the first such institution for girls in all of Central India. It had begun not with an academic orientation, but rather as a scheme devised by a senior ordained missionary embroiled in mission politics: he had urged the WFMS to finance a boarding school exclusively for Christian girls. The WFMS's 1886 *Annual Report* indicates that, at the time, it was prepared to go along with his suggestion and fund the type of approach that proved to be such a tragic strategy in Canadian residential schools: "By separating these [Christian girls] from home associations, and bringing them up more in harmony with our civilized and Christian ideas, in one generation, as much will be accomplished as could otherwise be done in three or four."[30] That a different, academic, direction was ultimately taken for the school reflected not just opposing pressures in mission politics and the role of women missionaries themselves in establishing a more academic kind of institution but also the developing local market for a school that would meet the wishes of non-Christian parents for a Western-style education for their daughters provided without insistence on accepting the foreigners' religion.

The institutional emphasis in the India mission, particularly among women missionaries, was stronger than in the church's missions in China and elsewhere, but at the same time not unusual. Indeed, there were plenty of precedents for and parallels to such an approach. American missionaries in particular were noted for their social gospel or "civilizing" approach, and women missionaries generally were "perforce civilizing agents more than evangelists."[31] Certainly, ordained male missionaries did more in the way of direct evangelization, but even for them, and especially perhaps for the ablest, the pressures of institutional work created demands that could not easily be set aside.

While their institutions won the missionaries friends in high places (local imperial officials and maharajas) and gave them, at least potentially, a captive audience for the gospel, they could not deliver conversions. The mission in fact produced strikingly few converts. Writing about its work for *Canada's Share in World Tasks*, the Rev. A. A. Scott chose not to provide numbers or focus on what had been accomplished by way of "establishing a definite Christian Church" and instead argued for the mission's achievement in "Christianizing the whole atmosphere of the district."[32] Indeed, such "converts" as the mission achieved over the years had resulted mainly from the rescue of orphans of both sexes during local famines in 1897 and 1900, who were subsequently raised in residential mission institutions. Later, there were also conversions among largely un-Hinduized tribal peoples and other depressed classes. Here again, the pattern of drawing converts primarily from among a society's most marginalized and vulnerable people may have been particularly pronounced in this and other denominations' missions in India, but similar patterns can be seen in other missions in this period, including the large Canadian Presbyterian and Methodist missions in China.[33]

When Congregationalists, Methodists, and a majority of Presbyterians came together in 1925 to create the United Church of Canada, they brought with them almost all of their overseas missionaries, all but 17 out of 655 in total, and all major mission fields. The United Church operated three missions in China, and one in each of Japan and Korea. Together these five missions employed more than two-thirds of the church's overseas personnel.[34] When *Rethinking Missions* was published in 1932, some of these missionaries were comfortable with at least some of its recommendations and in fact had contributed their own insights and experience to the research studies on which it drew.[35] A few may have quietly agreed with its overall philosophy. And yet when the United Church published *A New Church Faces a New World* in 1937 under the authorship of the Rev. Jesse H. Arnup, Secretary of the Board of Foreign Missions, there was no reference whatever to the controversial American publication. Overall, Arnup's book sounded a decidedly traditional note about the purpose of overseas missions and the peoples served by his church. The latter were categorized by race and colour and described in nonpejorative but exceedingly condescending terms. Behind all the arguments in favour of creating the United Church of Canada, Arnup wrote, "the ultimate object was always set down as the evangelization of the world."[36]

What is one to make of these differences and, at the same time, of the fact that, notwithstanding the sharp cutbacks in resources brought on by the Great Depression and the theological controversies opened up by the public and controversial rethinking of missions, Canada's mainstream missionary

enterprise maintained much of its essential character, or at least its traditional image, until the post–World War II era? In contrast to the open and
divisive theological splits that were occurring within US Protestantism,
diverse strands were largely contained *within* the United Church of Canada.
Different perspectives and discourses about what missions should be therefore continued to coexist, reflecting such variables as age and experience.
Arnup's perspective was not that of a missionary working on the ground
and living through the turbulence created by the era's powerful nationalisms
and a no-longer-subservient Other, but rather that of a long-serving missions bureaucrat anxious to maintain his constituency's belief in the ongoing
value of missions. His enigmatic pronouncements could sound decidedly
old-fashioned, as if he were pining for the traditional evangelism that had
been missions' foundational goal, or, at other times, as if he were in harmony
with the new mood.[37]

Many of his church's missionaries, though, would undoubtedly have agreed
with a former British missionary who told a Cambridge University audience
in 1934 that the central challenge of missionary work had passed "from enun-
ciation of doctrine to the compelling power of the Christian life." What was
required most now of the modern missionary was "a life lived and not a message delivered."[38] One of those modern missionaries was Queen's University
graduate Donald Faris, who would later play an indirect role in the founding
of CUSO. Faris had gone as an ordained missionary to China in 1925 from an
Ontario farm background with the expectation that he would do the kind of
work expected of a missionary clergyman. But his interest shifted to what was
quite literally grassroots rural development. The kinds of upgrading courses he
took and the contacts he made on his interwar furloughs reflected the growth
of his interest in experimenting with crops that could help peasants in and
beyond the turbulent north China mission to escape from impoverishment.
Faris returned to Canada in 1942 in an exchange of wartime detainees.[39] Even
if unknowingly, he was experiencing the end of an era. Imperial high noon
was over. So also was missionary high noon.

From Missions to NGOs

From the Victorian era onward, China had been, along with India, the largest
mission field for Britain, the United States, and Canada. With the triumph
of the Chinese Revolution under communist Mao Zedong's leadership in
1949, access to China was effectively closed off for decades, though it would
take a few years for that to become perfectly clear. Elsewhere, however, as old
empires crumbled and as former colonies won their independence, Western
humanitarians, including Canadians, became involved in new ways of living

and working in the Global South, most strikingly through the NGO phe-nomenon in both its faith-based and secular forms.

Within the United Church, the missionaries who had experienced the upheaval in China seem to have been the readiest to recognize that it could no longer be business as usual for mission work anywhere in the Third World. Donald Faris, who had served on UN rehabilitation and relief projects in China in the late 1940s, made a final, unsuccessful, attempt to return to that country to do rural development work as a United Church missionary in 1950. This was followed by an attempt, also futile, to persuade his church to support him in grassroots agricultural work in India in an unconfining rela-tionship with its notably conservative mission there. Pondering these closed doors, Faris observed in a letter to his son in 1951 that the kind of work he wanted to do and for which his experience had prepared him was "some-thing that the church has no machinery or thinking prepared to use. It forces me to a conclusion that . . . my best contribution to the world now, perhaps is outside the church organization. . . . The exodus from China and growing sentiment in all countries of the world . . . make the older concept of mission a complete impossibility." In the same year, another former United Church China missionary, Katharine Hockin (she was also a "mish kid"), reflected in a similar vein on the past—and the future—of her church's mission work: "Why have we failed so badly. . . ? Where do we go from here. . . ? Does it not mean that the whole missionary venture needs re-vamping and a con-secrated self-examination?"[40]

The kind of revamping that Hockin perhaps had in mind in 1951 and in which she would play a significant role did not begin for another dec-ade, despite the fact that in 1948 the United Church had been a founding member of the World Council of Churches (WCC), whose growing repu-tation for liberal positions would increasingly worry conservative Christian groups. But when changes to the United Church's approach to mission did come, they were far-reaching, for they were spurred on by a larger pattern of social upheaval affecting the entire "Liberal Protestant Establishment" in 1960s' Canada, especially as "what had been a creeping process of seculariza-tion became an avalanche." The changes began with the restructuring of the United Church's missions bureaucracy and with new terminology. In 1962, the Board of Overseas Missions became the Board of World Mission (BWM). The new adjective and the dropping of the *s* signified that the Board's sense of responsibility was global, like the WCC's, rather than confined to its his-toric mission "fields." The Board's rebranding was accompanied by another (and controversial) modernizing step: the official end of gender separation in the church's overseas mission responsibilities as the work of the Woman's Missionary Society (WMS) was folded into the BWM.

Meanwhile, in the same year that the BWM came into existence, the church's Twelfth General Council commissioned "an independent and fundamental study of how The United Church of Canada can best share in the World Mission of the Church." By the time that the resulting *Report of the Commission on World Mission* was issued in November 1966, many of its recommendations were already being adopted or put into practice by the BWM. These included a call for a broader, more flexible, more ecumenical approach to the church's "task in mission": "technical assistance," for instance, and refugee and emergency aid; repentance for "all arrogance, whether racial, cultural, or ecclesiastical" in past mission practice; and "dialogue with people of other faiths." As well as partnerships with autonomous Third World churches, there was to be cooperation with governments and international aid organizations in a mission field now understood to be of global dimensions. Overall, as A. C. Forrest, editor of the church's official periodical pointed out, the recommendations signalled a "serious and radical departure from what many people still considered missions." When the most conservative member of the commission, its chairman, Donald Fleming, a former minister in John Diefenbaker's government, tried to argue that the *Report* did not represent a departure from the church's traditional evangelical emphasis or "my name would not have been attached to it," Forrest was quick to challenge his claim. With the publication of the *Report* and then, in 1972, with another bureaucratic change, the folding of the Board of World Mission into the new Division of World Outreach (DWO), the United Church was signalling the nature of the changes that were already taking place in the philosophy and practice of its overseas work and its future directions. Not only was the very word "mission" absent from the new organization's name; under the heading "Responsibilities," the DWO constitution contained nothing that could be construed as evangelizing. And long-familiar tasks such as teaching and medical work were no longer justified or described in those terms.

Whether undertaken overseas or within Canada, many of the specific changes sought during this decade by the United Church's core group of mission reformers were interrelated. They were also fraught with challenges and internal contradictions. This was strikingly the case with its attempts to work out new relationships with the Indigenous churches that had come into being as a result of the missionary activities of its predecessor denominations. The new language was that of "partnership." But in reality some of the Indigenous churches still needed considerable financial support or were much more theologically conservative than their Canadian partner. Or, they were unsuitable partners for the kind of humanitarian work that the Canadian church now wanted to support. Here the biggest challenge came from the church that had grown out of the mission established by Canadian

Presbyterians in India almost a century earlier. It was not the only, but perhaps a particularly egregious, example of an Indian Christian community demoralized by its history of poverty, marginalization, and dependency, and internally divided by the legacy and the spoils of mission colonialism. In such circumstances, though it still sent some missionaries, the United Church was especially anxious to contribute to work in India through ecumenical channels, including those initiated and orchestrated by the WCC, and to development tasks for which it was receiving funds from the federal government, beginning on a regular basis with the establishment in 1968 of CIDA.

In the course of the decade, the BWM became involved in an array of aid and development projects in cooperation with secular and ecumenical partners, a water-drilling project in India with CIDA funding, for instance, and family planning work with the Christian Medical Association of India (CMAI). Its project work in the developing world was accompanied at home by a range of critiques of colonialism and racism. Portugal's ongoing control of Angola, Ian Smith's white-minority regime in Rhodesia (Zimbabwe), and South Africa's apartheid policies became particular targets. In Angola, where in 1925 the new United Church had become heir to the mission work begun in the 1880s by Canadian Congregationalists, some of the most prominent missionaries became increasingly critical of Portuguese policy. They believed that by staying on there they appeared to condone the colonial regime and its brutal treatment of freedom fighters, or, if they were known for their criticisms of the regime, put African associates at risk. The most vocal critic, medical missionary Sidney Gilchrist, opted to relocate to a base in the Congo where he could be part of "a team to train front-line workers for a healthier Africa." Meanwhile, though it had no history of missionary activity in either Rhodesia or South Africa, the church became vocal on freedom struggles in both regions and increasingly in the late 1960s and early 1970s made Canadian government policies, or inactions, the target of its criticisms. Political stances were also expressed in financial aid to like-minded organizations, as with a small donation in 1969 to the Canadian Committee for Zimbabwe. More controversially, in 1971 the BWM decided to fund a WCC initiative that channelled aid to antiracist groups in southern Africa, notwithstanding the acknowledged reality that some of the aid might wind up supporting guerrilla organizations.

Inevitably, the Board's critiques of colonialism and neocolonialism also turned inward. Engagement in critical self-reflection about past and contemporary mission practices included inviting speakers and publicizing books designed to further the self-critical process. One speaker, an ordained Canadian then working with the Student Christian Movement (SCM) in Bangalore, India, told the Board that far from regretting the passing of "the

days when the missionary and the Church had a much more central position and a place of privilege," mission constituencies should welcome the
opportunity to be "on the frontier of God's mission today" and "in a unique
position to become the Church of the Poor." Certainly the BWM should
continue some of its "traditional ways of service to countries going through
rapid social change," by providing "doctors, nurses, educationalists, etc." But
more was required: "As we increasingly take our stance as the Church of the
Poor we will begin to ask such questions as 'Are we standing in solidarity
with the poor unless we send medical supplies to the Viet Cong, unless we
provide nurses, doctors and teachers for those who are seeking to overthrow
the racist regimes in Rhodesia and South Africa?'" Far from thinking that
their young guest speaker had gone too far, the executive committee of the
Board discussed the possibility of distributing his three addresses across the
denomination and to media beyond its own.

Not surprisingly, during the tumultuous 1960s the BWM also did much
soul-searching about the matter of recruiting and appointing missionaries.
After a recruitment crisis early in the decade there was a brief upsurge in
applicants under the stimulus of a popular recruitment secretary with missionary experience in China and India. There were still many young people
who wanted to live lives of Christian service overseas, he believed, but who
were unable to "describe their inner convictions in words . . . traditionally
accepted by the Church." A document produced by a BWM study committee on recruitment made pertinent observations about dilemmas facing the Board and raised questions about future directions. It was agreed
that the policy of recruiting "only in response to requests from overseas
organizations" had to be maintained. And yet how was the Board to deal
with such challenges as the fact that while increased food production was
clearly essential in the developing world, not a single agriculturalist had been
requested in the preceding year? And how should the Board respond to
ongoing requests for teachers of academic subjects when it knew that in
India and some other countries there were numerous unemployed young
people with arts or other degrees? Given frequent requests from applicants
for short-term appointments and the Board's increasing inability to offer
longer-term appointments, was there even a future for career missionaries?
Moreover, weren't there now plenty of other opportunities for Canadian
Christians to serve in the developing world? This question seemed so pertinent that it was formulated in several different ways:

> Has the time come when we should encourage the young to join CUSO,
> the middle-aged to join External Aid [predecessor to CIDA], and the
> older to join Canadian Executive Service Overseas? Should the Board of

World Mission be finding more outlets for its staff in service with secular agencies such as local national governments? . . . With the increasing number of government and private agencies becoming involved in development programs overseas, does the Board of World Mission have a distinct role to play or should it encourage Christians to become involved in these secular organizations?

To the extent that the Board answered its own questions, it continued both to send out its own short-term missionaries on request and to encourage and support women and men with an interest in serving overseas under secular agencies such as CUSO. As an editorial in the *United Church Observer* put it in 1968, "The idea is you don't have to wear a church label, let alone a denominational label, to witness effectively to your faith in the neediest parts of the world." Earlier that year the *Observer* had reported only one ordained minister among the new group of missionary appointees. Two years later, of 27 newly appointed missionaries, most were under 30 years of age, some were not from United Church backgrounds, and not one was a clerical appointment.

In a parallel development, in 1968, for the first time in its history the church chose a layman, Dr. Bob McClure, as its moderator, its most senior official. McClure's exuberant showmanship on behalf of the church's development work following a high-profile career in China and India (in the latter country he had been regarded by some within the CMAI as the father of its family planning program) made him excellent copy in the mainstream media as well as the church press. Like the leading proponents of mission modernizing within the BWM, McClure had a personal faith that was important to him, but it was his quotable challenges to traditional Christian theology and his medical activism in the developing world ("he would rather preach family planning than salvation," wrote his biographer) that made him such an appropriate ambassador for the new face of mission in the United Church of the 1960s.

The selection of McClure as moderator might have been expected to be an effective complement to the work that the BWM had done during the decade to tutor the church into a new understanding of mission. Yet as the church entered a new decade Board spokesmen experienced a sense of frustration that their message was not being heard. In 1971 Board chairman Dr. C.W.M. Service, a practicing surgeon and a former China medical missionary, gave an address on "The Changing Face of Mission." In his address, Service declared that the "man in the pew" was "still generally living with a Nineteenth Century concept of mission." Even the clergy seemed unaware of "what this Board is doing and what it stands for in the 70s.

The communication gap is *colossal*." To illustrate his message, Service presented a "Then" and "Now" list: a list of the ways that missionaries, and understandings of mission, had changed in the course of a century.

His exasperation was palpable. Despite a decade of effort it appeared that neither the United Church's "man in the pew" nor many of its clergy was attuned to the changing face of mission. It should thus come as no surprise that neither those organizing CUSO in 1961 nor many of the young adults who became its volunteers were able to see beyond outdated stereotypes. CUSO was determined to create something fresh and new, an organization for overseas service free of mission associations and the odious taint of colonialism. That, at least, was the vision. In reality, there would be significant links as well as tensions between the new secular NGOs and their faith-based counterparts in the mainline Protestant and Catholic churches, and not only for pragmatic reasons.

In Canada, as elsewhere in the Western world, the 1960s was a decisive decade for the expansion, transplanting, and creation of development-focused NGOs. In this decade, for instance, the Mennonite Central Committee and the Canadian Catholic Organization for Development and Peace, both faith-based, and the secular Oxfam Canada became important Canadian NGOs with roots or ties in other countries. Organizations to send young volunteers from industrialized to developing countries multiplied internationally, and here, perhaps especially, the zeitgeist fostered and required a secular orientation. The Peace Corps, a state agency established by executive order in March 1961 by President Kennedy and designed to flood the developing world with well-educated young Americans, was explicitly secular. Beyond the idealism and the early confidence about Western volunteers' ability to contribute to modernizing the Third World, there was a sense of urgency arising from the Cold War context. CUSO, then, was part of a larger Western pattern.[41]

CUSO was officially established during the June 1961 meeting of the National Conference of Canadian Universities and Colleges. Student-initiated organizations with rudimentary plans for sponsoring overseas volunteers already existed at several Canadian universities. The first and most solid of these organizations, Canadian Overseas Volunteers (COV), was based at the University of Toronto. Before merging with CUSO at the end of 1962, COV sent two cohorts of volunteers to Asia. COV's founder, Keith Spicer, a doctoral student researching Canada's role in the Colombo Plan, had been motivated by reading Donald Faris's 1958 book, *To Plow with Hope*. Inspired by a brief passage in which Faris had called on educated young Westerners to get involved in development, Spicer and a handful of supporters approached service clubs, businesses, and churches for funding.

They also turned to the churches for help with such matters as orientation for would-be volunteers.

Unlike Spicer and COV, CUSO's organizers initially wanted to keep the churches and the missions establishment entirely out of their planning. No representatives of missionary societies were invited either to CUSO's founding meeting or to an earlier consultative meeting in March 1961. However, mission groups associated with the ecumenical Canadian Council of Churches (CCC) did receive information about the March meeting from a young man who represented the national SCM on the CCC and who had attended it as an SCM representative. Donald Wilson told the groups that there had been "a general air of not wishing to accept anything from the churches, apart from money," and a "rather obvious feeling on the part of some members present that the whole movement must be kept clear of any religious implications." Several months later, following a recruitment tour of Western Canadian universities for CUSO, on whose first executive he served, Wilson reported a climate of distaste for anything associated with the churches' missionary work. University students, he wrote, would consider it to be "a compromise of their integrity" to "go overseas under church auspices." Though most volunteers going out under CUSO had come from Christian homes, many of them were "deliberately choosing a secular channel rather than the church." Nor was the negative attitude to missions confined to students. "By and large," Wilson wrote, "the university community has a complete emotional and intellectual bloc [sic] to the word 'missionary,' as they understand it."

The antipathy toward anything that resembled missionary activity was both clear and widespread. But because of their long history, missionaries could not be so easily sidelined. As this book suggests, various Canadians had political and economic ties with the developing world in this era. However, the churches' mission establishments had a unique and extensive knowledge of life in the developing world as a result of their involvement in Third World peoples' daily lives through educational and health work and religious outreach and a long-term presence in numerous communities. Given this reality, CUSO soon found itself turning to the churches for guidance as well as financial assistance. In the autumn of 1962, CUSO's first full-time executive director, formerly with COV, asked the CCC's Department of Overseas Missions for assistance with such matters as orientation for newly selected volunteers. During the next few years, Protestant and Catholic church personnel were also involved with CUSO's recruitment and selection activities and overseas placements. A young Presbyterian missionary, for instance, coordinated CUSO's first years of work in Nigeria, while a Catholic priest with decades of experience as a missionary educator in southern Africa remained a prominent figure in CUSO's recruitment, selection, and orientation programs well into the 1970s. In Asia, Africa, and Latin America there would be numerous placements for volunteers in educational and medical institutions founded by Protestant and Catholic missionaries from all parts of the Western world.

In 1965 CUSO began receiving financial assistance from the federal government. By the end of the decade it was obtaining by far the largest part of its revenue from CIDA's NGO division. By the mid-1960s CUSO also had a sizable pool of returned volunteers (RVs) to whom it could turn for expertise following their two years abroad. RVs served on recruitment and selection committees; some became CUSO administrators in Ottawa or field staff abroad. Although in these circumstances the organization outgrew many of its early links with the mainline churches, it continued to seek even small sums from them and from service organizations and businesses as a way of avoiding total dependence on CIDA.

Furthermore, other links with the mainline churches emerged by the late 1960s—links based not on dependency but rather on strategic considerations and a desire to influence government policy and public opinion. As the United Church and CUSO itself became more politicized, they increasingly interpreted the problems of the developing world as outcomes of colonialism, neocolonialism, and racism rather than as temporary difficulties that could be resolved with large doses of Western-style modernization. They were thus prepared to cooperate or join forces to identify and publicize shortcomings in the Canadian government's development and foreign policies. *The Black Paper: An Alternative Policy for Canada Towards Southern Africa*, published in 1970, was a striking example. BWM secretary Garth Legge and University of Toronto political science professor Cranford Pratt were the lead authors on the pamphlet, but two CUSO RVs were also named. All four had experience working in eastern or southern Africa. *The Black Paper* provided a carefully documented critical analysis of the Trudeau government's proposed policies on southern Africa as set out in its recently released white paper on foreign policy before proposing alternative policies. Canada, it urged, should take a more critical, activist, clearly antiracist approach to the region, including nonmilitary aid to liberation movements (as Sweden and some NGOs were already said to be doing), and it should cease trading with South Africa. In the 1970s there would be more such ad hoc coalitions, involving other secular NGOs and other Protestant, and Catholic, church groups. Especially as a result of reforms stemming from the Catholic Church's Second Vatican Council, 1962–65, and, later in the decade, the growth of "liberation theology" (explained in this book by Sean Mills) in and beyond Latin America, groups such as the Canadian Catholic Organization for Development and

Peace had become desirable coalition partners. Not surprisingly, some coalition initiatives, such as multifaceted support for refugees who had fled from Rhodesia to Zambia, would engender sharp criticism. Even if only indirectly, critics charged, such projects made use of Canadian government funds to assist "terrorists" or "Communist-front" groups.

Meanwhile, as the 1970s began it was clear that when it came to placing personnel overseas, strength in numbers lay with the secular CUSO rather than with the United Church of Canada, the largest of the mainline Protestant mission-sending agencies. CUSO entered the 1970s with more than 1,300 volunteers serving in more than 40 countries. For its part, the United Church had just 232 overseas personnel, serving in 24 countries. Many of CUSO's volunteers had come out of church-going families, often United Church families. But by the time they attended university and went on to volunteer, as products of the new zeitgeist they were commonly opting out of the religious observances and moral codes of their parents' generation. Thus, the very notion of mission, even in NGOized form, did not capture their enthusiasm or speak to their idealism in the way that the new organization did.

Yet if the understandings held by both these sending agencies about the rights and needs of people in the developing world were broadly similar, wherein lay the differences once they were actually on the ground? Primarily, perhaps, in the nature of the organizational and personal relationships their respective personnel established. In principle, both organizations were committed to respecting local priorities by sending workers only on request. Early CUSO volunteers in India, recognizing practical problems with that principle (many institutions had no idea that qualified young Canadians were available to fill staffing needs), sometimes sought out suitable new placements for the next cohort or advised against replacing themselves when their two-year assignment was up. But generally volunteers were placed in response to requests, especially as Africa became more of a focus, and particularly in Nigeria, by far CUSO's biggest placement country. Although they had assignments in agriculture and medical work and much else, volunteers were most commonly deployed as teachers. Requests for teachers led to placements in a variety of different types of schools, often, as noted, mission-founded schools. But even these did not typically involve volunteers being dragooned into religious activities, since CUSO field staff quickly learned to avoid placements in schools, whether Protestant or Catholic, that insisted on volunteers' active religious engagement. For the United Church, requests for personnel often came, as seen, from or through partner churches, whose religious observances they could presumably not bypass even if those observances were more conservative theologically or more exuberant than those they were familiar with in Canada. Moreover, in the 1960s Canadians had choices about the vehicles through which they could render service in the developing world, as the United Church's "Reflections on Recruiting Personnel" readily acknowledged. Canadians who chose to go out as missionaries were thus making a statement about their own personal faith as well as linking themselves to faith groups as their primary overseas communities. CUSO volunteers, meanwhile, whether in teaching or other assignments, were eager to establish social and personal lives of their own choosing both within and beyond their workplaces. The West's sexual and gender revolutions and the beginnings of more capacious thinking about "race" became part of what they brought in their cultural baggage, especially from the mid-1960s, with the result that cross-race friendships and, in some places, casual sexual relationships and marriages became common. Among 1960s' United Church missionaries who went to their assignments unmarried, there were certainly those who came back from the developing world with partners. But it seems unlikely that even "modern" mainstream missionaries were able to experience the developing world with the same degree of openness to personal and intimate relations or with the same zest and opportunities for exploring new cultural horizons as their young secular counterparts. As RVs, the latter signalled their sense of what they had gained from their (usually) two-year sojourn in the developing world by reversing the early CUSO slogan, "To serve and learn," and emphasizing that they had learned far more than they had served.

Personal growth was all very well, but did NGOs make any tangible, practical difference in the developing world? *Can NGOs Make a Difference?* was the title of a collection of articles published in 2009 by NGO insiders. Arising from an international conference in Manchester, England, the book was one of many publications in the early twenty-first century to reflect the soul-searching of engaged scholars and NGO activists as they acknowledged both increasing constraints on their ability to make a positive difference and their awareness of concerns that big, Western-conceived development schemes have often done more harm than good.[42] It was perhaps small comfort that development critics, mindful of NGOs' typically small-scale and grassroots approach, have generally left them out of their condemnations or found specific initiatives to commend. Molly Kane's chapter in this collection takes up this question of what Canadian NGOs contributed to the developing world. In *Canada's Global Villagers* I briefly discussed what CUSO volunteers themselves thought they accomplished during the first quarter-century of their organization's existence and noted their lack of complacency.[43] Like the United Church in the 1960s, CUSO was already engaging in critical self-reflection by the 1970s. Self-reflection did not, obviously, lead to a cessation of its overseas work, though pragmatists wanted it to become more businesslike and developmental ("Development is our business" replaced "To serve and learn" as a slogan), while some politicized RVs urged scaling back or even ending volunteer placements. Politicization did lead, though, to more efforts at home in the realm of development education and, as noted, more criticisms of federal government foreign and aid policies.

Did pressure tactics of the sort employed by CUSO and other NGOs make any practical difference? Writing in the late twentieth century, Cranford Pratt, a veteran scholar of Canada's aid and development policies, concluded that pragmatic considerations rather than what he called "humane internationalism" were the most typical drivers of such policies. His colleague David Morrison, focusing specifically on CIDA, was somewhat more inclined to perceive instances in which pressure on the political process from humanitarian groups did have some impact. CUSO RVs who reflected back from a twenty-first-century perspective tended to believe that it was back in Canada that they had been able to contribute most to the developing world: through national and local global consciousness-raising and support for aid and solidarity work, through careers in other NGOs such as Oxfam, and as insiders in government agencies such as CIDA and the International Development Research Centre (IDRC).

If we return the focus to the mainline churches, it seems clear that from the early post-Confederation period, the mainline Protestant denominations had good reason to believe that their overseas concerns as well as their domestic agendas were taken seriously by governments. As noted earlier, a viceroy of India who had formerly served as governor general of Canada had acted informally during a visit to Central India to help lessen early opposition to the Canadian Presbyterian mission there. Although Canada had no foreign policy independent of Britain until after World War I, it could seek to bring attention to its missions' concerns through personal and informal channels. Later, as the Protestant church that was not only Canada's largest but the one that most confidently saw itself as a *national* church—"a church with the soul of a nation"—the United Church expected that it should and could have the ear of politicians. Indeed, in 1952 Secretary of State for External Affairs Lester B. Pearson "urged the United Church to take a greater interest in Canada's foreign policy." He assured the church that its attentiveness to international issues was helping "to ensure that Christian principles and endeavour are directed to the task of promoting a just and peaceful world order."[44] As prime minister in the 1960s, Pearson may have been less happy with the church's readiness to provide not just advice but criticisms of his government's foreign and aid policies. But he remained mindful of the Western churches' historic role, through their mission work, in tasks analogous to those being taken up in the 1960s under the rubric of development. Since he was the son of a minister and the colleague and friend of men and women with backgrounds and ongoing associations with the world of mainstream missions, it could hardly have been otherwise. After his retirement as prime minister, Pearson chaired a commission on development for the UN and subsequently wrote its report, *Partners in Development.* The report dealt only briefly with private and voluntary aid, but in that section he referred to the significance of the work being done by volunteers from developing countries and the historic role played by missions in pioneering educational work, especially in Africa.[45] Meanwhile, Pearson's successor as Canadian prime minister, Pierre Trudeau, was quicker to react with impatience when faith-based and secular NGOs turned from "good works" abroad to vigorous pressure tactics at home, as was the case when they took up the cause of breakaway Biafra in Nigeria's civil war and urged his government to come to Biafra's aid.

Both in terms of the kinds of work-related and personal relationships they established in the Global South in the "Development Decades" and in regard to the kinds of developing-world causes for which they became advocates, Canada's faith-based and secular NGOs saw themselves as having made a decisive break with the attitudes and assumptions of the imperialist past, including its missionary past. Recall the "Then" and "Now" paradigm invoked by the BWM's Dr. Service in 1971 to call his church's attention to the changes in understandings about mission, and the determination of CUSO's founders a decade earlier to keep their new organization secular. Significantly, though, when the SCM's Donald Wilson reported on the March 1961 meeting that led to the founding of CUSO, he was struck by the irony of the fact that while the CUSO founders wanted to keep the new organization free of "religious implications," there was at the same time "a general flavour of the spirit which I imagine pervaded early SVM days when the world was to be helped, and renewed by the youthful vigor of a North American generation."[46] Likewise, when in 2008 the editors of *Can NGOs Make a Difference?* looked back on the 1960s, they regarded at least some of the transnational initiatives of that time as having emerged "from the legacy of colonialism," and here they included "volunteer programmes sending experts to 'under-capacitated' countries or [to] organizations that derived from missionary interventions."[47] And Kevin O'Sullivan, writing in 2014 about NGOs' responses in Britain and Ireland to the Biafran humanitarian crisis, observed that the NGOs' responses were "in practice rooted in a very Western understanding of humanitarian responsibilities and a very Western image of the Third World." He concurred, too, in the suggestion that their vision of a suffering "'common humanity' was more appealing to the West when it was expressed with a local accent and a 'white face.'"[48]

There can be no gainsaying these continuities, or perhaps their inevitability, whether one is focusing just on Canadian NGOs or on the phenomenon generally. "Now" could not easily transcend "Then," particularly at a time when Canada, like Britain and Ireland, and by extension their NGOs, had not yet been transformed by the changed immigration policies that would progressively alter the country's "white face." In the 1970s a variety of Canadian NGOs would sponsor national tours by African liberation movement leaders still fighting white regimes, as well as visits by other Third World leaders. In these and many other contexts, Indigenous leadership was on display. Also undeniable was the fact that Canadian agencies were taking steps, sometimes comparatively bold if naïve steps, to help African nationalists defeat the most obdurate instances of formal colonialism.[49] It was a long way from George Monro Grant's belief in a "providential" British Empire.

Conclusion: From Missions to Development . . . to Twenty-First-Century Evangelical Missions

In 1887, several years after being rebaptized and experiencing faith healing, the Rev. Albert Benjamin Simpson, a Maritime-born Presbyterian like Grant, founded the Christian and Missionary Alliance (C&MA) in New York. He did so as a means of pursuing mission and healing activities in his adopted country and in order to foster a greater urgency and a more direct focus on the overseas task of saving souls. The latter became his passion. The C&MA eventually became a distinct evangelical Protestant denomination, first in the United States and, in 1981, in Canada. In 2014 its national website in Canada reported almost 130,000 people attending more than 430 churches, and over 250 missionaries working among "least-reached peoples in more than forty countries."[50] Although the website does not say so, its best-known member is Canada's twenty-second prime minister, Stephen Harper. Simpson's 1880s initiative is a reminder that even during imperial high noon and the heyday of mainstream Protestant missions there had been individuals and organizations with an urgent, direct, and exclusive focus on making conversions and a consequent disinclination to engage in institution-building for seeking those converts through social outreach. One of the most distinctive of such organizations, the China Inland Mission, which Canadians enthusiastically joined, became particularly noteworthy for its missionaries' adoption of native dress.[51] The early twentieth century saw the emergence of Pentecostal missionaries as well as the growth—and increasing combativeness—of self-styled fundamentalists and other evangelical Protestant groups.

Nevertheless, it was only in the second half of the twentieth century as the mainline churches increasingly abandoned even the language of evangelism at home and abroad that conservative Christians who prioritized making converts in their overseas work found their way into groups like the C&MA and Pentecostalism and became the leading edge of what was effectively the reinvention of the missionary movement. A historian of modern evangelical Protestantism identifies the 1980s as the decade when it first became "a prominent new force in Canada."[52] By the early 1960s, though, Protestants who were still strongly missions-minded were already showing their preference for an approach that gave primacy to evangelization. A 1962 survey conducted by the ecumenical CCC revealed that by far the largest number of Canadian Protestant missionaries was serving with conservative Canadian mission boards (i.e., boards not affiliated with the CCC or the WCC) or with congenial US mission boards. In 1966, a breakaway group in the United Church formed the United Church Renewal Fellowship. Its members were, among other things, "zealous supporters of foreign missions," and for them the church's emphasis on social issues was "a diversion from its main business of converting individuals."[53]

A significant number of twenty-first-century Canadian evangelical denominations are involved in mission activity in the Global South. They partake in work with existing Christian communities and in missionizing that involves outreach to so-called unreached peoples, including those living in countries where missionary activity is illegal. Even taken together, though, these evangelical denominations certainly do not make Canada one of the world's top missionary-sending countries. Evangelicals make up a much smaller proportion of the Canadian population than is the case in the United States, which in 2010 was very much the largest sending country, with 127,000 missionaries. Almost half of the world's top missionary-sending countries are now in the Global South, with Brazil, South Korea, and India reportedly in the lead.[54] The sending of missionaries from these and many other non-Western countries is a reflection of the fact that by the early twenty-first century some 60 per cent of "professing Christians" lived in "the global South and East," with Africa the most Christianized of continents.[55] The latter statistic is not a reflection of the long-term success of the pioneer mainline missionaries in Africa, whom some scholars have come to regard as no more than "'detonators' of new and indigenous forms of Christianity." Nor do such scholars attribute the Christianization of Africa to recent missionary successes but rather to the fact that at an early date Indigenous Christians themselves became proselytizers.[56]

As well as having a very small place in the global growth of present-day evangelical missions, Canadian proponents of the movement generally operate below the radar within Canada. In contrast, for instance, to the days when the SVM had high visibility on campuses across the country, urging young men and women to consider a missionary vocation, today's university students are unlikely to be aware of mission activism unless they are themselves associated with evangelical churches. And yet such churches and their overseas work are not without significance for our government's relationship with the Global South and for foreign policy more generally.[57] Lobbying may not be as evident as it was in the heyday of the United Church and other mainline churches, which took pride in demonstrating their access to national leaders. But Ottawa watchers do not take this as evidence that such lobbying does not exist, as was seen, for instance, in 2014 in critical observations about the absence of provision for abortion aid in the Harper government's high-profile global maternal and childcare policy.[58] Moreover, present-day Canadian evangelical churches no longer eschew action on social issues in their missionary work. Rather, they have become a new kind of faith-based NGO: making converts may well remain the priority in their work, but it does not preclude social outreach activities for which they seek federal foreign-aid funding.[59] Even Pentecostal Christianity, noted for its ongoing adherence to such beliefs as faith healing and "the eternal doom of the unregenerate in the lake of fire," has by now become sufficiently engaged in the practice of development to warrant the holding of an international conference on the subject.[60]

Canada's secular character makes it a country much less attuned to the goals and activities of twenty-first-century evangelical missions than was the case for their nineteenth-century predecessors, who were very much a part of the fabric of the larger society. Canada in the 1960s was likewise a congenial place and time for the founding of such secular NGOs as CUSO and the transplanting of others such as Oxfam. On the face of it, the current faith-based outreach enterprises of Canada's evangelical churches seem to represent a distinct break with earlier stages in our country's historic person-to-person relationships with the non-Western world. Continuity does exist, however, in the ongoing transnational character of today's faith-based outreach enterprises: they continue to be characterized by links with other sending agencies as well as with non-Western societies. Meanwhile, as both Kane's and Mills's contributions to this volume show, numerous secular NGO actors, many of them relatively recent, are still going to the Global South, on justice and solidarity and humanitarian aid work, as voluntourists, and so on. Whether faith-based or secular, these transnational NGOs go to parts of the world where religion matters in ways that it no longer matters in Canada. Understanding that reality will continue to play a crucial role in their ability to make safe and sensitive interventions.[61]

Box 5.1

Donald K. Faris (1898–1974) was involved from the late 1940s in UN-sponsored aid and development work. Near the end of his 1958 book *To Plow with Hope*, he called on educated youth to take up service in "the world's neediest villages" and thereby supplement the work of "balding experts" like himself. His appeal struck a chord with the idealism of many 1960s' CUSO volunteers.

From *To Plow with Hope*[62]

Our youth possess a tremendous potential of energy, idealism and enthusiasm, just waiting to be tapped. The one reagent needed is the challenge that life's fullest expression is found in serving others. To this end, visualize placing not just a few thousand balding experts in the field to cope with the advancing enemy but a hundred thousand young people to supplement the older and more seasoned men and women—teams of junior experts who would, after an intensive period of orientation, be prepared to go into any country where they were invited. They would be available for loan to governments or private agencies to work with indigenous leaders in the world's neediest villages. . . .

If we were aware of all that is involved we would willingly pay this price for solid friendship. In war we send our best youth by the millions to kill or be killed: in two world wars approximately a million volunteers went from sparsely settled Canada alone, not asking for comfort or safety. They accepted it for an ideal—survival of their way of life. Today our own survival is again at stake. Now comes a call for an army of volunteers to wage another world war, this time against poverty, ignorance and disease—enemies that destroyed not 22 million in six years, as in World War II, but 180 million in the same period. The last war wiped out $4 trillion in capital; another could end in a "take all." By contrast, the cost of every intelligent, constructive effort on our part is infinitesimal.

The officers functioning in the elite programs are still indispensable, but slogging foot soldiers are also needed to help in the waging of this constructive war which could well outmode destructive conflicts. If, in addition to technical skills, these junior experts were equipped with humility and courage, with sincerity and wisdom, they would be able to transmit not only physical satisfactions to the needy but also lasting values such as friendship, goodwill and understanding.

Even now the forces of regeneration are emerging in the less developed areas: in Thailand we see Buddhist monks with robes off helping villagers build roads, bridges, schools; in India, Hindus working in vast village programs; in Pakistan, Moslems active in numerous field projects; and, working by their side, representatives of the Christian community—all in their own way obeying the imperative of love. In this brotherhood of man all barriers are down; no lines are drawn. Old nations are being born anew, vitality once again is stirring in men and women, hope is returning to eyes long grown dull.

Will this hope attain fulfillment if we stand idly by, our compassion grown stale, while all of these, our neighbors, struggle unaided? In confronting their destitution our own religious insight becomes adult. Across space, divergent traditions, with or without gratitude, and sometimes, so it seems, against our own self-interest, the imperative still operates. It demands of us that we put all our weight alongside these peoples straining, as they are, to break through the triple barriers of disease, poverty and ignorance to find a wider basis for dignity and self-realization.

Discussion Questions

1) Historians are fascinated by the ironies of unintended consequences. How are such ironies illustrated in long-term outcomes from missionary and development work?

2) Many African nationalists were educated in mission schools. And even in post-independence India, girls from non-Christian, middle-class families often continued to be sent to schools founded by missionaries. What is the significance of these educational patterns in considering themes of "cultural imperialism" and "Indigenous agency"?

3) Mainstream Canadian missionary committees believed that their best-educated and most able missionaries should be sent to Asia rather than assigned to First Nations work in Canada. Consider the possible significance of these decisions for later tragic outcomes in Canada's residential school system.

4) To Third World men and women on the receiving end of interventions by Canadian aid workers in the 1960s and 1970s it was perhaps neither easy nor important to determine whether they were sent by a faith-based or a secular NGO. Discuss.

5)   Whether inspired by religious motives or secular humanitarianism, Canadian missionary and aid workers from the nineteenth to the early twenty-first century have been part of larger people-to-people movements from the West to the Global South. Given the transnational character of these movements, what scope has there been for Canadians to stand out as distinctive global actors?

Further Readings

Achebe, Chinua. *Things Fall Apart*. Oxford: Heinemann, 1958.

Austin, Alvyn, and Jamie S. Scott, eds. *Canadian Missionaries, Indigenous People: Representing Religion at Home and Abroad*. Toronto: University of Toronto Press, 2005.

Brouwer, Ruth Compton. *Canada's Global Villagers: CUSO in Development, 1961–86*. Vancouver: UBC Press, 2013.

Brouwer, Ruth Compton. *Modern Women Modernizing Men: The Changing Missions of Three Professional Women in Asia and Africa, 1902–69*. Vancouver: UBC Press, 2002.

Cox, Jeffrey. *The British Missionary Enterprise since 1700*. New York: Routledge, 2008.

Eade, Deborah, and Ernst Ligteringen, eds. *Debating Development: NGOs and the Future*. Oxford: Oxfam GB in Association with Oxfam International, 2001. http://dx.doi.org/10.3362/9780855986858.

Freedman, Jim, ed. *Transforming Development: Foreign Aid for a Changing World*. Toronto: University of Toronto Press, 2000.

Hutchison, William R. *Errand to the World: American Protestant Thought and Foreign Missions*. Chicago: University of Chicago Press, 1987.

Notes

1   Jesse H. Arnup, *A New Church Faces a New World* (Toronto: United Church of Canada, 1937), 37–47; Barbara Lawson, "Collecting Cultures: Canadian Missionaries, Pacific Islanders, and Museums," in *Canadian Missionaries, Indigenous People: Representing Religion at Home and Abroad*, ed. Alvyn Austin and Jamie S. Scott (Toronto: University of Toronto Press, 2005), 235–61.

2   Jeffrey Cox, *The British Missionary Enterprise since 1700* (New York: Routledge, 2008). Although Cox pushes the start of the modern mission movement back to the beginning of the eighteenth century, it has been more common to refer to the period 1792–1914 as "the Great Century" and to associate the movement's beginnings with the evangelical revival of the late eighteenth century.

3   John G. Stackhouse Jr., *Canadian Evangelicalism in the Twentieth Century: An Introduction to Its Character* (Toronto: University of Toronto Press, 1993), 7. It is important to note that the core beliefs of today's evangelicals were also core beliefs in mainstream Christianity and the larger Canadian culture in the nineteenth century. Drawing on a heritage from the Protestant Reformation, evangelicals emphasize "the unique authority of Scripture and salvation through faith alone in Christ."

4   On Grant see *Dictionary of Canadian Biography*, vol. 13 (Toronto: University of Toronto Press, 1994). For the quotation see Ruth Compton Brouwer, *New Women*

for God: Canadian Presbyterian Women and India Missions, 1876–1914 (Toronto: University of Toronto Press, 1990), 80.

5 As quoted in Brouwer, *New Women for God*, 80.

6 Cox, *British Missionary Enterprise*, Chapter 10.

7 Ibid., Chapter 7.

8 For women at the home base see Patricia R. Hill, *The World Their Household: The American Woman's Foreign Mission Movement and Cultural Transformation, 1870–1920* (Ann Arbor: University of Michigan Press, 1985); for women missionaries' increasing numbers, see William R. Hutchison, *Errand to the World: American Protestant Thought and Foreign Missions* (Chicago: University of Chicago Press, 1987), 101; and Cox, *British Missionary Enterprise*, 17.

9 Connie Shemo, "Directions in Scholarship on American Women and Protestant Foreign Mission: Debates Over 'Cultural Imperialism,'" *History Compass* 10, no. 3 (2012): 270–83. Shemo notes that imperial historian Andrew Porter and others have critiqued the concept of cultural imperialism for failing "to allow sufficient room for the agency of people in host cultures." See Porter, "Cultural Imperialism and the Protestant Missionary Enterprise, 1780–1914," *Journal of Imperial and Commonwealth History* 25, no. 3 (1997): 367–91. As Shemo observes, "All scholars of women missionaries must wrestle with the basic problem . . . How does one balance an exploration of the power of people in the host culture to shape missionary projects while recognizing the importance of the imperial context in which women missionaries operated?" (275).

10 Emily J. Manktelow, "The Rise and Demise of Missionary Wives," *Journal of Women's History* 26, no. 1 (Spring 2014): 135–59.

11 For a telling concern in the Canadian context about what would later be called a "brain drain" see Brouwer, *New Women for God*, 196.

12 Chinua Achebe, *Things Fall Apart* (Oxford: Heinemann, 1958), first published in African Writers Series in 1962 and reprinted 30 times by 1986.

13 Brian Stanley, *The Bible and the Flag: Protestant Missions & British Imperialism in the Nineteenth & Twentieth Centuries* (Leicester: Apollos, 1990) 104–09, 136. In *New Women for God*, 180–81, I briefly discuss Canadian Presbyterian missionaries' moral dilemmas over the opium trade in India given its commercial importance in the part of India where they worked. Andrew Porter's "Religion, Missionary Enthusiasm, and Empire," in *The Oxford History of the British Empire: The Nineteenth Century*, ed. Andrew Porter (Oxford: Oxford University Press, 1999), 222–46, provides a broad overview and concludes by observing that "religion and empire frequently mingled, but were as likely to undermine each other as they were to provide mutual support." Jeffrey Cox's *The British Missionary Enterprise since 1700* has done an excellent job of synthesizing and critiquing recent decades of research on missions as well as relevant new research in imperial history, postcolonialism, and gender studies in order to challenge old assumptions about invariably close ties between missions and Britain's empire. Cox also complicates binary distinctions "that threaten to obliterate the complexity of the past" and foregrounds new insights about such topics as the roles of women and the missionized in the missionary enterprise.

14 See, for instance, Inger Marie Okkenhaug, *Gender, Race and Religion: Nordic Missions 1860–1940* (Uppsala: Studie Missionalia Svecana XCI, 2003), which

shows that, as in other parts of Europe and North America, women were activists for the cause.

15 Cox, *British Missionary Enterprise*, 214.

16 Andrew Preston, *Sword of the Spirit, Shield of Faith: Religion in American War and Diplomacy* (New York: Anchor Books, 2012), 192 for "advance agents of *American* imperialism" (italics added), 182 for "internationalism . . . ways."

17 The SVM has several mentions in Preston, *Sword of the Spirit*, and is discussed routinely in studies of the American foreign missionary movement. John R. Mott, inaugural chairman of the SVM, wrote *The Evangelization of the World in This Generation* in 1900, after which his book's title became a widely adopted slogan well beyond the SVM.

18 Hutchison, *Errand to the World*, Chapter 5. I elaborate on the waning of the separate spheres approach and its significance in Ruth Compton Brouwer, *Modern Women Modernizing Men: The Changing Missions of Three Professional Women in Asia and Africa, 1902–69* (Vancouver: University of British Columbia Press, 2002).

19 Hutchison, *Errand to the World*, Chapter 5.

20 Alvyn J. Austin, *Saving China: Canadian Missionaries in the Middle Kingdom, 1888–1959* (Toronto: University of Toronto Press, 1986), 85.

21 Erin F. Phillips, "The Impact of the Second Vatican Council on the Scarboro Foreign Missionary Society," in Canadian Catholic Historical Association, *Historical Studies* 52 (1985): 97–112. On Canadian Catholics' work in China see Austin, *Saving China*, Chapter 8.

22 H.C. Priest, *Canada's Share in World Tasks* (Toronto: Canadian Council of the Missionary Education Movement, 1920).

23 Ibid., 11.

24 Brouwer, *New Women for God*, 92. Unless shown otherwise, the information that follows about the church's mission in India draws on this book.

25 As quoted in Brouwer, *New Women for God*, 68–69.

26 Edward W. Said, *Orientalism* (New York: Pantheon Books, 1978).

27 As quoted in Brouwer, *New Women for God*, 24.

28 Brouwer, *New Women for God*, 114–15.

29 Brouwer, *New Women for God*, 60–61; Rosemary R. Gagan, *A Sensitive Independence: Canadian Methodist Women Missionaries in Canada and the Orient, 1881–1925* (Montreal: McGill-Queen's University Press, 1992), Chapter 5.

30 As quoted in Brouwer, *New Women for God*, 109.

31 Ibid., 128.

32 Priest, *Canada's Share*, 101.

33 See Porter, "Religion, Missionary Enthusiasm, and Empire," and Margo S. Gewurtz, "'Their Names May Not Shine': Narrating Chinese Christian Converts," in *Canadian Missionaries Indigenous Peoples*, ed. Alvyn Austin and Jamie Scott (Toronto: University of Toronto Press, 2005).

34 Arnup, *A New Church Faces a New World*, 97–98.

35 Brouwer, *Modern Women Modernizing Men*, 55.

36 Arnup, *A New Church Faces a New World*, 96–98.

37 See scattered references to Arnup in Phyllis D. Airhart, *A Church with the Soul of a Nation: Making and Remaking the United Church of Canada* (Montreal: McGill-Queen's University Press, 2014), and 83 for her point that the church's interwar missionary movement spoke with "many voices."

38 Quoted in Brouwer, *Modern Women Modernizing Men*, 11.

39 Ruth Compton Brouwer, "Faith in Development: Donald K. Faris's Path to a New Mission in the Postcolonial Era," *Historical Papers 2011/Canadian Society of Church History* (2011): 189–210.

40 Unless shown otherwise, the following discussion of "NGOization" in the mainstream churches and the emergence of CUSO draws on my article "When Missions Became Development: Ironies of 'NGOization' in Mainstream Canadian Churches in the 1960s," *Canadian Historical Review* 91, no. 4 (2010): 661–93. Citations for Faris's and Hockin's observations and for other quoted passages are given there.

41 The discussion of CUSO that follows draws on my book *Canada's Global Villagers: CUSO in Development, 1961–86* (Vancouver: University of British Columbia Press, 2013) as well as on Brouwer, "When Missions Became Development," unless shown otherwise.

42 Anthony J. Bebbington, Samuel Hickey, and Daina C. Mitlin, eds., *Can NGOs Make a Difference? The Challenge of Development Alternatives* (London: Zed Books, 2008).

43 Brouwer, *Canada's Global Villagers*, esp. the conclusion.

44 Airhart, *Church with the Soul of a Nation*, 203.

45 Lester B. Pearson, *Partners in Development: Report of the Commission on International Development* (New York: Praeger, 1969), 185–89.

46 As cited in Brouwer, *Canada's Global Villagers*, 15–16.

47 Bebbington, Hickey, and Mitlin, *Can NGOs Make a Difference?*, 11.

48 Kevin O'Sullivan, "Humanitarian Encounters: Biafra, NGOs and Imaginings of the Third World in Britain and Ireland, 1967–70," *Journal of Genocide Research* 16, no. 2–3 (2014): 1–14.

49 Maggie Black, *A Cause for Our Times: Oxfam the First 50 Years* (Oxford: Oxford University Press, 1992), 171–72; Dick Bird, *Never the Same Again: A History of VSO* (Cambridge: Lutterworth Press, 1998), 154. It is worth noting that Black, writing about Oxfam, maintains that Oxfam Canada by the late 1960s had a more radical streak than its UK counterpart. Likewise, Bird, historian of Britain's Voluntary Service Overseas (VSO), believed that CUSO came to have a broader understanding of what "development" involved than its British counterpart. CUSO radicals who were longtime supporters of Zimbabwe's protracted independence struggle had particular reason to be dismayed by Robert Mugabe's later betrayal of that struggle.

50 For background, "Simpson, Albert Benjamin (1843–1919)," http://www.bu.edu/missiology/missionary-biography/r-s/simpson-albert-benjamin-1843-1; for statistics, http://www.cmacan.org/.

51 Austin, *Saving China*, Chapter 1.

52 Stackhouse, *Canadian Evangelicalism in the Twentieth Century*, 3. See also Sam Reimer, *Evangelicals and the Continental Divide: The Conservative Protestant Subculture in Canada and the United States* (Montreal: McGill–Queen's University Press, 2003), which argues for basic similarities between Canadian and American evangelicals except in the realm of politics. Reimer finds Canadian evangelicals less inclined than their American counterparts to engage in heated and confrontational rhetoric with fellow citizens who hold different political views.

53 Brouwer, "When Missions Became Development," 692 (for statistics), 689–90 (quotation).

54 Reimer, *Evangelicals and the Continental Divide*; "The Surprising Countries Most Missionaries Are Sent From and Go To," *Christianity Today*, July 2013.

55 Lamin Sanneh and Joel A. Carpenter, eds., *The Changing Face of Christianity: Africa, the West, and the World* (New York: Oxford University Press, 2005), preface, vii.

56 Cox, *British Missionary Enterprise*, Chapter 11, 252, 260. Cox provides an overview of theories about reasons for church growth in Africa and challenges the argument that, there and elsewhere, missionaries were mere "'detonators' for indigenous non-western forms of religion freely chosen by, and transformed by, non-western peoples." If that were the case, he argues, "the imperial taint of missions then disappears." But in fact even in the postcolonial age and perhaps especially in the "new age of mission focus on responsive and unreached peoples, the relationship . . . inherently involves inequality of power and influence."

57 This fact was made evident in the summer of 2014 in connection with the case of Kevin and Julia Garratt, evangelical Christians running a coffee shop in Dandong, China, and from there conducting mission outreach across the border with North Korea. The couple were detained by Chinese officials on suspicion of espionage after the Canadian government had accused China of spying in Canada. See Charles Burton, "Canadians Detained in China Are Pawns in a Bigger Game," *Globe and Mail*, August 8, 2014. Likewise, the Harper government's stalwart support of Israel in its conflict with Hamas was seen as part of an ongoing effort "to curry favour with Jewish and evangelical voters." See Konrad Yakabuski, "What Gaza Tells Us about Canadian Politics," *Globe and Mail*, August 7, 2014.

58 Paul Wells, "A Matter of Life and Death," *Maclean's*, May 21, 2014; "Mr. Harper's Maternal and Child Health Summit, Part 3: Delusions about International Leadership," http://www.mcleodgroup.ca/2014/05/27/mr-harpers-maternal-and-child-health-summit-part-3-delusions-about-international-leadership.

59 See Charmain Levy, "Bringing Religion into Development Studies: An Introduction," in the special issue of *Canadian Journal of Development Studies* 34, no. 2 (2013), and the final two articles, which deal with government funding of faith-based NGOs in Canada in recent years. While the first of these articles, by Vander Zaag, determined that such NGOs were less dependent on government funding than their secular counterparts in the period 2005–2011 and that a change in government during the period did not affect funding patterns, the second, by Francois Audet, dealing with the period 2001–2010, argued that funding to NGOs engaged in proselytizing significantly increased under the federal Conservative government.

60 For the beliefs cited here see "What We Believe," https://paoc.org/family/what-we-believe. On plans for the September 2014 conference see "8th GloPent Conference: Pentecostalism and Development," http://www.glopent.net/Members/webmaster/london-2014/pentecostalism-and-development. See also Michael Wilkinson, *Canadian Pentecostalism: Transition and Transformation* (Montreal: McGill-Queen's University Press, 2009).

61 On this matter, see Joanne Benham Rennick, "Is Religion a Force for Good? Reformulating the Discourse on Religion and International Development," *Canadian Journal of Development Studies* 34, no. 2 (2013): 175–88. Rennick's focus is on parts of the developing world where religious beliefs are strongly held, but my closing sentence is written with places such as North Korea and China also in mind.

62 Donald K. Faris, *To Plow with Hope* (New York: Harper & Brothers, 1958), 202–03.

6

Foreign Policy, Diplomacy, and Decolonization

DAVID WEBSTER

Introduction

A hundred years after World War I, Canada's government unleashed a flurry of commemoration and celebration of the war as the period when Canada came of age as an international player. The war saw Canada start to carry out its own diplomacy, signalled by Conservative Prime Minister Robert Borden's signature on behalf of Canada on the treaty ending the war in 1919, and underlined by Liberal Prime Minister Mackenzie King's signature of treaties in the 1920s and the concurrent opening of Canada's first diplomatic missions overseas. The location of these new missions—at the League of Nations in Geneva and in the capitals of Britain, France, the United States, and Japan—indicated where Canada's diplomatic priorities lay.[1]

None of those diplomatic outposts can be considered to be in the Third World, had the term even existed when Ottawa took its first hesitant steps into international diplomacy. With one exception, they lay within the North Atlantic world that Canadian policy makers saw as the space within which their country had been born and grown up. Opening an embassy in Japan indicated an interest in a rising Pacific power and also carried a watching brief for the Asian continent, but it was not until the 1940s that Canadian embassies opened in China, Brazil, and other major countries in the Global South. The South was peripheral to Canadian diplomacy, leaving Canadian engagement in the hands of nonstate actors, from traders to missionaries to soldiers, as many of the chapters in this book explore. Canada–Third World relations cannot be considered mainly through a state-to-state lens, the approach that dominates the first book titled *Canada and the Third World*.[2] But neither can the role of the Canadian state be omitted, as is done by the essays in *Conflicts of Interest: Canada and the Third World*.[3]

Though peripheral, the Third World was not absent from Canadian diplomatic horizons. Canada and Canadians approached it through the lens of empire, as British subjects in a world-spanning imperial community. Policy makers in Stephen Harper's Conservative government donned similar lenses in the early twenty-first century: they viewed Canada as part of a Western alliance of developed democracies based within the North Atlantic world, even while seeing the Global South as a zone of opportunity. The centenary of World War I saw Canadian diplomacy looking to the Third World, in ways that reflected policy makers' visions of Canada's place in world affairs. While conflict between Israel and Palestinians drew unequivocal Canadian government support for the Israeli government, a civil war in Syria saw Ottawa just as unequivocal in opposition to the government. Foreign minister John Baird assailed Syria's "obscene and brutal repression" and demanded a political solution. "Canada will continue to work with our allies to ensure that all Syrians have a better, brighter future," Baird said. He highlighted Canadian humanitarian aid for refugees of the conflict and called for Syria's government to end the conflict, while situating Canada very much within the Western alliance system.[4] Early images of Canada as part of a British empire and more recent images of Canada as part of a Western alliance share one thing in common: they see the Global South as a zone of conflict, peripheral to Canada's national interests. These images are deeply racialized, implicitly seeing Canada as a "white" nation.

Central through the later years of the twentieth century and into the twenty-first has been a Canadian diplomatic self-image of this country as a voice for justice, a defender of the weak, and an advocate for a more just global order. Concepts of global justice are no longer tied to the concept of a civilizing British empire, but they cannot be entirely separated from this inheritance, from the idea that human rights are those embraced in the Western world and to be transmitted to the South. "Canada has been a consistently strong voice for the protection of human rights and the advancement of democratic values, from our central role in the drafting of the Universal Declaration of Human Rights in 1947/1948 to our work at the United Nations today," proclaims the foreign affairs department.[5] Even nongovernmental sources sometimes repeat this claim uncritically,[6] although it is highly debatable, glossing over Canada's resistance to the Universal Declaration and to the promotion of international human rights for most of its history.[7] It illustrates the self-image of Canada as a voice for justice: one that is far more real among Canadian nongovernmental organizations than it is as a description of Canadian government policy.

Canadian government diplomacy and foreign policy toward the Third World has often trailed, rather than led, nonstate interactions. This has been possible because policy makers have often viewed the Third World as peripheral, and kept their gaze locked tightly on the North Atlantic core of what they have perceived as Canadian national interests. There is nothing inevitable about the North Atlantic focus of Canadian diplomacy, however. It was shaped by the mental maps of the men (and more recently, some women) central to making Canadian foreign policy. This chapter uses the concepts of mental maps, the way policy makers imagine the world spatially, to describe the background against which Canada approached the decolonization of the Global South.[8] It traces Canadian policy toward regions often treated by the government as peripheral, using the central problem of colonialism and political decolonization to illustrate dominant themes in Canadian diplomatic approaches to the Third World. In doing so, it notes the gaps between the Canadian diplomatic self-image and the less altruistic practice of Canadian diplomacy. The role of racialized perceptions is examined primarily in a textbox that looks at two case studies.

A Northern Empire

Canadian mental maps prior to 1945 draw on two powerful inheritances explored in Carl Berger's classic study *The Sense of Power: Studies in the Ideas of Canadian Imperialism, 1867–1914*: "New World" and "North."[9] European explorers coined the term "New World" to describe the Americas, yet the term's power derives from the way it was used by settler societies. Like Edward Said's Orient, the "New World" was an object created by the discourse about it, then represented territorially.[10] In this case, however, the major figures drawing the representations were settlers within the New World. Standing aloof from Europe's quarrels, they suggested, the New World could become a place of purity and refuge, of peace as opposed to Europe's wars, of the "world's longest undefended border." Canadians, Berger wrote, "came to see themselves not as the agent of an Old World culture charged with civilizing the New, but as beings uplifted and restored by their New World environment whose duty it was to regenerate the Old."[11] Especially after Europe descended into World War I, the idea grew that Canada was part of a New World that could teach the Old. Canada's longest-serving prime minister, Mackenzie King, was far from alone when he decried Europe as a continent "which cannot run itself" and which Canada "should not feel called upon to save periodically."[12]

Canadian mental maps also had to allow for difference from the United States. Thus, Canada was presented as a "Northern" nation, less adulterated by the republican and racial contaminations than the United States and the Latin America republics to its south. "Who, considering our present and looking back upon the past, can doubt but that a great future is before these colonies?" asked Ontario-Manitoba politician Alexander Morris as the Northwest Territories (then including most of what is now the prairie provinces) was joined to the fledgling Dominion of Canada. "Nay, is it not manifest that the day must come when they will play no mean part in the world's history, and amid the ranks of nations?"[13] A great "Northern" destiny, it was hoped, could also bind together English and French-speaking populations, embracing northernness/*nordicité* and its linked values of purity and vigour. These themes echo through more recent years, from John Diefenbaker's "Northern Vision" to Stephen Harper's "Northern Agenda."[14]

There was also the continued idea of an imperial tie with Britain, a mental map that reinforced the idea of Canada as living "between" the United States and Britain. The 1898 postage stamp that adorns the cover of *The Sense of Power* is a powerful picture of Canada's place on the globe. The stamp depicts a map of the world, with the British Empire coloured red. With North America at the centre, Canada dominates: it is the largest and most central red tract, topped with the royal crown. Canada, rather than Suez and India, link an oversized Britain to Australia. The empire was an enterprise in which Canadians participated, even if somewhat less enthusiastically than (for instance) Australians. Journalist Gordon Sinclair's bestselling tales of travel in India and Afghanistan published in the 1930s were both written and read in the context of an imperial understanding. He wrote as a self-consciously brash colonial, but echoed British images of effeminate Hindus in India and masculine, wild martial races in Afghanistan. His tales were popular enough to be reissued, without editing, in the 1960s.[15]

Into Africa and the Indies

Canada's government followed Britain's, and the imperial-minded public opinion of much of English Canada, into the empire's African conflicts. Diplomatically, Canada played a limited role in British wars of conquest in Sudan and South Africa in the late nineteenth century, but men from Canada fought in both. A Canadian force fought as part of British forces against an Islamic resistance movement in the Sudan (1884–85). It included veterans of the Red River expedition in which the Canadian state had fought Louis Riel and his Métis resistance in Manitoba.[16] The main effects were domestic: the South African (Boer) War of 1899–1902 split the cabinet between imperial-minded members and those less inclined to participate in overseas wars (mainly Quebeckers). This foreshadowed later Canadian attitudes to a more recent American empire.[17] A similar split over conscription would occur in World War I. It informed one of the major documents in Canadian external policy, the 1947 Gray lecture by Louis St. Laurent (then foreign minister, and later prime minister) that argued the key basis of Canadian foreign policy should be to maintain unity between English-speaking and French-speaking Canadians.[18]

This did not mean Canadians did not look abroad. World War I saw Australia, New Zealand, and South Africa acquire colonies under a "mandate" from

Figure 6.1 The cover of Carl Berger's book *The Sense of Power: Studies in the Ideas of Canadian Imperialism 1867–1914* (1971)

the newly formed League of Nations. There were no German colonies close enough to tempt Canada into becoming a subimperial power, but Robert Borden's Conservative-led government did look south to consider taking on a colonial empire of its own, made up of British possessions in the Caribbean basin. This was already a region of Canadian commercial interest; Canadian imperialists began in the late nineteenth century to see it as a potential miniature Canadian empire. As early as 1911, some in the Bahamas entertained the idea of confederating with Canada. "There is a grandeur about the vision which it opens up which is very attractive, and hard times intensify the glamour," wrote the governor of the colony.[19] The Confederation impulse may have been encouraged by Canadian adventurers. Commercial and imperial motives combined in this consideration for union.

Trade agreements between Canada and the West Indies started in 1912. Borden's government contemplated political union as well. Allowing that the proposal of a Canadian empire might be "chimerical," Borden nevertheless thought it might increase Canada's importance and influence, allow the production of tropical products and thus give Canada better ability to compete with the United States, build markets for Canadian industry, add weight to his campaign for a strong Canadian navy, and make Canadians more imperial-minded as they took up the burden of "governing subject races."[20] Though the British government was open to handing some colonies to Ottawa, it felt that wartime was not the right time for the transfer. Still, leading British imperial thinker L.S. Amery felt that Britain "cannot do it all," and would need Canadian capital and assistance in ruling. There might even emerge "a Greater Dominion of British America including Newfoundland, the Bermudas, the West Indies, and even, if you liked to have them thrown in, the Falkland Islands."[21]

Borden did indeed like the notion. In the aftermath of World War I, he repeated the advantages of the idea as lying in production of tropical goods and trade, as well as the boost to domestic support for sea power and the "increased sense of responsibility due to administration of a territory inhabited largely by backward races." On the other hand, there would be costs to develop the new colonies and the problem of three million new citizens, many of them black, who would insist on the same right to vote already held by black men living in Canada.[22] Opting to pursue commercial union before political, Ottawa signed trade agreements with most British colonies in the Caribbean basin, but proved unwilling to invest the capital required to maintain weekly steamship connections. Canadian imperial interest in the region lingered, however. In 1932, two Canadian destroyers even disembarked troops in El Salvador to protect British interests, since they were the closest British empire vessels during a revolution in the country. They did not face battle, but their presence may have indirectly helped the government suppress a popular uprising.[23]

Missionaries, Media, and Mandates: Canada Considers a Colony in Armenia

World War I had been fought, according to some Canadians then, and to some historians since, by an "Anglo-Saxon alliance."[24] Global imperial sentiments clashed with the desire to remain safely within what Senator Raoul Dandurand famously described as a "fireproof house" in North America.[25] This often pitted cautious political leaders against internationally minded church figures. Attitudes toward the 1919 Korean movement for independence from Japan are illustrative. Canadian missionary Frank Schofield, a close confidant of Korean nationalist leaders, drew on Korean nationalist imagery of a highly civilized, industrious, inventive, pro-Western, and Christian-inspired small nation fighting for its freedom against the "heathen militarist rulers" and "Savages" of Japan.[26] Policy makers in Ottawa, on the other hand, saw Korea as too remote to merit any response to the appeal by Schofield and other Canadian missionaries for any support for the cause of Korean independence.

Genocide in Armenia also engaged Canadian church and public sympathy, but the Canadian government was reluctant to get involved. A part of the Ottoman empire before World War I, Armenia had been slated for a potential League of Nations mandate administered by the United States, a counterpart to European mandates over other parts of the Ottoman empire (France in Syria, Britain in Palestine, and so on).[27] When the United States remained outside the League, the search was on for other possible mandatory powers. First-choice Norway proving unwilling, British delegate Lord Curzon then informed a League meeting that Canada would take the mandate.[28] The news came as a surprise in Ottawa, which issued a swift denial that any such proposal was under consideration.

That Canada could be announced as committed was the result of extensive campaigning by missionaries and *The Globe* newspaper for relief aid to Armenians facing mass killings. The relief campaign drew on images of Turkish cruelty and the persecution of Armenian Christians. George Munro Grant and other stalwarts of Canadian imperialism had raised $30,000 for Armenian relief in the 1890s; a campaign in *The Globe* in the early months of 1920 raised $300,000.[29] As Australia, New Zealand, and South Africa assumed colonial mandates under League of Nations auspices, it was natural that some Canadians considered taking on the same "duty." *The Globe*, for instance, ran a front-page cartoon suggesting that Canadian troops might have to accompany Canadian relief supplies.[30]

Elite voices in Canada called for the country to take up the "duty" of a mandate. Canada, argued H.F. Angus in *The University Magazine*, had the qualities needed for a mandatory power: strength adequate to the task, disinterestedness, enterprise, responsibility, idealism, and reasonableness.[31] The Canadian cabinet fuelled expectations that it might take on the mandate by noting that it was "absolutely opposed to return of any Armenian provinces of Turkey to Turkish rule."[32] That month (April 1920), Curzon made his claim that Canada stood ready to take on a mandate. In November, the League passed a resolution calling for an armed force to halt hostilities in Turkish Armenia and invited Canada among others to take part; in a one-sentence telegram, Prime Minister Arthur Meighen's government refused to do so.[33] Meighen was soon out of power, but Mackenzie King was no keener to deploy troops to Turkey. Meighen's government did respond to public sympathy for the Armenians by voting (with just seven others, and in opposition to Britain and the other Dominions) to admit Armenia to the League of Nations in December 1920.[34] And advocacy of the Canadian mandate proposal continued. A mandate would be "a fine thing," in the words of one typical appeal from 1921:

> Such an act would put Canada "on the map" in international affairs; would give Canada a new sense of nationhood arising out of the assumption of a new responsibility; would place on Canada her share of the "white man's burden" and thus serve to justify the fast-waning confidence of the Armenian people in the humanitarian idealism of the Anglo-Saxons, and finally would give Canadian enterprise, political, industrial and commercial, a fine field for effort and adventure.[35]

Canadian debates over the possibility of taking on a colonial mandate over a Third World territory underlined the link between empire and an emerging Canadian diplomatic self-image as an advocate of justice—driven more by nonstate voices than by government. The conclusion of a new treaty more favourable to Turkey in 1923 ended talk of a mandate for Armenia once and for all. Canada, however, had very definitely considered becoming a colonial power overseas. The pressure to do so had drawn on images of a backward and barbaric Turk and on the duties that fell to noble humanitarian Anglo-Saxons—Canada as much as other colonial powers. It was safer, however, for policy makers to remain within their New World "fireproof house."

Opening New Embassies

Only the shock of World War II jolted Ottawa out of its isolated stance. The Nazi sweep across Europe had the incidental effect of shuttering some

Canadian embassies in Europe; the pioneering embassy in Japan closed soon after. The consequent availability of diplomats, along with Ottawa's willingness to take on a more global role as part of the war effort, prompted a more open attitude to requests coming from the South for diplomatic relations with Canada, even as the diplomatic priority went to new high commissions in Commonwealth countries (Australia, New Zealand, South Africa, and Ireland). Brazil and then a host of other Latin American countries sought an exchange of embassies, turning Canada into "the belle of the ball," wooed by an array of South and Central American states.[36] O. D. Skelton, Undersecretary of State for External Affairs, "hoped that a presence in Latin America would appeal to opinion in Quebec, thereby making it easier politically to carry out his projects of expanded relations with the dominions," the historians of the Department of External Affairs wrote.[37] With European markets cut off, allies needed, and trade prospects seen in South America, Mackenzie King agreed to open embassies in Brazil and Argentina in 1940 despite his earlier fears that "South America will be a trouble zone while this war continues."[38] Mexico and others followed once the first two embassies were open.

So too did China, which had been pressing Canada for an exchange of embassies. General Victor Odlum arrived as the first Canadian ambassador in 1942, and Canada offered a $60-million credit to China in 1946.[39] But the embassy was makeshift, rats ate the First Secretary's soap at night, and there was little meeting of the minds between Canada and Chiang Kai-shek's Republic of China. Chinese civil war caused reconsideration of that credit and less Canadian willingness to sell military equipment.[40] The subsequent advances of the Chinese communists led to the evacuation of Canadians beginning in December 1948 and the suspension of further credits to the Republic of China.[41] Although Canada initially planned to recognize the new communist-led People's Republic, it had not followed the lead of India, Britain, and others in doing so by the time the Korean War broke out. With Chinese and American forces at war in Korea, recognition was deferred—as it happened, until 1970.[42]

The Challenge of Decolonization

Before World War II, Canadians had felt safe behind their oceans. Afterwards, new military technology left Canada sandwiched between the two superpowers, where once it had been safe and secure in New World isolation. All at once, the "fireproof house" was in danger. Fisheries minister Robert Mayhew, speaking on Canada's engagement with the Pacific, updated the image for a new and more dangerous age: "Our world of today is a very small world.

If I may use a humble metaphor, it is like a haystack. It does not matter on which side the fire is started; if the wind is favourable, all will be destroyed."[43]

The Cold War world was swiftly cloven into "two camps," a term used by both American evangelist Billy Graham and Soviet ideologue Andrei Zhdanov.[44] This was the mental map on which many Western policy makers saw the world: torn in two, one part free, one part enslaved by communism. It is a view that shaped Canadian diplomatic perceptions as official Ottawa faced a fast-changing colonized world. "If, through aggression or folly or inertia, the whole of Asia were to be allowed to fall under Communist domination, the free world would be tragically maimed and would be exposed to even greater dangers," worried Lester B. Pearson, the diplomat who became the chief architect of Canadian foreign policy in the 1940s and 1950s.[45]

Postwar Canada existed within a potent mental map of "the North Atlantic triangle."[46] The North Atlantic Treaty Organization (NATO) appeared as the realization and refinement of the triangle, a British-American-Canadian scheme that added the rest of Western Europe to the British corner. It was a "natural creation," in Pearson's words.[47] The Canadian commitment to NATO seemed almost spiritual, but it also required support to noncommunist Asia, as Louis St. Laurent, prime minister from 1948 to 1957, argued. To him, Canada's NATO membership was all about the defence of "civilization" against the newest threat, Soviet communism. "But we have to recognize at the same time that there is another side to the preservation of civilization," he said in a speech at the University of Toronto in 1950. "To preserve civilization, we have to nurture the spirit within. . . . We cannot neglect the less fortunate within our own midst, nor can we ignore the plight of nations less fortunate than our own. The preservation of civilization requires us to help those untold millions, most of them in Asia, to improve their standards of life and to achieve a situation they will feel it is worthwhile to defend."[48] Civilization was equated, implicitly, with whiteness (this racialized thinking is explored further in Box 6.1). St. Laurent was far from alone in his evocation of the West as the land of civilization and in linking Canada into this North Atlantic zone. Arnold Heeney, the chief civil servant in External Affairs, made a similar speech soon after. "For us in North America the shrines of Western Europe are no mere items of geography. In Britain, in France, in Italy are the vital well-springs of our civilization."[49]

The North Atlantic triangle was a zone of comfort for Canadians. In a broad grouping including the United States, Britain, and France, Pearson argued, "we can be comfortable and secure. We will be far happier there, if I may put it this way, than we could ever be in a double bed with any one of the three."[50] So, too, for the lingering British Empire, rebranded as the Commonwealth. Again and again, Canadian officials called the Commonwealth a "bridge" between the West and Asia. Canadian Asia policy aimed to somehow make east and west meet by bringing "free Asia" into the "free world." R.G. Nik Cavell, administrator of Canada's Colombo Plan aid to Asia, highlighted this theme in a 1952 speech, declaring "that if the free world were to be kept in existence, it would have to be expanded and strengthened, and that could not possibly be done if the Asian countries disappeared behind the Iron Curtain, as China had done."[51] Although China had "disappeared" into the communist world, the rest of Asia could still be saved.

Amidst World War II, Ottawa avoided comment on decolonization debates between the United States and Britain, but was "deeply interested in the effect on Anglo-American relations of problems of Colonial policy."[52] In other words, it prioritized harmony within the North Atlantic triangle. Within the Commonwealth, Canadian voices tended to side with Britain and South Africa in resistance to Australian and New Zealand pressure (later joined by India, Pakistan, and other new members) for greater international oversight of colonial empires.[53]

The Canadian Model of Decolonization

The new United Nations, formed after World War II, rejected American pressure to place all colonies under a new UN system of "trusteeship," but it did put former League mandates under that system and ask colonial powers to report on their administration. This added to the global pressures for all colonial powers to pay at least lip service to the idea that, in the end, colonies would become independent countries. But how would that be done? In Canadian government eyes, Canada offered a good model. Decolonization should be orderly, evolutionary, nonconfrontational, constructive. "It is our task to build, not to tear down," Canadian representative Senator Wishart Robertson solemnly told the UN's fourth (trusteeship) committee as it convened in 1946. Canada, he said, spoke as a country that "has not been entrusted with the responsibility of administering non self-governing territories, of a nation that has not secured, and does not desire to secure[,] additions to its territory as a result of war."[54] (The claim that Canada had no non-self-governing territories came up against the reality of the Canadian North, which Ottawa had been careful to stress was not to be considered a colonial territory.[55]) Robertson continued with a defence of British rule in Africa, reading the Canadian experience directly onto a different continent:

> I have never been to Africa, but I do know that I am a citizen of a country that was once a non self-governing territory under the administration of the United Kingdom and I can testify to this Assembly that in my humble

opinion no nation on earth has a prouder record in the field of human relations than has the United Kingdom.[56]

Canada, in short, offered a model of political and economic development that Canadian policy makers thought newly emerging countries would do well to follow. One of the best summaries of the philosophy underlying Prime Minister Louis St. Laurent's foreign policy was that he wanted to offer the entire world "the peace of Compton." Everywhere in the world should be more like St. Laurent's home village in Quebec's Eastern Townships, an industrious community where French and English Canadians lived in peace and harmony with one another (and a place built on erasure of the original Abenaki presence).[57] Policy makers did not share the American dilemma of balancing sympathy for self-determination on the one hand, against Cold War solidarity with European allies on the other.[58] Nor had there been any notable earlier Canadian advocacy for independence in the colonized world. Canadian diplomacy was not exerted to preserve Chinese control of Manchuria when Japan invaded in the 1930s. There was some advocacy from the Canadian mission in Geneva to defend Ethiopia in the face of Italian invasion, but Mackenzie King ensured that Canada did not act to defend Ethiopian independence even with the imposition of sanctions on Italy. The question has normally been addressed by historians as a failure of collective security. This is not wrong, but the Ethiopian crisis equally marked Canadian acquiescence in a case of late colonization. The Ethiopian crisis was not simply prelude to World War II. It also demonstrated that Canada, like the major European powers, would not act to protect a country's independence. Empire remained superior.

What resonated in postwar Ottawa were notions of European tutelage leading gradually toward self-government. When British officials began to plan tentatively to shed some colonial territories, official Ottawa initially worried that the pace was too fast, not too slow. The Canadian model of decolonization proposed in effect that other countries follow Canada's path "from colony to nation" in an orderly, evolutionary fashion, one that did not cast off the colonizer's legacy but built upon it. Independence did not mean a break with the former colonial power: links remained in the political (Commonwealth), strategic (NATO), economic, and ideological realms.

India: The Decolonization of the Raj

So when Britain's postwar Labour government decided it would have to give in to nationalist pressure and "quit India," there was no pressure from Ottawa for British leaders to move any more quickly than they had opted to do. Canadian policy makers worked quietly in support of British counterparts to ensure that India's independence meant independence within the Commonwealth. India, along with Pakistan and Ceylon, was persuaded to accept "Dominion" status modelled on the separate-yet-connected status of Canada. As historian Hector Mackenzie has written, "ultimately this was a multilateral rather than a bilateral process and . . . to achieve its ends, Britain needed support from other members of the Commonwealth. . . . Canada became Britain's principal ally among the 'Old Dominions' in the elaboration and implementation of a solution which not only redefined the constitutional basis of the Commonwealth but also repositioned it politically." So important was the retention of India within the Commonwealth that India's continued membership was arranged even after its government's decision to drop the links with the British Crown that held other members together.[59] The result was a "New Commonwealth" that permitted the decolonization of the British Empire's Third World components while ensuring that the new states were still linked to Britain and to its "Old Dominions"—especially Canada, the earliest and most enthusiastic proponent of the new order. A later British prime minister, for instance, recalled that Pearson was one of those Canadian leaders who were "happy with the old Commonwealth but happier with the new."[60]

Other Decolonizations within the Commonwealth

The same hopes were expressed when the "new Commonwealth" expanded again to permit independence for Malaya and Ghana in 1957 (and incidentally, even up the numbers—five "Old Dominions" with European majorities, and five "new Commonwealth" states with nonwhite majorities). This came as part of a policy announced in the mid-1950s to grant independence within the Commonwealth to five new states: Ghana (then Gold Coast), Nigeria, a Central African Federation of three British colonies, a federation of Malaya, and a federated British West Indies. External Affairs worried that British decolonization plans risked opening up a potential power vacuum into which Soviet influence could flow. As one memorandum mused: "We wonder whether the speed at which the United Kingdom proposes to proceed with political emancipation, particularly in West Africa, may not inspire nationalist agitation in territories where the French, Belgians and Portuguese have attempted to impose a political 'quarantine' until such time as there is a solid economic and social base for political participation by the native population." But with independence a certainty, the new African states would need to be wooed. Canada would have to offer aid and open a high commission (the Commonwealth term for embassy) in Ghana, the first black-majority state to receive independence.[61] In the early years of Kwame Nkrumah's government, including around his visit to Ottawa in 1958, Canadian observers hailed Ghana's loyalty to the Commonwealth, its Atlantic world orientation, and its constructive attitude to global problems. They tended to see Canada as a more effective Western mentor for Ghana than the British, the former colonizers, or the Americans, for whom the Cold War contest dominated all.

Prime Minister John Diefenbaker's government, rhetorically committed to moving the Commonwealth to the centre of Canadian foreign relations, opened high commissions in both Malaya and Ghana and was represented by cabinet ministers at each country's independence celebration. In Ghana, minister of mines and surveys George Prudham noted that "they were beginning to travel the same road as we in Canada had travelled." Because Britain was the former colonial power, there was "a great responsibility on other members of the Commonwealth, perhaps more especially on Canada," to guide the new country.[62]

Hopes and imagery were similar on the other side of the world, where minister without portfolio J.M. Macdonnell represented Canada at Malaya's independence celebrations. Canada had a special role as a Commonwealth older brother to Malaya, with similar racial diversity (in the parlance of the day, French-speaking and English-speaking Canadians were two different "races," much as Malaya had Malay, Chinese, and Indian "races"). Canada, he insisted, had no colonial past, which made it a good friend for Malaya. He continued:

> Two main points impressed themselves on me during my week in Kuala Lumpur [the Malayan capital]. The first was the very great need to assist non-committed South East Asian nations in their determination to resist Communism. The second was the very warm and genuine regard which the Malayan leaders have for Canada. Malaya, as an independent and democratic nation within the Commonwealth, is in a position to be a strong bastion against Communism, and it is partly in this context that I think we should regard her.[63]

Malaya was indeed an anticommunist bastion—its government was composed in large part of elite Malays and Chinese financiers who had backed the British colonizers in the "Malay emergency" that pitted British forces against communist-led independence fighters earlier in the 1950s. There, British officers pioneered counterinsurgency tactics that would later be attempted with less success by American forces in Vietnam. Malaya continued to be a pro-Western voice in Southeast Asia thereafter. In 1963 it eased the British decolonization of Singapore and colonies on northern Borneo by absorbing them and becoming a new Federation of Malaysia. Singapore would not remain in the federation long, but Malaysia and a new independent Singapore remained pro-Western bastions in Southeast Asia—and favoured Canadian partners—as a result, until attention shifted from Malaysia to Indonesia in the 1970s and onwards.[64]

Canada looked on with vague benevolence as the British Caribbean colonies gained their independence. The Diefenbaker government launched an aid plan for the English-speaking Caribbean and a Canada-Caribbean prime ministers' meeting hosted by Diefenbaker's successor as prime minister, Lester B. Pearson. Aid, trade, and raw materials for Canadian corporation Alcan, however, led diplomacy in Canadian relations with the English-speaking Caribbean.[65] The hoped-for West Indies Federation did not succeed, but Canadian trade and political interests in the region remained substantial as each island gained its separate independence.

Decolonization by Revolution: Indonesia and Vietnam

Canadian policy makers were far less keen on independence achieved through revolutionary means. The first anticolonial revolution to reach the United Nations was the Indonesian struggle for independence from the Netherlands. Indonesian nationalists declared the end of the Dutch East Indies and their transformation into an independent Republic of Indonesia in 1945. It took four years of negotiation, warfare, and international diplomatic pressure before the Dutch recognized Indonesian independence in 1949. Looking back a decade later, Pearson wrote about this first unwilling decolonization in characteristically mild yet telling terms:

> The experience of Indonesia is in fact part of a longer and larger story which now takes on a clearer and more compelling meaning in a shrinking world where all peoples must learn to live and work and progress together, if we are to live at all. This cannot be done if people who wish political freedom cannot achieve it by peaceful change—or at all. But it also cannot be done if freedom means only national narrowness and prejudice and suspicion of others. . . . Indonesia, I know, is now independent, and that is good. But the reality of its independence might be deeper, and more secure, if it had been achieved in a more peaceful, orderly and co-operative fashion.[66]

In other words, Indonesia would have done well to pursue a more evolutionary and cooperative path toward independence—a path more like the Canadian model.

This attitude had shaped Canadian action at the UN as Canada served its first term on the Security Council, in 1948 and 1949. Faced with the issue of Indonesian decolonization, Canadian policy makers looked first to the Netherlands to consider the effect of this Third World issue on a European colonial power. Dutch prosperity was seen as dependent on the riches of the Indies trade, and thus when Ottawa extended postwar reconstruction aid to Europe, it included the Dutch East Indies as the only non-European territory to receive Canadian reconstruction dollars. As Indonesian nationalists were fighting Dutch attempts to recolonize the Indies (occupied by Japan from 1942 to 1945), Canadian policy makers were far more concerned with the formation of NATO, which would tie the United States to the defence of Western Europe. After the Indonesian Republic crushed a communist rising in mid-1948, it gained the full-throated support of the United States. The Truman administration even threatened to withhold Marshall Plan money earmarked for the Netherlands if the Dutch did not come to the bargaining table and negotiate Indonesian decolonization. For their part, the Dutch threatened to wreck the talks toward forming NATO. Concerned over this growing rift between allies and the threat to North Atlantic unity, Canada's Security Council delegation managed to broker a compromise in which the Netherlands agreed to host a round-table conference with Indonesian nationalists. The result was the creation in 1949 of an independent Indonesian state anchored in a Netherlands–Indonesian Union. The model, clearly, was the Commonwealth. Canadian diplomats had supported Indonesian decolonization in principle, but their efforts aimed above all to repair a North Atlantic rift and assist the Netherlands out of an untenable position. This was no great Canadian campaign for the independence of colonized peoples. Still, it helped construct a Canadian diplomatic self-image as helpful advocates of peaceful solutions and friend of the Third World.[67]

The Indonesian case was resolved relatively quickly. UN pressure had been important, as the Security Council for the first time ordered a colonial power to move toward decolonization. The same could not be done in Vietnam, where a French veto would have prevented similar action by the Security Council. Indeed, with respect to French colonies in North Africa (Morocco and Tunisia), Canada initially supported the French presence partly out of concern that France remain in common European defence arrangements and retain its presence in Indochina.[68] Canada's stance on Vietnam's independence struggle, which also began immediately after World War II ended in 1945, was equally circumspect: in principle, France should decolonize, but only if responsible, moderate nationalists were to take over afterwards. With the Vietnamese independence movement led by communists, a sharp contrast to Indonesia, this option did not seem available. Canadian diplomats instead urged their French allies to work with "moderate Vietnamese nationalists" who were best placed to "prevent possible Communist domination of all of East Asia."[69] It took a Vietnamese military victory at the French Indochina fort of Dienbienphu and an international peace conference before France agreed in 1954 to accept Vietnamese independence in the north, along with a new regime in southern Vietnam led by American-backed noncommunist nationalists. Canada never pressed France very hard up to this point to decolonize. It did agree to serve on the Indochina (Vietnam, Laos, and Cambodia) truce supervision commissions created by the 1954 peace accords, which drew Canadian diplomats into the problems of postcolonial peace monitoring (see below). Canadian attitudes toward the French war to retain control of Algeria in the latter half of the 1950s echoed those of the early 1950s in Indochina. Ottawa continued to prioritize North Atlantic alliance priorities over support for decolonization, even voting on the French side at the UN in opposition to decolonization policies that Canadian diplomats thought France would be well advised to adopt. Alliance solidarity trumped all else until French leader Charles de Gaulle opted to pull out of Algeria, a decision taken in 1959 and implemented by 1962.[70]

Canada and the End of Empires in Southern Africa

Nor was pressure very severe in the early years at the southern tip of Africa. South Africa is not normally viewed as a decolonization issue, yet its white settler population was a minority ruling over a black majority and Indian and "coloured" minorities. It inhabited the Commonwealth, but was increasingly at odds with new Commonwealth members. When India hauled its Commonwealth partner South Africa up before the UN General Assembly over racist treatment of Indians in South Africa, Canada opposed a resolution on the grounds that it was domestic jurisdiction; Canadian diplomats even avoided mediating, as "Canada's position in regard to the status of East Indians here is not above criticism" and it would be unwise to "concentrate attention on our own position and extend the controversy to include us."[71]

South Africa had its own colonial mandate to rule over Namibia (formerly German South West Africa) but refused to place the territory under the United Nations trusteeship system. In this, it had early Canadian support. Only as the Namibia issue gained force internationally with the independence of other states in southern Africa did Canada's stance begin to shift. Canadian governments—those of Conservatives John Diefenbaker and Brian Mulroney in particular—have often been portrayed as leaders in the anti-apartheid campaign. It is true that Canadian policy makers had little sympathy for the blatant racism that allowed only whites to vote for South Africa's government and consigned nonwhites to a constrained, subject existence, governed by "pass laws" and other forms of racial discrimination. But Ottawa was also in accord with its allies on the importance of South Africa as an anticommunist power, and early Canadian policy makers agreed with South African arguments that the country's domestic affairs were its own concern, not that of the UN or the international community more broadly. Canada was at best an "ambiguous champion" of the anti-apartheid cause. Ottawa policy makers were "pushed" into international advocacy by domestic public opinion within Canadian civil society and the perceived need to save the Commonwealth, rather than acting from moral motives.[72]

Diefenbaker and his officials promoted the ideal of racial equality as a principle binding throughout the Commonwealth. This linked up well with moves the government was taking domestically, such as the passage of a bill of rights. "Any association that hopes to play an effective role in the world must ... endeavour to bring about co-operation and understanding between races," Diefenbaker said.[73] Thus, when South Africa transformed itself into a republic (with whites alone permitted to vote and rule), Diefenbaker argued that it could not rejoin the Commonwealth while retaining its racist policies. If it did, the Commonwealth would lose its Asian and African members and thus the dream of a "new Commonwealth" could die. With a multiracial, multicontinental Commonwealth cast as a force in holding back communism, this would harm multiple aspects of Canadian foreign policy.

In opting to part ways from Britain, Australia, and New Zealand by not backing the South African stance, Canada had acted from a pragmatic calculation that this was the way to preserve the Commonwealth, an association that the Diefenbaker government placed at the centre of its foreign policy. The stance, nevertheless, won applause from the newer Commonwealth states, all led by nationalists who had struggled for their countries' independence. Canada appeared as an adversary to racism and an advocate of racial equality. This has helped build up the image of Canada as a friend to Third World independence and a voice for human rights and racial equality globally. Such was not necessarily the principal goal of Canadian diplomacy, but it was one important result. It fed into the Canadian diplomatic self-image as a friend of the Third World, which would revive again when a later Conservative prime minister, Brian Mulroney, took a similar stance within the Commonwealth on apartheid.

Mulroney's government, normally supportive of American and British Cold War strategies, diverged from Canada's major allies in calling for a stronger world response to apartheid. The image of Mulroney standing up to British Prime Minister Margaret Thatcher for a more multiracial and fair

Commonwealth has become ingrained in the Canadian diplomatic memory. Beyond the strong words, Canadian concrete sanctions were deliberately restrained in scope and followed a similar trajectory to those imposed by other Western governments. Instead, as political scientist Linda Freeman has chronicled, "Canadian policy was limited, and the claims made for it excessive."[74] Here lies a common theme in Canadian foreign policy: strong words, accompanied by carefully constrained actions. The end of apartheid in 1994 was the result of action within South Africa and international solidarity work, in which Canadian championing of the anti-apartheid cause was more rhetorical than concrete, and came from a country still constrained by its Commonwealth and North Atlantic ties.

For the time being, however, South Africa's apartheid regime seemed secure. Decolonization swept Africa, with 1960 and 1961 seeing a host of former British and French colonies join the UN and tip the balance of the world body much more toward the South. Tacking with what British prime minister Harold Macmillan called the "wind of change," Britain moved to hand power to reliable noncommunist nationalists in most of its African empire. France followed by granting a form of independence with links to France to most of its African colonies in 1961.[75] As Britain began to move to decolonize, its officials consulted Canadian counterparts, finding support for the general path along with some worry that the pace might be too swift. Canadian diplomats looked on with similar attitudes as France agreed to grant conditional independence to most of its Sub-Saharan colonies. Consummate Atlanticist diplomat Pierre Dupuy, while ambassador to France, toured the French African colonies. He reported that Canada provided a valuable model for the continent. (At times this reached the point of self-caricature: "Canadians have the reputation of being simple, easy-going, gay, dynamic, hospitable and interested in sports. No background would appear more attractive to Africans.")[76] The idea of Canada as potential model for Third World decolonization broadened out into a diplomatic self-image of Canada as friend of the Third World.

There were holdouts from this wave of decolonization, most of them in southern Africa. Africa's most intractable decolonization challenge lay in the Portuguese colonies. Although Belgium pulled out of its Congo colony abruptly (see Box 6.1), Portugal refused to budge. National liberation movements sprang up in Angola, Mozambique, and Guinea-Bissau and turned to armed struggle as the Portuguese government made it clear that it had no intention of following Britain and France down the decolonization path. The United Nations, with a voting majority from Africa and Asia, regularly called for Portugal to grant independence rather than continuing to claim that its colonies were "overseas provinces" and thus as integral a part of

Portugal as, for instance, Hawaii was of the United States. In Ottawa, there was some sympathy for Portugal as a NATO ally. Some Canadian diplomats, indeed, saw Portugal as a relatively progressive power as the decolonization wave took hold in earnest in Africa. One discussion paper, issued in 1959, noted: "The situation in Portug[u]ese Africa apparently remained stable; the Portug[u]ese practice of establishing real equality between natives and European Portug[u]ese eliminated a cardinal cause of anti-colonial feeling. The intention of the Portuguese was to develop, as far as capital shortages permitted, their overseas provinces for the good of all local inhabitants."[77] Canadian rhetoric started shifting in the 1960s. At the UN, Canada tended to back the large majority calling on Portugal to decolonize. Yet Canadian government comments in debate still indicated a preference for negotiated solutions and a refusal to back the armed struggle paths of the liberation movements. Canada, meanwhile, was a top market for Angolan products—the premier market for oil from Angola, for instance—and Canadian companies sought investments in Mozambique. Pierre Trudeau's foreign minister Mitchell Sharp argued, in a traditional Canadian line, that "trade helps to bring about contacts that do in fact influence policy."[78] In 1974 Portugal's army, tired of colonial wars, backed a popular "Carnation Revolution." The subsequent Portuguese government swiftly moved to dismantle its centuries-old colonial empire. Throughout the ending of this last great European empire, the Canadian stance remained one of favouring independence by evolution rather than revolution, negotiation rather than armed force. Canada did not take the path of some northern European countries that openly backed the national liberation movements, nor did it take the hardline stance of backing the colonial power.

Bandung, Birthplace of the "Third World"

The idea of a Third World was born at Bandung in 1955, the first gathering of independent Asian and African states, hosted by Indonesia's revolutionary president Sukarno. The term was coined by a French journalist as a parallel to the "Third Estate," the commoners of the French revolution. Bandung, a conference rejecting the Cold War as the guiding principle in international affairs, made the concept geographical: refusing to be characterized as allies of one side or the other, the governments present implicitly presented themselves as a third camp. What held them together was the struggle to end colonialism. The conference alarmed the United States government, while appearing as an opportunity to win friends for the young communist regime in China. Canadian diplomats saw no real danger from the gathering, noting the leading role of Indian prime minister Jawaharlal Nehru and other moderate nationalists. Though Sukarno's opening oration cast the global decolonization struggle as akin to the American Revolution, only Canada among Western governments smiled on Bandung. Prime Minister Louis St. Laurent sent the sole formal message of greeting from a Western head of government, according to Canadian diplomatic reports. "We regard the Conference as a natural development arising out of the concern of the countries of the area to meet and discuss common problems, and significant of the increasing importance of the Asian countries," Pearson cabled the high commission in New Delhi. He hoped above all that the conference would be "constructive."[79] So it was, in the view of External Affairs' resident Asia expert Arthur Menzies, who called the final declaration "a thoughtful and construct[ive] document." The conference, Menzies wrote, "seems to have given the independent nations of Asia and Africa a new sense of confidence which will not only increase their authority but may have the final result of bringing closer the time when Asia will be able to co-operate with the West without any of the after-thoughts of colonialism which have impeded good relations until now."[80]

In decolonization, the Third World found a mission statement and Canada found a process that it might gently support, while seeking to channel it in "constructive" directions. Canada first approached the "Third World" as it was starting to come into being, new states appearing on the map where once all had been coloured in the imperial kaleidoscope of red, blue, and so on. To policy makers in Ottawa, the Third World emerged initially as a problem of decolonization—the end of empire. Yet even as formal imperialism began to end, informal forms of influence of North upon South continued. Official Ottawa was concerned to ensure that a new gulf did not emerge between the Western states and the new independent states of the South, at a time when a new bipolar Cold War order was coming into being. There was no advocacy for independence. "Though we have sympathy for those who seek self-government, we also have a strong interest in preventing the development of trouble-spots that would endanger western defence," as Canada's delegation to the United Nations wrote.[81] In other words, the next angle after decolonization through which Canada viewed the Third World was the Cold War, in which Canada was embedded as a member of the Western alliance system.

Cold War Alliances and Third World Wars and Diplomatic Self-Image

Canadian diplomacy from the 1940s to the end of the 1980s was dominated by the Cold War, in which Canada was a clear partisan of one side.

A "free world" that could "contain" communism was a potent mental map.[82] In Asia, the Cold War turned hot on several occasions. Most prominently for Canadian diplomacy, that meant war in Korea (1950–53) and Vietnam (from the 1950s into the 1970s). In both cases American troops were on the ground in force, distracting the United States from the North Atlantic priorities that Ottawa always saw as central. Canadian policy makers perceived a clear national interest in seeing these Asian wars resolved peacefully. Ideally that meant keeping Korea and Vietnam as free of communism as possible, but above all it meant containing the wars rather than allowing them to spread, and ending them in ways that would see American priorities return to Western Europe and the North Atlantic, not the more "peripheral" eastern Asia.

The Cold War has been portrayed as a "long peace" by some scholars.[83] In the European context, this is true. But if the Cold War headed off World War III, it was only by diverting much conflict to the Third World, where several domestic conflicts were exacerbated by the Cold War titans each backing one side or another in civil wars, from Cambodia to the Congo. Canadian direct diplomatic interests in most of these conflicts were minimal, but diplomats worried about the effect on more direct Canadian interests. This meant, in most cases, the North Atlantic alliance. Canadian participation in the wars in Korea and Vietnam is addressed in the chapter by McKay and Swift on military connections. But Korea, where Canada took part as a belligerent, also saw foreign minister Pearson and his officials work out a role that would later be sanctified in the Canadian diplomatic self-image as mediator and peacemaker. Canadians worked especially closely with India in a series of efforts to find a peaceful solution to the Korean War that would not see Korea fall entirely to communism, but would accept a solution short of the American military goal of all-out victory. This has often been described as "the diplomacy of constraint."[84] Constraint on some limited matters there may have been, but Canada was equally constrained by the needs of alliance politics not to depart too far from the American line. After all, both countries shared a broad commitment to anticommunist alliances and collective security. This "guaranteed that differences between Canada and the United States during the Korean War would be tactical, not strategic," writes historian Robert Bothwell. "Differences there would be, but as far as Canada was concerned they would never bring into question the existence of an alliance with the United States, or its basic purpose. . . . Nor should it be forgotten that during the Korean War there were several, sometimes many, American points of view, some of them identical to what the Canadian government was saying."[85]

The Suez Crisis, the "Special Relationship" with India, and Truce Supervision in Vietnam

At the UN in the 1950s, Canada tended to seek the middle ground—as one set of instructions to the UN delegation put it, to adopt "the classical position of the silent abstainer in the face of directly conflicting attitudes by the United States and the United Kingdom."[86] Ottawa's preference for a back seat began to shift as Canadian diplomats took a position on decolonization similar to that of the United States, and Canadian activism reached its climax with the Suez crisis of 1956. This conflict saw Egypt nationalize the Suez Canal, which ran through its territory, angering the traditional imperial powers in the region, Britain and France. The two powers secretly arranged with Israel that it would invade Egypt, providing an excuse for Britain and France to intervene to "protect" the canal. This revival of "gunboat diplomacy" enraged most independent Third World governments, who would no longer blithely tolerate such attempts to flex colonial muscle. African and Asian governments demanded that Britain and France pull back. So too did the Eisenhower government in Washington, which saw its global strategies undermined by freelance imperialism by its allies. The United States government was far from enamoured of Egypt's neutralist course in international affairs and Arab nationalism, but it saw no reason to back a Franco-British adventure launched without notice to the leader of the West.

Louis St. Laurent's government in Ottawa was no keener. Suez can be seen as the first major divergence of Canadian and British foreign policy during the early Cold War. When the British sought support from the "Old Dominions," they received it from Australia and New Zealand, but St. Laurent offered them no comfort. The age of such blatant imperialism was over, he implied in a chilly message to British Prime Minister Anthony Eden. Canada could not back Britain for three reasons, he wrote. First, there was the effect on the UN. Furthermore, the invasion was sparking division within the Commonwealth. Above all, there was "a matter of deep and abiding interest to Canada, the deplorable divergence of viewpoint and policy between the United Kingdom and the United States." Canada could not look indifferently at a crisis that put Washington and London on opposite sides of the issue.[87] "The chasm opening between Britain and the United States alarmed the Canadian government and brought Canada into the Suez crisis," as historian Michael Carroll writes.[88]

Pearson, then Canada's respected foreign minister, jumped on a remark by Eden that Britain was merely seeking to keep the peace and proposed that the United Nations create and run a peacekeeping force, in which Canada was willing to play a leading role. With American backing, Pearson presented the plan at the UN, and the world body endorsed it. Britain and France gave way, under US as much as UN pressure. The United Nations Emergency Force, the original "blue helmet" peacekeeping army, was born. For this proposal, Pearson won Canada's first (and still only) Nobel Peace Prize. As McKay and Swift elaborate in this volume, for years afterwards, the incident echoed through Canadian diplomatic memory, hallowing a "cargo cult of peacekeeping" at home even as actual Canadian peacekeeping contributions declined.[89] It was true that Canadian diplomacy, in this crisis as in others, had been deft and creative. The motivation, however, was to heal a rift between Canada's key North Atlantic allies, and to avoid a situation in which the Third World would be united against Britain and France. Canada worked for peace, certainly, but above all that meant peace between allies.

Another Canadian concern was the desire to preserve the Commonwealth "bridge" between North and South. The core of this bridge, for some Canadian diplomats, was the "special relationship" between Canada and India. Ottawa and New Delhi collaborated on peacemaking efforts in a number of 1950s crises. Ties were cordial and cooperation frequent. Escott Reid, the most prominent high commissioner to India, was the key advocate of the "special relationship" before and after his India tenure. Although Pearson and several other diplomats did indeed value good working relations with the Third World's largest non-Commonwealth state, when push came to shove Ottawa prioritized North Atlantic interests above Indian links.[90]

On matters where Canadian interests were limited, Canada could defer to Indian leadership. So for instance when China cracked down harshly on Tibetan demonstrations for greater autonomy in 1959, leading to the Dalai Lama's flight to India, Ottawa did not try to make anticommunist hay. "The useful lesson in Communist imperialism may well be lost on the Asians if the Western Powers show too much eagerness to exploit it for what will seem to the Asians western Cold War purposes," as one message from the Department of External Affairs stated.[91] Canada backed a joint resolution on Tibet presented by Ireland and Malaya, but avoided comment in debate. On the other hand, when India and the United States were at loggerheads over whether to pursue the Korean War, Canadian desire to work with India took a back seat to the need to appease American emotions. India was one of the smaller players in a United Nations effort to defend anticommunist South Korea against North Korea starting in 1950. The United States was very much in command of an ostensibly UN military effort. When American-led forces drove back the North Koreans, there was a debate over whether the UN army should cross into North Korea and in effect conquer the North on behalf of the South. US pressure carried the day, and the border was crossed. China then signalled that if American armies came close to their borders, they would intervene. The signals came through India's ambassador in Beijing. They were discounted in Washington, but China duly threw its own armies into battle, driving the Americans back south (the final armistice line, today's border between the two Koreas, is not far distant from the pre-1950 border). In controversies over whether to cross the border and whether to heed Chinese warnings, India and the United States took opposite stances. Canadian policy makers often saw the wisdom in India's stances, but always felt they had to side with the United States: alliance solidarity had to prevail at key moments.[92] In the end, Canada would side with its allies, right or wrong. The Canada-India "special relationship" foundered after Ottawa accepted an invitation to serve on the truce supervision commissions created in 1954 for Vietnam, Laos, and Cambodia after France agreed to decolonize. Part of the motivation for Canada to accept an offer to serve on the commission was the need to help France out of its Indochina quagmire; another part was the chance to work with diplomats from India, who were to chair the commission (the third member, Poland, represented the Soviet bloc and was not seen as a potential collaborator). In practice, Canadian and Indian diplomats rarely saw eye to eye. The Canadians more often than not shared the opinion of American counterparts, whose anticommunist stance increasingly drew Canadians into the defence of the South Vietnamese regime. India's representatives, committed to nonalignment in the Cold War, charted a middle course between the two sides. Canadian diplomats on the ground saw this, more often than not, as flabby, amoral pandering. Given the large numbers of Canadians who served on the truce commissions, an entire generation of diplomats became more likely to be cold warriors. The bloom was off the "special relationship" rose. It faded further as the Diefenbaker government showed more sympathy with the anticommunist military government in Pakistan than with India, and vanished altogether when India used Canadian nuclear technology to explode a "peaceful nuclear device" in 1974.

Resisting Secession: Pierre Trudeau and Third World Decolonization

Coming to power in 1968, Prime Minister Pierre Trudeau's government promised to sweep away the sentimentalities and alliance preoccupations it perceived as the core of previous Canadian foreign policy. Canada would henceforth approach the world pragmatically, with an eye to promoting Canadian trade, and with a more global approach—or so the new government declared in the first formal review of Canadian foreign policy, published in 1970. There would be new, special attention paid to the Third World and to the quest for development, Trudeau declared in one of his first speeches as prime minister. Never mind that previous governments, too, had sought what they saw as Canada's national interests, worked to promote Canadian trade, and so on: the new brooms would sweep clean the cobwebs, restore vigour to Canadian foreign relations, and toss in the global perspective that world traveller Trudeau, unlike his predecessors, could offer. Yet the North Atlantic did not, as it turns out, move so very far from the core of Canadian preoccupations. When the Trudeau government sought a "third option" to diversify trade away from Canada's increasing dependence on the United States, it targeted Western Europe as prime partner. Japan, and to a lesser extent the rest of Asia, were added as afterthoughts, partly on the urging of Western Canadian voices. In the end, Trudeau's foreign policy ended up much like the policies he had promised to shelve.[93]

Trudeau-era sympathy for the Third World was best reflected through the continuation and expansion of Canadian development assistance. Trudeau worked well with Third World nationalists from Fidel Castro of Cuba to Lee Kuan Yew of Singapore. That many of these were not democrats was hardly relevant: Trudeau's promotion of human rights at home was not matched by any such advocacy abroad. Indeed, one major characteristic of Trudeau's foreign policy was to be continued under successor governments headed by Brian Mulroney, Jean Chrétien, and Stephen Harper: vocal rhetoric about human rights, accompanied by a frequent absence of any action to back up words and even active complicity with human rights violators who welcomed Canadian trade and investment.

The Trudeau government maintained the old focus on national unity in its battle with Quebec for the support of newly independent French-speaking African governments.[94] This was an issue not just of national unity, but also of how Canada would approach decolonization in action. It did so, first and foremost, as part of a domestic political struggle: Canadian mental maps placed Canada first. Nor would Canada show any sympathy for attempts to continue decolonization after the independence of African states. The attempted secession of Biafra from Nigeria became a cause célèbre among Canadian nongovernmental activists, especially as Biafrans began to starve in vast numbers. For Trudeau, battling Parti Québécois efforts to secede from Canada, this was an issue of defending the territorial integrity of an existing state, no matter how new and how fabricated that state might be. "Where's Biafra?" he famously asked.[95] He knew, of course, but his point was that it had no international legal existence as a state, and its future was no official concern of Canada's. Quebec nationalists had in many cases been inspired by the global wave of decolonization into casting their own struggle as a decolonization battle. One writer famously called the Québécois the "nègres blancs d'Amerique."[96] For the federal government, this was an invalid comparison, but it also helped to inform Canadian opposition to most efforts at secession from new states—all the more so when secession movements used the language of decolonization.

Human Rights and the Decolonization of East Timor

This applied even when secession movements were trying to reverse foreign invasion. The case of Timor-Leste (East Timor) is illustrative of Canadian opposition to secession and lack of Canadian advocacy on human rights, even in the face of one country taking over another.[97] East Timor was a former Portuguese colony that in 1974 seemed to be setting out on the same path to independence as Portugal's African colonies. That independence was aborted when Indonesian armed forces invaded at the end of 1975 and annexed East Timor as the twenty-seventh province of Indonesia. The Trudeau government raised no objection, maintained Indonesia's place as a priority country for Canadian development assistance, and quickly offered Indonesia a new line of credit. Canada would soon be siding with Indonesia against UN condemnations of its invasion and the high toll in human life of its military occupation—200,000 people, more than a quarter of the population, was a common estimate of the number of people who died under the occupation.

Prime Minister Brian Mulroney used the 1991 Commonwealth Heads of Government meeting in Zimbabwe to declare that Canada would henceforth withhold aid to chronic human rights violators. Less than a month later, Indonesian troops gunned down more than 250 Timorese pro-independence protesters. The government responded with expressions of concern and a freeze on three planned future aid projects for Indonesia, but carefully sought to insulate Canadian trade and diplomatic interests in Indonesia from these semi-sanctions. Ottawa endorsed, before and after the 1991 killings, the "territorial integrity" of Indonesia—meaning it opposed Timorese independence. Prime Minister Jean Chrétien's government increased aid to Indonesia, pushed hard for Canadian investment and trade (which duly soared), and even authorized the supply of military equipment to Indonesia (which had been suspended for Mulroney's final two years in office).

Only when Indonesia's military regime toppled in 1998 did the Canadian government endorse self-determination for East Timor, backing the decolonization of the last remnant of the Portuguese colonial empire. (Macau, Portugal's other Asian outpost, was slated for return to China in 1999.) The final decolonization of East Timor came after a 1999 referendum, the pro-independence results of which could not be derailed even by a last-ditch campaign of killing, burning, and deportation orchestrated by the Indonesian military. Canada came late to the aid of this decolonization. In doing so it prioritized Canadian trade with Indonesia, the desire to keep the rest of Indonesia united, and regional stability. The Chrétien government couched its support in the language of foreign minister Lloyd Axworthy's "human security" agenda, linking it to larger Canadian diplomatic initiatives such as Axworthy's campaign for a ban on land mines.

After the Cold War

The Cold War's end removed the central organizing frame of late-twentieth-century international relations. Gone, too, was one of the Third World's unifying concepts as a third zone outside the superpower contest. Canadian mental maps would no longer see the Global South as a Cold War battleground. But the Third World did not move to the centre. It remained a zone of conflict, seen by Canadian policy makers and the public as an often undifferentiated zone of poverty, conflict, and state failure.

The central Canadian diplomatic self-image of relations with the South has been one of a friend of Third World decolonization and development. An analysis of government policy can only conclude that this is wrong. The Canadian government has offered rhetoric on these issues, but has rarely acted out of anything other than its perceptions of Canada's national interest. As Sean Mills's contribution to this volume elaborates, it is only once we move beyond the realm of government actions that we can see the claimed altruism. Canada is not a voice for human rights or an antipoverty actor. But Canadians outside the government, increasingly, have been.

Box 6.1 Racialized Perceptions in Canadian Foreign Policy Making

The Third World spans the large majority of the world's surface and encompasses an even larger majority of the world's population. Yet Canadians' mental maps sometimes see it as a vast zone of poverty and conflict, much the same from country to country. This is especially true of Africa—not one country, as some popular accounts imply, but 54 at last count (plus two territories, Western Sahara and Somaliland, seeking their independence). Canadian policy makers have often looked at the Third World and seen sameness. The Canadian southward gaze has also been shaped by racialized perceptions—a point often overlooked in accounts of Canadian interactions with the Third World.[98] This textbox attempts to make explicit what is implicit in the body of the chapter: the role of racialized perceptions in Canadian foreign policy making. Canadian approaches toward one region have often been shaped not by the local situation itself, but by attitudes toward other regions and other conflicts.

In 1961 and 1962, for instance, two unrelated conflicts were drawing world attention toward the Congo and West New Guinea (now West Papua). The Congo dominated central Africa. Joseph Conrad famously dubbed this region "the heart of darkness." It had been colonized by a private company on behalf of King Leopold of Belgium before becoming a formal colony as the Belgian Congo. Leopold's notorious forced labour programs moderated but did not end under Belgian rule.[99] Belgium did little to prepare the Congo for independence before reluctantly acceding to Congolese demands for freedom in 1960. But Belgian troops intervened soon afterwards, and the United Nations sent peacekeepers to deal with a civil conflict. As in other decolonizations, there was no pressure from Canada on Belgium to decolonize. One Canadian ambassador wrote that the Congo was "inhabited by very backwards peoples few of whom can have any concept of government"; thus it was "inconceivable" that they could govern themselves in less than 20 years. Racialized perceptions shaped press accounts and diplomatic reporting. As independence saw Congolese troops mutiny against their Belgian officers, the *Toronto Star* headlined "Panic-Stricken Europeans Flee Congo Troop Bayonets." Canada sent off peacekeepers to join a UN force, but ensured they were not housed with nonwhite soldiers, who made up the majority of UN troops, or forced to eat too much curry with rice, the standard fare for South Asian soldiers. External Affairs asked its delegate to the UN to "exercise a restraining influence" on African and Asian diplomats who might push the UN to "extreme positions." Racist language was enough of a problem that Canadian troops had to be told to avoid calling Congoloese "Blacks, Black Bastards, Jigaboos, and Coloured."[100]

And yet, the Congo was independent and the struggle was over who was to rule, and how much freedom the country would be permitted by larger outside powers. The outcome was different in the last Asian colony of the Netherlands: West New Guinea. Indonesia claimed this territory, which had been retained by the Dutch when they recognized the independence of the rest of their Indonesian colony in 1949. The Indigenous Papuans began to claim a separate future of self-government when they saw Black American troops liberating Japanese-occupied territories in 1944. Dutch anthropologists, meanwhile, categorized the black-skinned, frizzy-haired Papuan peoples as "Pacific negroids," distinct from the "Asian" inhabitants of Indonesia. This anthropological distinction was the justification for the Dutch staying on in West New Guinea. In vain did Indonesians call it racial pseudoscience. Papuan nationalists, in common with nationalists in other countries, were soon mobilizing to demand decolonization. In 1961 the Dutch government offered to prepare its colony for independence by the decade's end; the following year it offered to give West New Guinea to the UN and let the world body supervise decolonization. Papuan nationalists made a play for African support by announcing that they were a "Pacific people" quite unlike the Indonesians, appealing on behalf of "the negroids of the Pacific to the negroids throughout the world," and declaring their country to be "New Africa." In Ottawa, images of backward Papuan headhunters and cannibals helped prevent any Canadian advocacy for decolonization. "Civilization is still in a very primitive stage" and self-government "out of the question," an early Canadian memorandum noted. Indonesian claims were also dismissed as mere "emotionalism." Only after Indonesia acquired Soviet arms and began to prepare for an invasion did Ottawa take notice. By this point, Canada's ambassador to Indonesia wrote, it did not matter too much who was "trying to tempt the Papuans down from the tree-tops." The point was to try to head off a conflict between a white NATO member and an Asian neutral state that Canada wished to keep on friendly terms with the West. Papuan independence claims, to Western diplomats, merely evoked fears of "another Congo." Where Papuan nationalists had tried to make race a diplomatic asset in Africa, this merely evoked racialized fears in Canada and its North Atlantic allies. Afraid of seeing Indonesia "go communist," US President John F. Kennedy's government intervened to force the Dutch to transfer West New Guinea to Indonesian rule, via an interim UN administration.[101]

In neither the Congo nor Papuan cases did Ottawa advocate decolonization. In both, perceptions of Africa—and the Pacific "New Africa"— as zones of conflict and primitivism played a role in shaping Canadian decisions. Indeed, the West New Guinea struggle was seen as simply a replica of the Congo conflict, in which Canada was already embroiled. Thus the Diefenbaker government rejected invitations to mediate the Dutch-Indonesian conflict and scrupulously avoided replying to Papuan calls for Canadian advocacy for their cause. Racism did not determine Canadian policy. Rather, it was more complex: racialized perceptions were part of the background to policy decisions. The same point could be made with regard to multiple Canadian approaches to the Global South.

Discussion Questions

1) To what extent were Canadian approaches to Third World decolonization formed by Canada's own journey from colony to independent state within the Commonwealth?

2) Do you agree that "mental maps" were important in the formation of Canadian foreign policy?

3) Did Canada have a Third World policy, or was Canada's political approach to the Third World simply a function of its global foreign policy with a North Atlantic focus? If it did have a distinct Third World policy (or policies) toward different regions of the Global South, what defined that policy?

4) Are there different approaches taken by the Canadian government toward Africa, Asia, and Latin America?

5) How much has government diplomacy led the agenda in Canada–Third World relations?

Further Readings

Bothwell, Robert. *Alliance and Illusion: Canada and the World, 1945–1984.* Vancouver: University of British Columbia Press, 2007.

Carroll, Michael K. *Pearson's Peacekeepers: Canada and the United Nations Emergency Force, 1956–67.* Vancouver: University of British Columbia Press, 2009.

Donaghy, Greg. "Coming Off the Gold Standard: Re-assessing the 'Golden Age' of Canadian Diplomacy." Paper presented at the University of Saskatchewan, 2009, http://www.schoolofpublicpolicy.sk.ca/_documents/outreach_event_announcements/DFAIT_symposium/Coming_off_the_Gold_Standard.pdf.

Donaghy, Greg, and Bruce Muirhead. "'Interests but No Foreign Policy': Canada and the Commonwealth Caribbean, 1941–1966." *American Review of Canadian Studies* 38, no. 3 (2008): 275–94. http://dx.doi.org/10.1080/02722010809481715.

Freeman, Linda. *The Ambiguous Champion: Canada and South Africa in the Trudeau and Mulroney Years.* Toronto: University of Toronto Press, 1997.

Gendron, Robin S. *Towards a Francophone Community: Canada's Relations with France and French Africa, 1945–1968.* Montreal: McGill-Queen's University Press, 2006.

Gendron, Robin S. "Tempered Sympathy: Canada's Reaction to the Independence Movement in Algeria, 1954–1962." *Revue de la Société historique du Canada* 9, no. 1 (1998): 225–41.

Hilliker, John, and Donald Barry. *Canada's Department of External Affairs. Vol. 1, The Early Years, 1909–1946.* Montreal: McGill-Queen's University Press, 1990.

Hilliker, John, and Donald Barry. *Canada's Department of External Affairs. Vol. 2, Coming of Age, 1946–1968.* Montreal: McGill-Queen's University Press, 1995.

Lee, Steven Hugh. *Outposts of Empire: Korea, Vietnam, and the Origins of the Cold War in Asia, 1949–1954.* Montreal: McGill-Queen's University Press, 1995.

MacFarlane, Peter. *Northern Shadows: Canadians and Central America.* Toronto: Between the Lines, 1989.

Price, John. *Orienting Canada: Race, Empire, and the Transpacific.* Vancouver: University of British Columbia Press, 2011.

Spooner, Kevin A. *Canada, the Congo Crisis, and UN Peacekeeping, 1960–64.* Vancouver: University of British Columbia Press, 2009.

Stacey, C.P. *Canada and the Age of Conflict. Vol. 1, 1867–1921.* Toronto: University of Toronto Press, 1984.

Stacey, C.P. *Canada and the Age of Conflict. Vol. II, 1921–48.* Toronto: University of Toronto Press, 1981.

Touhey, Ryan M. *Conflicting Visions: India in Canadian Foreign Policy 1941–1976.* Vancouver: University of British Columbia Press, 2015.

Webster, David. *Fire and the Full Moon: Canada and Indonesia in a Decolonizing World.* Vancouver: University of British Columbia Press, 2009.

Notes

1   J. L. Granatstein, *The Greatest Victory: Canada's One Hundred Days, 1918* (Toronto: Oxford University Press, 2014); C. P. Stacey, *Canada and the Age of Conflict, vol. 1: 1867–1921* (Toronto: University of Toronto Press, 1984); John D. Meehan, *The Dominion and the Rising Sun: Canada Encounters Japan, 1929–41* (Vancouver: University of British Columbia Press, 2006).

2   Peyton V. Lyon and Tareq Y. Ismail, eds., *Canada and the Third World* (Toronto: Macmillan, 1976).

3   Jamie Swift and Brian Tomlinson, eds., *Conflicts of Interest: Canada and the Third World* (Toronto: Between the Lines, 1991).

4   Department of Foreign Affairs, Trade and Development Canada (FATDC), "Canada Marks Third Anniversary of Syrian Crisis," March 14, 2014, http://www.international.gc.ca/media/aff/news-communiques/2014/03/14a.aspx.

5   "Canada's International Human Rights Policy," http://www.international.gc.ca/rights-droits/policy-politique.aspx.

6   Pitman Potter, Sharon Hom, Douglas Horswill, Joseph Ingram, and Robert Wright, *Advancing Canada's Engagement with Asia on Human Rights* (Vancouver: Asia Pacific Foundation, 2013), http://www.asiapacific.ca/research-report/advancing-canadas-engagement-asia-human-rights. The claim is even repeated implicitly at times in book-length journalism or scholarship. Andrew Cohen, *While Canada Slept: How We Lost Our Place in the World* (Toronto: McClelland and Stewart, 2004); Constantine Melakopides, *Pragmatic Idealism: Canadian Foreign Policy, 1945–1995* (Montreal: McGill-Queen's University Press, 1998). Excellent correctives to hagiographies of a Canadian foreign policy "golden age" are Greg Donaghy, "Coming Off the Gold Standard: Re-assessing the 'Golden Age' of Canadian Diplomacy" (paper presented at the University of Saskatchewan, 2009), http://www.schoolofpublicpolicy.sk.ca/_documents/outreach_event_announcements/DFAIT_symposium/Coming_off_the_Gold_Standard.pdf; and Adam Chapnick, "The Golden Age: A Canadian Foreign Policy Paradox," *International Journal* 64, no. 1 (Winter 2008–09): 205–21.

7   William A. Schabas, "Canada and the Adoption of the Universal Declaration of Human Rights," *McGill Law Journal* 43 (1998): 403–41; Andrew Lui, *Why Canada Cares: Human Rights and Foreign Policy in Theory and Practice* (Montreal: McGill-Queen's University Press, 2012); Jennifer Tunnicliffe, "'The Best of a

Bad Job': Canadian Participation in the Development of the International Bill of Rights, 1945–1976" (PhD diss., McMaster University, 2014).

8   Alan K. Henrikson, "Mental Maps," in *Explaining the History of American Foreign Relations*, ed. Michael J. Hogan and Thomas G. Paterson (Cambridge: Cambridge University Press, 1991); Peter Gould and Rodney White, *Mental Maps* (Harmondsworth, UK: Penguin, 1974); Howard F. Stein and William G. Niederland, eds., *Maps from the Mind: Readings in Psychogeography* (Norman: University of Oklahoma Press, 1989); Gearóid Ó Tuathail, *Critical Geopolitics: The Politics of Writing Global Space* (London: Routledge, 1996); Thongchai Winichakul, *Siam Mapped: A History of the Geo-Body of a Nation* (Honolulu: University of Hawai'i Press, 1994).

9   Carl Berger, *The Sense of Power: Studies in the Ideas of Canadian Imperialism 1867–1914* (Toronto: University of Toronto Press, 1970).

10 Edward Said, *Orientalism* (New York: Vintage, 1978); Maria Todorova, *Imagining the Balkans* (Oxford: Oxford University Press, 1997).

11 Berger, *Sense of Power*, 31.

12 King quoted in Robert Bothwell and Norman Hillmer, *The In-Between Time: Canadian External Policy in the 1930s* (Toronto: C. Clark, 1975), 141.

13 Berger, *Sense of Power*, 52.

14 Harper made the comparison explicit in a 2008 speech in Inuvik. "Prime Minister Harper Announces the John G. Diefenbaker Icebreaker Project," August 28, 2008, http://pm.gc.ca/eng/news/2008/08/28/prime-minister-harper-announces-john-g-diefenbaker-icebreaker-project#sthash.RaxwseXx.dpuf.

15 Gordon Sinclair, *Footloose in India* (1932; Toronto: McClelland and Stewart, 1966).

16 An evocative account appears in Peter Piggott, *Canada in Sudan: War Without Borders* (Toronto: Dundurn Press, 2009), 56–75.

17 Stacey, *Canada and the Age of Conflict*, 57–74; Carmen Miller, *Painting the Map Red: Canada and the South African War 1899–1902* (Montreal: McGill-Queen's University Press, 1993); Robert Bothwell, "Back to the Future: Canada and Empires," *International Journal* 59, no. 2 (Spring, 2004): 407–41.

18 Louis St. Laurent, *The Foundations of Canadian Policy in World Affairs: Duncan & John Gray Memorial Lecture* (Toronto: University of Toronto Press, 1947), http://www.russilwvong.com/future/stlaurent.html.

19 Governor of Bahamas to Colonial Secretary, April 4, 1911. *Documents on Canadian External Relations (DCER)* 1: 687.

20 Prime minister to acting Canadian high commissioner, June 3, 1916. *DCER* 1: 715.

21 Amery to Borden, August 19, 1918. *DCER* 1: 717.

22 Borden to F.H. Keefer MP, January 1, 1919. *DCER* 3: 758. For a detailed consideration that foregrounds race, see Paula Hastings, "Territorial Spoils, Transnational Black Resistance, and Canada's Evolving Autonomy during the First World War," *Histoire sociale/Social History* 47, no. 94 (June 2014): 443–70.

23 Peter MacFarlane, *Northern Shadows: Canadians and Central America* (Toronto: Between the Lines, 1989), Chapter 4.

24 A quotation taken from one of the chapter titles in Stacey, *Canada and the Age of Conflict*.

25 Dandurand himself was more subtle than later users of his metaphor. Stéphane Paquin, "Raoul Dandurand: Porte-Parole de la Conscience Universelle," in *Architects and Innovators/Architectes et Innovateurs: Building the Department of Foreign and International Trade, 1909–2009/Le développement du ministère des Affaires étrangères*

et du Commerce international, 1909–2009, ed. Greg Donaghy and Kim Richard Nossal (Montreal: Queen's Policy Studies Series, McGill-Queen's University Press, 2009), 42.

26 "Declaration of Independence," Korean Red Cross pamphlet, 1919, Korean American Digital Archive, Rev. Soon Hyun papers, box 5; Louise Yim, *My Forty Year Fight for Korea* (New York: A.A. Wyn, 1951), 120; "Korean Inventions and Discoveries," Korean National Association press release, March 12, 1920, KADA, KNA papers, box 11. Schofield likened the Japanese to a "Prussian war machine" rolling over innocent Belgium. Dorothea E. Mortimer, "Dr. Frank W. Schofield and the Korean National Consciousness," in *Korea's Response to Japan: The Colonial Period 1910–1945*, ed. Eugene Kim and Dorothea Mortimer (Kalamazoo Center for Korean Studies, Western Michigan University, 1977).

27 Margaret Macmillan, *Paris 1919: Six Months that Changed the World* (New York: Random House, 2003).

28 Edwin L. James, "Canada Offers to Take Mandate for Armenia," *New York Times*, April 23, 1920: 1.

29 Aram Adjemian, "Canada's Moral Mandate for Armenia: Sparking Humanitarian and Political Interest, 1880–1923" (MA thesis, Concordia University, 2007).

30 "Perhaps This Boy Is Needed Along with the Relief," editorial cartoon, *The Globe*, February 25, 1920.

31 H.F. Angus, "Next for Duty," *The University Magazine* 19, no. 1 (February 1920): 24–30.

32 Governor-General to Colonial Secretary, March 5, 1920. *DCER* 3: 69; Administrator to Colonial Secretary, April 1920. *DCER* 3: 70.

33 High Commissioner in London to Prime Minister, November 29, 1920, *DCER* 3: 73; PM to High Commissioner, December 1, 1920, *DCER* 3: 74.

34 Richard Veatch, *Canada and the League of Nations* (Toronto: University of Toronto Press, 1975), 52.

35 L.P. Chambers, "Give Canada Mandate for Armenia," *The Globe*, February 19, 1921, 23.

36 A chapter title from J.C.M. Ogelsby, *Gringos from the Far North* (Toronto: Macmillan, 1976).

37 John Hilliker and Donald Barry, *Canada's Department of External Affairs, vol. 1: The Early Years, 1909–1946* (Montreal: McGill-Queen's University Press, 1990), 189–90.

38 Ogelsby, *Gringos*, 44.

39 Secretary of State for External Affairs to Ambassador in China, January 3, 1946. *DCER* 12, http://epe.lac-bac.gc.ca/100/206/301/faitc-aecic/history/2013-05-03/www.international.gc.ca/department/history-histoire/dcer/details-en.asp@intRefid=11796.

40 Report on Meeting of Cabinet Committee on External Trade Policy, March 4, 1947. *DCER* 13, http://epe.lac-bac.gc.ca/100/206/301/faitc-aecic/history/2013-05-03/www.international.gc.ca/department/history-histoire/dcer/details-en.asp@intRefid=14102, Chester Ronning, *A Memoir of China in Revolution* (New York: Pantheon Books, 1974), 59.

41 Extract from Cabinet Conclusions, December 1, 1948. *DCER* 13, http://epe.lac-bac.gc.ca/100/206/301/faitc-aecic/history/2013-05-03/www.international.gc.ca/department/history-histoire/dcer/details-en.asp@intRefid=10799;

Extract from Cabinet Conclusions, December 16, 1948. *DCER* 13, http:// epe.lac-bac.gc.ca/100/206/301/faitc-aecic/history/2013-05-03/www. international.gc.ca/department/history-histoire/dcer/details-en.asp@ intRefid=10804.

42 Paul M. Evans and B. Michael Frolic, eds., *Reluctant Adversaries: Canada and the People's Republic of China 1949–1970* (Toronto: University of Toronto Press, 1991); Paul Evans, *Engaging China: Myth, Aspiration and Strategy in Canadian Policy from Trudeau to Harper* (Toronto: University of Toronto Press, 2014). See also the essays in John Meehan and David Webster, eds., "A Deeper Engagement: People, Institutions, and Cultural Connections in Canada-China Relations," *Journal of American-East Asian Relations* 20, no. 2–3 (2013).

43 Mayhew speaking in Parliament, June 29, 1950. *Canada House of Commons Debates* 4: 14370–4374.

44 Zdanov cited in Ruth McVey, *The Soviet View of the Indonesian Revolution* (Ithaca, NY: Cornell University Press, 1957); Billy Graham cited in Stephen J. Whitfield, *The Culture of the Cold War*, 2nd ed. (Baltimore, MD: Johns Hopkins University Press, 1996).

45 Pearson, "The Development of Canadian Foreign Policy," *Foreign Affairs* 30, no. 1 (October 1951): 17–30.

46 John Bartlett Brebner, *North Atlantic Triangle: The Interplay of Canada, the United States and Great Britain* (New Haven, CT: Yale University Press, 1945).

47 Pearson, "Development."

48 St. Laurent, "The Preservation of Civilization," *External Affairs Statements and Speeches (S&S)* 50/43 (speech to University of Toronto convocation, October 27, 1950).

49 Heeney, "Canada and the Atlantic Community," *S&S* 51/11 (speech to Canadian Club, Montreal, March 19, 1951).

50 Pearson, "The North Atlantic Community," *S&S* 52/6 (speech at Commercial Club, Halifax, January 26, 1952).

51 "Canada and the Colombo Plan," speech by R.G. Nik Cavell to the Empire Club, Toronto, December 4, 1952, http://speeches.empireclub.org/60071/data.

52 SSEA to SSDA, December 23, 1942. LAC, RG 25, file 180(s).

53 See for instance London letter A.52, January 29, 1946, LAC, RG25, vol. 3686, file 5475-N-40C [1]; Holmes memorandum to the minister, December 22, 1949, RG25, vol. 3686, file 5475-N-40C [4.1].

54 New York telegram 179, November 14, 1946, LAC, RG25, vol. 3686, file 5475-N-40C [3].

55 USSEA to SSEA, from San Francisco, May 26, 1945, LAC, RG25, vol. 5773, file 180(s).

56 New York telegram 179, November 14, 1946, LAC, RG25, vol. 3686, file 5475-N-40C [3].

57 Dale Thomson, *Louis St. Laurent: Canadian* (Toronto: Macmillan, 1967). Compton, ironically enough, exists on lands originally home to the Abenaki peoples, whose presence has now been erased by both the Canadian and American governments, its name an erasure of earlier names. This echoes the fate of the Iroquois homeland in what is now upstate New York, where "an alien historical landscape has been laid down like a rug beneath which the real history has been swept. Iroquois places have been renamed Syracuse, Rome, Ithaca, Homer, Ovid,

as if a place could be transformed by logomancy from one world to another." Ronald Wright, *Stolen Continents: The "New World" Through Indian Eyes* (New York: Houghton Mifflin, 1992): 121. The names suggest, indeed, that it is settler society that has been here since time immemorial.

58 Robert J. McMahon, *Colonialism and Cold War: The United States and the Struggle for Indonesian Independence, 1945–49* (Ithaca, NY: Cornell University Press, 1981).

59 Hector Mackenzie, "An Old Dominion and the New Commonwealth: Canadian Policy on the Question of India's Membership, 1947–49," *Journal of Imperial and Commonwealth History* 27, no. 3: 84.

60 Oral history interview of Lord Home (formerly Alec Douglas-Home), by Peter Stursberg, October 1, 1978, Cold Stream Scotland, LAC, Peter Stursberg fonds, MG31 D78, vol. 28.

61 Memorandum from Under-Secretary of State for External Affairs to Secretary of State for External Affairs, December 9, 1955. *DCER* 22.

62 Report from Minister of Mines and Technical Surveys George Prudham, Canada's Special Envoy to the Ghana Independence Celebrations, to Prime Minister, March 28, 1957. *DCER* 22.

63 McDonnell letter to Diefenbaker, September 11, 1957. LAC, vol. 4300, file 11038-AB-17A-40.

64 Richard Stubbs, *Hearts and Minds in Guerrilla Warfare: The Malayan Emergency, 1948–1960* (Singapore: Oxford University Press, 1989); Richard Stubbs and Mark S. Williams, "The Poor Cousin? Canada-ASEAN Relations," *International Journal* 64, no. 4 (Autumn 2009): 927–39; Richard Stubbs, "Canada's Relations with Malaysia: Picking Partners in ASEAN," *Pacific Affairs* 63, no. 3 (Autumn 1990): 351–66.

65 Greg Donaghy and Bruce Muirhead, "'Interests but No Foreign Policy': Canada and the Commonwealth Caribbean, 1941–1966," *American Review of Canadian Studies* 38, no. 3 (2008): 275–94.

66 Lester B. Pearson, foreword to *Indonesian Independence and the United Nations*, by Alastair Taylor (Ithaca, NY: Cornell University Press, 1960).

67 David Webster, *Fire and the Full Moon: Canada and Indonesia in a Decolonizing World* (Vancouver: University of British Columbia Press, 2009), Chapter 1.

68 Instructions to Canadian delegation to UN General Assembly and memorandum to cabinet, October 8, 1952. *DCER* 18.

69 "USSEA memorandum for SSEA," memorandum for file on meeting with French ambassador by acting head American and Far Eastern Division Arthur Menzies, October 18, 1949. *DCER* 15; Steven Hugh Lee, *Outposts of Empire: Korea, Vietnam, and the Origins of the Cold War in Asia, 1949–1954* (Montreal: McGill-Queen's University Press, 1995), 55–57.

70 Robin S. Gendron, "Tempered Sympathy: Canada's Reaction to the Independence Movement in Algeria, 1954–1962," *Revue de la Société historique du Canada* 9, no. 1 (1998): 225–41.

71 Consul General in New York to Secretary of State for External Affairs, November 30, 1946. *DCER* 12, http://epe.lac-bac.gc.ca/100/206/301/ faitc-aecic/history/2013-05-03/www.international.gc.ca/department/ history-histoire/dcer/details-en.asp@intRefid=11969; Secretary of State for External Affairs to Consul General in New York, November 2, 1946. *DCER*

12, http://epe.lac-bac.gc.ca/100/206/301/faitc-aecic/history/2013-05-03/ www.international.gc.ca/department/history-histoire/dcer/details-en.asp@ intRefid=12215.

72 Linda Freeman, *The Ambiguous Champion: Canada and South Africa in the Trudeau and Mulroney Years* (Toronto: University of Toronto Press, 1997).

73 Diefenbaker cited in Freeman, *Ambiguous Champion*, 25.

74 Freeman, *Ambiguous Champion*, 5.

75 Robin S. Gendron, *Towards a Francophone Community: Canada's Relations with France and French Africa, 1945–1968* (Montreal: McGill-Queen's University Press, 2006); Thessa Girard-Bougoin, "La Politique Étrangère Canadienne à l'Égard de la Décolonization de l'Afrique de 1945 à 1960" (PhD diss., University of Ottawa, 2013).

76 Extract of Report by Ambassador in France, December 1960. *DCER* 27, http://epe. lac-bac.gc.ca/100/206/301/faitc-aecic/history/2013-05-03/www.international. gc.ca/department/history-histoire/dcer/details-en.asp@intRefid=13148.

77 Record of discussion by Canadian heads of mission, Paris: October 29, 1959. *DCER* 26, http://epe.lac-bac.gc.ca/100/206/301/faitc-aecic/history/ 2013-05-03/www.international.gc.ca/department/history-histoire/dcer/ details-en.asp@intRefid=11273.

78 John S. Saul, *Canada and Mozambique* (Toronto: Development Education Centre, 1974), 70.

79 Secretary of State for External Affairs to Canadian High Commission in New Delhi, April 12, 1955. *DCER* 21: 1615–16.

80 Secretary of State for External Relations circular on Bandung, July 27, 1955. *DCER* 21: 1616–25.

81 Chairman, Delegation to the General Assembly of the United Nations, to Secretary of State for External Affairs, December 29, 1951. *DCER* 18, http://epe. lac-bac.gc.ca/100/206/301/faitc-aecic/history/2013-05-03/www.international. gc.ca/department/history-histoire/dcer/details-en.asp@intRefid=3708.

82 Alan K. Henrikson, "The Geographical 'Mental Maps' of American Foreign Policy Makers," *International Political Science Review* 1, no. 4 (1980).

83 Most prominently, John Lewis Gaddis, "The Long Peace: Elements of Stability in the Postwar International System," *International Security* 10, no. 4 (1986): 99–142.

84 Lee, *Outposts of Empire*; Denis Stairs, *The Diplomacy of Constraint: Canada, the Korean War and the United States* (Toronto: University of Toronto Press, 1974); Robert Prince, "The Limits of Constraint: Canadian-American Relations and the Korean War 1950–1," *Journal of Canadian Studies*, 27 (Winter 1992–3): 129–52; Greg Donaghy, "Pacific Diplomacy: Canadian Statecraft and the Korean War, 1950–53," in *Canada and Korea: Perspectives 2000*, ed. Rick Guisso and Yong-sik Yoo (Toronto: Centre for Korean Studies, 2001), 81–96; John Price, "The Cat's Paw: Canada and the United Nations Temporary Commission on Korea," *Canadian Historical Review* 85, no. 2 (June 2004), 297–324.

85 Robert Bothwell, *Alliance and Illusion: Canada and the World, 1945–1984* (Vancouver: University of British Columbia Press, 2007), 84–85.

86 "Final Report on Item 60, The Question of Tunisia," January 15, 1953. *DCER* 19.

87 Eden to St. Laurent, October 30, 1956. *DCER* 22; St. Laurent to Eden, October 31, 1956. *DCER* 22.

88   Michael K. Carroll, *Pearson's Peacekeepers: Canada and the United Nations Emergency Force, 1956–67* (Vancouver: University of British Columbia Press, 2009), 3.

89   Robert Bothwell, "The Canadian Isolationist Tradition," *International Journal* 54, no. 9 (1998–99): 86.

90   Escott Reid, *Envoy to Nehru* (Toronto: Oxford University Press, 1981); Greg Donaghy and Stéphane Roussel, eds., *Escott Reid: Diplomat and Scholar* (Montreal: McGill-Queen's University Press, 2004); Ryan M. Touhey, *Conflicting Visions: India in Canadian Foreign Policy 1941–1976* (Vancouver: University of British Columbia Press, 2015).

91   Secretary of State for External Affairs to Permanent Representative to United Nations, April 7, 1959. *DCER* 26; for early Canada-Tibet relations and links to key documents, see the Canada Tibet Committee's chronology at http://www.tibet.ca/en/tibet_and_canada/government_relations.

92   John Hilliker and Donald Barry, *Canada's Department of External Affairs, vol. 2: Coming of Age, 1946–1968* (Montreal: McGill-Queen's University Press, 1995), 80–81.

93   Department of External Affairs, Foreign Policy for Canadians (Ottawa: Queen's Printer, 1970); Ivan Head and Pierre Trudeau, *The Canadian Way: Shaping Canada's Foreign Policy, 1968–1984* (Toronto: McClelland and Stewart, 1995); J.L. Granatstein and Robert Bothwell, *Pirouette: Pierre Trudeau and Canadian Foreign Policy* (Toronto: University of Toronto Press, 1991).

94   Gendron, *Towards a Francophone Community.*

95   Bothwell, *Alliance and Illusion*, 307.

96   Pierre Vallières, *Nègres blancs d'Amerique* (Montreal: Parti Pris, 1968); David Meren, "An Atmosphere of Libération: The Role of Decolonization in the France-Quebec Rapprochement of the 1960s," *Canadian Historical Review* 92, no. 2 (2011): 263–94.

97   This section is based on Webster, *Fire and the Full Moon*, Chapter 6.

98   John Price, *Orienting Canada: Race, Empire, and the Transpacific* (Vancouver: University of British Columbia Press, 2011).

99   Adam Hochschild, *King Leopold's Ghost: A Story of Greed, Terror, and Heroism in Colonial Africa* (London: Macmillan, 1998).

100 Kevin A. Spooner, *Canada, the Congo Crisis, and UN Peacekeeping, 1960–64* (Vancouver: University of British Columbia Press, 2009), 18, 27, 73, 140, 153.

101 Webster, *Fire and the Full Moon*, 105, 119, 121.

7

Military Intervention and Securing the Third World, 1945–2014

IAN MCKAY AND JAMIE SWIFT

The Somalia Scandal

Around 8:45 p.m. on March 16, 1993, 16-year-old Shidane Abukar Arone entered an empty US army compound just to the west of that occupied by No.2 Commando of the Canadian Airborne Regiment Battle Group (the "Airborne") near Belet Huen, Somalia. What followed would come to be regarded as a revealing moment in Canada's relationship with the Third World in general and its traditions of peacekeeping and military intervention in particular.

For over a century Somalia, strategically positioned for entrepreneurs shipping oil and other commodities through the Suez Canal, served as a geopolitical pinball for Europe's great powers. Somalia became independent in 1960, and its predominantly nomadic and pastoral people lived under a succession of authoritarian regimes, backed by various Cold War patrons seeking to control the territory. After the regime of one Soviet-supported dictator collapsed, amidst brutal campaigns against his opponents, the United Somali Congress failed to unify the country, and Somalia began its descent into the chaos of a "failed state" (in the fashionable expression of some international relations specialists). By 1992 the capacity of Somalis to feed themselves had been depleted by years of conflict, and their country was awash with imported weaponry. A complex, clan-based society was fractured and people began to flee, with Canada a destination of choice. The Red Cross estimated that 4.5 million people faced starvation and issued a warning: "Only a global approach can prevent a disaster on an unprecedented scale." The Red Cross found itself spending 20 per cent of its total world-wide budget on emergency aid to a single country. Estimates of malnutrition reached "horrifying levels" in the area around Belet Huen and in the refugee camps near Merca.[1]

The Canadian military arrived in early 1992, part of "Operation Deliverance." The troops were operating not as a traditional "Chapter Six" UN peacekeeping force—lightly armed and responsible for investigation, mediation, and conciliation—but a "Chapter Seven" mission, authorized to use force. Many of them said they were glad to be involved in a peace-enforcement operation that meant "real soldiering," and not a traditional UN peacekeeping mission with its blue berets, complicated negotiations, and often indecisive outcomes.[2]

Yet, after three months, the soldiers were frustrated by the Somalia they had encountered—the dust, the punishing heat, the looting. Some, having come through training exercises that combined brutality with racism, despised the very people they were supposedly helping. On the morning of March 16 their commanding officer had ordered his men to set up a patrol to catch any intruder and make an example of him: "Abuse [the intruders] if you have to," he was remembered to have said. Did he mean to say that the soldiers had the right to use force to apprehend an intruder? Or did he mean that they had the right to harm a prisoner after capture, to make an example out of him?[3]

When Sgt. Joseph Hillier caught sight of Arone entering the compound, he immediately assumed the teenager was a looter. He chased him. The fleeing teenager spotted a portable toilet and ran inside. Hillier wrenched open the door, pulled him out, and applied plastic handcuffs. Arone offered no resistance. He was wearing loose-fitting civilian clothes—ones unsuitable for any nighttime looting raid on the compound. Very likely he was doing what he told the Canadian peacekeepers he was doing—looking for a lost child.

Earlier that same month, soldiers from the Airborne, conventionally described in media accounts as an "elite" outfit, had gunned down Abdi Hamdare and Ahmad Aruush, allegedly for breaching the compound's security fence. Hamdare and Aruush were shot from behind as they fled; Aruush was finished off at close range. Captain Michel Rainville was charged in connection with the incident but acquitted on the grounds that he was following orders. He stated that when local Somalis breached the wire border the act "clearly" constituted "an act of sabotage or an act of terrorism." (The Canadians, it later came out, were putting out food and water as bait to attract intruders.) Rainville's superior, Lieutenant-Colonel Carol Mathieu, congratulated his man on his performance. Army commanders in Somalia apparently saw the shootings as part of the hard work of peacekeeping. Mathieu was also acquitted after being charged with negligence. Army physician Major Barry Armstrong examined the dead and wounded Somalis after the shooting and wrote to his wife about "a very big racist thing going on here."[4]

Close to 10 p.m., Arone was left alone with two of his captors. At least one had been drinking heavily. They proceeded to torture the teenager. They struck him on the shins and on the face with an iron bar. They kicked him with their combat boots. They used a cigar to burn the soles of his feet.

One of them told another: "You've got a good trophy there, sir." They took photographs.

While the ordeal was going on, some 80 soldiers, according to one estimate, could hear the teenager's screams. One soldier compared Arone's cries to an experience he remembered from his rural childhood when animals were slaughtered on the family farm. "If an animal was not put down properly then as they were finished off they would still be alive and conscious, and that sound was very close to what I heard." Arone died around midnight.[5]

Most of the facts eventually came to light due to Major Barry Armstrong's refusal to go along with the military's attempted cover-up, and to the persistence of a handful of journalists. The military hierarchy attempted to stymie the release of information. Only two days after the army had attempted to showcase its "hearts and minds" humanitarian effort at Belet Huen by opening a school it had rebuilt, the CBC reported the first allegations of a cover-up in the murder of Shidane Arone. The two years that followed saw a steady drip-drip of revelations that prolonged public interest in Canadian crimes in Somalia. Several soldiers— but no one over the rank of major—were convicted in relation to the killings in Somalia. Not one would serve more than two years in prison. By January 1995 the CBC was broadcasting videotapes of the Airborne Regiment's hazing rituals. They showed simulated acts of sodomy, a black soldier smeared with feces spelling out "KKK," and a soldier declaring that Somalis were not starving but that "they never work, they're lazy, they're slobs, and they stink."[6]

By March 1995 Somalia and the Canadian Airborne Regiment were attracting so much attention that then Prime Minister Jean Chrétien's Liberal government disbanded the regiment and appointed a three-person Commission of Inquiry to look into what had become known as "The Somalia Affair." The commission was stonewalled by the Department of National Defence, delaying repeatedly in the face of orders to produce all documentation related to the scandal. With an election looming, a nervous government ordered the commission to complete its work immediately. An old boys' network seemed intent on containing the story. General Jean Boyle, the Chief of Defence Staff, was forced to resign in disgrace, but ultimately the inquiry was shut down before it could reach any conclusions about the wider significance of Arone's death. The investigators never did visit Somalia. Much of the story—including what Somalis themselves made of the Canadians—remains untold.[7]

The incident came to crystallize three distinct ways of looking at Canada's frequent post-1945 military interventions into the Third World.

For one increasingly powerful and energetic group—call them the *New Warriors*—Arone's death came about because Canadians had forgotten they are a warrior nation. According to this perspective, the country, coddled by a maternalistic and suffocating welfare state, perhaps softened by the peace-and-love ethos of the 1960s, had forgotten the true nature of war and of Canada itself. Arone's killing proved the country had taken a wrong turn in the 1960s (or perhaps, some said, the 1940s) when it turned its back on soldiering and smiled upon social welfare. The crimes in Somalia were committed by men who were neither true soldiers nor true Canadians. They were products of a system that failed to weed out the unfit and incompetent and did not provide opportunities for soldiers to be "blooded"—brought under actual fire—for until that happened, no one could know who were the fittest, who deserved to survive, and those who were the misfits who deserved to be weeded out.[8] For some New Warriors, the Somalia Affair was, among other events in the 1990s, a call-to-arms to return to the martial and global glories of the British Empire, and to create in Canada a culture celebrating militarism, hierarchy, and the "British Race."

For a second group, the *Liberal Internationalists*, Arone's death came about because of a few bad apples, not because of a fundamental flaw in Canada or in its stance toward the Third World. The killers were in no way typical of a country founded upon multiculturalism, global peacekeeping, and global citizenship, committed to a strong social safety net and to a consensual, collaborative, community-oriented approach to shared problems. Within this liberal framework, Canadian history at home and abroad is a history of the reasonable compromises achieved by a fair-minded people, offering a politics of civility, compassion, and humanitarianism to a wanting world. Lester B. Pearson and his tradition of peacekeeping is often cited as the best example of Canadian liberal humanitarianism. If things sometimes go wrong, as in Somalia, far more often they go right—in the work of Canadian NGOs, in the valiant efforts of Canadian soldiers from Egypt to Afghanistan to bring order and good governance to Third World populations, and in all the institutions Liberal Internationalists have so painstakingly created and in which they take great pride—the World Trade Organization, the World Bank, the North Atlantic Treaty Organization, and the United Nations.

Finally, there has recently arisen a third approach, one we shall call *Critical Realism*, which encourages a different way of looking at Canada in the world. Within this framework, Arone's death was just one of thousands either directly perpetrated or indirectly facilitated by Canadians in many years of engagement with the Third World, in Africa as part of British imperialism and in Vietnam as collaborator with the United States. Paralleling patterns of imperial conquest and cultural genocide within Canada itself, Canadian soldiers and civilians have often sought to impose their own ideas of free enterprise and liberal governance outside the country—peaceably if they can, violently if they must—often through the policies of the very institutions Liberal Internationalists cherish. As Dubinsky and Epprecht explore further in this volume, in 2013 the federal government announced it was making "economic diplomacy" in service of business the centrepiece of its foreign policy. It was merely making explicit what had long been implicit: Canada's complicated, intense, often violently exploitative, and generally pro-business relationship with the Third World.

Our core argument is this: the militarists we call the "New Warriors" have since the 1990s launched a systematic and well-funded official campaign whose ultimate objective is the negation of the central myths and symbols of the postwar Canadian state—the peaceable kingdom, the just society, multicultural tolerance, parliamentary democracy, and reasoned public debate—and their replacement by vastly different conceptions: the warrior nation, universal commodification, racial profiling, leadership from the top down, and permanent political polarization. Placing Canada on a permanent war footing, they see in each military intervention into the Third World an opportunity not just to change the target of the intervention but the culture and politics of Canada. Their agenda can only be understood if one grasps the underlying contradictions of Canada's position with respect to the Third World.

The "New Warrior" Framework

The crimes against Arone and other Somalis could be explained, said one of the key New Warriors, David Bercuson, as products of a system that failed to weed out the unfit and incompetent and did not provide opportunities for soldiers to be blooded—brought under actual fire. They were the results of a softened Canada addle-brained by talk of peace and neglectful of its martial past and future. They arose in an institution and a country in which misfits had not been weeded out and the fittest not placed in positions of leadership. Writing in *Significant Incident: Canada's Army, the Airborne, and the Murder in Somalia* (1996), Bercuson uses Arone's death as a confirmation of his case against government spending on health and other social services—the welfare state—whose complete destruction ("with gusto") he had urged two years before.[9] *Significant Incident* was an early New Warrior manifesto for a new army and a new Canada. It not only celebrated the martial virtues of a bygone age, but also called out for a great leader capable of defending those values in the future. The military and civilian leaders of the 1990s were not up to the job. They had forgotten an eternal truth: war is a permanent, unchanging, essential, and precious aspect of humanity, as "old as civilization itself," a constant "since the first dawn." To avert your eyes from this stern Darwinian truth (or to engage with the extensive anthropological counterevidence that radically complicates it) is to engage in liberal daydreams. Abandoning war means abandoning this fundamental evolutionary truth, threatening to rob soldiers of their moments of manliness. The true Canadian exults in the awful beauty of war, in horizons alight with gun flashes, with the devotion of soldiers to their comrades-in-arms.

Significant Incident is an early outline of the arguments that would later become a taken-for-granted feature of Canadian politics. Canada is founded on war. Its warriors are its heroes. Its best leaders understand that, founded upon war, the country can only flourish through war—which is the basis of our economy and whose discipline and hierarchy should set the pattern of our daily lives. Those who question this position merely reveal their defective Canadianism. As the popular bumper sticker says, "If you don't stand behind our troops, you are welcome to stand in front of them." At the heart of the crisis gripping the army in 1996, and by extension the country, was the search for great leaders, "true warriors," those whose excellence and courage in battle would "set the tone for the entire chain of command."[10] A Canada that turns its back on battle, a Canada run by bureaucrats and civilian busybodies: here is the Canada that killed Shidane Abukar Arone. He died because, in the decades of darkness in which Canada forgot its martial nature, its best soldiers were not sent to Somalia.

Some might say that Bercuson was an extremist voice crying in the wilderness. Yet just over a decade later, his views became part of a comprehensive, often state-sponsored, well-funded chorus of militarists. In *Whose War Is It? How Canada Can Survive in the Post-9/11 World* (2007), historian and Canadian War Museum director J.L. Granatstein detailed what a real leader would tell Canadians. He would tell them that they are engaged in a global war on terror, one that calls upon each of them to be vigilant at all times against enemies within. And this tough-minded spirit should animate Canada as it engages with a wider world rife with terrorists. This re-energized Canada will have escaped from the "harmful idealization of peacekeeping" and will now stand ready to defend, militarily, its *hard* interests—an "open economy," a "pluralistic society," and, of primary importance, a positive relationship with the United States. For the man considered by some to be "Canada's national historian," to be a Canadian is to understand that the Canadian past was basically about war and the Canadian present is basically about accommodating the United States, the country's "largest customer, best friend, and ultimate defender." Only misguided romantics—prone to what Granatstein calls "naïve foolishness"—could miss these truths about history. They also hold "moralizing" views and are often anti-American purveyors of "a poison afflicting the Canadian body politic."

For Granatstein, perhaps the poison-purveyors' most odious nest can be found in "deeply pacifist and anti-military Quebec." For him, that province played a damaging role in preventing Canada from uniting with its US-led allies to invade Iraq in 2003. Perhaps a future prime minister—or even the one elected while Granatstein was writing his book—would finally level with Canadians who cling to romantic dreams of a peaceful world. Granatstein imagines what he might say: "Canada has a dominant cultural pattern comprising Judeo-Christian ethics, the progressive spirit of the Enlightenment, and the institutions and values of British political culture."[11]

The views of Bercuson and Granatstein have become part of an ambitious official attempt to reshape Canadian history and politics. New museums are built, and old ones redesigned, to suit the New Warrior agenda. Remembrance Day is transformed from a commemoration of the young victims of war to the celebration of Canadian victors. Expressways become highways of heroes. Streets and squares, radio serials and politicians' soundbites all sing the praises of our valiant armed men and women.

In some respects—as in the federal government's blatant harnessing of foreign policy to the demands of business, especially, as Dubinsky and Epprecht show in this volume, Canadian mining multinationals—this program is breaking new ground. By plainly making Canadian Business into the Business of Canada, we see a broader agenda of what is known as "neoliberalism," that is, the imposition of market criteria on every feasible aspect of social and economic life. Yet in many other respects, this framework for Canada borrows its concepts of race and nationhood from an older British imperialism. The antique concept of the "British Race" had once been consigned to the attic, but it has nowadays been dusted off and put to new use. Prime Minister Stephen Harper proclaimed the achievements of this Race, ones that have worked "to the joy, and peace, and glory of mankind."[12] In the Harper government's revamped *Citizenship Guide*, aspiring Canadians are taught to revere a succession of Canadian heroes, some going well before the country's Confederation in 1867. These men included those British soldiers who were complicit in mass death in India in the 1850s and administrators responsible for concentration camps in South Africa in the 1900s. The old ideals of a *Pax Britannica*—the "White Man's Burden" of Rudyard Kipling—are once again in common currency. Such terms as "Dominion" and such ideals as "Monarchism" regain their lost lustre.[13] Although in the new Imperialism the Empire's headquarters have shifted across the Atlantic to the United States, it still speaks for the "English-speaking peoples" and their higher values. As Winston Churchill once explained in his multivolume *History of the*

English-Speaking Peoples, Anglos—that "special edition of humankind"—had been the world's great successes—in war, commerce, and politics—because they remained true to the individualistic insights of liberalism.[14] Now, confronting worldwide conspiracies in the Third World, first Communist subversion and now "Islamo-fascism," Anglo-America fights for the entire planet.

Under the New Warriors, spending on defence skyrocketed, attaining its highest level since 1945, exceeding the levels attained in the Cold War. The $492-billion Canada First Defence Strategy, introduced in 2008, linked vastly enhanced military spending to what it calls "Canadian values." What are these? In the New Warriors' conception, some countries—those with strong leaders, strong armies, strong corporations—will win. Weak countries—whose armies are burdened with peacekeeping and whose soft-hearted governments have not confronted the eternal realities of blood and soil that define true masculinity and real nationhood—will lose. Only a Canada that is not afraid to stand side by side with its partners in the United States and Britain can measure up to a world threatened as never before by cunning and cruel enemies whose ways are not our ways. Thus it follows that not only high policy but daily life itself must be militarized. School-children must be instructed in the patently false notion that Canada was born on Vimy Ridge in 1917; dissenting Islamic Canadians must be disciplined and in some cases imprisoned without due process; and the country must sign on to war after war—with Afghanistan and Libya seemingly the first in a long series—to police the boundaries of the West. If much of the New Warriors' move on the Third World is blatantly motivated by corporate interests, it would be a mistake to overlook how much it is also shaped by age-old notions of white Britons teaching salutary lessons to peoples of colour around the globe.

The New Warriors' stance with respect to the Third World thus becomes clear: the staunch defence of transnational corporations, an insistence on Canada's civilizational superiority, and a celebration of the country's enhanced military might to achieve the wider objectives of the Anglosphere—that union of the United States and Britain that carries forward the liberal heritage of the "English-speaking peoples."

The "Liberal Internationalist" Framework

Critical realists cast a skeptical eye upon the New Warriors, seeing in their work a rerun of ancient myths of racial superiority and imperial progress that come with a proven track record of toxicity. Yet they are not any more convinced by the Liberal Internationalists. Preaching humanitarianism to the world, they too have often acted in the callous ways of empires the world over.

Much of the New Warrior worldview was developed in Canada after the 1990s, and was intended explicitly to undermine the liberal (and often Liberal) assumptions that New Warriors blame for softening Canadians and blinding them to the realities of the world. For New Warriors, the very words "peacekeeping" and "Pearson" have become anathema—which explains the 2013 demise (primarily because of a shortage of federal funds) of the Lester B. Pearson Canadian International Peacekeeping Training Centre. When opened in the mid-1990s at the former Canadian Forces Base Cornwallis in Nova Scotia, the centre was regarded as a world leader in peacekeeper training. For New Warriors, the entire peacekeeping tradition savours of a romantic sentimentality regarding a jungle-like world. When it comes to Canada's relations with the Third World, peacekeeping is out—and corporate investment, and if necessary the military muscle to defend it, is in.

But the New Warriors are greatly oversimplifying the views of their liberal enemies. Young Pearson was as much an admirer of the British Empire as Stephen Harper: in one scholarly piece he wrote in the 1920s as a university professor, he extolled the "westward march" of an Empire in which the "recognition" of cultural differences would provide a basis for a "deeper unity." Pearson praised an Empire in which all manner of people, even those he termed "low specimens" of humanity, might be wisely governed and slowly civilized, as they gradually assimilated the culture of their imperial betters.[15] As Webster also explores in this book, Pearson was one of the key thinkers behind the North Atlantic Treaty Organization (NATO), which he thought offered the West a wonderful opportunity "to promote the economic well being of their peoples, and to achieve social justice, thereby creating an overwhelming superiority of moral, material, and military force on the side of peace and progress."[16] When Canada entered its first post-1945 war in the Third World in Korea (1950–53), Pearson expressed private misgivings—he even thought the war might be illegal under international law and was aghast at American plans to use atomic bombs in both Korea and China—but public support. He was an enthusiastic Cold Warrior, who crusaded vigorously against the peace movement and went along with purges of suspected radicals from the civil service (he likened the government's struggle against the Canadian Peace Congress to the battles waged by "our forefathers" against "savages lurking in the woods"). The Liberal government also launched a furious campaign against homosexuals in the civil service as well as people suspected of harbouring pro-Soviet sympathies, many of whom were persecuted and hounded from their jobs.[17]

Webster has, in this volume, explained Canada's ambiguous positions with respect to decolonization. Canadian commitment to the US side of the Cold War binary always trumped any imagined sympathies for nations attempting, especially through revolutionary means, to attain sovereignty. Canada's perspective on Vietnam provides a classic example. Through a quarter-century of French and American attempts to stop a revolution in Vietnam (1950–75), Pearson crafted a Canadian role of "Quiet Diplomacy" that amounted to "Quiet Acceptance" of US policies in Southeast Asia and throughout the Third World. Canadian businesses made handsome profits from the war, marketing everything from weaponry to the famous Green Berets. Throughout the Vietnam War, Canada proclaimed peace and abetted war.[18]

In the post-1945 period Pearson became a key figure in establishing a treaty that returned the world to conventional balance-of-power diplomacy, placing national armies and military alliances once more at the centre of world affairs. The Third World would soon become the place where the rival power blocs fought proxy wars through client states. Pearson did not break with, but preserved an "Atlanticist" approach to the Cold War that saw Canada, for the first time, permanently affiliated with (and subordinate to) US foreign policy. He was as much a Cold Warrior as anyone.

So why would New Warriors resist him and seek to erase this legacy? Because Pearson also came to represent an alternative voice at a time of enormous international anxiety—one that offered the non-Anglo world, even the Third World, some small measure of recognition. Pearson, the winner of the Nobel Prize for Peace in 1957, is also remembered as a master diplomat, a father of the United Nations, a self-deprecating man of peace, and the prime minister who helped usher in medicare, bilingualism, and Expo '67—the very "liberal Canada" the New Warriors have sworn to uproot. And however accommodating to US interests Pearson may have been, he was no militarist. On the fiftieth anniversary of the Battle of Vimy Ridge, Pearson reminded veterans at an Ottawa dinner of the "stupid bloodletting" that characterized so much of World War I.[19]

Like his predecessors Mackenzie King and St. Laurent, Pearson wanted an orderly international world engineered through an international regime of collective security; he did not want entanglements that might draw Canada into a potentially endless series of distant wars. Canada's most famous diplomat hoped, vainly as it turned out, that the Atlantic pact would be more than "an instrument of unimaginative militarism." Even when it came to designing military alliances such as NATO, he worked hard, if unsuccessfully, to use Article 2 of the NATO Treaty—it came to be called "the Canadian article"—to make the alliance into one that promoted cultural, social, and economic cooperation among the European and North American signatories. Pearson also wanted the United Nations to become an agency that worked alongside NATO to make war a distant memory.

The concept of peaceful mediation of international disputes came to be firmly attached to his name. Pearson introduced a motion in the United Nations in November 1956, at a time when Israel, France, and Great Britain had invaded Egypt, to create a peacekeeping force—ultimately known as the United Nations Emergency Force (UNEF)—designed to preserve peaceful borders while a lasting settlement was being worked out. The motion and its consequences won Pearson the Nobel Prize and caused Canadian chests to swell—although in fact the motion had been drafted by the US ambassador, Henry Cabot Lodge, and its on-the-ground implementation was the work of General E.L.M. (Tommy) Burns, the Canadian commander of the UN's first major peacekeeping force. To this day, postage stamps, high schools, institutes, and the country's largest airport have all come to be attached to Pearson's name. And in much of the world, despite the past two decades and a good deal of countervailing evidence, Canada is still celebrated as a supporter of peacekeeping—the "peaceable kingdom" working for a peaceable world.

For the Liberal Internationalists, Canada's role in the UN in general and peacekeeping in particular stand out as inspiring moments in the country's history—ones in which Canadians stood for something distinctive and humane in the world, a North American democracy that provided an alternative to British and US gunboat diplomacy. Although the Canadian military had already been involved in truce supervision along the India-Pakistan border and in Indochina, UNEF marked the beginning of an era termed "classical peacekeeping"—the positioning of UN forces between two warring parties that have agreed to a ceasefire. It has been the image of lightly armed Canadians doing this dull but often dangerous work that, in the decades that followed, came to have such wide appeal in Canada.

Tommy Burns, the on-the-ground implementer of Pearson's scheme, was a much-decorated World War I combat veteran and a top Canadian general in World War II. (He would later describe his post-1945 experiences pungently: "I learned something about the attitude of Asian, Middle Eastern and South American peoples towards the monster of the age, Imperialism."[20]) For Burns, peacekeeping meant much more Canadian contact with the burgeoning anticolonial nationalism of the Third World. Egypt, with a long history of indirect but potent British colonial rule, in particular had no use for soldiers of the Queen, and Canadian soldiers patrolling the Suez Canal Zone, dressed somewhat like their British counterparts, aroused resistance. It soon became evident that such a new force needed a new public identity—and hence the distinctive helmets of the UN came into common use. The whole affair helped spur the push for Canada to adopt (at last) a national symbol that did away with any trace of the British connection, and after Suez Pearson began to suggest openly that his country needed a distinctive flag. At the level of symbols as well as concrete policies, Liberal Internationalism was thus linked with a new Canadian nationalism: one more reason why Canadians could feel proud of Canada lay in the country's amiable, civilized, and peaceable deportment in a world crowded with countries that shared none of these characteristics. From the end of World War II until Canada's support for UN peacekeeping operations began to decline in 1997, partly as a result of the Somalia Affair, the country was a leading contributor to all such ventures in the world's intractable conflicts.

Pierre Trudeau, from this liberal perspective, inherited Pearson's mantle. Through the formation of the Canadian International Development Agency in 1968, charged with administering foreign aid programs and coordinating the efforts of both public and private agencies, Trudeau seemingly inaugurated a new era in Canadian relations with the Third World. He also changed immigration policy, replacing overtly racist restrictions with a merit-based point system. He irritated the Americans by refusing to play along fully with the arms race against the Soviets, cozying up to Cuba, and even launching his own peace crusade in the 1980s to bring the rival superpowers to their senses. Canadians overwhelmingly accepted their country's status as the UN's prized peacekeeper, with Canadian soldiers playing peacekeeping roles that included everything from what are known as traditional interpositional forces (Cyprus, Ethiopia/Eritrea) to observer missions (Georgia/Abkhazia, Lebanon), transitional administrations (Eastern Slavonia and East Timor), and the most controversial and difficult multidimensional operations—Bosnia, Rwanda, Somalia, Haiti, Sierra Leone. The work was routine enough that participation in an operation such as the United Nations Transition Assistance Group (UNTAG) went largely unnoticed in Canada. In 1989 UNTAG supervised successful elections in Namibia, the newly independent southern African country that had been victimized by decades of domination by Germany and South Africa. The United Nations Observer Group in El Salvador (ONUSAL) in 1991–1992 helped to bring an end to a civil war of unsurpassed brutality. During the Cold War, Canada sent more troops on UN peacekeeping operations than did any other country, suffering the highest number of fatalities.[21]

As Pearson once remarked, foreign policy was just domestic policy with its hat on. However marginalized and even occupied they might feel, with their own parliamentarians not even allowed to inspect defence installations in the nominally Canadian Arctic, Canadians could nonetheless take some pride in supporting and even inspiring such apparently liberal institutions as NATO and the UN. Lacking many of the necessary ingredients to forge a strongly imagined community within Canada—a common language, a nationalism unifying both major language groups and a multitude of other rooted identities, or even much in the way of an independent Canadian economy—the Pearsonians used the international sphere to develop a network of myths and symbols testifying to Canada's world-reshaping role. Canadians could imagine their country to be at the heart of a more enlightened approach to a conflict-ridden international world—one that, from the 1960s to the 1980s, often seemed, despite Canadians' best efforts, one misstep away from nuclear Armageddon.

Yet there were warning signs that this liberal era was coming to an end. The tragedy in Somalia was one. The 1994 genocide in Rwanda, a tragedy UN peacekeepers and a Canadian general had been unable to avert, was another. Leading liberals began to move away from Pearson's UN, an organization they increasingly identified with a stifling bureaucracy and inaction on urgent files. Some, like Lloyd Axworthy, backed "soft power" and non-government organizations (NGOs) as agents of a more activist humanitarian foreign policy, one oriented to the world's "responsibility to protect" those threatened by their own states. After the fall of the Soviet Union, many other Canadian liberals embraced notions of "robust peacekeeping" that encompassed war-making in such places as Iraq, Afghanistan, and Libya. A turning point for many of them were the major conflicts in the Balkan Peninsula in the 1990s (1991–95 and 1999–2000), whose implications—at least for those raised to respect the United Nations and Canada as a peaceable kingdom—were troubling. In 1995, after the failure of a UN force to stop vicious killings in Bosnia, the Security Council for the first time subcontracted a military operation to NATO that encompassed mass bombings and ethnic cleansing—for the first time, a blitzkrieg on a civilian population was officially presented as a form of peace-making.

And four years later, going even further to prevent assumed genocide in Kosovo, NATO—the organization Pearson had so hoped would play a civilizing and cultural role in the world—launched under American direction an attack on another state, one in which precision targeting and high-altitude bombing demonstrated the potency of the Empire's new armaments. A one-sided "war," based on equally one-sided and partial evidence, could be launched upon a recognized state, because, Liberal Internationalists now argued, human rights trumped the principles of sovereignty. In the same year, operating under the provisions of the Iraq Liberation Act of 1998, the United States dropped about 400,000 tons of bombs on Iraq—without even bothering to declare war. Throughout the following decade, this would become the pattern, one generally endorsed by liberals: peace through war.

Many Liberal Internationalists became, though they were often reluctant to admit it, New Warriors.

Throughout the world, many people had hoped the end of the Cold War would usher in an era of peace. What happened instead was the arrival of an American Empire unashamed to exercise its power. The post-Soviet "new normal" is that of undeclared conventional wars: leaving perhaps 130,000 dead civilians in Iraq, thousands more in Afghanistan and Libya, and a growing number of casualties in Pakistan from the operations of unmanned aerial vehicles (or drones)—the weapon of choice of liberal President Barack Obama. In a unipolar age of unabashed US unilateralism, Pearsonian peacekeeping—which had at its heart the interposition of UN forces between countries whose sovereign rights were respected and which enforced "international law"—seemed a thing of the past. In the space of a decade and a half, Canada dropped from its cherished position as first among UN peacekeepers to virtually the last.

Like conquistadores developing elaborate justifications for slaughtering and enslaving Indigenous peoples in the Americas, today's new imperialists construct impressive bodies of historical and social theory to explain why they have the natural right to be lords of humankind. The colonized (or those about to be colonized) are represented as unknowable and primitive, inscrutably inaccessible to our modes of reason, imprisoned in a static past. Today's indispensable Others are often Muslims living on or near coveted energy resources (or the pipelines and sea routes necessary for the secure passage of those resources to the West). Framing Muslims as civilizational enemies living in "failed" (or, if war is coming, "rogue") states gives soldiers and their political masters a comfortable way of justifying military expenditures and ill-defined and open-ended missions. Old-style Pearsonians can be wooed by promises that wars in and on Third World countries will be accompanied with lots of development programs—as in the once-acclaimed model of the "Three Block War," in which heavy conventional fighting in one block could be aligned with winning hearts and minds in another. By the twenty-first century, many liberals were championing New Warrior doctrines of unilateral militarism, the detention of prisoners under security certificates, and a vast standing army. Coming from very different places, New Warriors and Liberal Internationalists have often arrived at remarkably similar twenty-first-century destinations, in an age of an unchecked American Empire.

The "Critical Realist" Framework

From the Critical Realist perspective, both New Warriors and Liberal Internationalists present mystifying and increasingly convergent concepts of

Canada's position in the world. After wars in Somalia, the Balkans, Afghanistan, and Libya, the turn to the Warrior Nation drew support from people who also profess an attachment to the Pearsonian tradition. Often they invoke the responsibility to protect vulnerable minorities, whose fate should not be entrusted to rogue regimes. Increasingly, as in Somalia, peacekeeping and peacemaking come to look more and more like war. In Afghanistan, what was obviously a fairly conventional counterinsurgency war fought to maintain a regime friendly to the West—albeit one dominated by warlords and druglords—was often justified in terms of the responsibility to protect the women, children, and "civil society." In Pakistan, US drones—those enforcing the "ordered freedom" of Western civil society—routinely violate the airspace of a sovereign state ambivalently allied with the West. In the new order, Anglos—above all Americans—have the right to impose a death sentence, without even the pretense of due process, on those they deem terrorists, and upon any civilians, including children, unlucky enough to be in the vicinity. The boundaries of warfare have changed: in much of the world policed by the West's Empire, no war need be declared, no battles waged, and no rules of war engaged. War becomes a permanent part of daily life, in which once clearly demarcated boundaries between civilians and soldiers have disappeared.

It is tempting—and to some extent necessary—to mark the extraordinary distance many liberals have travelled since the 1960s, as they now routinely commend policies that Pearson (and most of his contemporaries) would have judged criminal. Yet this can often retain the oversimplified form of a "Battle of Canadian Mythologies"—Warrior Nation versus Peaceable Kingdom—that threatens to conclude merely with a frustrating stand-off between rival certainties. To move beyond this dualism calls for a new framework of analysis, one that analyzes more closely the origins of Canadian policies toward the Third World in Canada's own geohistorical position.

From a critical realist perspective, one key to the resilience of the myths propounded by New Warriors and Liberal Internationalists lies in the intrinsic difficulties of saying what exactly Canada is. At no time in the nineteenth century did Canadians decide to constitute themselves as a sovereign political community. When a mid-nineteenth-century state called "Canada" did emerge in northern North America, it did so only because Great Britain, the world's largest and most powerful empire, and the United States, the continent's emergent powerhouse, had agreed—with a lot of economic and diplomatic friction persisting to the 1920s—not to go to war over their rival claims in this area. From 1867 to 1931, Britain exercised in Canada many of the rights normally associated with

a sovereign state. Canada was, in a real sense, a colonial white dominion of British settlement, one imposed upon preexisting Amerindian and
francophone societies. It was able to emerge because the United States,
notwithstanding the most belligerent claims of proponents of Manifest
Destiny, did not go to war with its British rivals. Was this nonsovereign
Dominion of Canada a country or a colony? And, if the latter, whose
colony was it? In 1931, the Statute of Westminster declared it the equal of
any self-governing country in the Commonwealth. Until then Britain had
been vested with final say over many questions regarding Canada's foreign
policy. British citadels (like Kingston's Fort Henry), naval stations, and the
famous redcoats testified to this reality—as did, more subtly, the absence of
any discussion of foreign policy in the *British North America (Constitution)
Act* of 1867. After 1939, when the United States had manifestly supplanted
Britain as the preeminent power in North America and the world, Canada
would slip more and more into a US orbit, seeking from the United States
the military protection and profitable economic advantages it had once
sought from Britain.

Some Canadians wanted to create their own country, and in the 1930s
and 1940s especially, they had reason to think they had done so—but they
continually came up against the brute, hard facts of their own position on
the cusp of two empires whose mutual cooperation was a precondition
of Canada's very existence and of the security and power of its business
class. And such nationalistic Canadians were powerfully divided among
themselves, lacking in fact a foundational "war of independence," a unifying language, a common set of social objectives, a shared set of heroes and
villains—in short, what authorities on nationalism call a shared myth-
symbol complex. If no state can long survive in the modern era without the
capacity to elicit the active loyalty of its citizens, the foundational challenge
of all Canadian statecraft has always been to form some sort of nationalism,
however weak, that might do so.

From this critical realist perspective, then, the New Warriors, struggling
to develop a coherent and inspiring story of the Canadian State, are just
trying to do what nationalists everywhere try to do, but which in northern
North America is very difficult to pull off. In their case, Canada is to be
revered because it is the inheritor and defender of British freedoms extend-
ing right back to the Magna Carta in 1215—freedoms now most enshrined
in the United States that we must now defend, forcibly if need be, around
the world. The New Warriors' nationalism is peculiar in world terms because
it so resolutely focuses on another country, the United States. *Their country,
right or wrong* could be its motto. For them, the neoliberal principal of market
sovereignty is everything: the market is the ultimate source of meaning and

purpose. And the Promised Land of the Market is to be found in the United States.

Yet, when it comes to winning the loyalty of citizens—let alone persuading young Canadians they should sacrifice life and limb for their country—so blatant a commercial Canada, one that treats Canadians like customers rather than citizens, seems unsustainable as the centrepiece of nationalism. One might prefer, as a consumer, one store to another: Wal-mart, say, to Costco. Yet it is doubtful if many people would lay down their lives for either. A country that increasingly justifies itself primarily as a commercial enterprise, a Costco writ large, whose foreign policy is now officially and bluntly reduced to the furtherance of business interests, can hardly find within such commercialism a myth-symbol complex upon which nations, by definition, rely. Yet, in a world the New Warriors think is more and more like a jungle, wherein only the strong shall survive, myths and symbols that might well persuade citizens to lay down their lives are all the more necessary. Hence the appeals to much older imperial models of loyalty—to heroic men, to apostles of a masterful race, to missionaries of Judeo-Christian civilization, to the monarchy, and to the world domination of particular versions of humanity—to lend the magic of nationalism to the hard cash-driven pragmatism of Empire.

It may seem—and in logic it is—contradictory to have a government preaching belt-tightening austerity and the withdrawal of social programs on the one hand and open-ended, unclearly defined, and extremely expensive overseas adventures on the other. Yet, in real-world politics, a skilled and determined leadership can craft convincing strategies that conceal such contradictions. And in this case, vast expenditures on equipping and celebrating the *warfare* state—defended on the grounds of national security to a population persuaded it is at grave and perpetual risk of terror from maligned Others—then make it possible to say that expenditures on the *welfare* state are an extravagance. Age-old myths of Nation, Race, and Chosen Peoples thus pave the way for the new definition of Canada as a vast corporation, not all of whose shareholders were created equal, but all of whom are expected to defer to the Leader. It is a Canada that reveres the notional soldier, depicted in shining romantic colours in the *Citizenship Guide*—but claws back benefits, even funeral benefits, from the actual soldiers who were injured or killed doing a job for their country.

A similar challenge also confronted—and still confronts—the inheritors of the Liberal Internationalist tradition who seek to craft a "Canada" that might survive in a world of rival empires. From 1945 on, they too wrestled with Canada's ambiguous character as something less than a free-standing country. Pearson, the Liberal Internationalists' hero, was a bundle of revealing contradictions. Even his speech accepting the Nobel Prize, which opens with sentiments about peace, ends with a sabre-rattling refusal to imagine a permanent détente with an unreformed Soviet bloc. When the Americans embarked on Operation Rolling Thunder—massive bombing campaigns against North Vietnam, followed by equally devastating raids on Cambodia—Pearson was privately aghast but publicly solicitous. Defenders of Pearson's claim to be the apostle of the Peaceable Kingdom invariably cite his Temple University speech of April 2, 1965, in which Pearson broke with diplomatic convention and criticized the host government for its bombing campaign in Vietnam. They recall conversations in which Pearson called the bombing of the North "obscene." They forget the many more moments when Pearson bent his knee to Johnson and his Cold War crusade.

Similarly, such ranking liberals as Pearson and Trudeau often expressed misgivings about a world divided between two superpowers, with NATO assuming an ever-more-prominent role as an international military alliance firmly under US control. The first tried to convert NATO into a benevolent agency for the elevation of all the world; the second briefly contemplated outright Canadian withdrawal from the organization. Both were acutely sensitive to Quebec—which, Granatstein is right to remind us, has often been resistant to militarism. Both of them sensed that in a place like Canada—lacking any unifying sense of itself as a sovereign political community—a drive to impose imperial war-making from above raised the prospect of destroying the Canadian state from within. What both would strive to do is to convert grassroots hostility to war into support for foreign and military policies seemingly designed to make it less likely. Thus, thanks to Pearson, NATO—as was the United Nations—was seen by many Canadians as an almost moral force for the reordering of the world, one in which they should take deep pride. He sought to enmesh powerful countries in a new global fabric that would constrain their aggressiveness, a worldview perpetuated by Trudeau.

Here too the contradictions were patent: English Canadians came to express nationalistic pride in a Western alliance perpetuating, indeed accentuating, their subordinate status within North America and the world. Like the New Warriors, the Liberal Internationalists vested much of their nationalistic pride in events and people and places outside Canada. Often they preached peace and practiced war. Canada's activity in Vietnam, Congo—where peacekeepers were complicit in the murder of President Patrice Lumumba—and Cyprus was not in effect a peaceable alternative to Cold War bullying, but rather its complement. To the outright coercion of applied US imperialism in Vietnam and Belgian colonialism in the Congo, Canada would add the more consensual politics of investigation, invigilation, and mediation. The contradictions of Canada's own position were glaring: a sovereign state that was also dependent and compliant. It was little comfort to Vietnam's napalmed villagers or the murdered rebels of Congo that the so-very-complicated Canadians were there to murmur words of conciliation.

In neither the 1940s and 1950s, when the Liberal Internationalists sought to redefine Canada's place in the world, or in the late 1990s and early 2000s, when the New Warriors have undertaken to reverse their work, have those constructing such realignments felt the need to base themselves upon the democratic decisions of a sovereign people. Just as Confederation itself was never put to anything resembling a popular vote—it likely would not have passed—so too do neither New Warriors nor Liberal Internationalists feel obliged to seek democratic legitimacy for Canada's definition of itself in the world. In both cases, the foreign-policy and military "revolutions" they championed (and they *were* revolutions, at least in the sense of entailing vast changes in the prevailing doctrines of Canadian nationalism) were "passive revolutions," effecting top-down changes geared to safeguarding the country's contribution to the modern capitalist world-system, not ones proceeding from a foundational decision-making process on the part of Canadians themselves.[22]

And so a critical and realistic reconnaissance of Canada's position in the world, and its often violent and exploitive relationship with the Third World in particular, would begin by acknowledging the extent to which both the New Warriors and the Liberal Internationalists have not only built upon this tradition of nonsovereignty and non-democracy, this passive revolution, but have also projected this messy compromise overseas. In the first case, the New Warriors have enthusiastically joined a project of imposing a US-led empire of capital upon the planet—a process that not only proceeds without the assent of those upon whom it is imposed, but entails the evaporation-through-trade-agreement of their future rights to shape the most important forces impinging on daily life. In the second case, Liberal Internationalists, who now find themselves echoing New Warrior policies while sometimes deploring the crudity and violence of the rhetoric in which they are couched, offer their qualified support to much the same project.

Peacekeeping in either its pacific Pearsonian or bellicose Harperian formulations is the projection of passive revolution, seeking to contain internal conflicts, favour privileged economic groups, and impose short-term and frequently superficial answers—as is the case with the short-term domestic prosperity promised by pipelines—to smouldering social and economic contradictions. Missions abroad follow the same pattern, offering often the semblance, but not the reality, of genuine peace. Often, as scholars such as Mark Neufeld, Sherene Razack, and Sandra Whitworth have suggested, such peacekeeping ventures have further camouflaged imperial agendas by other means.

Critical realists, proceeding from a genuine regard for democracy, would go beyond either framework. Rather than dismiss Pearsonism as an idle dream, they would note how deeply and pervasively the ideal of a peaceful world has resonated with Canadians. Even after a saturation campaign to persuade citizens that the War of 1812 was the "Birth of a Nation"—and not in fact an indecisive bloody conflict whose one concrete outcome was the obliteration of First Nations' dreams of a free-standing polity in North America—Canadians *en masse* were quietly unpersuaded by this warlike version of their own history. Canadians, like anyone else, can be swayed by campaigns that aim at their humanitarian instincts—as much of the sales campaign for the Afghanistan debacle demonstrated. Yet Canada's defeat in Kandahar left the vast majority of Canadians unimpressed by the war and unenthusiastic about further such adventures. Many Canadians were inundated with messages urging them to participate in the Anglo-American invasion of Iraq. They refused to do so.

It is not, from a critical realist perspective, that Canadians have an inherently peaceful nature. Rather, Canadians share the historical experience of living in a vast and divided country on the cusp of two empires. This is a country whose very existence has historically required these empires' peaceful coexistence. It is also one in which major wars have opened chasms separating the two predominant linguistic communities. One New Warrior laments that peacekeeping seems to have failed, "except in the minds of the Canadian people."[23] He is lamenting not a collective illusion but something more like a general understanding of Canada's particular geohistorical position. It has not been one that has lent itself to the celebration of a made-in-Canada militarism.

For example, many of the actual soldiers of 1914–1918 remembered a completely different war than the majestic "Birth of the Nation" we shall be enjoined to celebrate in 2017. They remembered a hypocritical class system, senseless and horrific violence, official incompetence, corrupt profiteering, and moral ambiguity—in a war that left a growing number of Canadians at odds with their government. Many soldiers returned home with revolutionary ideas—unfocused but powerful—of changing a hidebound Victorian order from top to bottom, and building a Canada whose independence would forestall any recurrence of such mass murder. Similarly, many a World War II veteran returned with schemes to build the very welfare state the New Warriors have sworn to dismantle. And many recently arrived Canadians from the Third World are also reluctant to embrace militarism as a culture, with fresh memories of the many wars waged by the imperial West that have plainly been about the extension of regimes of property and profits, not the advancement of human rights and social development. In Canada, enthusiasm for war seems inversely proportional to the actual prospect of enduring one.

Sandwiched between superpowers, in a country whose vast terrain with such a small population would be indefensible in any conventional war, and always occupied by an imperial presence exerting many of the powers of a sovereign state, Canadians have in the main inherited a skeptical attitude toward militarism. The very absence of a great complex of myths and symbols making Canadians citizens of a unified nation renders many of them less likely to contemplate invading other countries to right historic wrongs or seize their assets. Canadians have rarely shared that national mythology so widespread in the United States—the mythology of a distinctively North American people who, as clear-eyed defenders of their freedoms, always defeated their enemies and gained strength and unity through war. Inducing Canadians to accept such American-style nationalism—and one centred on militarized imperial narratives in which Canada plays but a minor supporting role—is unlikely to succeed in the long term. Nationalistic sabre-rattling does not align with traditions well-developed within Canada; more basically, it aligns even more poorly with the long-standing patterns that determine Canada's geohistorical position in the world.

One of the most striking things about the Somalia Affair—which in retrospect hardly stands as the worst enormity Canadians perpetrated in the Third World, and which today is dwarfed by the depredations of Canada-based mining companies—was how shocked Canadians were about it. This can be read, of course, as evidence of their innocence and credulity in the face of the harsh facts of the new global capitalism. It can be also interpreted as an indication that, when many Canadians did come face to face with the cruelties of imperialism, they did not like what they saw. It is very likely that one, often confused, liberal model of UN peacekeeping has expired. But from the critical realist perspective, the fall of the ideal of UN peacekeeping warrants neither a return to the fantasies of the British Empire nor to those of an equally imperial liberal humanitarianism—but rather to the development of a new approach to Canada in the world, founded upon the country's long-standing historical patterns, an approach both critical of past practice and realistic in its assessment of the country's actual geohistorical position.

Nor should the new global realities lead to any conclusion that peace activism itself has failed. In new forms of solidarity movements far removed from the Washington Consensus and the UN, such activism is an increasingly coherent force with deep Canadian roots. As Mills explores in this book, values of peace activism and social justice have animated social movements repeatedly in Canadian history: against nuclear weaponry and the American war in Vietnam; in divestment and boycott for liberation in South Africa when Nelson Mandela was routinely denounced as a "terrorist" by security zealots; in support of American war resisters from the 1960s to the 2000s; and, as Dubinsky and Epprecht reveal in this volume, in opposition to the corrosive activities of Canadian mining corporations.

"Canada, Canada," cried Shidane Abukar Arone on that terrible night in 1993. For the New Warriors, his death called out for yet more soldiers occupying yet more Third World countries. For the Liberal Internationalists, his death was merely a troubling sidebar to the uplifting story of Pearsonian idealism. But critical realists respond quite differently. In reconstructing what made this moment possible—Canada's tight connections with imperialism and its inheritance of long-standing doctrines of racial superiority—they also acknowledge the deep human solidarities that link Somali teenagers and Canadian citizens. And they imagine, both critically and realistically, how a world without such crimes might emerge—projecting, not as dreams but as strategies, a future in which affective ties among the many can resist the all-consuming greed and violence of the few.

Discussion Questions

1) What was the "Somalia Affair" and why has it become such an important way to consider the activities of the Canadian Armed Forces in the Global South?
2) What were some of the central myths and symbols of Canada's international role since 1945, and how are they changing now?
3) Has Canada ever been a "peacemaking" country?
4) Who are the "New Warriors" and what is so "new" about them?

Further Readings

Bercuson, David. *Significant Incident: Canada's Army, the Airborne, and the Murder in Somalia.* Toronto: McClelland and Stewart, 1996.

Campbell, Lara, Michael Dawson, and Catherine Gidney, eds. *Worth Fighting For: Canada's Traditions of War Resistance from 1812 to the War on Terror.* Toronto: Between the Lines, 2015.

Granatstein, J.L. *Whose War Is It? How Canada Can Survive in the Post-9/11 World.* Toronto: HarperCollins, 2007.

McKay, Ian, and Jamie Swift. *Warrior Nation: Rebranding Canada in an Age of Anxiety.* Toronto: Between the Lines, 2012.

Neufeld, Mark. "'Happy Is the Land That Needs No Hero': The Pearsonian Tradition and the Canadian Intervention in Afghanistan." In *Canadian Foreign Policy in Critical Perspective*, ed. J. Marshall Beier and Lana Wylie, 126–38. New York: Oxford University Press, 2010.

Razack, Sherene H. *Dark Threats and White Knights: The Somalia Affair, Peacekeeping, and the New Imperialism.* Toronto: University of Toronto Press, 2004.

Whitworth, Sandra. *Men, Militarism, and UN Peacekeeping: A Gendered Analysis.* Boulder, CO: Lynne Rienner, 2007.

Notes

This chapter is based on *Warrior Nation: Rebranding Canada in an Age of Anxiety* (Toronto: Between the Lines, 2012), which contains a fuller documentation of its argument.

1   Quoted in Africa Watch and Physicians for Human Rights, "Somalia: No Mercy in Mogadishu, the Human Cost of the Conflict and the Struggle for Relief," *Africa Watch*, March 26, 1992. For the Cold War background, see Odd Arne Westad, *The Global Cold War* (Cambridge: Cambridge University Press, 2007), 331–32.

2   See Sandra Whitworth, *Men, Militarism, and UN Peacekeeping: A Gendered Analysis* (Boulder, CO: Lynne Rienner, 2007).

3   David Bercuson, *Significant Incident: Canada's Army, the Airborne, and the Murder in Somalia* (Toronto: McClelland and Stewart, 1996), 7; Sherene Razack, *Dark Threats and White Knights: The Somalia Affair, Peacekeeping and the New Imperialism* (Toronto: University of Toronto Press, 2004).

4   Details in this and the following paragraph from "Information Legacy: A Compendium of Source Material/Commission of Inquiry into the Deployment of Canadian Forces to Somalia," 1997, cited in Razack, *Dark Threats and White Knights*, 80–84.

5   Ibid., 98.

6   Cited in Peter Desbarats, *Somalia Cover-Up: A Commissioner's Journal* (Toronto: McClelland and Stewart, 1997), 343–49; Razack, *Dark Threats and White Knights*, 4–5.

7   Desbarats, *Somalia Cover-Up*.

8   Bercuson, *Significant Incident*, 242, 32, 28–29.

9   David Bercuson and Barry Cooper, *Derailed: The Betrayal of the National Dream* (Toronto: Key Porter Books, 1994), 209.

10 Bercuson, *Significant Incident*, 114.

11 J.L. Granatstein, *Whose War Is It? How Canada Can Survive in the Post-9/11 World* (Toronto: HarperCollins, 2007), 52n, 26, 153, 149, 202. For a useful contrast, see Linda McQuaig, *Holding the Bully's Coat: Canada and the US Empire* (Toronto: Doubleday Canada, 2007).

12 Stephen Harper, speech at the Canada–UK Chamber of Commerce, London, July 14, 2006, http://www.monarchist.ca/en/quotations.

13 Citizenship and Immigration Canada, *Discover Canada: The Rights and Responsibilities of Citizenship, Study Guide*, 2010 ed. (Ottawa: Minister of Public Works and Government Services Canada, 2009).

14 As cited in Peter Buitenhuis, *The Great War of Words: British, American, and Canada Propaganda and Fiction, 1914–1933* (Vancouver: University of British Columbia Press, 1987), 6.

15 Citations from John English, *Shadow of Heaven: The Life of Lester Pearson, vol. 1: 1897–1948* (Toronto: Lester and Orpen Dennys, 1989), 36, 34.

16 As cited in Reginald Whitaker and Gary Marcuse, *Cold War Canada: The Making of a National Insecurity State, 1945–1957* (Toronto: University of Toronto Press, 1994), 265.

17 Pearson as cited in Stephen Endicott, *James G. Endicott: Rebel Out of China* (Toronto: University of Toronto Press, 1980), 276, 277, 286; Gary Kinsman and Patrizia Gentile, *The Canadian War on Queers: National Security as Sexual Regulation* (Vancouver: University of British Columbia Press, 2009).

18 For Pearson on Vietnam, see Mark Neufeld, "'Happy Is the Land That Needs No Hero': The Pearsonian Tradition and the Canadian Intervention in Afghanistan," in *Canadian Foreign Policy in Critical Perspective*, ed. J. Marshall Beier and Lana Wylie (New York: Oxford University Press, 2010), 130; Charles Taylor, *Snow Job: Canada, The United States and Vietnam 1954–1973* (Toronto: Anansi, 1975), 188; Victor Levant, *Quiet Complicity: Canadian Involvement in the Vietnam War* (Toronto: Between the Lines, 1986).

19 *Toronto Star*, April 10, 1967.

20 E.L.M. Burns, *Between Arab and Israeli* (Toronto: Clarke Irwin, 1962), 7–8.

21 For useful overviews, see Desmond Morton, *A Military History of Canada*, 5th ed. (Toronto: McClelland and Stewart, 2007); J.L. Granatstein, "Canada: Peacekeeper (A Survey of Canada's Participation in Peacekeeping Missions)" in *Peacekeeping: International Challenge and Canadian Response*, ed. Alastair Taylor, David Cox, and J.L. Granatstein (Toronto: Canadian Institute of International Affairs, 1968).

22 See Ian McKay, "The Canadian Passive Revolution, 1840–1950," *Capital and Class* 34, no. 3 (2010): 361–81.

23 Jack Granatstein, *Ottawa Citizen*, December 6, 2008.

8

A Decade of Change:
Refugee Movements from the
Global South and the Transformation
of Canada's Immigration Framework[1]

LAURA MADOKORO

Most of the new refugee problems bear little similarity to the classical European
problem and the real genius of the current service to refugees is its recognition
of this fact, its refusal to apply old remedies to new ills and its recognition that
different problems require different solutions.
—*Elfan Rees, World Council of Churches, 1967*[2]

Introduction

On October 15, 1970, Tsering Dorjee Wangkhang and Jampa Dorjee
Drongotsang landed in Toronto. They were the first to arrive of 240 Tibetan
refugees resettled to Canada from India in 1970 and 1971. Their presence
in Canada was at once an ordinary story of global migration and an extraordinary story of refugee resettlement (the act of providing protection by
moving people across national borders, beyond potential danger). In the
early post–World War II period, Canadian officials had been reluctant to
reach out to refugees beyond the Cold War in Europe.[3] Tsering and Jampa's
resettlement marked a critical juncture in the history of the international
refugee regime,[4] and the evolving relationship between Canada and the
Global South.

The 1970s were a significant moment in the history of immigration
and specially refugee policy in Canada. These years were bookended by the
small, discrete settlement of Tibetan refugees and the massive resettlement of
69,000 refugees from Indochina. In between, the Canadian federal government resettled people expelled from Uganda in 1972, individuals caught up
in the political turmoil following the Pinochet coup in Chile in 1973, and
the relatives of Canadians fleeing conflicts in Cyprus, Angola, Mozambique,
and Lebanon from 1974 to 1976. These discrete programs were significant
for their ad hoc and loosely defined character and because they indicated
an unprecedented willingness on the part of the Canadian government to

Figure 8.1 Tsering Dorjee Wangkhang and Jampa Dorjee Drongotsang reporting for training at the Bata Shoe Factory in Batawa, Ontario, 1970. Photo by Ronald Thorton, *Trentonian*, 21 October 1970.

Source: Refugees—Tibetan Movement—General, RG 76, Volume 1218, File 5786–1, Part 9, LAC

use its immigration programs as humanitarian tools to assist refugees and displaced persons outside of Europe.

This chapter examines how Canada's immigration programs evolved in this critical decade by tracing two strands of policies that emerged to deal with the movement of refugees globally. The first stemmed from Canada's signing of the UN Convention Relating to the Status of Refugees in 1969 and the subsequent introduction of refugee determination processes to consider the situation of individuals claiming refugee status in Canada. These regulatory changes, ultimately codified in the 1976 *Immigration Act*, enabled anyone, regardless of their country of origin, to seek protection in Canada under the terms of the 1951 UN Convention. The second development was the use of discrete resettlement schemes to assist refugees, such as Tsering and Jampa, caught up in various kinds of political turmoil in the Global South. Together, the introduction of refugee determination processes and the expanding use of resettlement as a form of protection marked a decade of change that fundamentally transformed the composition of the Canadian populace, the nature of Canada's engagement with the world's refugee populations, and the very manner in which the term "refugee" was understood.

In order to understand the context and the significance of Canada's commitment to the 1951 UN Convention and the introduction of refugee determination processes, as well as the use of humanitarian immigration policies to assist refugees in the Global South, this chapter focuses on the contested policy deliberations that led to important changes in how Canada conceptualized its responsibilities and relationships vis-à-vis refugees outside of Europe. There is some attention to the work of NGOs and the experience of the migrants themselves, but this chapter is primarily intended to shed light on the mindsets of the policy makers charged with creating and implementing refugee determination processes and discrete humanitarian policies. Exploring the thinking behind the decisions that shaped the introduction of refugee determination processes, as well as the scope and structure of refugee resettlement programs, helps us acknowledge and account for the initial skepticism with which Canadian officials viewed the merits of assisting refugees from the Global South.

In addition to providing an overview of the legal and administrative changes that transformed Canada's relationship with refugees in the Global South, this chapter examines the Tibetan refugee resettlement pilot project to explore the manner in which Canadian policy makers viewed population displacements in the Global South in the early years of the 1970s and how radically this perspective changed over the course of the decade. Not only did Canada implement the terms of the 1951 UN Convention after 1969, beginning in the 1970s policy makers demonstrated a willingness to help refugees in the Global South that had been unheard of in previous years. Authorities developed programs and regulations that enabled the government to assist people beyond the limited confines of the international refugee regime associated with the 1951 UN Convention. Through the introduction of refugee resettlement programs and the implementation of refugee determination processes, Canada met its legal obligations under the terms of the 1951 UN Convention and went even further, assisting people who did not meet the strict convention definition of a refugee. Many of the 100,000 people assisted through special resettlement programs came from the Global South, marking a radical departure in how Canadian authorities viewed their humanitarian obligations.

A Note on Terminology

In 2013, the United Nations High Commissioner for Refugees (UNHCR) estimated the world's refugee population at 16.7 million people, not counting the estimated 33.3 million internally displaced people (essentially refugees who remain within their countries of origin rather than crossing international borders—the majority of whom are in Africa) and the 4.8 million registered refugees in the Middle East. Given their positions on the UN Development Index, the top "refugee-producing" countries were all in what might be called the Global South. At the time of the survey, the UNHCR counted 499,500 refugees from the Democratic Republic of the Congo, 2,556,556 refugees from Afghanistan, 2,468,400 from Syria, 273,034 from Eritrea, and 1,121,738 from Somalia. In 2014, these countries were respectively listed as 186th, 169th, 118th, and 146th in terms of development out of 187 ranked countries (Somalia was not listed).[5] The sheer numbers of refugees from developing countries suggests there are valid grounds for using "Third World refugees" or "refugees from the Global South" as shorthand for the massive displacement that has taken place in developing countries over the past several decades. To do so, however, is to lose sight of the particular local contingencies and regional dynamics that caused people to leave. It also removes any sense of a unique historical relationship between distinctive parts of the world, and suggests that the historic engagement of a country such as Canada with different refugee groups stemmed from Global North–Global South dynamics as opposed to a range of multifaceted relationships defined by imperial and commonwealth ties as well as linguistic and cultural affinities.

This chapter recognizes that the language of the Third World and the Global South potentially erases the unique dynamics that attended Canada's engagement with particular refugee movements. Although the term "Global South" is used to discuss the movement of refugees in developing countries, this chapter treats Canada's historic response to refugee movements and population displacements not as an answer to the Global South as such but as a reaction to particular events and situations that, in turn, shaped the overall trajectory of Canada's engagement with the Global South. Doing so allows us to gauge how Canada became involved with refugee situations outside of Europe by the 1970s, how the country's involvement with different humanitarian situations enhanced its perceived role as benefactor in its evolving relationships with people and places in the Global South, and the profound impact these relationships had on Canada's demographic trajectory and the country's global humanitarian outlook.

The Long European Gaze

International laws defining refugee status and the organizations established to protect refugees in the interwar period used a very narrow definition of *refugee*, which deliberately limited the international community's scope of responsibility for the refugee situation in Europe. Similarly, after World War II, the refugee definition and infrastructure for refugee protection created by delegates to the United Nations, which operated unchanged for almost two decades, centred almost entirely on the plight of people in Europe. The situations of other displaced and uprooted people were written out of the framework for refugee protection governed by the 1951 UN Convention Relating to the Status of Refugees (hence the notion of a long European gaze).

The 1951 UN Convention, which was drafted in response to the continued displacement of millions of people in Europe after World War II and whose character was shaped by liberal democracies fearful of the spread of communism,[6] defined a refugee as an individual who

> owing to well-founded fear of being persecuted for reasons of race, religion, nationality, membership of a particular social group or political opinion, is outside the country of his nationality and is unable or, owing to such fear, is unwilling to avail himself of the protection of that country; or who, not having a nationality and being outside the country of his former habitual residence as a result of such events, is unable or, owing to such fear, is unwilling to return to it.[7]

Signatories had the option of limiting the application of the convention to refugee situations arising out of events in Europe prior to January 1, 1951. All of the original signatories did so. As suggested by the application of temporal and geographic limitations, the focus on the individual, and the use of persecution as the defining element of the refugee experience, the convention reflected the polarizing tensions of the Cold War as they played out in Europe. Implicit in the language of the convention was the idea that persecution would come at the hand of communist or fascist oppressors; the convention was not intended for mass displacements arising from civil wars or environmental disasters.

Canada participated in the drafting of the convention but did not sign the international legal instrument until 1969. In the immediate postwar period, Canadian policy makers desired to contribute to global peace and stability, but they were concerned, as were other nations, about the country's postwar economic recovery. As Walker has explored in this volume, they also worried about the impact of admitting people whose racial make-up jarred with the country's vision of its future.[8] Officials therefore balked at signing the refugee convention for fear that it would impede their capacity to determine admissions to the country. In keeping with the country's foundations as a white settler society, Mackenzie King's Liberal government privileged migration from the British Isles and Northern Europe while admitting 250,000 displaced persons and Ukrainian, German, Austrian, Jewish, Latvian, Lithuanian, Hungarian, Czech, Dutch, and Russian refugees from 1947 to 1962. At the same time, the government ignored the massive displacement of people in Asia following the defeat of the Japanese empire and its subsequent withdrawal from Southeast Asia, the violent partition of India in 1947, turbulent decolonization movements in Malaya and Indonesia, and the establishment of a communist regime in Beijing in 1949.

Instead of committing to the expansion of the emerging international refugee regime or attending to refugees outside of Europe, the government focused on the selection of displaced persons on the European continent, using relaxed eligibility criteria outlined in the 1952 *Immigration Act*. This meant that people who had family in Canada or skills that could contribute to the country's economic development were given priority for admission. Immigration policy in postwar Canada, even in its most humanitarian incarnation, was designed with the Canadian economy first and foremost in mind. The relaxation of established criteria to select people in difficult circumstances was the main method by which the Canadian government used its immigration policy to provide humanitarian assistance. This strategy was used to assist 37,000 refugees who fled the Hungarian Revolution in 1956 and 11,000 refugees who escaped the suppression of the Prague Spring in 1968. By the mid-1970s, it was a strategy that the government began to use to assist people in the Global South (see Box 8.1 for details).

A Landscape Transformed

Part of the change in how broadly the Canadian government extended its humanitarian immigration programs was due to an evolution in thinking about race-based immigration preferences. The horrors of World War II, Canada's membership in the United Nations, the strength of decolonization movements in the Global South, and cross-border civil rights campaigns made it difficult to rationalize exclusion on the basis of race, as did the introduction of a Bill of Rights in Canada in 1960. In 1962, Canada cancelled the most discriminatory of its race-based immigration regulations and issued new ones that authorized immigration officials to accept people regardless of their country of origin as long as they were capable of successfully establishing themselves and meeting Canada's roughly defined labour market needs (reflecting continued concern about the Canadian economy and a desire to limit access to the social welfare system).[9] This system was refined in 1967 when the government adjusted the points system for the selection of skilled workers regardless of origin, making it possible, and mandatory, to apply a more objective set of criteria. The points system was designed to ensure that selected migrants were well-suited to the needs of the labour market and were capable of adapting to life in Canada. The 1967 regulations also universalized sponsorship rules for the families of Canadian citizens and permanent residents, creating a family class category for close relatives and a nominated class for more distant relatives such as cousins.

Refugee programs evolved in tandem, characterized by latent fears about admitting less than desirable migrants to the country. In 1962—the same year that visa officers were instructed to select people on the basis of their labour market skills—the first group of non-European refugees were resettled to Canada. This group consisted of one hundred families who left the economic and political upheavals triggered by the Great Leap Forward experiment in the People's Republic of China and who joined hundreds of thousands of others in the overcrowded British colony of Hong Kong. The arrival of new waves of migrants after the 1967 reforms, including refugees from Haiti and Iraq in 1969, and the introduction of an official multiculturalism policy in 1971 transformed the landscape in which policy makers considered the movement of people globally. It was a rapidly transforming landscape. As the editors of *The Age of Migration* observe, the 1970s were "dominated by massive northward flows of both regular and irregular migrants from all areas in Latin America towards the industrialized countries of North America and Europe" as a result of an increased demand for foreign labour.[10] This, combined with political instability and natural disasters in the Americas, Africa, and Asia, contributed to the growth in global migration numbers.

In Canada, migration from the Caribbean, for instance, grew from 5.52 per cent of the total migrant population in 1968 to 11.89 per cent of the total in 1987. Similarly, migration from Africa grew from 3.82 per cent of the total in 1968 to 6.10 per cent in 1987, and migration from Latin America grew from 0.88 per cent of the total in 1968 to 7.64 per cent in 1987.[11] These numbers only hint at the significant change underway. Four decades after the points system was introduced, government statistics show that the Philippines, India, and Haiti were among the top ten source countries for permanent residents to Canada, suggesting that the full impact of structural changes that began in the 1960s were only felt in subsequent decades.[12]

Alongside the reforms to the selection of independent workers and the sponsorship of family-class migrants, Canadian policy makers and Canadians also reconceptualized their global humanitarian responsibilities over the course of the 1970s. In 1969, Canada signed the 1951 Convention and the associated 1967 Protocol, which removed the temporal and geographic limitations built into the original convention. Canada's signature suggested a deeper and more broad-based commitment to refugee protection than had existed previously. This commitment was tested by the advocacy work of the leaders of major religious denominations in Canada, along with the activism of international NGOs, who homed in on the implications of the signature.[13] The commitment was further tested over the subsequent decade by the wide variety of refugee situations that emerged globally, including in many parts of the Global South. Together, these factors encouraged the federal government to formalize some aspects of its previously ad hoc approach to refugee issues while continuing to create selective resettlement and humanitarian immigration schemes. The result was an initial approach that involved the adoption by Canada of the Convention's refugee definition to determine eligibility for resettlement, the setting out of rules to determine admissibility, the development of an "Oppressed Minority" policy, and the establishment of a small committee to examine requests for recognition of refugee status from people within Canada or upon arrival at the country's borders.

Affirmed by the federal cabinet in September 1970, this three-part refugee policy grew out of a recognition that signing the Convention and Protocol required changes to Canadian operating procedures (legal changes would come in 1976). The term "refugee," for instance, was redefined domestically according to the Convention definition, and refugee selection was to be

> on the basis of the norms of assessment as set out in the Immigration Regulations and on the understanding that examining officers (had) the discretion to admit such refugees, notwithstanding their inability to meet these norms, when the information available indicates that there is sufficient private and/or government assistance available, to ensure the applicant's successful establishment in Canada.[14]

Refugee selection depended not only on the needs of the refugees but also on the amount of support available to them in Canada. This approach would change within a few short years with amendments to the *Immigration Appeal Board Act* that recognized refugee status and allowed, but did not mandate, that the Immigration Appeal Board cancel deportation orders if someone was deemed a Convention refugee. Crucially, as one observer notes, "this was not a requirement," and refugee status therefore "remained a privilege rather than a right in Canada."[15]

Still, the federal government was becoming aware of the ongoing importance and permanence of refugee situations globally—particularly in the Global South—and subsequently began to develop mechanisms to adjudicate refugee claims. In 1973, an ad hoc interdepartmental committee was established to review refugee claims and make recommendations to the minister of immigration regarding an individual's status. This process became formalized under the 1976 *Immigration Act*, with the establishment of the Refugee Status Advisory Committee (RSAC). Members of the committee examined written transcripts and made decisions about refugee status accordingly. The number of applications proved greater than the RSAC could handle, and in the 1980s the government began to take administrative measures to both curtail the number of refugee claims being made and the speed with which they were considered.[16] Despite the tumultuous administrative changes that followed that ultimately led to the establishment of the Immigration and Refugee Board in 1989, the development of quasi-judicial processes to determine refugee status in the 1970s meant that people fleeing persecution in the Global South, and elsewhere, had a novel way of making their claims to protection heard by Canadian officials.

Parallel to the development of administrative processes, the federal government introduced programs that reflected the historic use of immigration policy as a form of humanitarianism. Beginning in the 1970s, this humanitarianism was increasingly formalized and, significantly, applied to situations beyond the conventional Cold War paradigm in Europe. The Oppressed Minorities policy, introduced in 1970 at the same time as the first efforts to adjudicate refugee claims, provided

> for the selection of members of oppressed minorities on the basis of the norms of admissibility set out in the Immigration Regulations and on the understanding that the inability to meet selection requirements notwithstanding, examining officers have the discretion to admit such applicants when the information available indicates that there is sufficient private and/or government assistance available to ensure the applicants' successful establishment in Canada.[17]

The impetus for the policy came from lobbying that had taken place on behalf of "Jews and Armenians in Arab States and some Christian sects in Turkey and a variety of persons in communist countries."[18] The critical difference between someone eligible for selection as a Convention refugee and someone covered by the Oppressed Minorities policy was that the former, by definition, was someone who had fled their country of citizenship or permanent residence due to a well-founded fear of persecution, while the latter was someone suffering from oppression while still residing in their country of citizenship or permanent residence. In developing the policy, the Canadian government indicated that it was prepared to proactively assist individuals in need, rather than waiting for them to present themselves at the Canadian border and ask for protection.

The 1970 refugee reforms, including the selection criteria for both Convention refugees and Oppressed Minorities, barely anticipated the pressures that would be placed on the Canadian government to provide humanitarian assistance throughout the 1970s. Changes in communication and transportation technologies meant that Canadians were increasingly aware of refugee situations around the globe. As a result of these changes, migrants were much more capable of making their situations understood by fleeing sites of violence and political upheaval. Persistent advocacy work by NGOs and voluntary agencies furthered awareness about refugee situations in the Global South.

From the earliest days of the Convention's existence, the UNHCR and a network of global NGOs and humanitarian organizations worked to foster a climate that made it difficult for governments to ignore the plight of the displaced and persecuted (as was generally the case prior to World War II). Volunteers with the Canadian University Service Overseas (CUSO) were among the many voices that called on Western governments to pay more attention to issues of poverty, political instability, and displacement in the Global South. The work of activists as well as the growth in the numbers of people displaced globally in the 1970s—from 2.5 million in 1970 to 8 million in 1980—gradually forced Canadian policy makers to rethink their approach to refugees beyond the Cold War in Europe.[19]

In response to NGO activism and the movement of people in the Global South, Canadian policy makers used the lenses of development and anti-communism to conceptualize solutions that simultaneously addressed global security concerns and domestic imperatives to provide some kind of humanitarian assistance. The result was the creation of an unprecedented number of humanitarian programs for refugees throughout the 1970s. As the case of the Tibetan refugees resettled to Canada from 1970 to 1971 will demonstrate, although it is tempting to celebrate the diversity of the people Canada assisted in the 1970s, it is also critical to temper celebratory narratives with an understanding of just how much anxiety the initial resettlement and admission of people from "nontraditional" source countries caused officials responsible for designing and delivering the programs. As Mike Molloy, former Director of Refugee Policy for the Department of Manpower and Immigration, explains,

> The unspoken fear was that change that was too rapid and too visible would provoke a racist backlash from elements of the Canadian population. The fear that "exotic" people might not be able to "establish successfully" was

partly just that, partly uneasiness at the potential provincial reaction if too many of these people landed on provincial welfare rolls. It also reflected the lack of real data and experience about how people as different as the Tibetans would react when dropped into a developed society.[20]

An Accidental Pilot Project

The resettlement of Tibetan families was a singularly important moment in the evolution of Canada's immigration and refugee policies. There was no Tibetan community in Canada at the time the refugee resettlement program was initiated in 1970, and the program was therefore treated as an experimental pilot project that would determine the future trajectory of Canada's resettlement efforts. The complicated manner in which the pilot project was crafted, the precautions the government adopted in selecting refugees for resettlement, and the extraordinary measures the Department of Manpower and Immigration took to ensure the migrants' successful settlement and assimilation were unique in their depth and breadth. Still, the Tibetan refugee pilot project marked the beginning of a decade of change in Canada.

Following the occupation of Tibet by the People's Republic of China in 1959, 200,000 Tibetans joined their spiritual leader, the fourteenth Dalai Lama, in exile. Many were aristocrats, educated monks, former government employees, peasants, and craftspeople. Most moved to India, though some went to Nepal, Sikkim, and Bhutan. Shortly after arriving in India, the Dalai Lama issued a worldwide appeal in the hopes of securing resettlement assistance for the stranded refugees. He worried about the future livelihoods of his followers. In India, the majority of the refugees lived in 41 camps scattered across five large agricultural settlements; about half were employed in road construction camps. There seemed to be little in the way of long-term prospects for them in India.

The Dalai Lama's initial appeal met with only cursory interest among Canadian officials. An almost simultaneous proposal from James M. Morton, of the Molson Brewing Company, and Colonel Ilia Tolstoy, of the Explorers Club of New York, triggered more engaged—if ultimately equally dismissive—consideration. Their idea, for a yak development project and refugee program, was inspired by their concern for the Tibetan refugees' plight. Morton and Tolstoy proposed to have yaks, for which Tibet was famous, sent to Canada and established on a reserve in the north. They suggested that handlers for the yaks could be selected from among the refugees and included in the relocation scheme. The response among officials to this proposal reveals the popular impressions of Tibetan life. Staff from the Department of Northern Affairs declared: "[W]e are of the view that we should seek settlers with an agricultural background rather than nomadic peoples who at best would simply eke out a bare existence."[21]

With this, early discussions about the Tibetan refugee situation in Canada languished. Although the UNHCR was involved in resettlement efforts on behalf of the Tibetan refugees, the organization met with little success in finding countries willing to accept people who were considered culturally backward and unassimilable as a result.

In response to the generally lacklustre international support, the Dalai Lama sent a direct appeal to Prime Minister Lester B. Pearson in 1966, asking for the Canadian government's assistance in organizing a group resettlement scheme for Tibetan refugees. The Dalai Lama desired to have the Canadian government assist with a group resettlement program so that the refugees could stay together and better preserve their unique cultural heritage. This time, the Dalai Lama's petition met with more serious consideration as the prime minister commissioned a survey among the relevant departments to determine what kind of assistance Canada might offer. The deliberations that followed reveal how anxious Canadian immigration officials were about Tibetan life and culture and how cautious they were about undertaking any resettlement program to Canada. Still, the discussions marked the beginning of a slow process that would eventually lead to an experimental pilot project involving the resettlement of 60 Tibetan families.

For the purposes of conducting the departmental survey, an interdepartmental committee was established to consider the pros and cons of resettling refugees in Canada. At the time the survey was struck, Canada was sending millions of dollars in aid to India under different Colombo Plan arrangements and export financing programs. As a result, there was initial interest in furthering relations with India by providing relief support to ease the perceived burden the refugees were placing on India's economy. The High Commissioner to India, James George, took a personal interest in the refugees' plight, and Judy Pullen, a CUSO volunteer, was in regular contact with officials in both the Department of External Affairs and the Department of Manpower and Immigration about the refugees' situation. Overall, however, there was little substantive interest, either among officials in Ottawa or the general Canadian public. The most active group was the Tibetan Refugee Aid Society (established in 1962 by George Woodcock, a professor at the University of British Columbia), which raised funds to support the Tibetan refugees. Other than the prime minister's instructions, there was no appetite for a resettlement project among officials, including members of the committee. R.B. Curry of the Department of Manpower and Immigration questioned the merits of the program by asking "if anyone had ever asked the Tibetans if they want to come here," arguing that their situation might be "like the Arab refugees in the Middle East" who were "unwilling to move so far away from their real homeland."[22] Immigration officials expressed additional doubts about resettling the Tibetans as a group, citing "unfortunate experiences" with "closed" settlements, such as the Doukhobours, Hutterites, and Amish settlements, and voicing their objections to "self-contained colonies, isolated from the mainstream of Canadian life."[23]

Committee members displayed healthy doses of curiosity and skepticism about the Tibetan refugees' best interests and their capacity to adapt to Canadian society. According to the representative from the Department of Manpower and Immigration:

> The Tibetan Refugees come from a society so different from the Canadian [one] in almost every respect as to render integration slow and difficult, even with extensive and sustained assistance. These are problems created by differences in religion, education, marriage customs, social attitudes and values.[24]

The government's desire for permanent, employable residents meant that the committee had conflicting objectives about the ultimate purpose of the admission program. Helping those most in need was not necessarily in the interest of Canadian society; many officials were conscious of the country's slowing economy. The need to ensure that migrants contributed fully to the social and economic life of Canada therefore seemed all the more pressing. At the same time, there was a working assumption that any resettlement program should provide tangible benefits to India and the Tibetans, not just the Canadian economy (though labour market considerations pervaded officials' deliberations throughout the exploratory stage). The committee observed:

> Any programs of resettlement must of necessity entail the selection of the better-educated and better qualified Tibetans. Their selection would deprive the Tibetan refugee communities of the very individuals they need to improve their situation. Canada might be criticized for accepting refugees from a more primitive culture when we have not solved the problems related to our own native groups.[25]

The last line is telling, suggesting that a refugee resettlement program risked drawing attention to the unequal power relations between Canada and the Global South and to the ongoing marginalization of First Nations in the federal landscape. The committee did not want to do anything to attract attention to either of these realities, even as it implicitly acknowledged the country's privileged position. Humanitarian admissions hinged on the notion of a privileged group assisting a less-privileged group, but the funds invested for the resettlement of refugees raised questions about the government's social and fiscal priorities.

As there was little in the way of precedent in Canada for refugee resettlement involving people from what policy makers believed was an undeveloped and entirely foreign part of the world, the committee expended considerable research and energy on understanding how countries that became involved with the Tibetan refugee question had fared. Their queries focused in particular on the experience of Switzerland and Denmark in assisting Tibetan refugees. In 1961, the Swiss government passed a law to allow for the admission of 1,000 refugees from India and the Himalayan States with the idea that they might revive farming in the "higher and bleaker valleys from which the Swiss themselves have retreated."[26] By 1969, 600 Tibetans had arrived in Switzerland in small family groups. In addition, over a hundred children were adopted into Swiss homes under a foster parent program. Denmark, meanwhile, created a vocational training program to help young Tibetan refugees gain skills that they could then use to help their families upon their return to India.

Based on the research into these various initiatives—and following extensive internal deliberations discussed previously—the ad hoc committee determined that there were three possible ways for Canada to assist Tibetan refugees. The first was a vocational training program for young Tibetans, the second was a foster parent program of the sort undertaken in Switzerland, and the final option was "a program for the resettlement of families in small groups." Departmental representatives expressed considerable misgivings about each of these options, and the committee therefore concluded that, "on balance, the resettlement of Tibetan families in Canada does not seem to be a practicable or desirable proposition." Noting that the Swiss government had spent $700,000 on the resettlement of Tibetan refugees, with more funds "urgently needed," the committee decided "such sums might be better used in providing help for the refugees in India and Nepal."[27] The committee proceeded to outline possible aid contributions that would address the financial burden the refugees presented to the Indian government. These included the sponsorship of individual Tibetans for vocational training in India and grants to the Canadian voluntary agencies who gave assistance to the Tibetans under External Affairs' matching grants program.

Following the deliberations of the interdepartmental committee, the government sent an ambivalent reply to the Dalai Lama. By this time, Canada had a new prime minister. Pierre Trudeau approached refugee questions from a rather cerebral perspective, and he began by following the advice of the committee and indicating to the Dalai Lama that resettlement to Canada was not a viable option.[28] Still, Trudeau noted, "Canada's immigration policy is non-discriminatory" and "people of any origin whatever are free to come to Canada as immigrants." He indicated to the Dalai Lama that the Canadian government was "prepared to relax these requirements for refugee families and give them special assistance to aid in their establishment here." He then explained that the Canadian government would "accept a limited number of applicants on a family or individual basis. If suitable employment could be found the Government would be prepared to make arrangements for transportation, training, and resettlement assistance." Trudeau's suggestions went far beyond the deliberations and recommendations of the interdepartmental committee.[29]

In his reply, the Dalai Lama expressed gratitude for the consideration extended by the Canadian government and encouraged follow-up. Officials in the Department of Manpower and Immigration were subsequently instructed to make arrangements for a "pilot project" to select and admit refugee families. Suddenly the government was involved in a resettlement program that went far beyond the developmental assistance proposed in the recommendations of the interdepartmental committee. Not surprisingly, there was a great deal of opposition to this "new and probably costly venture," despite the prime minister's enthusiasm.[30] Nevertheless, in 1970, the federal cabinet finally authorized the pilot project. In the Memorandum to Cabinet, immigration officials emphasized that "because the Tibetans come from a culture which is in many respects years behind that of Canada and because of the importance of religion in their daily lives, their successful settlement is going to involve social, cultural, economic, and psychological adjustments of the most difficult kind." To this end, the Department of Manpower and Immigration requested financial support to provide transportation to Canada from India, as well as "clothing, accommodation, furniture and supplies, extensive basic education, orientation, language and skill training courses" for one year or longer "in order to prepare the refugees for employment." The department estimated the costs at $3,000 per person for a total of $794,000. Cabinet ultimately approved a program for 240 people, with a $694,000 budget, based on expected support from the provinces and from voluntary agencies. It was agreed that if the experiment proved successful, a future program for refugees from Tibet might be orchestrated. The one condition was that there would be a "minimum of publicity in connection with this settlement program during the current negotiations with China on recognition (announced 13 October 1970) and exchange of diplomatic representatives."[31]

Despite this condition, the Department of Manpower and Immigration did issue a press release to alert the Canadian public to the experiment upon which the government was embarking. In announcing the pilot project, the government emphasized the difficult conditions in which the Tibetan refugees currently found themselves in order to garner support and sympathy for the resettlement experiment:

> [T]he majority are in refugee camps in northern India where they are without work. Others live in work camps in high mountain areas building roads under primitive conditions. Large numbers are children who are either orphaned or separated from their parents. The children lack educational facilities, regular food supplies, and medical attention. Due to malnutrition, diseases and the climate, the mortality rate is extremely high, particularly among the children.[32]

The government stressed the difficult challenges that lay ahead and emphasized that "the friendly assistance that Canadians have traditionally provided to refugees will certainly be required in addition to the services of government." The government was clearly anxious about the pilot project. In piece after piece of interdepartmental correspondence, government officials emphasized the "experimental" nature of the resettlement initiative. James Bissett, a senior official in the Department of Manpower and Immigration, underscored that the "experimental" nature of the program required that "the selection, processing and movement of the refugees be conducted as efficiently and effectively as possible." The whole process required "careful planning and effective communication" from beginning to end.[33] As a result, Canadian officials attended to both selection issues and settlement details.

In selecting refugees for resettlement, the government opted to select young families. This decision served to emphasize the humanitarian nature of the resettlement project. Instructions from James Bissett reminded selection officers, "the movement is motivated primarily from a humanitarian point of view[;] therefore an attempt should be made to make a representative selection from among the refugees." Bissett cautioned against accepting "only those who are reasonably well established now in India." To do so would fail to "alleviate the plight of the Tibetan Refugees generally." It further risked "legitimately" evoking "criticism from the Government of India." Ottawa's strategy was to concentrate "on younger couples and their children, who appear adaptable and sincerely wish to come to Canada."[34] Age and potential adaptability were the cornerstones of the selection process, as were ensuring an even distribution among the four main religious schools of Tibetan

Figure 8.2 From left to right: Canadian Immigration Officer Cliff Shaw, the 14th Dalai Lama, and Canadian High Commissioner to India James George.

Courtesy of Cliff Shaw

Buddhism: the Gelugpa, Kagyugpa, Nyingama, and Sakyapa. Among those selected for admission to Canada were monks, farmers, soldiers, nuns, and carpenters.

Settling Success

When it came time to prepare for the practical aspects of welcoming the 240 Tibetan refugees to Canada, discussions revolved around the key issues of assimilation and employment. Officials in the Department of Manpower and Immigration remained concerned about seemingly unbridgeable cultural differences. News that "it was not uncommon for Tibetan women to have two or three husbands" did not sit well with many. Some officials referred to the Tibetans' "medieval culture." George Woodcock of the Tibetan Refugee Aid Society sought to assuage concerns on this front, noting the "considerable effect" that "coming out of Tibet into India has had upon the refugees." He explained that the refugees "are now very far from the medieval people who originally fled ten years ago, since Indian society is far more westernized than Tibetan society was up to 1959, and they have already been subjected in diluted form to many of the influences that would bear upon them if they came to Canada."[35]

The first refugees to arrive settled in Batawa, Ontario, a planned community built around the local Bata shoe factory. Their settlement in October 1970 was the result of a private initiative. When the owner and founder of the company, Thomas Bata, had visited operations in India the previous year, he witnessed the plight of the refugees first-hand. He subsequently indicated to the federal government that he was prepared to employ three or four refugees in the Batawa factory. This was exactly the kind of private initiative the federal government desired. The small group resettlement, with employment offer attached, meant that the government could avoid the kind of large-scale group resettlement championed by the Dalai Lama and which fed the federal government's fears about possible cultural isolation. The guarantee of employment, moreover, helped assuage concerns about how the Tibetan refugees might settle into life in Canada.

As a result of the enthusiasm among federal officials for the Bata Shoe Company's initiative, there was a fair bit of fanfare when Tsering Dorjee Wangkhang and Jampa Dorjee Drongotsang arrived. They were met by a string of local dignitaries and officials at the airport. E.G. Staub, a settlement officer with the Department of Manpower and Immigration who was present for their arrival, reported with delight, "both refugees speak English very well." Staub spent two days with Tsering and Jampa, acquainting them with Canadian "restaurants, shops, supermarkets, laundromats, and other institutions." In addition,

> (they) purchased warm clothing in limited amounts, groceries and personal effects. Also an alarm clock and working clothes were needed as we have reason to believe that, in view of their surprisingly good knowledge of English and adaptation to Western habits, they shall be working at the Bata Shoe Company in the very near future.

Staub reported, this was "their desire, because they do not wish to cost the Canadian government a great deal and want to become useful citizens of this country at the earliest possible moment."[36]

Within two months, Jampa and Tsering were deemed by the Department of Manpower and Immigration to be settling in well. At a citizenship ceremony they were invited to attend in December, Tsering "told the audience that (he and Jampa) liked the Bay of Quinte area very much and how friendly the people had been to them."[37] It was a celebratory narrative that set the tone, and the expectations, for how the arriving Tibetan refugees and receiving Canadians would behave. Stories of lice-filled hair, tuberculosis, and difficulties in adjustment—particularly in Quebec where there was resentment about the requirement to learn French and more limited employment opportunities—detracted from the general way in which Canadians, and federal officials especially, were pleasantly surprised by the "highly motivated" Tibetans and their capacity to adapt to life in Canada.[38]

The refugees adapted to life in Canada while at the same time preserving many of their cultural traditions. Namgyal Nangsetsang, whose parents were selected for resettlement, remembers, "The families that we knew, with all the difficulties and challenges they went through, they all bought a home within ten years of coming to Canada." Her father was a monk and so he "was pretty strict about our Sunday prayers." There was both a shrine and altar room in the Nangsetsang home, and Namgyal recalls that the community was very close, "Every Sunday Tibetan families would take turns hosting prayer sessions. Now and then they'd gather for picnics."[39] In the case of the Tibetan refugees, officials in Ottawa ultimately viewed the preservation of their cultural practices with benign curiosity. The small numbers of resettled refugees, and their dispersal across the country, countered the more concerning elements of the project in terms of the government's assimilationist strategy. Ironically perhaps, the most pointed criticism about settlement arrangements was directed at the federal government, which had presumed to dictate rather than discuss arrangements with the arriving refugees. As one of many follow-up studies stated,

> Activities during the resettlement program should have been planned through mutual discussion. The Tibetans are adults and are neither childlike nor dependent. Much confusion arose at various times and places during the program because of the failure of the officials and Tibetans to arrive at mutual expectations. It would have been more appropriate to treat them as individuals than as a group from the start.[40]

Despite this criticism, there was a generally euphoric sentiment about the resettlement of the Tibetan refugees from India to Canada. The refugees far surpassed government expectations in terms of their capacity to integrate. In the following few years, thousands of people fled the violence of Cold War conflicts, political upheaval, and decolonization in the Global South, and the Canadian government was repeatedly called upon to assist refugees. Family reunification and concerns about assimilation continued to direct the depth and breadth of Canada's response to refugees. Unlike the early postwar period, however, Canadians and the federal government were willing to extend consideration to refugees outside of Europe. They proved less inclined, however, to extend the same kind of comprehensive financial assistance provided to the Tibetan refugees.

Humanitarianism in 1970s' Canada

Following the resettlement of Tibetan refugees from India, the Canadian government received a number of appeals to provide humanitarian assistance to people fleeing political and military violence. In 1972, the British government asked the Canadian government to assist with the resettlement of refugees following Idi Amin's expulsion of Ugandan Asians. In 1973, NGOs and church organizations pressed the federal government to assist Chileans fleeing the Pinochet coup. When 17 Chileans took shelter in the Canadian Ambassador's residence in Santiago, the government felt the pressure even more keenly. The government responded to these pressures and admitted people from Uganda and Chile. Following domestic pressure in Canada from citizens who wanted to help their relatives leave dangerous conditions, officials also extended humanitarian assistance to people fleeing the Turkish invasion of Cyprus in 1974, the civil wars in Angola and Mozambique in 1975, and the civil war in Lebanon in 1976.

Taken together, the rapid succession of events in Uganda, Chile, Cyprus, Lebanon, Mozambique, and Angola, along with the growing numbers of people making refugee claims upon arrival in Canada (which grew from 200 to 400 annually in the mid-1970s to several thousand annually by the 1980s),[41] alerted the federal government to the fact that it no longer had the luxury to custom-design ad hoc refugee resettlement programs, as it had for the Tibetan refugees in 1970. As the decade progressed, there appeared to be growing global tumult—particularly in Southeast Asia, where refugees started to leave Vietnam and Cambodia in significant numbers in 1975. Canadian politicians therefore embraced the idea of further formalizing the country's scattered and discrete resettlement efforts, just as it was doing for the parallel refugee determination processes in Canada.

The sheer number of population movements with which the Canadian government engaged from 1970 to 1976 and the limited scope of the 1951 Convention suggested the need for a much more formalized system than the one that existed as a result of the 1970 cabinet decisions. In 1974, a special task force of experts prepared a Green Paper on Immigration policy. A Special Joint Committee then held 50 public hearings across Canada on the future of Canada's immigration program. The Green Paper and the results of the hearings became the basis for the *Immigration Act* that was drafted in 1976 and implemented two years later. Some of the central recommendations from the consultation process appeared as Canada resettled refugees from Uganda and Chile and the first wave of Indochinese refugees arrived. As a result, the recommendations insisted that Canada should continue to be "a country of immigration for demographic, economic, family, and humanitarian reasons." The principle of nondiscrimination in immigration on the basis of race, creed, nationality, ethnic origin, and sex was also to be set out in the *Immigration Act*. Moreover, the committee recommended "a clear statement" on the substance of Canada's refugee policy.[42] This statement would come in the form of specific clauses introduced in the *Immigration Act*.

Using the language of the 1951 Convention, the 1976 *Immigration Act* defined the term "refugee" in Canadian law for the first time. It was a significant piece of legislation, for in addition to providing a legal definition of a refugee and the mechanisms for more formalized determination processes (discussed previously), it introduced the possibility of private refugee sponsorships. Under the terms of the act, groups of five Canadians or more, along with institutions such as churches, could undertake to provide for the settlement and adaptation of a refugee for one year. This initiative demanded a commitment from ordinary Canadians to provide durable solutions to refugees, shifting some of the government's assumed responsibility from previous years to the general public. This clause had an immediate impact. There were 7,300 refugees admitted in 1977. In 1979, there were 27,900.[43] Even more revealing of the breadth of change underway in government circles was the introduction of the Designated Class category.

The idea for the Designated Classes came from the Oppressed Minorities policy initiated in 1970 and reflected the government's efforts at using immigration policy as a humanitarian—and to some extent a development—tool in the intervening years. The Designated Class category was meant to address the needs of refugees who did not meet the strict Convention refugee definition. Refugees selected under the terms of the Designated Class had to demonstrate that they were capable of becoming "successfully established" in Canada, meaning that they were employable and capable of assimilation. In January 1979, the government introduced three designated classes: one for the Indo-Chinese, another for the Latin American Political Prisoners and Oppressed Persons, and a final one for the Eastern European Self-Exiled Persons. The first category applied to people leaving Vietnam, Cambodia, and Laos. The second applied to persons still resident (unlike Convention refugees who were outside their country of origin) in Argentina, Chile, and Uruguay who could demonstrate a genuine fear of persecution. The last category applied to Jewish refugees and anticommunists in Poland and other parts of Eastern Europe.

As a result of the three categories, thousands of people were admitted or resettled to Canada. The most notable, in terms of numbers, were the Indo-Chinese refugees who were resettled in the late 1970s. By the time the international effort on behalf of refugees in Southeast Asia concluded in the early 1990s, there were almost 69,000 new arrivals in Canada. More than half of these came as the result of private sponsorship agreements signed by churches, NGOs, and community groups with the federal government. The impressive scale of the Indo-Chinese refugee movement revealed the growing willingness, on the part of the Canadian government and Canadians, to provide assistance to people in the Global South by having them resettled or admitted to the country as refugees—a process that began in earnest with the resettlement of Tibetan refugees a decade prior.

Conclusion

How can we understand the decade that stretched from the resettlement of 240 Tibetan refugees to the beginning of a program that saw the arrival of 69,000 refugees from Vietnam, Cambodia, and Laos? The numbers alone, specifically the 100,000 people assisted through various humanitarian immigration initiatives, speak to a major change in how the Canadian government viewed its responsibilities with regard to refugees in the Global South. What the numbers don't tell us is how this change came about; how the policy-making process in the early 1970s was fraught with anxiety; and how, incrementally, Canada's refugee policy shifted to become global in scope. That story lies in the introduction of refugee determination processes and the mechanics of each resettlement and humanitarian program the government initiated over the course of the 1970s, beginning with the Tibetan refugees.

The resettlement of 240 Tibetan refugees marked the cautious beginning of Canada's sustained interest in refugee issues outside of Europe. Crucially, the policies that successive Canadian governments developed in response to humanitarian situations in the Global South over the course of the 1970s were reactive in nature, not proactive. Authorities did not seek out opportunities to be humanitarian, or to connect in a more profound way with the Global South. Rather, the humanitarian need presented and described by activists and the relatives of people in dangerous conditions demanded profound self-reflection and an assessment of the kind of country Canadians desired to have, as well as the kinds of people they wanted to be. Over the course of the decade, the people charged with developing and delivering Canada's immigration and refugee policies proved increasingly committed to providing concrete humanitarian solutions to the world's refugees. As Mike Molloy, himself a former visa officer, recalls,

> there were politicians like [Pierre] Trudeau, [Robert] Andras, [Bud] Cullen, and [Ron] Atkey who really believed in Canada's refugee mission and they were seconded by mandarins like [Jack] Manion, [Richard] Tait, [Jim] Mitchell, and most especially Kirk Bell who really believed and were in a position to push the changes through.... Then there were the minions like Don Cameron, Gerry Campbell and me and many, many more for whom a chance to work on a resettlement program was the best part of the job.[44]

Refugee movements and population flows from around the world, and especially from the Global South, forced Canadians and their governments to confront the extent to which they were prepared to actively facilitate a transformation of Canadian society through the resettlement and admission of people beyond the traditional source countries of the British world and northern Europe. The process that began in the 1960s with the introduction of a points system for independent migrants was tested repeatedly in the following decade by the refugee movements that emerged from Cold War confrontations, violent decolonization efforts, and evolving political landscapes in the Global South. In the case of the Tibetan refugees, the government experimented with a pilot resettlement project. Although authorities were pleased with the results, the comprehensive resettlement scheme was a costly investment and one that the government was not inclined to repeat until the massive exodus of millions of people out of Indochina after 1979 (even then, private sponsorships were responsible for more than half of the refugees resettled to Canada). Still, the Tibetan refugee movement influenced how subsequent refugee situations were addressed. Learning from the Tibetan experience, the federal government relaxed admission requirements and provided different levels of financial and settlement support for people leaving Chile, Uganda, Angola, Mozambique, and Lebanon as a result of various conflicts. Combined, these wide-ranging strategies led to the arrival of thousands of people from the Global South throughout the 1970s, as well as thousands of others who immigrated as independent workers under Canada's changing terms of admissions.

The number of humanitarian situations that emerged globally over the course of the 1970s prompted the Canadian government to formalize its refugee policies, moving from the ad hoc strategies that characterized its early postwar efforts to domestic legislation that defined refugees according to the 1951 Convention while at the same time providing a structural solution, in the form of Designated Classes, for those who did not meet the

Convention's narrow terms. The tentative manner with which the federal government resettled the small number of Tibetan refugees from 1970 to 1971 ultimately led to significant changes in Canada's legal landscape and global humanitarian outlook. Perhaps even more critically, the movement of refugees from the Global South marked a closer relationship between Canada and the people and places that were historically marginalized in the country's national imagery.

Box 8.1 A Timeline of Humanitarian Assistance in 1970s' Canada

In 1972, General Idi Amin ordered the expulsion of 50,000 Asian residents from Uganda. The citizenship of Asian residents was later revoked. In response to an appeal from the British government, Canada dispatched a selection team to Uganda in September 1972 and proceeded to admit over 6,000 people.

General Augusto Pinochet assumed power in Chile in September 1973 following a coup d'état that overthrew President Salvador Allende. In the following decade, an estimated 200,000 Chileans fled or were forced into exile due to their opposition to the new regime. As a result of active lobbying by churches, labour unions, and NGOs, Canada admitted 8,000 people, though the Trudeau government was roundly criticized for its seemingly slow response. The government initially planned to admit only 300 to 1,000 individuals.

The Turkish invasion of Cyprus in July 1974 created large-scale displacement, with an estimated 200,000 people forced to leave their homes as a result of the fighting. The Canadian government responded to pressure from the Greek community by loosening selection and processing procedures so that family-class members or nominated relatives could make their way to Canada. Seven hundred people did so.

In the same year, a revolution in Portugal marked the end of its empire in Africa. Civil wars later erupted in Angola and Mozambique, leading to the flight and displacement of 200,000 Portuguese settlers. In 1976, as a result of the worsening conditions in the two countries, the Canadian government relaxed admissions criteria for the relatives of Portuguese Canadians. As a result of this humanitarian initiative, 2,100 people came to Canada.

In 1976, civil war broke out in Lebanon. Canada responded, using Cyprus as a precedent, and processed relatives rapidly under loosened regulations. Lebanese who were in Canada temporarily under the nominated relatives category were given permission to work, and independent immigrants who were in the country temporarily were allowed to stay and work until conditions improved. A total of 1,100 people were admitted to Canada as a result of this program.

Following the end of the Vietnam War in 1975, people sought to leave the chaotic postwar conditions in Vietnam and Cambodia, and 9,000 were resettled to Canada. Conditions worsened in subsequent years, and by 1979 a massive exodus of people was taking place. As part of the international community's response, Canada resettled 60,000 people from Cambodia, Laos, and Vietnam. More than half of those resettled people came to Canada under private sponsorship agreements introduced in the 1976 *Immigration Act*.

Discussion Questions

1) What does a humanitarian immigration policy entail?
2) What do the different resettlement and humanitarian efforts that the Canadian government introduced over the course of the 1970s have in common? How do they differ?
3) This chapter tells the history of refugees in 1970s' Canada from the perspective of the federal government. How might this history look if it was told from the perspective of an international NGO or someone fleeing difficult circumstances?
4) How would you characterize the Canadian government's approach to the resettlement of Tibetan refugees?
5) What is the relationship between global change and developments within Canada, in terms of immigration and refugee policies? How might domestic developments influence the global landscape, and vice versa?

Further Readings

Chimni, B.S. "The Geopolitics of Refugee Studies: A View from the South." *Journal of Refugee Studies* 11, no. 4 (1998): 350–74. http://dx.doi.org/10.1093/jrs/11.4.350-a.

Dargyay, L. "Tibetans in Alberta and Their Cultural Identity." *Canadian Ethnic Studies* 20, no. 2 (1987): 114–23.

Iacovetta, Franca. *Gatekeepers: Reshaping Immigrant Lives in Cold War Canada.* Toronto: Between the Lines, 2006.

Martin, Susan F., Sanjula Weerasinghe, and Abbie Taylor, eds. *Humanitarian Crises and Migration: Causes, Consequences and Responses.* New York: Routledge, 2014.

McLellan, Janet. "Religion and Ethnicity: The Role of Buddhism in Maintaining Ethnic Identity among Tibetans in Lindsay, Ontario." *Canadian Ethnic Studies* 19, no. 1 (1987): 63–76.

Nafziger, Wayne E., Frances Stewart, and Raimo Väyrynen, eds. *War, Hunger, and Displacement: The Origins of Humanitarian Emergencies.* Vols. 1 and 2. Oxford: Oxford University Press, 2000.

Raska, Jan. "Tibetan Immigration to Canada." https://www.pier21.ca/blog/jan-raska/tibetan-immigration-to-canada.

Notes

1   The author wishes to thank Don Cameron and Mike Molloy for their assistance in the preparation of this chapter.

2   Elfan Rees, "The Refugee and Development," *Ecumenical Review* 19, no. 2 (April 1967): 208.

3   Resettlement is defined by the United Nations High Commissioner for Refugees (UNHCR) as "the selection and transfer of refugees from a State in which they have sought protection to a third State which has agreed to admit them—as refugees—with permanent residence status." UNHCR, *Resettlement Handbook* (November 2004), 1–2.

4   The notion of an "international refugee regime" refers to "the collective ensemble of international agreements, conventions, protocols, as well as the institutions, policies and practices that have appeared since the 1920s to define, address and resolve the problem of human displacement across national borders." Nevzat Soguk defines an international "regime" as a set of "legal and institutional arrangements and mechanisms of collaboration—cooperation and coordination—among actors." *States and Strangers: Refugees and Displacements of Statecraft* (Minneapolis: University of Minnesota Press, 1999), 108. Although most scholars associate the origins of the international refugee regime to the post–World War II period, the creation of the 1951 United Nations Convention Relating to the Status of Refugees, the 1967 amending Protocol, and the establishment of the Office of United Nations High Commissioner for Refugees, the origins of the current international refugee regime date to the 1920s and the displacement that occurred in the wake of World War I as empires crumbled and national borders were drawn and redrawn.

5   *War's Human Cost* (UNHCR Global Trends 2013), http://www.unhcr.org/5399a14f9.html; *World At War* (UNHCR Global Trends 2014), http://unhcr.org/556725e69.html.

6   An estimated 20 million people were displaced during World War II. Two years after the war's end, there were still over a million displaced persons scattered across Europe. It was a situation that threatened the hoped-for postwar peace and stability. Western liberals believed that the desperate situation in the refugee and displaced person camps created situations ripe for the spread of communism. As a result, early efforts to resettle refugees and displaced persons were the product of Cold War anxieties as well as a desire to provide humanitarian relief and redress the wrongs and neglect that led millions to perish in the Holocaust. It was in this context that an international conference met to draft a refugee

convention to protect refugees. Daniel Cohen, *In War's Wake: Europe's Displaced Persons in the Postwar Order* (New York: Oxford University Press, 2012).

7   *Convention and Protocol Relating to the Status of Refugees* (Geneva: UNHCR, 2011), 14.

8   See Franca Iacovetta, *Gatekeepers: Reshaping Immigrant Lives in Cold War Canada* (Toronto: Between the Lines, 2006).

9   Canada's early immigration policies were exclusionary in nature. Chinese migrants, for instance, faced a progressive punitive head tax from 1885 to 1923 before the *Chinese Immigration Act* banned migration almost completely until 1947. Japanese migration was held in check after 1907 through a negotiated "gentleman's agreement," and migrants from the Indian subcontinent were excluded through "continuous journey" regulations introduced in 1908 and were subject to limited quotas in the postwar period.

10   Stephen Castles, Hein de Haas, and Mark J. Miller, eds., *The Age of Migration: International Population Movements in the Modern World*, 5th ed. (New York: Guilford Press, 2013), 131.

11   For a detailed breakdown of arriving migrants by region for these same years, see Shiva S. Halli, Frank Trovato, and Leo Driedger, eds., *Ethnic Demography: Canadian Immigration Racial and Cultural Variations* (Ottawa: Carleton University Press, 1990), 149.

12   "2012 Facts and Figures," Citizenship and Immigration Canada, http://publications.gc.ca/collections/collection_2013/cic/Ci1-8-2012-eng.pdf.

13   Human Rights Consultation, 1974—Constitution and Bylaws, MG 28 I37, Volume 185, File 8, Canadian Council of Churches Fonds, LAC.

14   Memorandum to Cabinet, "Selection of Refugees to Canada," July 27, 1970, RG2, Privy Council Office, Series A-5-a, Volume 6359, LAC.

15   Randy Lippert, *Sanctuary, Sovereignty, Sacrifice: Canadian Sanctuary Incidents, Power and Law* (Vancouver: University of British Columbia Press, 2005), 45.

16   In 1989, the process was further formalized with the establishment of the Immigration and Refugee Board, a quasi-judicial body that reviews claims to Convention refugee status. In 2011, the Immigration and Refugee Board heard claims to refugee status by nationals from 182 countries. This figure reflects the fact that, unlike the selective resettlement and protection of the Oppressed Minorities policy and Designated Classes policies discussed below, the legal developments following Canada's signing of the 1951 Convention Relating to the Status of Refugees meant that migrants could take the initiative in having their claims to protection considered.

17   Cabinet Conclusions, "Selection of Refugees for Resettlement to Canada," RG2, Privy Council Office, Series A-5-a, Volume 6359, LAC, September 24, 1970, http://www.bac-lac.gc.ca/eng/discover/politics-government/cabinet-conclusions/Pages/cabinet-conclusions.aspx.

18   Memorandum to Cabinet, "Selection of Refugees."

19   Freda Hawkins, *Canada and Immigration: Public Policy and Public Concern* (Montreal: McGill-Queen's University Press, 1988), 382.

20   Mike Molloy, email correspondence with author, August 7, 2014.

21   Department of Northern Affairs to the Department of Manpower and Immigration, RG 76, Volume 1217, Tibetan Movement—General, File 5786–1, Part 1, LAC, October 24, 1962.

22 Minutes of the first meeting of the Interdepartmental Ad Hoc Committee on Tibetan Refugees, RG 76, Volume 1217, Tibetan Movement—General, File 5786–1, Part 1, LAC, October 20, 1967.

23 "Subject: Possible Aid to Tibetan Refugees" (paper prepared for consideration by Committee), Tibetan Movement—General, RG 76, Volume 1217, File 5786–1, Part 3, LAC.

24 Ibid.

25 Ibid.

26 Memorandum to Cabinet, "The Settlement of a Limited Number of Tibetan Refugee Families in Small Family Groups in Canada," Tibetan Movement—General, RG 76, Volume 1217, File 5786–1, Part 3, LAC, April 30, 1970.

27 Ibid.

28 Jack Granatstein and Robert Bothwell, *Pirouette: Pierre Trudeau and Canadian Foreign Policy* (Toronto: University of Toronto Press, 1990), 218. When asked during a press conference in Jamaica about the admission of Rhodesian settlers, Trudeau replied, "I am certainly not panting to have this immigration movement take place.... If they are liberals, white liberals, they should stay and have nothing to fear after Rhodesian independence. If they're ... racist, why shouldn't you [Jamaica] receive them rather than us?" See also Tom Axworthy and Pierre Trudeau, *Towards a Just Society: The Trudeau Years* (Markham, ON: Viking, 1990), 188.

29 "For Tibetan Refugees Canada Was Literally the New World," *Toronto Star*, November 23, 2010, last modified August 4, 2014, http://www.thestar.com/news/world/2010/10/23/for_tibetan_refugees_canada_was_literally_the_new_world.html.

30 J.C. Morrison to Deputy Minister, 18 July 1969, RG 76, Refugees—Tibetan Movement—General Volume 1218, File 5786–1, Part 6, LAC.

31 Memorandum to Cabinet, "The Settlement of a Limited Number of Tibetan Refugee Families."

32 Memorandum to Cabinet, "The Settlement of a Limited Number of Tibetan Refugee Families in Small Family Groups in Canada," RG 76, Volume 1218, File 5786-1, Part 8, LAC, April 30, 1970.

33 James Bissett (Director of Foreign Service) to Immigration Attaché for Canada, New Delhi, Tibetan Movement—General, RG 76, Volume 1217, File 5786–1, Part 3, LAC, July 3, 1970.

34 Bissett to Immigration Attaché for Canada.

35 George Woodcock to Mr. G.C. Wallach, Refugees—Tibetan Movement—General, RG 76, Volume 1218, File 5786–1, Part 8, LAC, January 24, 1970.

36 E.G. Staub to R. Talbot, Director of Technical Services Branch, RG 76, Volume 1218, File 5786–1, Part 8, Refugees—Tibetan Movement—General, LAC, October 21, 1970.

37 J.R. Staveley to E.G. Staub, Tibetan Movement—General, RG 76, Volume 1217, File 5786–1, Part 3, LAC, December 11, 1970.

38 Duncan Campbell, ADM (Strategic Planning and Research), to Jean Edmonds, Tibetan Movement—General, RG 76, Volume 1219, File 5786–1, Part 16, LAC, February 2, 1976.

39 "Canada Was Literally the New World."

40 Will Smith, "The Tibetan Refugee Settlement Program," RG 76, Volume 1219, File 5786–1, Part 6, Tibetan Movement—General, LAC.

41 Ninette Kelley and Michael Trebilcock, *Making of the Mosaic: A History of Canadian Immigration Policy* (Toronto: University of Toronto Press, 2010), 403.
42 Hawkins, *Canada and Immigration*, 376.
43 Ibid., 383.
44 Mike Molloy, email correspondence with author, August 7, 2014.

9
Popular Internationalism: Grassroots Exchange and Social Movements

SEAN MILLS

Introduction

As previous chapters have shown, the "Third World" does not lie beyond Canada's borders, in a land far removed from its everyday realities. Canadian governments and businesses have intervened in the non-Western world with the goal of pursuing profits or advancing "Western civilization." Yet, even while these developments were taking place, many within Canada challenged the direction of Canadian corporations and governments, seeing themselves and their realities as being deeply entangled with those of the Third World. Canadians have travelled to the Global South and taken part in social movements, defended migrant rights within Canada, and engaged in myriad other forms of support and exchange. In a provocative study, scholar Leela Gandhi asks us why, in certain circumstances, individuals have chosen to give up "the privileges of imperialism and elected affinity with victims of their own expansionist cultures"?[1] There are many answers to this question, because there have been many moments in the past in which global ties of friendship and support emerged across national or racial boundaries. In this chapter, I try to answer this question through a tentative exploration of the history of what I am terming Canadian popular internationalism.

The complex histories of the various forms of popular internationalism in Canada have yet to be written, and in this chapter I therefore have the modest goal of offering an early reconnaissance of some of the different sites in which this alternative internationalism emerged.[2] By exploring these different forms of popular internationalism in Canada, I hope to show some of the ways in which "foreign relations" were forged not only by governments, but also by regular citizens and migrants, and by churches and social movements. Here we will learn about individuals and social movements that sought to build different types of relationships with the Third World from those being forged by governments and corporations. As others in this book have noted, there is a variety of different ways in which individuals from Canada have engaged with the Third World, from military campaigns to missionary and NGO work, all of which were shaped by an international outlook. How, then, does this differ from the forms of popular internationalism—which some have historically called international solidarity—discussed in this chapter?

In this chapter I define popular internationalism as encompassing movements that have sought to understand the interconnected histories of the First and Third Worlds, and that have sought to oppose the structural inequalities between the two. Historically, these movements have emerged out of social movements and religious groups, migrant communities, labour organizations, and the work of dissident intellectuals and activists. They have a long history that stretches deep into the past, but I intend to focus on the post-1960 period, when new forms of solidarity and activism emerged.[3] One particularly controversial question is whether popular internationalism can take shape among NGOs, tied as they often are to governmental programs of foreign aid. In recent years, as Molly Kane illustrates in this book, a debate about NGOs and their connections to governmental foreign aid and foreign policy has emerged in many quarters. In Canada, two recent contributors to this discussion are solidarity activists Nikolas Barry-Shaw and Dru Oja-Jay, both of whom chart their own politicization to their awareness of the ways in which Canadian NGOs often uncritically support Canadian foreign policy, and who argue that true solidarity can only emerge outside of publicly funded NGOs.[4] This debate—and the effort to see oneself as being connected to the Third World rather than separate from it—is not new, and has historically emerged out of many different movements and been fed by a variety of intellectual and political traditions.[5]

I want to begin by looking at the new forms of popular internationalism that emerged out of the social movements of the 1960s, paying particular attention to the importance of Third World thought in Quebec and new forms of political economy and anti-imperialism that were developed by intellectuals in English Canada. By questioning their relationship to American transnational capitalism, both francophone and anglophone activists began looking to the countries of the Global South, which they saw as facing connected challenges of economic dependency and underdevelopment. Second, by drawing on examples of Latin American and Caribbean migrants, I will explore the ways in which international solidarity with the Third World was developed at least partly out of the intellectual and political analyses that migrants from the Third World brought with them when they began arriving in increasing numbers in the 1960s and 1970s. And, finally, I'll look to the convergence of many of the above forces in the development in the 1970s and 1980s of solidarity with Latin America, a crucial site in the development of broader movements of popular internationalism that, in many different ways, continue to shape political life in the present.

Internationalism and the 1960s in English and French Canada

Like in many other countries throughout the world, the 1960s in Canada was an era of protest, contestation, and change, and it was a decade when many began thinking about their relationship to the world in new ways. While the politics of the Third World were having an impact throughout the country, it was in Quebec where they had some of their most transformative effects, as the theories of Third World decolonization became the ideological foundation for social movements that transformed the province's political and intellectual structures. For many Quebeckers in the 1960s, the idea of decolonization often implied that Quebec needed to become independent and gain control over its own economic affairs. In the early 1960s, French Canadians constituted the vast majority of the Quebec population while controlling only 20 per cent of its economy, and they were marginalized from the sites of economic and cultural power within the province. Before the 1960s French Canadians were often told to "speak white"—meaning "speak English"—when speaking French in downtown Montreal. Because of the inequalities that French Canadians faced in relation to anglophones both within Quebec and within Canada more generally, a whole generation began to imagine that they had more in common with black Americans and with the Third World than they had with mainstream North American society.[6]

The idea of Quebec decolonization certainly seems strange to us now—after all, how could francophone Quebec be decolonized, when the province itself was largely composed of a white population settled on Aboriginal land? But as contradictory as the ideas of decolonization sometimes were, they had an enormous power in the 1960s, and these ideas formed the foundation on which international solidarity would be built. The power of the ideas themselves cannot be understood outside of the international context in which they were formed. In her study *L'une et l'autre indépendance, 1954–1964*, Magali Deleuze argues that throughout the 1950s the Algerian War had an important effect in Quebec. Across the political spectrum, there was wide support for Algerian independence, as Quebec intellectuals spoke out against French colonialism. By watching the example of Algerians fighting for their independence against a dying French empire, many Quebec intellectuals became attuned to the idea of decolonization, the belief that colonized peoples could free themselves from imperial rule and build their own society on the basis of national sovereignty. It was in the particular atmosphere of 1950s' Quebec, Deleuze maintains, that the idea of Quebec decolonization first came into widespread circulation. This support for the Algerian war, and the relatively small fraction of French intellectuals—such as Jean-Paul Sartre and Simone de Beauvoir—who dissented and also supported the Algerian side, helped bring ideas of decolonization into Quebec.[7]

By the early 1960s, the idea of Quebec decolonization was gaining widespread prominence, being articulated by a new wave of activists and intellectuals. Journals emerged that articulated the ideology of Quebec decolonization, and the idea would become central to a constellation of social movements that sought to reimagine Quebec's place in the world. Drawing on the works of Frantz Fanon, Jean-Paul Sartre, Jacques Berque, Albert Memmi, and others, many authors sought to understand the power relations that shaped their society. Dissident authors and activists founded new publications, and they created new political movements that sought to bring about social change. Of all the movements that emerged, however, none has received more attention than the Front de libération du Québec (FLQ). Ideas of decolonization gave FLQ members the feeling of legitimacy in waging a campaign of armed struggle. The group's actions therefore highlighted many of the problems with mapping anticolonial theory, developed in very different circumstances, onto the complex realities of Quebec society. Because so much attention has focused on this group, however, the vast array of ways in which a diversity of groups worked for social change—all with their own ideas on how to bring about this change—has been obscured. Feminists formed organizations in their communities and on campuses, laying the groundwork for the women's liberation movement that would reshape gender roles within Quebec society. Student groups sought to democratize the province's education system, and municipal activists founded a new political party to run in municipal elections. The decision to take up arms to violently challenge the established order was a minority position, and only one part of a much more complicated and diversified whole.[8]

With the proliferation of political movements in Quebec during the 1960s and 1970s, Third World thought made a dramatic entry into Canada. Quebeckers had supported Algerians during the Algerian War, and the Vietnamese in their campaign against the United States during the Vietnam War. Avant-garde Quebec journals followed the American civil rights and black power movements closely, and covered liberation movements in Africa, Asia, and Latin America. This unprecedented political energy of the 1960s in Quebec paved the way for new forms of international solidarity in the 1970s. But the social movements of the 1960s were not the only origins of international solidarity. Ideas of solidarity also took shape within a rapidly transforming Catholic Church, an institution that was greatly affected by the atmosphere of the era.

Throughout the 1960s, the Catholic Church lost much of its power in Quebec. The Catholic clergy was having difficulty recruiting new members, there was a 36 per cent decline in church congregations in the years from 1962 to 1978,[9] and many began to see the decreased power of the church as a central component of Quebec's modernization. Yet the Catholic Church, both locally and internationally, was also undergoing its own process of modernization, and Vatican II ushered in a whole series of transformations in the relationship between the church and its followers. While many traditional elements remained, there were also new forces that drew from both earlier Catholic traditions and the new climate of change sweeping much of the world, one of the most influential of which was liberation theology. Liberation theology was a particular movement that emerged in Latin America, through which Catholics interpreted the Gospel as advocating for a "preferential option for the poor." The real meaning of Christianity, those influenced by liberation theology argued, was found in the fight for social justice and the empowerment of the marginalized. French-Canadian missionaries working in Latin America were influenced by liberation theology, and they would bring many of these ideas home with them when they returned to Quebec. Catholic groups would become central to the development of popular internationalism in Quebec throughout the 1970s. International solidarity in Quebec was therefore born of a variety of different sources, from radical anticolonialism to Catholicism.[10]

The ideas motivating internationally minded people in English Canada were just as varied. Amidst the fading power of the British empire and the polarizing impulses of the Cold War, in the early 1960s in the hip cafés of Yorkville, young people sipped coffee and sang folk songs against war. It was at the Purple Onion coffee house in Toronto that Cree singer Buffy Sainte-Marie wrote "Universal Soldier," a song that captured many of the sentiments of 1960s' North American counterculture, advocating a universal opposition to militarism. According to *Maclean's* magazine, the Purple Onion was "a Victorian parlour that was blown up by a gas explosion during a whist drive," and was a place in which "the customers sit at rickety card tables and look at the remains of a fretwork-fronted upright piano, fragments of bombazine sofas and aspidistra pots, fractured specimens of spelterware and bits of stuffed birds."[11] Places such as the Purple Onion acted as some of the sites where a new form of international sensibility was taking shape in opposition to war, while university campuses were also slowly developing into sites of revolt.

In the early 1960s the Cold War raged, and the focus of activists remained on the looming prospect of nuclear war. Throughout the 1950s and 1960s, a variety of antinuclear movements took shape, and a women's peace organization, the Voice of Women, had also long prepared the ground for the emergence of the antinuclear movement. The threat of nuclear war informed the founding of the Student Union for Peace Action (SUPA) in Regina in 1964, an organization formed on the principles of student syndicalism, with the idea that students needed to be actively involved in politics outside of the university as well as within it. SUPA went out from university communities, working with the poor and disenfranchised. For SUPA members of the 1960s, it was impossible to separate the internal and external aspects of Canadian life. As such, they organized protests against the Vietnam War, such as protests at the American consulate on University Avenue in Toronto in 1965. In 1967, a major protest was held at the American consulate in Montreal, which saw 46 people arrested and 20 injured.[12]

The Vietnam War wasn't the only focus of social movements, as many also began looking toward Latin America. In the aftermath of World War II, movements of democratic reform took hold throughout the continent, inspiring hopes for the possibilities of a new democratic future in Central and South America. But the region was also quickly becoming an important theatre in the Cold War. Beginning with Guatemala in 1954, the combined forces of the United States and powerful interests in Latin America—including the landed class and the military—used violence to suppress democratic movements. As historian Greg Grandin argues, "Washington found that it greatly preferred anti-Communist dictatorships to the possibility that democratic openness might allow the Soviets to gain a foothold on the continent."[13] When the Cuban Revolution came to power in 1959, activists and sympathizers throughout North America began to fear an American-backed overthrow of the new government, or perhaps even an American invasion of the island. A CIA-backed invasion was attempted at the Bay of Pigs in 1961 and, although it failed, it brought the prospect of Cuba—which had drawn the attention and support of the Soviet Union— acting as a catalyst to nuclear war that much closer.

With the looming threat of invasion and the possibilities of nuclear war that this entailed, Cuba held a great degree of symbolic importance for the emergence of solidarity movements throughout the 1960s. Cuba was one of the places where it appeared that nuclear war might break out, especially with the scare of the Cuban missile crisis of 1962. The Cuban missile crisis also helped bring North American currents of pacifism and anti-imperialism to Canada, such as in May 1963 when a delegation of American pacifists came to Quebec City to begin a Quebec-Washington-Guantanamo Walk for Peace. The walk was designed "to oppose nuclear weapons testing, nuclear missiles, racial discrimination, and the Cuba travel ban/trade embargo, and bring Canadian and US peace activists into closer cooperation." The group worked with local peace groups and marched through the United States, where they faced considerable difficulties with police and a sometimes hostile public.[14] The walk, uniting pacifists in both Canada and the United States, helped to bring a form of internationalization to political life in Canada in the early 1960s.

The Cuban revolution itself—particularly in its early years—held out the possibility for a different kind of development, one in which societies would be able to create an independent path that would not rely on the economic power of North America, and the political power that this economic weight necessarily carried with it. In the United States, "Fair Play for Cuba Committees" emerged throughout the country, hoping to fend off what they saw to be an inevitable American invasion of the island. In Canada, solidarity with the Cuban Revolution also became an important constituent of the emerging politics of those who sought to forge "foreign policy from below."[15]

In 1961, after a trip to Cuba, Vernel and Anne Olson founded the first Fair Play for Cuba Committee across Canada, a Canadian version of the movement that had taken shape throughout the United States. The Fair Play for Cuba Committees that emerged in Canada did so with a broad transnational imagination that sought to rethink Canada's role in the world. The reaction to the Cuban Revolution played out differently in Canada than it did in the United States. There were many reasons for this, including the salient fact that Canadian banks and companies were not nationalized by the Cuban government in the same way as were those of the United States. This would change the dynamic of Fair Play for Cuba Committees north of the border, which would have a much longer life than they would in the United States. In February 1961 the first meeting of Fair Play took place at the First Unitarian Church in Toronto, and in its aftermath Vernel Olson toured the country, speaking to crowds about Cuba and the Cuban Revolution. Many would even take the Fair Play for Cuba Committee up on its offer to bring Canadians on tours of revolutionary Cuba. As Cynthia Wright explains, "The Canadian FPCC also produced an important body of literature of its own. FPCC pamphlets were often very detailed eyewitness accounts from people who had recently visited Cuba, and included titles such as the very popular *Four Canadians Who Saw Cuba* (1963), *The Real Cuba As Three Canadians Saw It* (1964), and *Canadian Students in Cuba* (1965), which came out of the 1964 student tour."[16] The symbolism of the Cuban Revolution and the possibilities of a new anti-imperialist politics sparked the imaginations of many activists within Canada.

As David Webster explores in this book, Cuba formed one part of a broader politics of anticolonialism and global decolonization, one that had its roots not only in Latin America, but also in Africa and Asia. And, as mentioned above, the power of many of the ideas that emerged out of Third World decolonization resonated widely in Canada, including among Aboriginal groups. As Scott Rutherford has maintained in the opening chapter of this book, Aboriginals in Canada were long seen to be obstacles that needed to be overcome for Canada to develop. In the 1960s, Aboriginal groups were increasingly making it clear that they had no intention to disappear. Aboriginal resistance to colonialism stretches back to the sixteenth century and continued throughout much of the twentieth, but the 1960s and 1970s nevertheless marked the beginning of a prolonged Aboriginal renaissance that continues forward to this day. During the 1960s and 1970s, many drew examples and inspiration from movements of decolonization taking place across the Third World.[17] Throughout the 1970s, Aboriginal politics would come to significantly reshape Canadian society, bringing the legacy of empire to the forefront of public discussion, and in so doing engaging a redefinition of Canada itself. As Jane Jenson and Martin Papillon argue, because borders have been in dispute since the beginning of European settlement, in "their everyday lives as well as their politics, movements of indigenous peoples live the complex relationship between citizenship claims and transnational social movement action."[18] Aboriginal political movements of the 1970s often emerged out of the intersection of long-held local grievances and a broad transnational politics of decolonization.[19]

Canadian activists denounced Canada's complicity with the war in Vietnam, including its manufacturing of weapons, and the country itself increasingly became shaped by the thousands of Americans fleeing military conscription in the United States.[20] In the 1960s, it had been nearly two decades since many Canadians had been worrying about Canadian identity in the face of Canada's subordinate relationship to the vast economic power of the United States. But in the 1960s these concerns rose to the forefront of debate. A landmark moment came in 1965 with the publication of George Grant's *Lament for a Nation*, a heartfelt cry for the loss of a distinctive identity that came with Canada's integration into the American empire. Canadians from a range of political perspectives took this book as something of a founding document; it struck a nerve among those who felt threatened by American cultural and economic power over Canadian life.[21] The crisis over the feared power of the United States had deep roots in Canadian thought, and in the 1960s young intellectuals and economists began looking to theories of development and underdevelopment that were emerging in Latin America. The fear of the United States and its control of American culture led many to begin exploring the ways in which other societies living within the shadow of the United States thought about these questions. In the contested climate of the 1960s, when the worry about the American control of the Canadian economy increasingly shaped political discussion, "left nationalism" became a major framework through which many people began to understand their position in the world. Premised on the belief that it was necessary to curb American control of the Canadian economy, many advocated for increased political and economic national self-determination that would give the government a stronger ability to build a just society.

Box 9.1 Kari Levitt and the Idea of Canadian Dependency

One of the most influential statements of Canadian dependency theory was penned by McGill University economist Kari Levitt, a scholar who had close contact with the anglophone Caribbean and who had developed her theories of the Canadian economy alongside Caribbean economists. Levitt moved to Montreal in 1960 to take up a post at McGill University, and quickly became involved with the Canadian New Democratic Party (NDP), while simultaneously building close connections with anglophone Caribbean intellectuals. While working to develop theories of the plantation economy to explain Caribbean underdevelopment, Levitt began writing background papers for the NDP, and eventually published a long essay in the Caribbean-based *New World Quarterly* on "Economic Dependence and Political Disintegration: The Case of Canada." The essay was reprinted and distributed informally throughout Canada, becoming something of a cult classic on university campuses and in the burgeoning world of the political opposition. When Levitt published an extended version of the essay in a book entitled *Silent Surrender: The Multinational Corporation in Canada*, the book received a lot of attention, crystallizing a debate that had been taking place for some time. Levitt argued that as the Canadian economy became increasingly dependent on the United States, the country was losing its ability to democratically shape its future. "Present-day Canada," she famously argued, "may be described as the world's richest underdeveloped country."[22] Levitt's ideas had a considerable impact, but they were also controversial, and many intellectuals and activists opposed seeing Canada as a society dependent on the United States, arguing that this perspective minimized an understanding of class relations within Canada, as well as Canada's asymmetrical relationship with the Third World.

In the 1960s and 1970s, "left nationalism" held considerable sway over the labour movement, as well as among artists and intellectuals,[23] and many began to develop an understanding of a different kind of world order in which they hoped to form a part. It was therefore out of the complex mix of leftist, nationalist, and Third World ideas that new forms of popular internationalism emerged. As activists pushed from below to change Canadian foreign policy and steer it further away from that of the United States, they drew upon economic theories from Latin America and the Caribbean, and many would begin looking to Canada's own asymmetrical relationship with the Global South. Many would eventually conclude that Canada was not only a victim of imperial structures of power, but that it was also actively engaged in perpetuating these very structures, and the country often occupied these two positions simultaneously.

This awareness that Canada had its own unequal relations with the countries of the Third World did not happen on its own, and it was not just the result of international theory; it also came about in part because of the interventions of migrants from the Global South who were increasingly making Canada their home. As Laura Madokoro explains in this book, shifting immigration regulations of the 1960s and 1970s brought small but significant numbers of non-European immigrants to Canada from Africa, Asia, and Latin America. Many brought with them ideas and experiences that would change the nature of Canadian grassroots internationalism.

Migrants and Popular Internationalism

As Barrington Walker has demonstrated in this volume, for much of Canadian history the composition of the Canadian population was forged through various escalating forms of racial exclusion that sought to keep the Canadian population white. But in the 1960s immigration regulations began to change. The new regulations of 1962 and 1967 took steps toward deracializing Canadian immigration policy, meaning that Canada increasingly became a destination of migrants from the Global South. One important group of migrants in the 1960s and 1970s was from the anglophone Caribbean, and these migrants would become some of the most articulate proponents of an alternative narrative of Western history, one which looked to Canada not as a colony, but as a society that had long had its own relationship of power with the Global South. Throughout the 1960s Toronto and Montreal were quickly becoming important centres of Caribbean activism and intellectual thought. Montreal became home to a chapter of the New World Movement, and the Caribbean Conference Committee also began organizing major conferences on Caribbean affairs in the city. Conferences were held in 1965,

1966, and 1967, with speakers such as George Lamming and C.L.R. James invited to address the audience. Young Caribbean intellectuals were laying claim to a role in shaping Canadian public life, while simultaneously hoping to have a role in the future of the Caribbean.[24]

In the fall of 1968, two important conferences on black politics were held in Montreal. The first, held at Sir George Williams (now Concordia) University, focused on the question of black life and racism within Canada, while the second, generating quite a bit more controversy, was the Congress of Black Writers, held at McGill University. At the Congress of Black Writers, world-renowned Caribbean thinkers such as C.L.R. James, Walter Rodney, and Caribbean-American Stokely Carmichael addressed an enthusiastic audience, one that was eager to hear their message of global revolution against American imperialism. The 1960s was a particular moment when it appeared that everything was being put into question, and many began challenging the basic operating structures of their society. The Congress of Black Writers was no exception, and it, more dramatically than any other event of the era, brought Third World politics into the heart of Canadian society.

At the Congress, black writers talked about the global politics of empire. The spirit of the time was one that favoured revolutionary thinking, and once the Congress was finished, this mood of contestation remained, and would greatly contribute to the "Sir George Williams Affair" that took place in February 1969. The Sir George Williams Affair originated at the end of the 1967–68 school year with complaints that biology professor Perry Anderson had treated black students unfairly. When the university did not adequately address these complaints, the students continued their protests into January 1969, leading eventually to an occupation of the university's computer centre. After a tense standoff and a prolonged occupation, the riot police were called in to clear the students on February 11. After a fire broke out, 97 students were arrested and charged criminally, and a major racial backlash unfolded in Montreal, with many demanding that the non-Canadian students be deported. The impact of this event spread far beyond the Canadian border. As many of the students arrested were of Caribbean origin, and as it was widely believed that the students were being treated unfairly and in a racist manner, the Sir George Williams Affair initiated political revolts in Trinidad, Barbados, and elsewhere. Within Canada, many in the black community began rallying together in the aftermath of the event, working to develop new readings of history, and creating the foundations for new political and community organizations to defend their rights.[25]

The Congress of Black Writers and the Sir George Williams Affair were some of the first major events that brought the politics of the Third World into the heart of Canadian society, forcibly demonstrating that Canada—and the makeup of its population—had changed dramatically. The Congress of Black Writers had brought together black intellectuals and activists from various backgrounds, and in its aftermath black intellectuals in the city began rethinking Canada's role in the world. Soon immigrants began arriving from throughout the Global South, and would begin organizing and developing new demands for immigrant rights and international solidarity, helping to shape and reshape Canadian society in the 1970s and beyond. Although most of the participants at the Congress were anglophone, one of the Congress's co-organizers was a Haitian named Elder Thébaud, and his presence symbolized some of the ways in which Haitian migration was in the process of changing francophone Quebec.

The arrival of Haitian migrants in Quebec in the 1960s came about partly because of close ties between French Canada and Haiti that were reinforced in the 1930s and then especially during World War II, when both societies sought out new allies as occupied France could no longer act as the central site of intellectual production in the francophone world. When François Duvalier came to power in 1957, he began to persecute the country's educated elites, who fled in large numbers into exile. Because of the earlier connections that had been forged, and because Quebec was undergoing a rapid expansion of its public service and was looking for qualified French-speaking professionals, Quebec in general, and Montreal in particular, became important sites for the Haitian diaspora that was taking shape across the continent.

All throughout the 1960s, Haitian intellectuals and writers fled to Montreal, and they began building a community of exiles in which, through both writing and political movements, they could articulate their views of Haiti, Canada, and Quebec. The influx of large numbers of Haitians significantly altered the nature of political life in Montreal. Haitian professionals played important roles in the expanding education and health institutions, and intellectual and political exiles formed political and literary groups discussing global politics, as well as developments in both Quebec and Haiti. At meeting places like the Perchoir d'Haïti on Metcalfe Street in downtown Montreal, Haitian poets read their work and brushed shoulders with avant-garde francophone writers. Many Quebec writers learned about Aimé Césaire and Frantz Fanon—two authors who would profoundly affect intellectual life in Quebec in the 1960s and 1970s—from Haitian exiles. Many of the first generation of Haitian migrants—mostly professionals and intellectuals, highly qualified and French-speaking—reported that their integration into Quebec society was relatively straightforward.[26] Many close political and intellectual connections were forged.

This would not be the case with the second major wave of Haitian migrants. A major crisis occurred in 1974, when it was learned that roughly 1,500 Haitians living in Canada without legal status were threatened with deportation. These migrants, like the second wave of Haitian migrants generally, were poorer and less skilled than those who had come in the 1960s. Although they were consistently portrayed as francophones in the media, in many cases they spoke only Creole, like the majority of Haiti's population. Partly because of the politics of Quebec's Quiet Revolution that had led many in Quebec to believe that one of the central needs for the province was to attract French-speaking immigrants, the threatened deportation of the 1,500 Haitian migrants created an enormous amount of political controversy. During the crisis, Haitian migrants popularized an argument that had been developing for years, namely that the Canadian government, through its foreign aid programs, along with Canadian and Québécois capitalists, were providing crucial support that allowed the Duvalier regime to remain in power. And it was this very regime that forced migrants to leave, leading to a situation in which they would find themselves in situations of irregularity upon arriving in Canada. The politics of Canada's foreign presence in the Third World was therefore closely connected to its immigration policies. The arguments that they made gained a great deal of support among social movements that began rethinking their relationship to the Third World.[27]

The feared deportations created a major controversy in Quebec, and very much intersected with broader feelings of Quebec nationalism. But they also opened up new understandings of the interconnected nature of Quebec, Canada, and the Third World. The debate about Haitian migrants was just one of the sites of interaction between new vocal migrant communities from the Third World and social movements in Canada. Elsewhere in the country similar controversies were taking place, and similar attempts were being made to understand Canada's relationship with the Third World, and in particular the way in which the country reacted to moments of crisis. Throughout the 1970s, crises in Latin America, and in particular the coup in Chile in 1973 that removed Salvador Allende from power, had a profound effect on Canada. By looking at Chilean and Latin American solidarity, we can see the intersection of the dissident ideas of the 1960s with the lives and realities of Third World migrants in the 1970s.

Popular Internationalism and Latin America

The Cuban Revolution had marked a new point in creating bonds of solidarity between activists in Canada and Latin America, but for activists in the 1970s it was the coup in Chile in 1973 that created heightened political awareness. In 1970 the hopes of progressive people throughout the world were raised with the election of Salvador Allende and his Popular Unity party. Once in power he began taking the country down a democratic road to social reforms, including beginning a program of nationalization of certain industries. But after three years in office and a prolonged period of political turmoil, Allende was assassinated and Augusto Pinochet violently came to power in an American-backed coup d'état, sending shockwaves throughout much of the world. The full weight of the state was used to crack down on those who were considered opponents of Pinochet's regime, and tens of thousands of people were taken to Chile's national stadium to be interrogated, tortured, or killed. The Canadian government was extremely quick to recognize the CIA-backed Pinochet government, and was excessively slow in recognizing the plight of Chilean refugees attempting to flee the regime. It did not open the door to Chilean migrants in the same way that it had for those fleeing communist dictatorships in earlier periods, such as from Hungary in 1956 or Czechoslovakia in 1968.[28] In Quebec the labour movement and returned missionaries became involved in setting up the *Comité de solidarité Québec-Chili*, and a large rally at the Montreal Forum brought tens of thousands together in opposition to the coup government. The contacts that were made with Chile before the coup by religious and labour groups—including famed labour leader Michel Chartrand—became central to the development of solidarity with Chile in the post-1973 period.[29] Solidarity with Chile became one important component of a broader world of progressive Catholicism in Quebec, which was greatly influenced by the ideas of liberation theology that had been developed in Latin America.[30] The coup that removed Allende from power had a deep and lasting effect on Quebec's social movements.[31]

Throughout English Canada, church groups and local unions also worked to develop forms of international solidarity with Chile, and Chilean solidarity movements formed part of the cultural and political landscape of Canada during the 1970s. The forms of solidarity that emerged in the aftermath of the 1973 coup built on (often religious) connections that had been growing since at least the 1960s. Canadian churches helped to finance the Latin American Working Group in the mid-1960s, and it and other organizations followed developments in Allende's Chile closely. In 1972 church groups even organized a conference in Canada on developments in Chile. When the coup occurred, it was church groups that organized a major campaign to pressure Canada to accept Chilean refugees, a campaign that would eventually lead to major policy changes.[32] When Chilean exiles eventually did arrive in Canada (roughly 6,000 came from 1973 to 1978), they formed organizations that worked to denounce the military regime of Augusto Pinochet and its human rights abuses. Exiles held meetings and founded newspapers, took part in arts, literature, and politics, and engaged significantly with non-Chileans to build support for popular movements in Latin America in general. These early Chilean migrants were instrumental in the establishment of Spanish-language social services and, as the decade wore on, Chilean migrants also became involved with Latin American and Third World solidarity more generally. As one Chilean activist, Patricia Godoy, recalls, "Of course I was in the [Chilean] women's group here in Toronto. . . . I think all of us who arrived in that era got involved in everything. So I participated a lot with the Uruguayans, the Argentineans, we helped the *Madres de Mayo*, I was involved in all that kind of thing. We had fiestas, and through the fiesta we'd raise money to send to the countries."[33] Chileans, in other words, helped build local forms of popular internationalism that spread far beyond the specific case of Chile.

While the coup against Allende's democratically elected government in Chile in 1973 became the occasion for a great deal of international condemnation of the new dictatorship, the stream of refugees from Chile would themselves greatly contribute to the transformation of politics in Canada in the 1970s. Chilean migrants turned out to be only the first group of Latin Americans to flee a right-wing dictatorship and come to Canada. Groups and organizations such as the Comité Québec-Chili and the Centre internationale de solidarité ouvrière (CISO) in Quebec, and the Development Education Collective and the Latin American Working Group in English Canada, became both physical and metaphorical sites where a new politics of solidarity would take shape.[34]

The coup in Chile played an important role in the development of an international awareness, and Chilean exiles worked to create a broader consciousness of military dictatorships and human rights abuses in Latin America. Throughout the 1970s and 1980s, massive human rights violations in Central and South America also led to renewed forms of international solidarity. Churches often took the lead. As previous chapters have shown, churches have played a central role in connecting Canadians to what would later be called the Third World. The ties originally forged by missionaries would, in many ways, lay the foundations upon which later business and NGO developments would take place. In the 1960s and 1970s, Protestant and Catholic religious groups began to rethink their earlier missionary endeavours, and significant forces within Canada's major churches began to find ways to develop new forms of solidarity, and to work for social justice outside of the paradigm of superiority and charity that had animated their work in earlier periods. At times, some of the leading proponents of change were former missionaries themselves, as they had first-hand knowledge of developments in the Global South.

The progressive church movement (PCM) therefore became one of the leading proponents of change. This movement organized and held rallies, and worked to pressure and change Canadian government policy toward human rights abuses in Latin America. Throughout the 1970s the focus remained on the dictatorships in Chile and Argentina, before shifting to Central America in the 1980s. According to David Sheinin, "As in the United States, and primed in part by the international outcry over the assassination of Salvadoran Archbishop Oscar Romero by a right-wing death squad, the PCM spearheaded a vociferous denunciation of right-wing terror in the region in a manner that—as had Romero—linked human rights activisms, left politics, opposition to US foreign policy, and liberation theology." In 1977, the Inter-Church Committee on Human Rights in Latin America (ICCHRLA) emerged, and it became the new centre of the forging of popular internationalism with Latin America, maintaining "strong ties with the Comité Chrétien (Christian Committee on Human Rights in Latin America) in Montreal and with a number of Latin American immigrant and exile organizations in Canada."[35] Deeply disturbed by the growth of the right in the hemisphere and the role of the United States in supporting dictatorships, the PCM worked to develop new lines of solidarity. Throughout the 1970s, the Progressive Church Movement sought to denounce the human rights abuses of Latin American dictatorships, but it also denounced the Canadian government's "complicity in the success of right-wing terror in the Americas." Churches also often played a central role in helping refugees from Latin America who fled dictatorial regimes.[36]

Political economy, Christian ethics, and the analyses brought forward by migrants all converged to create broader movements of popular internationalism in the 1970s and 1980s.

Conclusion

Drawing on a few examples, in this chapter I've attempted to outline aspects of the complex confluence of forces that led to the development of international solidarity with the Third World in the post-1960 period. It would have been possible to choose other examples, such as the support for the anti-apartheid movement in South Africa, or Canadian support for Indochinese "boat people," to take just two of the more obvious campaigns of the 1970s and 1980s. Far from being insignificant, all of this work helped change Canadian political culture. Not only were new forms of international ties created and new services for immigrants developed, but foreign policy "from below" had real effects on shifting state policy "from above." Speaking specifically of the Progressive Church Movement, but with relevance for the world of international solidarity in general, Sheinin argues that these movements "produced significant and rapid change that included new, more generous refugee laws after 1977, the 1980s disappearance of the Cuban lightning rod for conservative cold warriors in Canada, a foreign policy generally sympathetic to the Nicaraguan Revolution, and a dramatic realignment of Progressive Conservative Party policy on human rights, most evident in the leadership of Prime Minister Brian Mulroney's government within the Commonwealth in isolating South Africa during the 1980s."[37] Fred Franklin, one of the central activists involved in organizing to support Chilean refugees, articulated some of the long-term impacts of the movement in a slightly different way: "We will never know," he stated, "just how much we lightened the burden of our Latin American brothers and sisters. We do know that we gained faith, insight and perspective, tools of analysis, and a much clearer understanding of our own situation and part in it."[38]

Through the work of solidarity activists, both those who were born in Canada and those from elsewhere, the politics of the Third World decisively entered the country's political sphere, shaping its debates and everyday realities. While the Canadian government would continue to act in ways that marginalized both the politics and the people of the Third World, it did not do so without the active opposition of a civil society mobilized to raise critical questions about its actions. By the 1990s, the campaigns of the 1960s, 1970s, and 1980s had waned, but the energy that had given them life was taking on new forms. By the late 1990s, the realities of economic and cultural globalization had brought the world increasingly under the control of global capitalism and multinational corporations. Third World solidarity began to take new forms in the antiglobalization movements of the late 1990s and early 2000s, such as in the popular mobilization for the Summit of the Americas in 2001 in Quebec City, and then in opposition to the Iraq and then Afghanistan Wars. In recent years, the necessity of combining international solidarity with migrant rights, alongside supporting the ongoing work of Aboriginal peoples in Canada against colonialism, has become a major focus of social movements.[39] Popular internationalism has therefore taken on new meaning. Although activists may not yet have succeeded in humanizing foreign policy in this century, they, like the activists who came before them, have demonstrated that different forms of human relationships are possible. Solidarity is born, Leela Gandhi argues, when "some of the selves who make up a culture loosen themselves from the security and comfort of old affiliations and identifications to make an unexpected 'gesture' of friendship toward all those on the other side of the fence." "There is no finality in this action," she continues, "no easily discernible teleological satisfaction." But there is a "breach in the fabric of imperial inhospitality."[40]

Discussion Questions

1) What is popular internationalism, and how did it emerge in Canada?
2) What similarities or differences are there between anti-imperialism and popular internationalism in English Canada and Quebec?
3) What are some of the motivations that have historically led individuals to participate in popular internationalism?
4) How have migrants participated in forms of popular internationalism in Canada's past?

Further Readings

Anderson, Kathryn. *Weaving Relationships: Canada-Guatemala Solidarity*. Waterloo, ON: Wilfrid Laurier University Press, 2003.

Austin, David. "All Roads Led to Montreal: Black Power, the Caribbean, and the Black Radical Tradition in Canada." *Journal of African American History* 92, no. 4 (Fall 2007): 516–39.

Gandhi, Leela. *Affective Communities: Anticolonial Thought, Fin-de-Siècle Radicalism, and the Politics of Friendship*. Durham, NC: Duke University Press, 2006.

del Pozo, José. *Les Chiliens au Québec: Immigrants et réfugiés, de 1955 à nos jours*. Montreal: Les Éditions du Boréal, 2009.

Sheinin, David. "Cuba's Long Shadow: The Progressive Church Movement and Canadian-Latin American Relations, 1970–87." In *Our Place in the Sun: Canada and Cuba in the Castro Era*, ed. Robert Wright and Lana Wylie, 121–42. Toronto: University of Toronto Press, 2009.

Wright, Cynthia. "Between Nation and Empire: The Fair Play for Cuba Committees and the Making of Canada-Cuba Solidarity in the Early 1960s." In *Our Place in the Sun: Canada and Cuba in the Castro Era*, ed. Robert Wright and Lana Wylie, 96–120. Toronto: University of Toronto Press, 2009.

Notes

1   Leela Gandhi, *Affective Communities: Anticolonial Thought, Fin-de-Siècle Radicalism, and the Politics of Friendship* (Durham, NC: Duke University Press, 2006), 1.

2   For the idea of reconnaissance, see Ian McKay, *Reasoning Otherwise: Leftists and the People's Enlightenment in Canada, 1890–1920* (Toronto: Between the Lines, 2008). For a brief overview of international solidarity in Quebec, see Pierre Beaudet, *Qui aide qui? Une brève histoire de la solidarité internationale au Québec* (Montreal: Les Éditions du Boréal, 2009).

3   See, for just a few examples, Carla Marano, "'Rising Strongly and Rapidly': The Universal Negro Improvement Association in Canada, 1919–1940," *Canadian Historical Review* 91, no. 2 (June 2010): 233–59; Paula Hastings, "Territorial Spoils,

Transnational Black Resistance, and Canada's Evolving Autonomy during the First World War," *Histoire sociale/Social History* 47, no. 94 (June 2014): 443–70; Stephanie Bangarth, *Voices Raised in Protest: Defending North American Citizens of Japanese Ancestry, 1942–49* (Vancouver: University of British Columbia Press, 2008); Lisa Rose Mar, *Brokering Belonging: Chinese in Canada's Exclusion Era, 1885–1945* (Toronto: University of Toronto Press, 2011).

4   Nikolas Barry-Shaw and Dru Oja Jay, *Paved with Good Intentions: Canada's Development NGOs from Idealism to Imperialism* (Halifax: Fernwood Press, 2012).

5   One could point to the long history of peace organizing. See many important essays in Lara Campbell, Michael Dawson, and Catherine Gidney, eds., *Worth Fighting For: Canada's Tradition of War Resistance from 1812 to the War on Terror* (Toronto: Between the Lines, 2015). For a look at debates about Canadian expansionism and racism in Canada in an earlier period, see Hastings, "Territorial Spoils."

6   Sean Mills, *The Empire Within: Postcolonial Thought and Political Activism in Sixties Montreal* (Montreal: McGill-Queen's University Press, 2010).

7   Magali Deleuze, *L'une et l'autre indépendance 1954–1964: Les médias au Québec et la guerre d'Algérie* (Outremont, QC: Les Éditions Point de Fuite, 2001), 55.

8   Mills, *Empire Within*, 8–9.

9   Lucia Ferretti, *Brève histoire de l'Église catholique au Québec* (Montreal: Les Éditions du Boréal, 1999), 164. The clergy decreased by 16 per cent from 1962 to 1969.

10 Catherine LeGrand, "Les réseaux missionnaires et l'action sociale des Québécois en Amérique latine, 1945–1980," *Études d'histoire religieuse* 79, no. 1 (2013); Beaudet, *Qui aide qui?*; Catherine Foisy, "La décennie 1960 des missionnaires québécois: Vers de nouvelles dynamiques de circulation des personnes, des idées et des pratiques," *Bulletin d'histoire politique* 23, no. 1 (2014).

11 Cited in Stuart Henderson, *Making the Scene: Yorkville and Hip Toronto in the 1960s* (Toronto: University of Toronto Press, 2011), 91.

12 Bryan Palmer, *Canada's 1960s: The Ironies of Identity in a Rebellious Era* (Toronto: University of Toronto Press, 2009), 269–73.

13 Greg Grandin, *Empire's Workshop: Latin America, the United States, and the Rise of the New Imperialism* (New York: Metropolitan Books, 2006), 41. Also see Greg Grandin, *The Last Colonial Massacre: Latin America in the Cold War* (Chicago: University of Chicago Press, 2004).

14 Bradford Lyttle, unpublished autobiography. My thanks to Mr. Lyttle for sharing his unpublished material with me. Also see Simone Monet-Chartrand, *Les Québécoises et le mouvement pacifiste (1939–1967)* (Montreal: Les Éditions Écosociété, 1993); Mills, *Empire Within*, 49.

15 Cynthia Wright, "Between Nation and Empire: The Fair Play for Cuba Committees and the Making of Canada-Cuba Solidarity in the Early 1960s," in *Our Place in the Sun: Canada and Cuba in the Castro Era*, ed. Robert Wright and Lana Wylie (Toronto: University of Toronto Press, 2009), 98. Wright is drawing upon Van Gosse, *Where the Boys Are: Cuba, Cold War America and the Making of a New Left* (London: Verso, 1993).

16 Wright, "Between Nation and Empire," 104–12. The above paragraph relies on Wright. Also see Gosse, *Where the Boys Are.*

17 J.R. Miller, *Skyscrapers Hide the Heavens: A History of Indian-White Relations in Canada*, 3rd ed. (Toronto: University of Toronto Press, 2000), 340; Lee Maracle, "The Context for Red Power Activism in the 1960s and Its Enduring

Importance," in *New World Coming: The Sixties and the Shaping of Global Consciousness*, ed. Karen Dubinsky et al. (Toronto: Between the Lines, 2009), 358–67.

18 Jane Jenson and Martin Papillon, "Challenging the Citizenship Regime: The James Bay Cree and Transnational Action," *Politics & Society* 28, no. 2 (2000): 245.

19 See Ken Coates, *A Global History of Indigenous Peoples: Struggle and Survival* (London: Palgrave/Macmillan, 2004), Chapter 9; Miller, *Skyscrapers Hide the Heavens*, 328; Maracle, "Context for Red Power Activism"; Scott Rutherford, "Canada's Other Red Scare: Rights, Decolonization, and Indigenous Political Protest in the Global Sixties" (PhD diss., Queen's University, 2011).

20 David S. Churchill, "American Expatriates and the Building of Alternative Social Space in Toronto, 1965–1977," *Urban History Review/Revue d'histoire urbaine* 39, no. 1 (2010): 31–44; Myrna Kostash, *Long Way from Home: The Story of the Sixties Generation in Canada* (Toronto: Lorimer, 1980); Lara Campbell, "'Women United Against the War': Gender, Politics, Feminism, and Vietnam Draft Resistance in Canada," in Dubinsky et al., *New World Coming*, 339–46. Also see Jessica Squires, *Building Sanctuary: The Movement to Support Vietnam War Resisters in Canada, 1965–73* (Vancouver: University of British Columbia Press, 2013).

21 George Grant, *Lament for a Nation: The Defeat of Canadian Nationalism* (Toronto: McClelland and Stewart, 1970).

22 Kari Levitt, *Silent Surrender: The Multinational Corporation in Canada* (Toronto: Macmillan, 1970), 25. Also see Mills, *Empire Within*, 191–92.

23 Palmer, *Canada's 1960s*, 32; Steven High, *Industrial Sunset: The Making of North America's Rust Belt, 1969–1984* (Toronto: University of Toronto Press, 2003); Jeffrey Cormier, *The Canadianization Movement: Emergence, Survival, and Success* (Toronto: University of Toronto Press, 2004); Joan Sangster, "Remembering Texpack: Nationalism, Internationalism, and Militancy in Canadian Unions in the 1970s," *Studies in Political Economy* 78 (2006): 41–66.

24 See especially the important works of David Austin: Austin, "All Roads Led to Montreal: Black Power, the Caribbean, and the Black Radical Tradition in Canada," *Journal of African American History* 92, no. 4 (2007): 516–39; Austin, *Fear of a Black Nation: Race, Sex, and Security in Sixties Montreal* (Toronto: Between the Lines, 2013).

25 For the most important works on black activism in the 1960s and its connection to the Caribbean, see the many works of David Austin: Austin, *Fear of a Black Nation*; Austin, ed. *You Don't Play with Revolution: The Montreal Lectures of C.L.R. James* (Oakland, CA: AK Press, 2009); Austin, "All Roads Led to Montreal." For a fascinating look at the way in which many of these ideas have lived on into the present, see Peter James Hudson, "Research, Repression, and Revolution—On Montreal and the Black Radical Tradition: An Interview with David Austin," *CLR James Journal* 20, no. 1 (2014): 197–232. Also see Mills, *Empire Within*, Chapter 4.

26 Samuel Pierre, ed., *Ces Québécois venus d'Haïti—Contribution de la communauté haïtienne à l'édification du Québec moderne* (Montreal: Presses internationales Polytechnique, 2007); Éloise Brière, "Mère solitude d'Émile Ollivier: apport migratoire à la société québécoise," *International Journal of Canadian Studies/ Revue internationale d'études canadiennes*, no. 13 (1996): 61–70; Paul Dejean, *D'Haïti au Québec* (Montreal: CIDIHCA, 1990). Also see Sean Mills, *A Place in the Sun: Haiti, Haitians, and the Remaking of Quebec* (Montreal: McGill-Queen's University Press, 2016).

27 Sean Mills, "Quebec, Haiti, and the Deportation Crisis of 1974," *Canadian Historical Review* 94, no. 3 (2013): 405–35.

28 Reg Whitaker, *Double Standard: The Secret History of Canadian Immigration* (Toronto: Lester and Orpen Dennys, 1987).

29 José del Pozo, *Les Chiliens au Québec: Immigrants et réfugiés, de 1955 à nos jours* (Montreal: Les Éditions du Boréal, 2009); Fernand Foisy, *Michel Chartrand, la colère du juste (1968–2003)* (Outremont, QC: Lanctôt Éditeur, 2003). For a discussion of Chilean exiles in Montreal, see Pierre Beaudet, *On a raison de se révolter. Chronique des années 70* (Montreal: Les Éditions Écosociété, 2008).

30 LeGrand, "Les réseaux missionnaires"; Gregory Baum, "Catholicisme, sécularisation et gauchisme au Québec," in *Religion, sécularisation, modernité: Les experiences francophones en Amérique du Nord*, ed. Brigitte Caulier (Québec City: Les Presses de l'Université Laval, 1996), 105–20; Gregory Baum, "Politisés Chrétiens: A Christian-Marxist Network in Quebec, 1974–1982," *Studies in Political Economy* no. 32 (1990): 7–28; Foisy, "La décennie 1960."

31 See Nikolas Barry-Shaw, "Rêve/Cauchemar: Allende's Chile and the Polarization of the Québec Left, 1968–1974" (MA thesis, Queen's University, 2014).

32 Joan Simalchik, "Part of the Awakening: Canadian Churches and Chilean Refugees" (MA thesis, University of Toronto, 1993), 8, 22–28.

33 Quoted in Francis Peddie, *Young, Well-Educated and Adaptable: Chilean Exiles in Ontario and Quebec, 1973–2010* (Winnipeg: University of Manitoba Press, 2014), 95. The above paragraph is drawn from Peddie.

34 Beaudet, *Qui aide qui?*

35 David Sheinin, "Cuba's Long Shadow: The Progressive Church Movement and Canadian-Latin American Relations, 1970–87," in Wright and Wylie, *Our Place in the Sun* (Toronto: University of Toronto Press, 2009), 122–23. Important information can also be found in Simalchik, "Part of the Awakening."

36 Sheinin, "Cuba's Long Shadow," 129–30; Simalchik, "Part of the Awakening." For a fascinating look at Canadian-Guatemalan solidarity, and in particular efforts to accompany returning Guatemalan refugees, see Kathryn Anderson, *Weaving Relationships: Canada-Guatemala Solidarity* (Waterloo, ON: Wilfrid Laurier University Press, 2003). Also see Allison McMahon, "From Charity to Solidarity: Liberation Theology, Dependency Theory, and Narratives of Parallel Struggle in the Canadian Nicaraguan Solidarity Movement, 1979–1990" (MA thesis, Queen's University, 2012), 2.

37 Sheinin, "Cuba's Long Shadow," 138.

38 Quoted in Simalchik, "Part of the Awakening," 87.

39 See Harsha Walia, *Undoing Border Imperialism* (Oakland, CA: AK Press, 2013).

40 Gandhi, *Affective Communities*, 189.

Glossary

Arone, Shidane: Shidane Arone was a 16-year-old Somali tortured and murdered by two members of the Canadian Airborne Regiment stationed in Somalia in 1993. Despite initial attempts to cover up the story, Shidane Arone's death led to a federal government investigation, which was not allowed to reach conclusions. "The Somalia Affair" was the catalyst for huge debates and competing interpretations of the role of Canadian forces in the Global South.

Bandung Conference: In April 1955, 29 Asian and African countries gathered in Bandung, Indonesia, for a conference to build cooperation between the two continents and to assert their adherence to a nonaligned movement in resistance to the polarization of the deadly Cold War rivalry between the Soviet Union and the United States. The Bandung Declaration captured a collaborative spirit of independence movements and the aspirations of the participating countries to make great strides in economic development of their societies within a new international order. The final communiqué also emphasized the importance of cultural cooperation among African and Asian countries; human rights and self-determination; and the promotion of world peace and cooperation. Canada was the only Western country to send greetings to the Bandung Conference.

Canadian International Development Agency (CIDA): CIDA was established by the federal government in 1968 and officially folded into the newly created Department of Foreign Affairs, Trade and Development in 2013. Founded by Prime Minister Pierre Trudeau, CIDA signalled a more sophisticated, robust, and enduring approach to international cooperation for development. With the creation of CIDA, Canada set in place the means to develop policies, programs, and expertise in development cooperation with greater autonomy and clarity of mandate.

Canadian University Service Overseas (CUSO): CUSO was founded in 1961. It was the first Canadian NGO to undertake development work from a secular stance and in a context of rapid decolonization, sending thousands of young Canadian volunteers to work abroad in the developing world.

***Chinese Immigration Act* (1885)**: Passed by the Canadian federal government in response to vehement agitation against the presence of Chinese immigrants in Canada, particularly in British Columbia. The act imposed a head tax of $50 on all prospective Chinese immigrants, later raised to $500. It was one of a series of discriminatory acts passed against Chinese people in this era, including prohibiting their right to vote and ultimately, in 1923, excluding them from immigration altogether.

Cold War: Usually defined as the period of military tensions between the United States and the Soviet Union that occurred between 1947 and 1991. Beyond these two powers, however, the entire world was drawn into these hostilities. The Third World was regarded by both sides as a proving ground for the universal applicability of their ideologies (communism vs. capitalism) and was often the site of proxy battles between the US and the Soviets. The military standstill between the two great powers was, in large measure, diverted into Third World territories. Canadian policy makers joined their counterparts in other Western countries assuming a world in two camps: one part "free," the other "enslaved by communism."

Colombo Plan: Canada engaged initially in development cooperation through its membership in the Commonwealth. Following a meeting of the Commonwealth Conference of Foreign Ministers held in Colombo, Sri Lanka, the Colombo Plan was launched in 1950 to provide a framework for cooperation around specific bilateral (country-to-country) projects in Asia and the Pacific.

Cuban Revolution: In January 1959, a revolutionary government took power in Cuba. Committing itself to a program of equality and national independence, it nationalized many industries previously owned by US business interests. Unlike the United States, Canada maintained relations with the government of Fidel Castro, and some Canadians organized support networks for the new Cuban regime through organizations such as the Fair Play for Cuba Committee.

Decolonization: The process of a country removing itself from the political structures of another country and establishing itself as a sovereign nation. As well as allowing a country to gain control over political and legal structures, decolonization has important cultural and social dimensions. This process is perhaps best expressed by Jamaican musician Bob Marley: "Emancipate yourselves from mental slavery, none but ourselves can free our minds."

Exploitative colonialism: Usually distinguished from settler colonialism. Most European powers first viewed territories in North America, Latin America, and the Caribbean not as places they wanted to live in, but instead as places over which they could rule to generate wealth to bring back home. They wanted to extract large amounts of resources as cheaply as possible, thus maximizing their profit.

Frantz Fanon: Martinique-born psychologist and philosopher, whose book *The Wretched of the Earth* (1961) became a foundational document in articulating the demands of many colonies around the globe for independence and national liberation.

Idle No More: The name of the most recent wave of Aboriginal rights organizing in Canada. In November 2012, four Indigenous women in Saskatchewan called a meeting to discuss Bill C-45, a federal "omnibus" bill that included significant changes to the *Indian Act* and drastic rollbacks on environmental protection. They organized under the banner "Idle No More," and word of the meeting and the slogan quickly spread through social media. The group helped both to galvanize opposition to Bill C-45 and also to draw attention to other pressing issues, including the housing crisis in Attawapiskat (which included a hunger strike by Chief Theresa Spence) and demands for recognition of the inherent and shared rights of Indigenous peoples.

Immigration Act **(Changes 1967)**: In 1967 Canada formally abolished explicit racial criteria for accepting immigrants and replaced race-based criteria with a points system based on labour-market needs. The points system was designed to ensure that selected migrants were well-suited to the needs of the labour market and were capable of adapting to life in Canada. The 1967 regulations also universalized sponsorship rules for the families of Canadian citizens and permanent residents, creating a family class category for close relatives and a nominated class for more distant relatives such as cousins.

Indian Act: Passed by the Canadian federal government in 1876, it consolidated laws that had been passed in the pre-Confederation era and applied to all the provinces and territories. Highly controversial, it defined who constituted an "Indian" in Canada. It has been called a paternalistic, assimilationist, colonialist, and even genocidal piece of legislation by many First Peoples. It was a foundational moment in how race was legally produced by the state in late-nineteenth-century Canada.

"Jim Crow": The informal name for the various systems of racial segregation and inequality most associated with—but not exclusive to—the southern states of the United States. In Canada social custom—evident in areas such as religion, social attitudes, and socioeconomic status—predominated over legal restrictions, with a few notable exceptions.

"John Chinaman": This was an imaginary character or archetype, invented by Caucasians, which expressed pervasive white supremacist anxieties that existed toward Chinese people in the nineteenth century. These anxieties emerged out of both the class and psychosocial worries that Chinese bodies produced in white people. In a variety of formal and informal settings, whites routinely described the Chinese as inscrutable, cunning, sexually perverse, filthy, and prone to vice and criminality including gambling and illegal drugs.

Komagata Maru: In 1913 members of the Indian community, spearheaded by a wealthy entrepreneur named Gurdit Singh, sponsored the arrival of 376 East Indian residents of Hong Kong, China, and Japan. Vancouver authorities did not allow the ship to come into port and its passengers were not allowed to disembark. Amidst a heated public debate that took place in the media and in parliament, the passengers of the *Komagata Maru* languished aboard the ship for two months. Immigration officials prolonged inquiries on the issue of individual passengers' admissibility, stalled the provision of food and medical care, and allowed the conditions aboard the ship to steadily worsen to an intolerable degree. Ultimately the boat was not allowed to land because it had violated the "continuous journey" regulation that required boats to arrive directly from their point of departure (a thinly disguised piece of legislation that restricted South Asian migrants). The ship was sent back to India.

Left nationalism: A political perspective that became popular in Canada in the 1960s. Left nationalists argued that the Canadian economy was increasingly dependent on the United States, and that Canada was losing its ability to democratically shape its own future. The ideas of left nationalism were articulated in an important book by Kari Levitt of McGill University, *Silent Surrender: The Multinational Corporation in Canada* (1970).

Marshall Plan: Named after the US Secretary of State George Marshall, this was a fund for European economic recovery after World War II, financed and directed by the United States from 1948 to 1952. During those four years the United States provided $13 billion in economic and technical assistance to the European countries that had joined the Organization for European Economic

Co-operation (OEEC, now the OECD). Much of the Marshall Plan funds were used to buy raw materials and manufactured goods from the United States and Canada, the other allied country that had emerged from the war without damage to its economic infrastructure. The allowance by the United States for the purchase of goods from Canada is an indicator of the integration and subordination of the Canadian economy to that of the United States in the postwar period. The unprecedented financial investments of the Marshall Plan were mobilized, not only for the direct benefit of Europe, but also as a bulwark against the perceived threat of Soviet antagonism to capital and its expansion of influence in the rest of the world.

Millennium Development Goals (MDGs): These are global targets, based on the United Nations Millennium Declaration that called for a reaffirmation of commitment to the principles of the Charter of the United Nations. The member states made ambitious pledges designed to alleviate poverty by 2015. The specific goals were:

- To halve the number of undernourished people
- To achieve universal primary education
- To promote gender equality and empower women
- To reduce child mortality
- To improve maternal health
- To combat HIV/AIDS, malaria, and other diseases
- To ensure environmental sustainability
- To develop a global partnership for development.

Popular internationalism: A term that we use for movements that have sought to understand the interconnected histories of the First and Third Worlds, and that have sought to oppose the structural inequalities between the two.

Racial historicism: A concept associated with US theorist David Theo Goldberg that illustrates how, in much of North American history, it was believed that "inferior" races needed the guidance of superior races to help them evolve to a higher order of humanity. The idea was that race was not determined by biological forces but rather is the product of historical, social, and cultural forces. Thus adherents to this position believe that lesser races can be brought to the level of superior races via education and religious instruction.

Racial naturalism: A term to describe the idea that race is characterized by fixed, unchanging biological essences.

Resource curse: A theory that attempts to account for the multiple problems that resource-rich countries of the Global South often experience. Mining-dependent developing countries are kept poor, by this argument, because of endemic corruption, inflated currencies, loss of competitiveness, a loss of development of other economic sectors, as well as unequal distribution of mining's benefits, such as employment and profits.

Settler colonialism: During the 1700s immigrants from Europe began to arrive in the territories of contemporary North America with the intention of permanent settlement. Though European powers still prized colonies for their richness of natural resources, they also began to see them as valuable places for the relocation and settlement of their own people. At its core, settler colonialism is about the ability of one group of people to impose their worldview and themselves upon another group of people.

Structural adjustment: Structural adjustment programs were imposed on countries of the developing world in the 1980s by international financial institutions, ostensibly to ensure that they serviced their growing debt. But the agenda of the creditors was also to use the debt "crisis" to open avenues for capital expansion, through extreme privatization and liberalization of Third World economies. States were declared "inefficient" (despite their considerable achievements in the short period since independence), and public services were first run down before being sold off to the oligopolies for a song. These states were prohibited from subsidizing agricultural production or investing in social infrastructure, with prohibitions also on capital investment in health, education, transport, and telecommunications. Eventually public goods were taken over by the "private" (read oligopolistic) sector. Tariff barriers to goods from the advanced capitalist countries were removed; access to natural resources opened up for pillaging; tax regimes were relaxed; and "export processing zones" were established to enable raw exploitation of labour without any regulations from the state or trade unions. Over time, privatization was extended to agriculture, land, and food production and distribution.

Suez Crisis: In 1956, the Egyptian government of Gamel Abdel Nasser nationalized the Suez Canal, which had been built by the British but was part of Egyptian territory. Israel, with the backing of Britain and France, invaded Egypt. The United States was opposed to the invasion because they believed this might push Egypt to the Soviet side of the Cold War. Canada was also opposed to the invasion, and Suez can be seen as the first major divergence of Canadian and British foreign policy during the early Cold War. Lester Pearson, then Canadian Foreign Affairs minister, presented a peacekeeping plan (with American backing) to the UN, and the world body endorsed it. The United Nations Emergency Force, the original "blue helmet" peacekeeping army, was born. For this proposal, Pearson won Canada's first (and still only) Nobel Peace Prize. For years afterward, the incident echoed through Canadian diplomatic memory, hallowing what might be called a "cult of peacekeeping" at home even as actual Canadian peacekeeping contributions declined.

Index

Aboriginal title, 29. *See also* Indigenous peoples
Achebe, Chinua, *Things Fall Apart*, 124
Acres International, 71
Adams, Howard, 30
Afghanistan War, 4, 103, 200, 205–7, 212, 262
Africa, 223. *See also* names of individual African
    countries
    illicit financial outflows from African
        economies, 108
    independence movements post–World War
        II, 91
    "scramble for Africa," 70
African Development Bank, 108
The Age of Migration, 223
Agent Orange, 4, 63
Algerian War, 2, 4, 171
    support in Quebec, 7, 248–49
Allende, Salvador, 258–60
American civil rights movement, 249
American Civil War, 51
American empire, 93, 206. *See also* United
    States
American imperialism, 125
American Indian Movement, 29
Anglosphere, 200
Angola, 135, 174, 217
Angus, H.F., 162
antiglobalization movements, 262
antinuclear movements, 251
Apale, Alisha, 12
apartheid, 37, 63, 171–72, 262
Armenia, 161–62
Armstrong, Christopher, 66–67
Arnup, Jesse H., 132
    A New Church Faces a New World, 131
Arone, Shidane Abukar, 193–96, 198, 214
assimilation policies, 22–23, 26–27, 39–40, 49
Atlantic pact, 202
"Atlanticist" approach to the Cold War, 202
Attawapiskat housing crisis, 31
Austin, David, 17
Axworthy, Lloyd, 205
    "human security" agenda, 182

Backhouse, Constance, *Colour-Coded*, 37
Baird, John, 156
Bandung Conference, 6–7, 91, 174–75
Bangladesh factory collapse, 60
Barrick Gold, 65, 71–73
Barry-Shaw, Nikolas, 247
Bay of Pigs, 251
BC *Immigration Act* (1884), 42

Beauvoir, Simone de, 249
Beckert, Sven, 11
Beijing Platform for Action (BPFA), 106
Bercuson, David, 199
    Significant Incident, 197–98
Berg Report, 98
Berger, Carl, *The Sense of Power*, 157
Berque, Jacques, 249
Best, Carrie, 52
Bethune, Norman, 1
Biafran humanitarian crisis, 144, 180
"Birth of the Nation," 212
Bissett, James, 232
Black Canadians, 47–49, 52–54
Black Paper, 140
black power movements, 249
Blackberry, 62
Board of World Mission (BWM), 133–37
Boer War, 66, 158
Bombardier, 62, 64
Borden, Robert, 155, 160
Bosnia, 205
Bothwell, Robert, 176
Brand, Dionne, 37
BRICS countries, 10.
British Colonial Development Act, 4
British Empire, 3–4, 7, 18–19, 23, 50–51, 201
British imperialism, 12, 124
British North America Act (1867), 207
"British race," concept of, 199
Buhari, Muhammadu, 75
Burns, Tommy, 203

Can NGOs Make a Difference?, 142, 144
Canada
    diplomatic self-image, 156–57, 162, 176.
        (*See also* Canadian foreign policy)
    extractive and engineering industries today,
        71–78. (*See also* Canadian mining
        companies overseas)
    military intervention into Third World,
        193–214
    missions to Third World, 120–31. (*See also*
        missionaries)
Canada, conceptions of
    as living "between" US and Britain, 158
    as "multinational country," 29
    as Northern country, 157–58
    as part of Western alliance of developed
        democracies, 155–56
    as UN peacekeeper, 201, 204, 206
Canada First Defence Strategy, 200

Canada in US orbit, 3, 208
Canada Pension Plan, 76
Canada's Share in World Tasks, 127–32
Canadian banking interests in Caribbean and
    Latin America, 66, 68
Canadian Bill of Rights (1960), 28, 222
Canadian businesses, 61–62, 67, 69–70. *See also*
    Canadian mining companies overseas
    abuse of human rights, 64
    ethics compared to others, 63, 68
Canadian Catholic Organization for
    Development and Peace, 138, 140
Canadian Commonwealth Federation (CCF), 44
Canadian Council of Churches (CCC), 139
Canadian Council of the Missionary Education
    · Movement, 127
Canadian dependency theory, 254
Canadian foreign policy, 1, 3, 5, 7, 10, 111,
    179, 246
    in 1940s and 50s, 164
    business-friendly, 64–65, 209
    Canadian Asia policy, 165
    Canadian embassies, 155, 162–63
    coherence, 102–3
    Conservative government (2006), 64
    development aid as instrument for, 90
        (*See also* development aid)
    racialized perceptions in, 182–84
    recognition of China, 231
    under St. Laurent, 158, 166
Canadian imperialism, 160–61
Canadian mining companies overseas, 62, 65,
    77, 111, 199, 213–14
    claims of job creation, 74
    corruption and scandals, 71
    environmental damage, 74–75
    government support for, 76
    Indigenous Guatemalan case against, 78
    lax domestic regulation, 72, 77
    outsourcing riskiest tasks, 73
Canadian Overseas Volunteers (COV), 138
Canadian Pacific Railway, 2, 67
Canadian Students in Cuba, 252
Canadian University Service Overseas. *See*
    CUSO
"Canadian values," 200
capitalism, 28, 30
carbon tax, 61
Caribbean Conference Committee, 255
Caribbean immigrants, 55, 223, 255
Carmichael, Stokely, 256
Carroll, Michael, 177
Carter, Jimmy, 5
Castro, Fidel, 180
Catholic Church, 25–26
    in Quebec, 250
Second Vatican Council, 140, 250
Centre internationale de solidarité ouvrière
    (CISO), 260

Césaire, Aimé, 257
Chartrand, Michel, 259
Chiang Kai-shek, 163
Chile, 259
    refugees from, 217, 237, 260
China Inland Mission, 145
Chinese Exclusion Act (1923), 43
Chinese Immigration Act (1885), 42
    head tax, 43
Chinese labour, 46
Chinese National Petroleum Company, 69
Chinese Revolution, 132–33
Chinese Tax Act (BC), 41
Chrétien, Jean, 180–82, 195
Christian and Missionary Alliance (C&MA),
    145–46
Christian Medical Association of India
    (CMAI), 135
Christianity in the New World, 24–25. *See also*
    missionaries
Christie, Fred, 52–54
Churchill, Winston, *History of the English-
    Speaking People*, 199–200
CIDA (Canadian International Developmental
    Agency), 1, 64, 101–2, 106, 135, 140,
    143, 204
    contracts with mining companies and
        NGOs, 88–89
    creation of, 96
    partnered with mining companies, 65
Citizenship Guide, 199, 209
civil society organizations (CSOs), 106
Clarion, 52
Clark, Joe, 101
Clarke, Austin, 1
Clarke, Robert, *Ties That Bind*, 10
Coates, Ken S., 18, 30
Cochrane, Thomas John, 66
Cold War, 4, 7, 138, 164, 174, 202, 251
    Canada's aid policy and, 103
    Canadian diplomacy and, 175–76
    diverted conflict to the Third World, 176
Colombo Plan, 94, 227
colonial mandates, 161–62
colonialism, 4, 9–10, 16, 94, 110, 140
    exploitative colonialism, 17–19
    global colonial project, 15–17, 23
    in *Indian Act*, 39–40
    legacies of, 91–92
    missionary colonialism, 121
    settler colonialism, 19–25, 27, 31, 41–42
colonization, 10, 15, 20
Columbus, Christopher, 15–16, 24
Comité Chrétien, 261
Comité de solidarité Québec-Chili, 259–60
Commonwealth, 164–65, 167, 171–72, 177
    Africa program, 95
    Caribbean Aid Program, 94–95
communism, 93, 164, 176

Compton Brouwer, Ruth, *Canada's Global Villagers*, 142
Congress of Black Writers, 256–57
Convention on the Elimination of all Forms of Discrimination against Women (CEDAW), 106
"Corporate Social Responsibility Strategy," 77
Critical Realism, 196, 206–14
Cuba, 251, 253
Cuban missile crisis, 251
Cuban Railroad Company, 67
Cuban Revolution, 251–52, 258
cultural genocide, 27, 29–30, 196
culture, 11, 20, 26–27, 127
    non-Western people's commitments to their own cultures, 126
    preservation, 235
    subjugation (from colonialism), 17
    Western cultural superiority, 5
CUSO, 120–21, 132, 137–38, 140–43, 147, 226
    cross-race friendships, sexual relationships, and marriage, 142
    founders' determination to keep secular, 144
    funding from federal government, 140
    turning to churches for guidance, 139–40
Cyprus, 204, 210, 217, 236

Dalai Lama, 178, 227, 230–31, 234
Dandurand, Raoul, 161
decolonization, 30, 121, 163–64, 181, 202, 253
    Africa, 174
    Canadian model of, 165–66
    Cuba, 253
    East Timor, 181–82
    India, 166–67
    Indonesia, 170
    Quebec, 248–49
    by revolution, 169–71
Deleuze, Magali, 249
    L'une et l'autre indépendance 1954–1964, 248
Denault, Alain, 72, 74, 76
Desmond, Viola, 52, 54
development aid, 60, 88–111
    alignment with interests of Canadian resource extraction, 89
    Canada as "developed country donor," 94
    Conservative government (2006), 64
    flow of resources, 108
    instrument of foreign policy, 88, 90, 103
    myth of superior knowledge and capacity, 107
    paradigm of technical solutions for social needs, 106
    partnerships with mining companies on, 65, 73, 89
    poverty reduction associated with, 92
    public support, 100
Development Assistance Committee (DAC), 95

Development Education Collective, 260
development tourism, 12
Diefenbaker, John, 28, 168–69, 171–72, 179
    "Northern Vision," 158
diplomacy of constraint, 176
Dresden (Alabama of the North), 54
Dubinsky, Karen, 89, 197, 199, 214
Dupuy, Pierre, 173
Duvalier, François, 257–58

"Economic diplomacy," 65
economic inequality, 61, 109, 111
ecumenism, 126
Eden, Anthony, 177
"Eight Istanbul Principles for CSO Development Effectiveness," 106
Electoral Franchise Act (1903), 43
Engle, Karen, 26
environmental degradation, 24
environmental justice movement, 79
environmental protection rollbacks (Bill C-45), 31
Epprecht, Marc, 89, 197, 199, 214
Escobar, Arturo, 107
Ethiopian crisis, 100–1, 166
evangelical Protestant groups, 6, 121, 145–47
Export Development Canada
    financing and insurance for Canadian mining industry, 76–77

Fair Accommodations Practices Act, 1954 (Ontario), 54
"Fair Play for Cuba" Committees, 252
Fairclough, Ellen, 28
faith-based NGOs, 121, 133, 138, 144
family class refugees, 223
Francophonie, 102
Fanon, Frantz, 20, 249, 257
    The Wretched of the Earth, 2
Fantino, Julian, 65, 71–73, 89–90
Farini (William Hunt, the "Great Farini"), 2
Faris, Donald, 132–33
    To Plow with Hope, 138, 148
Fast, Ed, 65
Ferier, Thompson, 48
First World, 9
Fleming, Donald, 134
Fontaine, Tina, 32
Ford, Rob, 7–8
"foreign policy from below," 252, 255. *See also* Canadian foreign policy
Forrest, A.C., 134
Four Canadians Who Saw Cuba, 252
franchise, 28, 39–40, 43, 49, 51
francophone Africa, 95
Franklin, Fred, 262
Franklin v. Evans, 52–54
Freeman, Linda, 63, 173
Front de libération du Québec (FLQ), 249
fur trade, 18, 25

Gaddafi, Muammar, 77
Gandhi, Leela, 6, 246, 262
GATT, 100
Gaulle, Charles de, 171
Geddie, John, 120
Generation NGO, 12
genocide, 5, 39–40, 69, 161, 205
Gerrior, Cathy, *A Native Perspective of Gold Mining in Guatemala*, 80
Ghana independence, 167–68
Gharbi, Rachid Liass, 2
Gilchrist, Sidney, 135
Global Financial Integrity, 108
Global Markets Action Plan, 65
Global South. *See* Third World
Godoy, Patricia, 260
Goldberg, David Theo, 38, 48–49, 55
Goldcorp, 74
Gordon, Todd, *Imperialist Canada*, 64
Granatstein, J.L., 199, 210
    Whose War Is It?, 198
Grandin, Greg, 251
Grant, George Monro, 121–22, 145, 161
    Lament for a Nation, 253
Grassy Narrows, 30
Green Paper on Immigration Policy, 236
greenhouse gases, 61
Greer, Allan, 25
Guatemala, 2, 5–6, 67, 73–74, 76, 251

Haitian migration, 257–58
Harper, Stephen, 145, 180, 201
    "Northern Agenda," 158
Harper government, 31, 147, 199
    Global South as zone of opportunity, 156
    linked foreign policy with expanding
        business interests, 64–65
Hartman, Saidiava, 110
Hillier, Joseph, 194
Hockin, Katharine, 133
Honest Accounts? The True Story of Africa's Billion Dollar Losses, 108
Hotel Act, 1963 (Quebec), 54
HudBay Minerals, 78
Hudson, Peter, 68
Hudson's Bay Company, 22
Human Development Index, 6
human rights, 54, 156, 182, 262
    abuses, 64, 75
    trumped principles of sovereignty, 205
    vocal rhetoric accompanied by absence of
        action, 180–81
humane internationalism, 97
humanitarian assistance, 65, 240–41
Hungarian refugees, 222

IAMGOLD Corporation, 65, 89
IDRC (International Development Research
    Centre), 96

immigrant assimilability, 47
Immigration Act, 38, 41, 44, 55, 218, 222–23,
    225, 236–37
Immigration and Refugee Board (1989), 225
Immigration Appeal Board Act, 224
immigration policy, 4, 7, 37–55, 258
    from British Isles and Northern Europe,
        222
    with Canadian economy first in mind, 222
    change to merit-based point system, 204
    in early post-Confederation period, 40–41
    humanitarian immigration policies, 218–19,
        224–25, 236–38
    principle of nondiscrimination, 237
    racism in, 38–39, 41–44
    refugee policy, 217–40
    struggle for civil rights in, 55
*The Impact of Canadian Mining in Latin America
    and Canada's Responsibility*, 75
Imperial Act (1883), 50
imperialism, 9, 15–18, 24, 27
INCO, 74
independence movements, 91, 97, 167–69.
    See also decolonization; secession
India, 124–25
    decolonization of, 166–67
    independence, 91
    institutional emphasis in the India mission,
        130
    "special relationship" between Canada and,
        178–79
"Indian," category of, 39–40
Indian Act, 31, 38–40
    assimilation policies of, 22, 26
    prohibition of cultural and spiritual
        practices, 27
    right to depose hereditary chiefs, 27
Indian wars in US, 23
Indigenous activism, 24, 28, 32
    confrontational tactics, 30
    global movements for change worldwide,
        28, 30
    Idle No More, 3, 22, 28, 31
    social media use, 31
Indigenous knowledge and kin networks, 18
Indigenous languages, 24, 26
Indigenous peoples, 2, 7, 15–32, 38, 47–48
    Aboriginal and Métis uprisings, 18
    Aboriginal women, 26
    dispossession of land from, 17, 19–24, 30, 37
    extinguishing land title from, 22–23
    franchise issue, 28–29
    missionary work among, 130
    murdered and missing Aboriginal women
        and girls, 3, 31–32
    as "our Third World," 7–8
    residential schools, 26, 32
    resistance, 111, 253, 262
    slavery, 17

starvation, 23
  Third World decolonization and, 253
  treaties and formal agreements, 19, 21–23
Indonesia, 169–70, 181
industrialization, 28, 30
Innis, Harold, 62
Inter-Church Committee on Human Rights
  in Latin America (ICCHRLA), 261
International Development Research Centre
  (IDRC), 143
International Missionary Council, 126
International Monetary Fund (IMF), 61, 74, 79
  IMF-approved Poverty Reduction Strategy,
  99
international NGOs, 100, 224
international solidarity, 247–48, 250, 259–60
Iraq Liberation Act, 205
Iraq War, 262
Ismael, Tareq, 10

James, C.L.R., 256
James Bay Cree, 29–30
Jenson, Jane, 253
Jesuits, 25
Jim Crow, 39, 48–49, 51–53
"John Chinaman," 41

Kane, Molly, 5, 121, 142, 147, 247
Kennedy, J.F., 138
"kill the Indian in the child," 26
King, Mackenzie, 155, 157, 162–63, 166, 202,
  222
Kipling, Rudyard, 199
Klein, Naomi, 111
K'naan, 1
Komagata Maru, 43–44
Korean independence, 161
Korean War, 163, 176, 178, 201
Kosovo, 205
Kuan Yew, 180

labour movement, 255, 259
labour organizations, 247
"labour used, labour discarded," 42
Lamming, George, 256
Latin America, 68, 247
  liberation theology, 140, 250
  popular internationalism and, 258–61
  refugees from, 223
Latin American Working Groups, 259–60
League of Nations, 155, 160–61
"left nationalism," 254–55
Léger, Raoul, 6
Legge, Garth, 140
Lester B. Pearson Canadian International
  Peacekeeping Training Centre, 201
Levitt, Kari, 254
Lewis, Stephen, 1
Liberal Internationalists, 196, 200–6, 209–11

"Liberal Protestant Establishment," 133
liberal racial order, 49–50
liberation movements, 249
liberation theology, 140, 250, 259, 261
Livingstone, David, 123
Lodge, Henry Cabot, 203
Lubka, Nancy, 53
Lyon, Peyton, Canada and the Third World, 10

MacDonald, David, 101
Macdonald, John A., 42, 66
  National Policy, 22–23
Mackenzie, Hector, 167
Macmillan, Harold, 173
MacMurchy, Marjory, 122
Madokoro, Laura, 55, 255
Madres de Mayo, 260
Malaysia, 167–69
Mandel-Campbell, Andrea, 62
  Why Mexicans Don't Drink Molson, 61
Mandela, Nelson, 214
Manji, Firoze, 98
Mao Zedong, 132
Maracle, Lee, 30
Marlin Mine, 74
Marshall Plan, 92–93, 170
Martin, Paul, 63
Mathieu, Carol, 194
Mayhew, Robert, 163
McClure, Bob, 137
McFarlane, Peter, 68
  Northern Shadows, 67
McKay, Ian, 4, 39, 49, 65, 176, 178
McKay, John
  Bill C-293 Official Development Assistance
    Accountability Act, 104
  Bill C-300 "Responsible Mining Act," 77
Meighen, Arthur, 162
Memmi, Albert, 249
Mennonite Central Committee, 138
Menzies, Arthur, 175
Métis, 23, 28
militarism, 210, 212–13
militarization, 200
Millennium Development Goals (MDGs),
  104–5
Miller, J.R., 18, 25
Mills, Sean, 7, 140, 147, 214
missionaries, 5, 24–25, 32, 124, 161
  agents of American imperialism, 125
  Canada's people-to-people contacts within
    the Global South, 121
  "Canadian" face to developing world, 120
  "civilizing" approach, 130
  colonialism and, 24–25, 121
  conservative Canadian mission boards, 146
  conservative missionaries, 126–27
  evangelical churches in Canada, 6
  evangelical missions, 145–47

French-Canadian missionaries in Latin
    America and Caribbean, 6, 250
interdenominational approach to mission,
    126
Pentecostal missionaries, 145–46
resurgent international missionary
    movement (late 20th and early 21st
    century), 121
women in missionary field, 123, 126–30, 133
missionary heroes, 122–23
missionary-sending countries from the Global
    South, 146
Molloy, Mike, 226
Montreal, 17
    Caribbean activism, 255
    Haitian diaspora, 257
Morris, Alexander, 157
Morrison, David, 143
Morton, James M., 227
Mulroney, Brian, 180–81
    leader in anti-apartheid campaign, 171–72,
    262
Munk, Peter, 73
murdered and missing Aboriginal women and
    girls, 3, 31–32
Murphy, Rex, 28

National Policy "protectionism" *vs.* free trade
    liberalism, 62
Native Alliance for Red Power, 29
Native Women's Association of Canada, 31
nativism, 39
NATO (North Atlantic Treaty Organization),
    164, 170, 196, 201–3, 205, 210
Negro Citizenship Association (NCA), 55
Nehru, Jawaharlal, 174
Nelles, H.V., 66–67
neocolonialism, 140
neoliberalism, 8, 97, 99, 199
    approaches to development, 100, 108, 111
    principal of market sovereignty, 208
    racisms of later 20th century (and now), 38
Neufeld, Mark, 212
New Democratic Party (NDP), 44
new global capitalism, 213
New International Economic Order (NIEO),
    96–97
New Warriors, 196–200, 206, 208–9, 211
    manifesto for a new army and a new
    Canada, 197–98
New World Movement, 255
New Zealand, 19
NGOs, 5, 11. *See also* secular NGOs
    activism on refugees, 226
    contribution to developing world, 142
    integration into development industry, 100
    international NGOs, 224
    partnership approach, 101–2
    popular internationalism and, 247

Nigeria, 75, 124, 167
1960s in Canada, 248–55
    worry about American control of Canadian
    economy, 254
Nkrumah, Kwame, 168
Nolin, Catherine, 74
North Atlantic, 155–56, 164–165, 171, 176
North Mara mine deaths, 73
numbered treaties, 22–23

Obama, Barack, 206
OECD, 61, 79, 92, 94
    Development Assistance Committee (DAC),
    95
    donors, 98–99
Office of the Extractive Sector Corporate
    Social Responsibility Counsellor, 77
Official Development Assistance Accountability Act,
    104
Oja-Jay, Dru, 247
Ojibway Warriors Society, 29
Oka (1990), 30
Olson, Vernel, 252
Ontario Human Rights Commission, 54
"Operation Deliverance," 193–94
Operation Rolling Thunder, 210
Oppressed Minorities policy, 224–26, 237
Orientalist concepts, 128
O'Sullivan, Kevin, 144
Oxfam, 138, 143, 147

Papillon, Martin, 253
Paris, John, 52
Paris Declaration on Aid Effectiveness, 105–6
Partnership Africa Canada (1986), 101
paternalism, 5, 23, 38–40
Pax Britannica, 199
peace activism, 214
Peace Corps, 138
peacekeeping, 65, 69, 176, 196, 203, 205,
    211–12
Pearson, Lester B., 28, 63, 95, 143, 167, 175,
    209, 227
    "business cooperation" element, 64
    on Canadian flag, 204
    Canadian role of "Quiet Diplomacy," 202
    chief architect of Canadian foreign policy
    (1940s and 50s), 164
    enthusiastic Cold Warrior, 201
    "liberal Canada," 202
    Nobel Peace Prize, 178, 202, 210
    in Suez crisis, 177–78
    tradition of peacekeeping, 65, 176, 196, 203
Pearson Commission report, *Partners in
    Development*, 95–96, 144
Pentecostal Christianity, 145–47
People's Republic of China, 91
Perchoir d'Haïti, 257
Perry, Adele, 32

Petrie, Frank, 63
Pinochet, Augusto, 259–60
Placer Dome, 71, 74
Plan Canada, 89
popular internationalism, 246–62
Portugal, 19, 173–74
post–World War II
    Canada's emergence as economic power,
        91–94
    perceived threat of Soviet antagonism, 92
    subordination of Canadian economy to
        US, 92
postcolonial peace monitoring, 171
postdevelopment movement, 79
Prashad, Vijay, 9–10
Pratt, Cranford, 90, 140, 143
Presbyterian Church in Canada, 26, 121–22, 127
Presbyterian Record, 129
Presbyterian work in India, 135
Preston, Andrew, 125
Project Accompaniment, 6
Purple Onion coffee house, 250

Quebec, 158
    development aid to assert influence in
        francophone world, 102
    foreign policy, 10
    Haitian diaspora, 257
    international relations, 102
    nationalism, 180, 258
    opposition to the coup in Chile, 259
    progressive Catholicism in, 259
    resistant to militarism, 210
    support for the Algerian War, 248–49
    Third World decolonization and, 248
    Third World thought in, 247
Quebec decolonization, 248–49
Quebec Foreign Missionary Society, 6
Quebec-Washington-Guantanamo Walk for
    Peace, 251–52

race and racism in Canada, 2–4, 17, 32, 37, 41,
        43–44, 48–49, 52, 68–70, 156–57
    change in racial attitudes (World War II), 54
    in foreign policy, 182–84
    historicist attitude toward race in British
        Empire, 38–39, 47, 50–51
Racial Discrimination Act, 1944 (Ontario), 54
racial hierarchies, 8, 38, 41, 47, 123
racial naturalism, 38, 49, 53
Rainville, Michel, 194
Ramos, Howard, 29
Razack, Sherene, 20, 69, 212
Reagan, Ronald, 5
The Real Cuba as Three Canadians Saw It, 252
refugee determination processes, 219, 224. *See
    also* immigration policy
refugee movements from the Global South,
    217–40

Chinese refugees, 223, 236
Southeast Asia refugees (Vietnam and
    Cambodia), 236, 238
Tibet (*See* Tibetan refugee resettlement
    pilot project)
refugee settlement in Canada
    changed composition of Canadian populace,
        219
    Designated Class category (of refugee), 237,
        239
    making refugee claims on arrival in Canada,
        236
    private sponsorship agreements, 238–39
Refugee Status Advisory Committee (RSAC),
    225
Reid, Escott, 178
remittances, 1, 43
Report of the Commission on World Mission, 134
reserves, 23
    as apartheid, 37
    centres of political organizing, 24
    likened to Third World slums, 24
    mortality rates, 28
    in urban setting, 24
residential schools, 26–27, 32, 129
responsibility to protect, 205, 207
"Responsible Mining Act," 77
Rethinking Missions, 126, 131
Rhodesia (Zimbabwe), 135–36
Riel, Louis, 23, 158
Rights Action, 76
Rio Tinto Alcan, 65
Rios Montt, Efrain, General, 5–6
Rodney, Walter, 256
Romero, Oscar, 261
Royal Proclamation (1763), 22
Russell, Graham, 76
Rutherford, Scott, 253
Ryerson, Egerton, 54

Sacher, William, 72, 74, 76
Said, Edward, 69, 128
    Orientalism, 20
Sainte-Marie, Buffy
    "Universal Soldier," 250
Sartre, Jean-Paul, 249
Saunders, Doug, 72
    "Canada's African Adventure Takes a
        Colonial Turn," 71
Sauvy, Alfred, 9
Schofield, Frank, 161
scientific racism, 39–40, 123
Scott, A.A., 131
Seagram's distillery, 62
secession, 180–81. *See also* independence
    movements
secular NGOs, 120–21, 133, 137, 147
    ad hoc coalitions with church groups, 140
    advocates for developing-world causes, 144

links and tensions with faith-based counterparts, 138
secularization in approach to missions, 133
Service, C.W.M.
"The Changing Face of Mission," 137–38
sexual assaults at Pogera mine in New Guinea, 73
Sharp, Mitchell, 174
Sheinin, David, 261–62
Sierra Leone, 50
Simcoe, John Graves, 50
Simpson, Albert Benjamin, 145
Sinclair, Gordon, 158
Singh, Gurdit, 44
Sir George Williams affair, 256
Six Nations of Grand River, 30
Skelton, O.D., 163
slavery, 17, 50, 66
Smillie, Ian, 109
SNC-Lavalin, 64, 77
social change, 107
social justice, 214, 260
social movements, 7, 214, 247
social progress, 106
social protest, criminalization of, 76
social welfare in developing countries, 100
"soft power," 205
Somalia scandal, 193–97, 204–5, 213
South African apartheid, 7, 63, 135–36, 262
Soviet Union, 91, 205
Spence, Theresa, 31
Spicer, Keith, 138
St. Laurent, Louis, 6, 164, 166, 175, 177, 202
Stairs, William, 66, 69–70
Stam, Valerie, 12
Stanger-Ross, Jordan, 24
Stanley, Brian *The Bible and the Flag*, 124
Stanley, Timothy, 43
Stouffer, Allen P., 51
Strong, Maurice, 96
structural adjustment, 98–100
Structural Adjustment Participatory Review Initiative (SAPRI), 99
Student Christian Movement (SCM), 135
Student Union for Peace Action (SUPA), 251
Student Volunteer Movement for Foreign Missions (SVM), 125, 144, 147
Sudan, 69, 158
Suez crisis, 177
Sukarno, 174–75
Summit of the Americas in Quebec City, 262
Swift, Jamie, 4, 65, 176, 178
Conflicts of Interest, 10
Swift, Richard, 10

Talisman Energy, 68–69, 74, 77
Taylor, Graham D., 62
Taylor, Sheldon, 55
technical assistance, 99, 134

technical solutions, 106
terminology
refugees, 220, 224, 237, 239
Third World, 7–10, 220
terra nullis, 20
Thatcher, Margaret, 172
Third World, 3, 6, 8–10, 220
catastrophes in factories, 60
causes of impoverishment today, 109
consumer items from, 60
economic ties between Canada and, 60
growth in, 61
impact of development aid, 88
and mining, 73–74
and neoliberal ideology, 97
omnipresence in everyday life, 10
as project, not place, 9–10
"resource curse," 75
reversals of gains (1970s), 98
social welfare, 100
structural adjustment, 98–99
terminology, 7–10
through lens of empire, 155
Western hegemony in, 4
as zone of conflict, 156
Third World solidarity, 262
Tibetan Refugee Aid Society, 228, 233
Tibetan refugee resettlement pilot project, 217, 219, 226–32, 239
preservation of cultural practices, 235
success, 233–35
Tolstoy, Ilia, 227
Tomlinson, Brian, 10
transnational Canadian history, 2, 11
"tropical capitalism," 66
Trudeau, Pierre, 96, 140, 144, 174, 210, 230–31
"business cooperation" element, 64
changes to immigration policy, 204
development assistance, 180
focus on national unity, 180
Indonesia's place as priority country, 181
Third World decolonization and, 179–81
Truman, Harry, 93, 95, 170
Truth and Reconciliation Commission on Residential Schools, 32
Twitter, 7–8

underdevelopment, 94, 98
United Church
"Reflections on Recruiting Personnel," 142
United Church Observer, 6–7, 137
United Church of Canada, 121, 131–32, 140, 143
changes in approach to mission, 133
ecumenical approach to mission work, 134–35
on evangelization of the world, 131
on freedom struggles, 135
partnerships in mission field, 134–35
residential schools, 26

United Church Renewal Fellowship, 146
United Nations, 91, 165, 196, 203, 205, 210
United Nations Convention Relating to the
    Status of Refugees (1951), 218–19, 224
  Canada's signing of, 218, 221, 224
United Nations Declaration on the
    Establishment of a New International
    Economic Order, 96–98
United Nations Declaration on the Rights of
    Indigenous Peoples (UNDRIP), 30
United Nations Emergency Force (UNEF),
    178, 203
United Nations High Commissioner for
    Refugees (UNCHR), 220, 228
United Nations Human Development Index,
    6, 220
United Nations Millennium Declaration, 104
United Nations Observer Group in El Salvador
    (ONUSAL), 204
United Nations Security Council, 170
United Nations Transition Assistance Group
    (UNTAG), 204
United States
  as expansionary industrial power, 66
  Jim Crow regime, 51
  move into "Indian territory," 19
  rise in Latin America, 67
  role in supporting dictatorships, 261
  US-dominated global capital markets, 68
  US drones (unmanned aerial vehicles),
    206–7
  US/ Guatemalan relations, 5
Universal Declaration of Human Rights, 91,
    156

Van Horne, Sir William, 2, 67, 70
Vietnam, 168
  Canada's stance on independence, 170–71
Vietnam War, 176, 251
  Canada's complicity with, 4, 253
  Canadian businesses profited from, 202
  Pearson's criticism, 210
  social movements opposing, 7
Voice of Women, 251
volunteer opportunities, 12
voluntourists, 147

Walker, Barrington, 4, 221
Walker, James, 54

War of 1812, 212
Ward, Peter, 41, 43
warrior image of Canada, 4
Warrior Nation *vs.* Peaceable Kingdom, 207
Weaver, John C., 22
Webster, David, 4, 6, 202, 253
Webster-Ashburton Treaty, 50
West Coast potlatch, 27
Western cultural superiority, 5
Western hegemony in the Third World, 4
Western-style education for girls, 130
Western universalized standards, 8
white Canada, 4, 37, 41, 43–44, 53, 156
"White Man's Burden," 199
White Paper on Indian Policy, 29
white settler society, 222
white supremacy (in immigration policy), 41
Whitworth, Sandra, 212
Wilson, Donald, 139, 144
Winegard Report, 101
Winks, Robin, 54
Wolfe, Patrick, 19
Wolseley, Garnet, Lord, 18
women in missionary field, 123, 126–30, 133
women's liberation movement in Quebec, 249
Woodsworth, J.S., *Strangers Within Our Gates*,
    39, 44–48
Working Group on Mining and Human
    Rights in Latin America, 75–76
Workingman's Protection Association in BC,
    42
World Bank, 10, 71, 98, 196
World Council for Indigenous Peoples, 30
World Council of Churches (WCC), 133, 135
World Trade Organization (WTO), 100, 196
World War I, 157–58, 212
  Canada's coming of age, 155
  Canadian imperialism following, 160
  fought by an "Anglo-Saxon alliance," 161
World War II, 162
  veterans, 212
Wright, Cynthia, 252

Young, Robert J.C., 16

Zambia
  FIPA deal with Canada, 74
  losses through illicit financial outflows
    (IFFs), 75